The
New England
Theology

The New England Theology

*From Jonathan Edwards
to Edwards Amasa Park*

Douglas A. Sweeney
and Allen C. Guelzo, editors

Baker Academic

Grand Rapids, Michigan

© 2006 by Douglas A. Sweeney and Allen C. Guelzo

Published by Baker Academic
a division of Baker Publishing Group
P.O. Box 6287, Grand Rapids, MI 49516-6287
www.bakeracademic.com

Printed in the United States of America

Library of Congress Cataloging-in-Publication Data
The New England theology : from Jonathan Edwards to Edwards Amasa Park / Douglas A. Sweeney and Allen C. Guelzo, editors.
      p.   cm.
   Includes bibliographical references and index.
   ISBN 10: 0-8010-2709-8 (pbk.)
   ISBN 978-0-8010-2709-3 (pbk.)
   1. New England theology. 2. Edwards, Jonathan, 1703–1758. 3. Calvinism.
   4. New Divinity theology. 5. Congregational churches—Doctrines. I. Sweeney, Douglas A. II. Guelzo, Allen C.
   BX7250.N49 2006
   230′.580974—dc22   2006019320

To
Joseph Conforti,
colleague and friend,
who got this started

Contents

Acknowledgments   11
Introduction   13

Part 1 Wellspring of the New England Theology: The Thought of Jonathan Edwards   25

Jonathan Edwards, *A Divine and Supernatural Light* (1734)   27

Jonathan Edwards, *Religious Affections* (1746)   38

Jonathan Edwards, *An Account of the Life of the Late Reverend Mr. David Brainerd* (1749)   47

Jonathan Edwards, *Freedom of the Will* (1754)   57

Part 2 The Emergence of a Movement: Early New Divinity Thought   69

Joseph Bellamy, *True Religion Delineated* (1750)   73

Joseph Bellamy, *A Dialogue between a Minister and His Parishioner Concerning the Half-way Covenant* (1769)   79

Samuel Hopkins, *An Inquiry Concerning the Promises of the Gospel* (1765)   86

Samuel Hopkins, *An Inquiry into the Nature of True Holiness* (1773)   91

Sarah Osborn, *Memoirs of the Life of Mrs. Sarah Osborn* (1799)   98

Nathan Strong, *On the Evidence of Forgiveness* (1798)   109

Nathanael Emmons, *The Deceitfulness of the Human Heart* (1842)   113

7

Nathanael Emmons, *The Duty of Sinners to Make Themselves a New Heart* (1812)   118
Jonathan Edwards the Younger, *Remarks on the Improvements Made in Theology by His Father, President Edwards* (1842)   123

Part 3 The Moral Government of God: Edwardseans and the Atonement   133

Stephen West, *The Scripture Doctrine of Atonement, Proposed to Careful Examination* (1785)   135
Jonathan Edwards the Younger, *Three Sermons on the Necessity of the Atonement, and Its Consistency with Free Grace in Forgiveness* (1785)   140
John Smalley, *The Sufficiency of the Atonement of Christ for the Salvation of All Men* (1814)   144

Part 4 Edwardsean Ethics: Antislavery and Missions   149

Samuel Hopkins, *A Dialogue Concerning the Slavery of the Africans, Showing It to Be the Duty and Interest of the American Colonies to Emancipate All Their African Slaves* (1776)   151
Jonathan Edwards the Younger, *The Injustice and Impolicy of the Slave Trade and of Slavery* (1791)   157
Society of Inquiry Respecting Missions, *Historical Sketch of the Society* (1833)   165

Part 5 The Exercisers and the Tasters   171

Nathanael Emmons, *Man's Activity and Dependence Illustrated and Reconciled* (1842)   173
Asa Burton, *Essay XXX* (1824)   179

Part 6 Theology in New Haven   187

Timothy Dwight, *Sermon III: Comparative Influence of Atheism and Christianity* (1818)   189
Nathaniel W. Taylor, *Concio ad Clerum* (1828)   194
Nathaniel W. Taylor, *Review of Spring on the Means of Regeneration* (1829)   205
Nathaniel W. Taylor, *Lectures on the Moral Government of God* (1859)   214

Part 7 Finney and the New Measures 219

James Harris Fairchild, *Oberlin Theology* 221
Charles G. Finney, *Lectures on Revivals of Religion*
(1835) 227
Charles G. Finney, *Lectures on Systematic Theology*
(1846–47) 237

**Part 8 Last of the "Consistent Calvinists": Edwards Amasa
Park 245**

Edwards Amasa Park, *The Theology of the Intellect and
That of the Feelings* (1850) 247
Edwards Amasa Park, *New England Theology* (1852) 256

**Part 9 Things Sublime and Eternal: The New England
Theology as Remembered by Harriet Beecher
Stowe 265**

Harriet Beecher Stowe, *The Minister's Wooing*
(1859) 267
Harriet Beecher Stowe, *Oldtown Folks* (1869) 273

Select Bibliography 279
Index 318

Acknowledgments

The production of this volume offered numerous opportunities to consult with other scholars. We gratefully acknowledge their contributions to our work. Kenneth Minkema, David Kling, and Gerald McDermott offered advice at several stages of production. André Gazal, Andrew Tooley, and Caleb Maskell helped to compile the bibliography. For scanning and checking texts, we thank Brandon Withrow, Matthew Harmon, Robert Caldwell, and John-Mark Yeats. For administrative support, we thank Christine Uggerud, Susanne Henry, and Gerri Wissinger.

Introduction

We beg leave, therefore, first of all, to explain the term, New England Theology. It signifies the formal creed which a majority of the most eminent theologians in New England have explicitly or implicitly sanctioned, during and since the time of Edwards. It denotes the spirit and genius of the system openly avowed or logically involved, in their writings. It includes not the peculiarities in which Edwards differed, as he is known to have differed, from the larger part of his most eminent followers; nor the peculiarities in which any one of his followers differed, as some of them did, from the larger part of the others; but it comprehends the principles, with their logical sequences, which the greater number of our most celebrated divines have approved expressly or by implication.

Edwards Amasa Park, *New England Theology* (1852)

In the spring of 1858, an Illinois newspaper editor looked around the landscape of America—which, among other things, included a major national financial depression, an upcoming senatorial contest, and the uproar over slavery in the Kansas-Nebraska territories—and decided that the most important news was about religious revival. "There is no one topic . . . so frequently the subject of discussion as the religious awakening now agitating the land," wrote Charles Lanphier. This revival of religion was "a natural reaction from the materialism of the last twenty years." But the "reaction" took the form of religious revival, partly because that was how Americans dealt "at periodical intervals" with the contradictions and stresses of their culture and partly because revivals had "received the sanction on this side of the Atlantic of Jonathan Edwards, the great metaphysician of his century."[1]

1. Charles Lanphier, "Religious Revivals," *Illinois State Register,* March 26, 1858, 2.

Editor Lanphier seems not to have noticed that he was placing this laurel on the head of Edwards almost exactly one hundred years after Edwards's death at Princeton. But the coincidence was a telling one. Ezra Stiles, who had grown up knowing Edwards and disagreeing with most of Edwards's thinking, was sure at that time that "in another Generation" Edwards would "pass into as transient Notice perhaps scarce above Oblivion, as Willard or Twiss, or Norton" and be "looked upon as singular and whimsical."[2] Stiles was a stalwart of what became known as Old Calvinism—the established, parish-based system of Congregationalist Calvinism that had been in place since the Puritan founding of Massachusetts Bay in 1630. Edwards's complaint had been that Old Calvinism had gone stale, substituting a civil but uninspiring version of Calvinism for the passionate and living piety of the Puritan founders. Edwards's sympathies lay in the direction of the new Pietism, whose best-known English-speaking apostles were John Wesley and George Whitefield. When Whitefield arrived in New England in 1739, preaching revival and renewal, Edwards fell in alongside him and became the primary defender of what would soon become known simply as the Great Awakening.

Edwards hoped, in his devout heart of hearts, that the Great Awakening was the overture to the day of judgment and the millennium, when "religion shall in every respect be uppermost in the world."[3] But the Awakening burned through its own energies, and when Edwards tried to force the Northampton church to rewrite its understanding of church membership, based on the more demanding piety of the revival, the members resisted him and then in 1750 fired him. Instead of hailing the "dawning of a general revival of the Christian church," Edwards took up the day-to-day routine of superintending the mission station of the Massachusetts Commissioners for the Propagation of the Gospel at Stockbridge, Massachusetts, where he preached to two hundred Stockbridge Mahicans (in English, using a translator; he never tried to learn the Mahican language, although his six-year-old son picked it up effortlessly and wrote a study of it, *Observations on the Language of the Muhhekanew Indians*, in 1788) and an English congregation that was not entirely eager to have him as its pastor. Edwards's own attention soon strayed back to his early enchantment with philosophy, and, between 1750 and 1757, he

2. Cited in Franklin B. Dexter, ed., *The Literary Diary of Ezra Stiles, D.D.*, vol. 3 (New York: Charles Scribner, 1901), 275.

3. Gerald R. McDermott, *One Holy and Happy Society: The Public Theology of Jonathan Edwards* (University Park, PA: Pennsylvania State University Press, 1992), 65; see also Jonathan Edwards, *Some Thoughts Concerning the Revival*, in *The Great Awakening, The Works of Jonathan Edwards*, vol. 4, ed. C. C. Goen (New Haven: Yale University Press, 1972), 353.

composed three great treatises in moral philosophy—on *Original Sin, Freedom of the Will,* and *The Nature of True Virtue*—all the while praying for a new awakening until the trustees of the infant college at Princeton invited him to take up the presidency there in 1757. But the books did not sell well, and Edwards fell ill from the complications of a smallpox inoculation at Princeton. He died there on March 22, 1758, "without the least appearance of murmuring through the whole."[4]

Although Ezra Stiles expected that Edwards's reputation would disappear in the same uncomplaining fashion, the result over the next century was the exact opposite. His students, Joseph Bellamy and Samuel Hopkins, took up in the 1750s and 1760s where Edwards left off, and the result, to Stiles's dismay, was the formulation of an Edwardsean "New Divinity," the first generation of a distinctively New England theology.[5]

Bellamy and Hopkins saw, as the Old Calvinists did not, how very directly Edwards's writings spoke to the central concerns of Americans as they descended into the storm of the Revolutionary decades. First, however much Edwards's dismissal from Northampton looked like New Englanders' repudiating revivalism as a device for stoking up the spiritual temperature of their churches, Bellamy and Hopkins were convinced that Edwards's fall only underscored the degree of New England's apostasy from true Calvinism and the need to redouble the effort to provoke revival. The weapon Edwards put into their hands was contained in the treatise *Freedom of the Will,* in which Edwards confected an ingenious reconciliation of absolute Calvinist predestination with a demand for immediate and utter surrender of a person's will to the demand for conversion and holiness.

When God decrees an act, Edwards wrote, that act becomes *necessary.* But acts can become necessary in one of two ways: God can physically compel someone, even while the person really wants to do something else. Or an act becomes necessary when a person already has a psychological inclination toward that act, and the more intense a person's inclination, the more likely it is that it will be acted on in a predictable fashion. Edwards called the necessity that involves force *natural necessity.* No one under the force of natural necessity can be held morally accountable for what he or she does. But the necessity that arises from

4. William Shippen to Sarah Edwards, March 22, 1758, cited in George M. Marsden, *Jonathan Edwards: A Life* (New Haven: Yale University Press, 2003), 494.

5. We use "New England Theology" (as it was used in the nineteenth century) to refer to the Edwardsean tradition or school of thought: the tradition beginning with Edwards, running through the New Divinity from Samuel Hopkins and Joseph Bellamy to Nathanael Emmons, and extending to more ambiguous figures who nevertheless claimed a linkage to Edwards, from Nathaniel W. Taylor, Lyman Beecher, and Charles G. Finney to the last of the school's stalwarts, Andover's Edwards Amasa Park.

people's own inclinations is *moral necessity*. Since no one is actually using force in moral necessity, such people can be held responsible for their actions; in fact, the *greater* the force of an evil inclination on their actions, the *more* accountable they are, precisely because they have all the natural, physical power they need to do otherwise. In practical terms, this meant that people could not excuse themselves from the call to repentance and conversion on the grounds of *inability*. They had arms and legs and lips and a brain, and they could use them to bow the knee in repentance—and do it *now*, without waiting for some external, natural necessity to get them to do it. If we were to look at this as a modern psychologist might, we would say that Edwards was creating a moment of catharsis by telling them that, despite their sinful inclinations, they were fully responsible to repent and believe.

Second, Edwards also confronted the incapacity of conventional Calvinism to deal with the blandishments of the Enlightenment. The skeptical luminaries of the British Enlightenment, from Hobbes to Hume, had turned Calvinism on its head, not by denouncing predestination but by co-opting it and making material substances and forces the absolute determiners of all human actions. To save any place for the activity of human spirit, Calvinist divines in England and New England diluted Calvin's determinism with doses of free willism—Arminianism, after the seventeenth-century Dutch opponent of Calvinism—and once they began diluting, there was not much they did not dilute, including the Trinity. Edwards, on the other hand, made it clear that the best defense against atheistic determinism was an aggressive Calvinistic offense, and the formulas he developed in the treatises of the 1750s allowed Hopkins and Bellamy to combine the most *ultra* forms of Calvinism with the rhetoric of free choice and to do it with demands for revival and moral purism that made the Old Calvinists blanch.

Third, the Edwardseans had an important lesson in civics to teach, based on Edwards's distinction between force and necessity (although it is safe to say that the Edwardseans were not entirely self-aware of it). Just as Edwards had taught that God rules human conduct by affecting the inclination and not by force, so the Edwardseans transformed New England Calvinism by basing its support on an appeal to public inclination rather than to tax collections reinforced by civil statute. In so doing, they demonstrated that the exclusion of religion from formal public establishment by the American republic's Constitution need not mean the end of the churches' influence on American public life. Closed off from making policy, they made converts. Unable to legislate, they organized independent societies for Bible distribution, for alcoholism reform, for observance of the Sabbath, for suppressing vice and immorality, for the end of slavery. When the French liberal Alexis de Tocqueville took his celebrated tour of the United States in the 1830s, he was amazed to find that while "in the United States religion" has no "influence on the laws or on the details of political opinions," nevertheless "it directs the mores" and through that "it works to regulate the state."[6]

But if Edwardsean-style revivalism was an important means for igniting public interest in religion, it was also a poor instrument for sustaining it. The demand for immediate repentance and "disinterested benevolence" was, at its most fundamental level, a reflection of the old Puritan weakness for separatism. The revivals called people to repentance, but they also called them out of society, out of their normal relations, out of their everyday moral lives to participate in an intensely demanding but very otherworldly version of Protestant Christianity. The very fact that a revival was judged necessary at all was a judgment on the failures of the regular churches and the impurities of conventional society, and its logical end was to turn people into come-outers of various sorts and to inflate a radical individualism.

Fearsome as the New Divinity became as preachers, they prided themselves just as much on the passion with which they wrote and studied. Nathanael Emmons stoically devoted himself for seventy-eight years to a regimen of ten to sixteen hours a day in his study and wore a gouge in the wainscoting where his feet were propped up. Hopkins met with two of his students to talk theology through the day, then at nightfall saw one of them out to the stable for his horse; they fell to talking some more, and eventually they noticed what they thought was the glow from a fire in the east. It was actually the sun coming up, the next day.[7]

Gradually, the contours of New England religion, during the Revolution and into the nineteenth century, sorted themselves out into three broad categories: the genteel congregations of upper-crust Boston, who eventually went the distance in their embrace of the Enlightenment and turned Unitarian; the Old Calvinists, who struggled to preserve some traditional sense of Calvinist orthodoxy within a state-established parish system in which baptism and communion defined church membership more than conversion; and the Edwardseans, who set the bar of church life as high as Edwardsean revival could put it. There is no "score" to say which of these persuasions eventually "won." But there is no question that the Unitarians became and remained a cultivated, Bostonian taste,

6. Alexis de Tocqueville, *Democracy in America*, ed. Harvey Mansfield and Delba Winthrop (Chicago: University of Chicago Press, 2000), 278.
7. Edwards Amasa Park, "Memoir of Nathanael Emmons," in *The Works of Nathanael Emmons, D.D.*, vol. 1, ed. Jacob Ide (Boston: Congregational Board of Publication, 1861), 60, 66, 105; Ann Douglas, *The Feminization of American Culture* (New York: Avon Books, 1977), 173; and Edwin Pond Parker, ed., *The Autobiography of the Rev. Enoch Pond* (Boston: Congregational Sunday-School and Publishing Society, 1883), 24–27.

while the Old Calvinists eventually dissolved by the 1860s into the first wave of American theological liberalism. The Edwardseans, however, captured the western New England hill country, struck westward along the Erie Canal and turned Upstate New York into the "burned-over district," followed the arrows of New England migration farther west into the Western Reserve of Ohio, and then went into Michigan, Indiana, Illinois, Wisconsin, and Iowa, founding churches, colleges, and moral reform movements and lighting up the sky with the glow of a Second Great Awakening—and then a third Awakening, the one Charles Lanphier described in 1858.

None of the New Divinity, however, cleared as wide a path for himself as Charles Grandison Finney. Born in western Connecticut, Finney moved to Upstate New York and trained as a lawyer. But in 1821, Finney was dramatically converted and embarked on a new career as a preacher of revivals. No one ever wielded the thunderbolts of immediate repentance and the requirement for perfect, "disinterested" benevolence more powerfully than Finney, and from 1824 to 1832, he ignited revivals all through the Mohawk River valley, advanced to the Chatham Street Chapel and the Broadway Tabernacle in New York City, and eventually became one of the leading lights in founding Oberlin College. Although Finney has been routinely cast as a sort of religious Davy Crockett, preaching free will Arminianism to freely willing American democrats, Finney's memoirs are teeming with the distinctive Edwardsean vocabulary, and in the 1840s, he was still rejecting "what the Arminians call a *gracious* ability, which terms are a manifest absurdity."[8]

But while the historical figure of Edwards continued to wax, the figure of his disciples eventually waned. It is possible to take up almost any history of American ideas before the 1980s and find almost no mention whatsoever of the New England Theology or the New Divinity. Henry May, writing in 1976 in *The Enlightenment in America*, gave them all of three pages and concluded that "by 1796, they were winning the pulpits and losing the people" in New England. Sydney Ahlstrom, who wrote *A Religious History of the American People* in 1972, feared that "they degraded Puritan theology by turning it into a lifeless system of apologetics," and in this Ahlstrom was following the judgment of Joseph Haroutunian in *Piety versus Moralism: The Passing of the New England Theology* (1932), who found Hopkins and Bellamy guilty of transforming Calvinism "into a vast, complicated, and colorless theological structure, bewildering to

8. Charles Grandison Finney, "Letters on Revivals—No. 4," *Oberlin Evangelist,* March 12, 1845, 44.

its enemies and ridiculous to its friends."⁹ Ezra Stiles's prediction had at last come true—but it was about the Edwardseans, not Edwards.

Just how an intellectual and theological movement of such vitality and scope could disappear almost entirely from the attention of American historians and theologians is a curious question. It stems, first, from the almost-entire failure and disappearance of the Edwardseans after the passing of Edwards Amasa Park and the capture of the New England Theology's most important citadel, Andover Theological Seminary, by the Andover liberals in the 1880s. The fall of Andover was followed in short order by a similar collapse into liberalism at two secondary Edwardsean outposts, Union Theological Seminary and Oberlin College, under the aegis of two Edwardsean-cum-nineteenth-century liberals, Henry Boynton Smith and Henry Churchill King. Unlike the Old School Presbyterians, who found in J. Gresham Machen an intellect of sufficient stature to hand on the legacy of Charles Hodge and Archibald Alexander once Princeton Theological Seminary fell into the hands of liberalism in the 1920s, the New England Theology had no one to carry forward the weight of its tradition. By the time George Nye Boardman and Frank Hugh Foster were writing comprehensive histories of the New England Theology in *A History of the New England Theology* (1899) and *A Genetic History of the New England Theology* (1907), they were also conscious that they were writing its obituary.

The Presbyterian conservatives of Machen's generation were certainly not inclined to spend much energy on preserving the memory of the New England Theology. Although Edwards ended his days as president of Princeton College, his eventual successor in 1768, the Scottish Presbyterian John Witherspoon, deliberately scoured out every aspect of Edwardseanism in Princeton he could find. Witherspoon was the Scottish equivalent of an Old Calvinist, and those who followed him at the college and later at Princeton Theological Seminary were wary of the theological peculiarities of the New Divinity, especially the suspicious way the New Divinity had played with the nature and extent of the atonement. The Princetonians, and those who succeeded them through Westminster Theological and Reformed Theological seminaries, could not avoid bowing in respect to the figure of Edwards, but it was an Edwards carefully sculpted to resemble Princeton Calvinism and an Edwards who had no heirs. When Benjamin Breckinridge Warfield wrote the entry on "Edwards and the New England Theology" for James Hastings's *Encyclopedia of Religion and Ethics* in 1912, he could not

9. Henry F. May, *The Enlightenment in America* (New York: Oxford University Press, 1976), 61; Sydney Ahlstrom, *A Religious History of the American People* (New Haven: Yale University Press, 1972), 405; and Joseph Haroutunian, *Piety versus Moralism: The Passing of the New England Theology* (New York: Henry Holt, 1932), 71.

avoid hailing Edwards as "the one figure of real greatness in the intellectual life of colonial America." But he was equally unable to recognize the Edwardseans as Edwards's legitimate offspring. "It was Edwards' misfortune that he gave his name to a party," Warfield wrote, because the New England Theology was "in many respects the exact antipodes of Edwards."[10] Consequently, modern conservative Reformed theology knows much of Edwards but almost nothing of Edwardseanism.

The New England Theology remained lodged in the dustbin until the 1970s. Sidney Mead wrote a marvelous biography of Nathaniel W. Taylor in 1942, and Ann Douglas included a sharply written chapter on the New Divinity in *The Feminization of American Culture* in 1977. But otherwise, except for unpublished Ph.D. dissertations by Dick van Halsema (1956) and Hugh Knapp (1971), material on the New England Theology was almost impossible to be had. Even when the New Divinity were invited in for a brief appearance, as they were in Stephen Berk's *Calvinism versus Democracy: Timothy Dwight and the Origins of American Evangelical Orthodoxy* (1974), it was usually to repeat Haroutunian's contemptuous dismissal. Then in 1977, Joseph Conforti, a student of William McLoughlin at Brown University, wrote a remarkable and sympathetic dissertation on Samuel Hopkins (which he published in 1981 as *Samuel Hopkins and the New Divinity Movement*), and in 1978, a Sydney Ahlstrom student at Yale, William Breitenbach, wrote an extraordinary (but still unpublished) dissertation titled "The New Divinity and the Era of Moral Accountability." These two Ph.D. dissertations finally restarted creative work on the New Divinity material, and their reassessment was taken up in a radical new synthesis of American intellectual history in 1985 by Bruce Kuklick, *Churchmen and Philosophers: From Jonathan Edwards to John Dewey*. The two most recent surveys of American theology, Mark Noll's *America's God: From Jonathan Edwards to Abraham Lincoln* (2002) and E. Brooks Holifield's *American Theology: Christian Thought from the Age of the Puritans to the Civil War* (2003), devote multiple chapters to the New England Theology.

With them, the New England Theology has been stood back on its feet, although this is a revival conducted as an act of historical research rather than as a devotional pursuit of what the New England theologians liked to call "Consistent Calvinism." For that reason, this revival might not be significantly different in its novelty from other academic revivals of obscure personae and movements in the American past, nor significantly differing from their tedium. But the reemergence of the

10. Benjamin Breckinridge Warfield, "Edwards and the New England Theology," in *Encyclopedia of Religion and Ethics*, vol. 5, ed. James Hastings (New York: Charles Scribner's Sons, 1912), 221, 226.

New England Theology as a major historical player in American intellectual and religious history does have a number of important claims to advance, suggesting that its staying power may be more than a little resilient. First, the claims of the New England Theology require students of American intellectual history to reconsider the once-prevailing consensus that the history of American ideas is largely a story about Boston, Unitarians, and Harvard—the great convention of American intellectual history, which implies that the whole business can be confined to a narrative that runs from Edwards to Emerson to William James—and to examine the extension of various Continental legacies and conversations into the provinces and into what Bruce Kuklick calls the tradition of "speculative thought."[11]

Second, recovering the ideas and texts of the New England Theology in general (and the New Divinity in particular) lays a foundation for understanding the strain of ethical absolutism that underlies nineteenth-century American reform movements. A great deal of this absolutism was owed to Kant and American readers of Kant, beginning with James Marsh and Ralph Waldo Emerson. But Romantic Kantian ethics of the Emersonian sort falls a great deal short of explaining the fiery urgency of William Lloyd Garrison and John Brown, and it is only when we have in hand the puzzle piece of the ethics of disinterested benevolence, which springs from the New Divinity, that we begin to understand what moved John Brown (who grew up under New Divinity preaching in Connecticut) or what makes the evangelical radicalism of the antislavery movement really comprehensible. By the same token, the recovery of the New England Theology makes it clear that the most distinctive form of that absolutism—moral perfectionism—was a Calvinist as much as a Methodist or Holiness innovation. At the end of the day, perhaps *nous sommes tous calvinistes*.

Third, the New England Theology compels us to revisit the history of Reformed theology in America and to broaden the scope of that history to include the multiple forms of evangelical Calvinism that dominated the American horizon in the nineteenth century, forms that could accommodate Charles G. Finney as much as Charles Hodge. Edwards commanded, and still commands, a healthy following among Calvinist Baptists. Isaac Backus, who is known for his writings on church-state separation, introduced Edwardsean views into Baptist thinking, and Jonathan Maxcy made a dent in the New Divinity doctrinal platform with his "Discourse

11. Bruce Kuklick, "The Place of Charles Hodge in the History of Ideas in America," in *Charles Hodge Revisited: A Critical Appraisal of His Life and Work*, ed. John H. Stewart and James H. Moorhead (Grand Rapids: Eerdmans, 2002), 64.

Designed to Explain the Doctrine of Atonement" (1796).[12] Early Southern Baptist leaders also appropriated Edwards. William Bullein Johnson, a faithful protégé of Maxcy, along with William Brantly, Luther Rice, and Jesse Mercer, are only the best-known examples of Edwardsean church leaders who played important roles in shaping early Southern Baptist life—most importantly through the founding of the Triennial Convention (1814), predecessor to the Southern Baptist Convention (1845). Even today, John Piper, pastor of Bethlehem Baptist Church in Minneapolis, publishes widely popular books on Edwards's thought and spirituality and heads a national center, named Desiring God Ministries, devoted in part to sharing Edwardsean views with others.[13] Within the Southern Baptist Convention, Edwardsean partisanship persists by means of the efforts of the Calvinistic Founders Movement.

The Princetonians, of course, disliked making any concession to the New Englanders and often disputed the New Englanders' title to Calvinism (as Benjamin Breckinridge Warfield did concerning the issue of Finney and Oberlin Perfectionism in a series of articles published posthumously in 1931 as *Studies in Perfectionism*). But however much the Princetonians criticized the New Englanders, it was still a family criticism. However much they might deplore Edwardseanism, from the time of the Great Awakening to the early twentieth century, Presbyterians north and south happily appealed to Edwards as a champion of Calvinist orthodoxy, despite the chronic fears of Old Schoolers regarding the dangers of infection from New England.[14] One modern heir of Princeton Calvinism, John Gerstner (a faculty member at Pittsburgh Seminary as well as Trinity Evangelical Divinity School) plied hundreds of pastors, seminarians, and evangelical laity with Edwards, devoted his summers to poring over Edwards's manuscripts at Yale, and published several books on Edwards's theology.[15] He also made disciples, most importantly

12. Jonathan Maxcy's "Discourse" was anthologized by Edwards Amasa Park in what has become the standard New Divinity volume on the subject: Edwards A. Park, ed., *The Atonement: Discourses and Treatises by Edwards, Smalley, Maxcy, Emmons, Griffin, Burge, and Weeks* (Boston: Congregational Board of Publication, 1859).

13. John Piper's Edwardsean publications include *Desiring God: Meditations of a Christian Hedonist* (Sisters, OR: Multnomah, 1986); *The Supremacy of God in Preaching* (Grand Rapids: Baker, 1990); *The Pleasures of God* (Sisters, OR: Multnomah, 1991); *God's Passion for His Glory: Living the Vision of Jonathan Edwards* (Wheaton: Crossway, 1998); and John Piper and Justin Taylor, eds., *A God Entranced Vision of All Things: The Legacy of Jonathan Edwards* (Wheaton: Crossway, 2004).

14. For a lengthier discussion of Baptist and Presbyterian Edwardseanism, see Douglas A. Sweeney, "Evangelical Tradition in America," in *The Cambridge Companion to Jonathan Edwards*, ed. Stephen J. Stein (Cambridge: Cambridge University Press, forthcoming).

15. John Gerstner's best-known publications include *Steps to Salvation: The Evangelistic Message of Jonathan Edwards* (Philadelphia: Westminster, 1959); *Jonathan Edwards on Heaven and Hell* (Grand Rapids: Baker, 1980); *Jonathan Edwards: A Mini-Theology*

R. C. Sproul, who established Ligonier Ministries in the early 1970s near Gerstner's home in western Pennsylvania. A deeply Edwardsean institution, Ligonier Ministries moved to Orlando, Florida, in 1984. Today it sponsors a radio show, a monthly magazine, a multimedia ministry, and numerous seminars. It also owns an Edwardsean firm named Soli Deo Gloria, which was founded by Don Kistler, another Edwards partisan.

Edwards, as befits a theologian who straddled at least one denominational fence (between New England Congregationalism and Middle Atlantic Presbyterianism), also managed to acquire a substantial theological following beyond conventional denomination circles. Iain Murray and his Banner of Truth Trust, based in Scotland, have prompted thousands of evangelicals to study Edwards's oeuvre.[16] Evangelical academics such as Paul Helm, George Marsden, Mark Noll, and Gerald McDermott have made the study of Edwards into a scholarly industry.[17] Even theologians within mainline churches, which otherwise seem to hold precious little of Edwards's ideas, have begun to "retrieve" Edwards for the work of constructive theology. Sang Hyun Lee is the best known. His tenure teaching at Princeton Seminary and his work on what he calls Edwards's "dispositional ontology" have contributed both to Edwards studies and to the field of theology.[18] Lee's student, the Japanese theologian Anri Morimoto, has adapted Lee's insights to the field of soteriology, recommending Edwards for use in Roman Catholic–Protestant dialogue.[19] Robert Jenson, though a Lutheran, has also recommended Edwards as

(Wheaton: Tyndale, 1987); and *The Rational Biblical Theology of Jonathan Edwards*, 3 vols. (Orlando: Ligonier, 1991–93). For more on recent evangelical uses of Edwards's thought, see Sweeney, "Evangelical Tradition in America."

16. Iain Murray's best-known work is a study of Edwards's life, *Jonathan Edwards: A New Biography* (Edinburgh: Banner of Truth Trust, 1987).

17. See, for example, Edwards's *Treatise on Grace, and Other Posthumously Published Writings*, ed. with an introduction by Paul Helm (Cambridge: James Clarke, 1971); George M. Marsden, *Jonathan Edwards: A Life* (New Haven: Yale University Press, 2003); Mark A. Noll, *The Scandal of the Evangelical Mind* (Grand Rapids: Eerdmans, 1994), 77–81; Gerald R. McDermott, *Seeing God: Twelve Reliable Signs of True Spirituality* (Downers Grove, IL: InterVarsity, 1995); and Gerald R. McDermott, *Can Evangelicals Learn from World Religions? Jesus, Revelation, and Religious Traditions* (Downers Grove, IL: InterVarsity, 2000). Also see the essays in D. G. Hart, Sean Michael Lucas, and Stephen J. Nichols, eds., *The Legacy of Jonathan Edwards: American Religion and the Evangelical Tradition* (Grand Rapids: Baker, 2003).

18. See especially Sang Hyun Lee, *The Philosophical Theology of Jonathan Edwards*, rev. ed. (Princeton: Princeton University Press, 2000); and Sang Hyun Lee, editor's introduction to Jonathan Edwards, *Writings on the Trinity, Grace, and Faith*, ed. Sang Hyun Lee, *The Works of Jonathan Edwards*, vol. 21 (New Haven: Yale University Press, 2003), 1–106.

19. See especially Anri Morimoto, *Jonathan Edwards and the Catholic Vision of Salvation* (University Park, PA: Pennsylvania State University Press, 1995).

"America's theologian," one who can aid us in negotiating the forces of the Enlightenment.[20]

This leads ineluctably to the questions of whether there is an identifiable Edwardsean theological legacy today and whether the New England theologians who followed Edwards are worth rehabilitating as a living component of modern Reformed thinking. It is very much because of those questions, as well as the questions posed by the scholarly revival of interest in the New England Theology, that we have undertaken this collection of the New England Theology's primary texts. The New Englanders' commitment to improving on the past, to recontextualizing even the best of their doctrinal inheritance, and to calling no man master has left the larger world with a set of rich, Edwardsean resources that have rarely been controlled by those opposed to innovation. We hope this volume will help students navigate these vast resources. We also hope it will be used by many present-day theologians who will engage America's first indigenous theological movement.

Most of the readings in this volume were published by Edwards and his followers and are reproduced here in abridged form. One of the texts printed below is published here for the first time. Thanks to Roland Baumann and the Oberlin College Archives for permission to transcribe, edit, and publish "Oberlin Theology" by James Harris Fairchild (James Harris Fairchild Papers, Oberlin College Archives).[21]

The readings have been edited very lightly. Bible references have been regularized, as have the headings within entries. Selections are reproduced verbatim, except where the original punctuation and spelling would prove confusing to modern students and where obvious typographical errors were corrected. The only changes in punctuation that affect our original sources' prose pertain to modern standards for the use of commas (which we have followed). Ellipses mark the spots where material has been deleted. The original authors' footnotes have been deleted without notice.

20. Robert W. Jenson, *America's Theologian: A Recommendation of Jonathan Edwards* (New York: Oxford University Press, 1988).

21. This manuscript was later revised and published as "Oberlin Theology," in *Cyclopaedia of Biblical, Theological, and Ecclesiastical Literature*, vol. 7, ed. John McClintock and James Strong (New York: Harper & Brothers, 1877), 277–78.

Wellspring of the New England Theology

The Thought of Jonathan Edwards

Ever since the turgid paper wars of the antebellum clergy, scholars have struggled with the relationship between Jonathan Edwards (1703–58) and his followers. Most have pitted Edwards against the bulk of his (self-professed) disciples, using the sayings of the master to measure the distances they strayed. Others allow for variegation in any living, breathing tradition, expecting Edwardsean adaptations of the work of Edwards himself. But whether viewing the permutations of the New England theologians more as salutary adjustments or as departures from the truth, nearly all now grant that they were drawn—legitimately or not—from the deep and plentiful wells of Edwards's spiritual estate.

Edwards's writings have been reprinted hundreds of times, in multiple languages, from English, Welsh, and Gaelic to Dutch, German, French, Swedish, and Italian—not to mention Arabic, Choctaw, Spanish, Chinese, and, most influentially in recent years, Korean. But none of Edwards's titles nourished the growth of the New England Theology as much as those that treated the hallowed doctrine of the new birth, or the soul's regeneration from spiritual death to life in Christ. Indeed, the New England Theology might be said to be a lengthy dialogue—at times, a family feud—about the nature of the new birth and the conditions under which it was most likely to transpire. From Edwards himself to Edwards Amasa Park, New England's greatest Calvinist thinkers devoted their lives to the development of a theological program that would support their region's revivals and promote their people's conversions.

This should come as no surprise given Edwards's role in making sense of New England's Great Awakening. Beginning in 1734, when a revival rocked Northampton and nearby Connecticut River towns—quickly reverberating throughout the entire Anglo-American world—Edwards found himself in the middle of an international struggle to renew the state churches of Great Britain and her colonies. Other ministers proved more important in preaching and organizing the work. George Whitefield (1715–70) outpreached Edwards. John Wesley (1703–91) did much more to channel the forces of renewal. Many others might be mentioned who traveled farther or spent more energy mustering troops to fight the good fight. But no one worked as hard to shape theological reflection on the phenomena of revival as Edwards. From his breathless *Faithful Narrative of the Surprising Work of God* (1737) to his final *Dissertation on the Nature of True Virtue* (published posthumously in 1765), Edwards devoted himself to elucidating the ways and means by which to distinguish true, twice-born religion from its fatal counterfeits.

The selections that follow feature Edwards's most significant attempts to shape perceptions of the nature and the outcomes of conversion. During his thirty-five years of ministry, he drafted several thousand pages pointing the way to spiritual life. But none of his sermons, tracts, or treatises played as great a role as these in fueling the rise or in steering the course of the Edwardsean tradition. Based on Matthew 16:17, Edwards's sermon titled *A Divine and Supernatural Light* (1734) is a gem. It is not nearly as well known as *Sinners in the Hands of an Angry God* (1741), but that is a shame, for it is the *locus classicus* of his conception of the experience of spiritual regeneration—as well as the celebrated doctrine of what he called "the sense of the heart." Edwards's treatise *Religious Affections* (1746) has long been seen as a spiritual classic. Extending the themes he published first in *A Divine and Supernatural Light,* it has played a greater role than any other book in Christian history in fleshing out what Edwards called "experimental piety" and in distinguishing true religion from hypocrisy. Edwards's *Account of the Life of the Late Reverend Mr. David Brainerd* (1749) proved to be his most popular book—and Brainerd himself his most important, carefully crafted, spiritual model. Finally, *Freedom of the Will* (1754) has proven most interesting to scholars. Its famed distinction between a sinner's "natural ability" and "moral inability" to repent was grist for the mills of countless New Englanders to the time of the Civil War.

Jonathan Edwards

A DIVINE AND SUPERNATURAL LIGHT (1734)

"And Jesus answered and said unto him, 'Blessed art thou, Simon Bar-jona: for flesh and blood hath not revealed it unto thee, but my Father which is in heaven'" (Matt. 16:17). So began Edwards's greatest sermon on the reality of spiritual light. First preached at the First Church of Northampton in August 1733, it was published the following year and has since become one of the most beloved items in his oeuvre (a body of work that includes nearly 1,250 sermons).

Sermons on Matthew 16 have most often focused on what follows in verses 18 and 19: "And I say also unto thee, that thou art Peter, and upon this rock I will build my church; and the gates of hell shall not prevail against it. And I will give unto thee the keys of the kingdom of heaven: and whatsoever thou shalt bind on earth shall be bound in heaven: and whatsoever thou shalt loose on earth shall be loosed in heaven." This text has stood for centuries as the basis of the Roman Catholic claim for Peter's supremacy as first among the apostles and of the papacy's power to bind and loose our sins on God's behalf (the power of the keys).

But this is not what captured Edwards's attention about this text. For him, the divine and supernatural *revelation* made to Peter proved more crucial for Christian practice than the donation of the keys. What mattered most to Edwards was that the Father had made himself known—supernaturally—to Peter, and the other apostles too, transforming their lives and giving them spiritual understanding. As he phrased the doctrine of this sermon: "There is such a thing, as a spiritual and divine light, immediately imparted to the soul by God, of a different nature from any that is obtained by natural means." (Edwards's sermons, like those of his Puritan forebears, were usually arranged in threefold fashion, with sections unpacking the text, propounding its doctrine, and detailing an application.) In other words, Peter's confession of Christ—like those of all with genuine faith—was enabled directly by God, who grants the gifts of spiritual light and spiritual sight.

For Edwards and his followers, this gift changed everything. Most importantly, it changed the way they perceived, or experienced, God. As Edwards explained in a passage pregnant with existential exigency, the divine and supernatural light that God has shined in the hearts of the saints is "a true *sense* of the divine excellency of the things revealed in the Word of God, and a *conviction* of the truth and reality of them." Many have heard about these things and have understood them cognitively, but only the saints have sensed their beauty and come to know them personally. Indeed,

> there is a difference between having an opinion that God is holy and gracious, and having a sense of the loveliness and beauty of that holiness and grace. There is a difference between having a rational judgment that honey is sweet, and having a sense of its sweetness. A man may have the former, that knows not how honey tastes; but a man can't have the latter, unless he has an idea of the taste of honey in his mind. . . . There is a wide difference between mere speculative, rational judging anything to be excellent, and having a sense of its sweetness and beauty. The former rests only in the head, speculation only is concerned in it; but the heart is concerned in the latter. When the heart is sensible of the beauty and amiableness of a thing, it necessarily feels pleasure in the apprehension.

The Edwardseans wanted desperately to see that pleasure in others, to extend the community of the saints, and to cultivate an awakened, truly spiritual sensibility in the hearts and minds of those to whom they ministered.

{{ornament}}

. . . What I would make the subject of my present discourse from these words, is this:

Doctrine

There is such a thing, as a spiritual and divine light, immediately imparted to the soul by God, of a different nature from any that is obtained by natural means.

In what I say on this subject at this time, I would:

I. Show what this divine light is.
II. How it is given immediately by God, and not obtained by natural means.
III. Show the truth of the doctrine.
And then conclude with a brief improvement.

I. I would show what this spiritual and divine light is. And in order to it would show,
First, in a few things what it is not. And here,
1. Those convictions that natural men may have of their sin and misery is not this spiritual and divine light. Men in a natural condition may have convictions of the guilt that lies upon them, and of the anger of God, and their danger of divine vengeance. Such convictions are from light or sensibleness of truth: that some sinners have a greater conviction of their guilt and misery than others is because some have more light, or more of an apprehension of truth, than others. And this light and conviction may be from the Spirit of God; the Spirit convinces men of sin: but yet nature is much more concerned in it than in the communication of that spiritual and divine light, that is spoken of in the doctrine; 'tis from the Spirit of God only as assisting natural principles, and not as infusing any new principles. Common grace differs from special, in that it influences only by assisting of nature; and not by imparting grace, or bestowing anything above nature. The light that is obtained is wholly natural, or of no superior kind to what mere nature attains to; though more of that kind be obtained than would be obtained if men were left wholly to themselves. Or in other words, common grace only assists the faculties of the soul to do that more fully, which they do by nature; as natural conscience, or reason, will by mere nature make a man sensible of guilt, and will accuse and condemn him when he has done amiss. Conscience is a principle natural to men; and the work that it doth naturally, or of itself, is to give an apprehension of right and wrong; and to suggest to the mind the relation that there is between right and wrong, and a retribution. . . .

The Spirit of God acts in a very different manner in the one case, from what he doth in the other. He may indeed act upon the mind of a natural man; but he acts in the mind of a saint as an indwelling vital principle. He acts upon the mind of an unregenerate person as an extrinsic occasional agent; for in acting upon them he doth not unite himself to them; for notwithstanding all his influences that they may be the subjects of, they are still "sensual, having not the Spirit" (Jude 19). But he unites himself with the mind of a saint, takes him for his temple, actuates and influences him as a new, supernatural principle of life and action. There is this difference; that the Spirit of God, in acting in the soul of a godly man, exerts and communicates himself there in his own proper nature. Holiness is the proper nature of the Spirit of God. The Holy Spirit operates in the minds of the godly, by uniting himself to them, and living in them, and exerting his own nature in the exercise of their faculties. . . .

2. This spiritual and divine light don't [doesn't] consist in any impression made upon the imagination. 'Tis no impression upon the mind, as though one saw anything with the bodily eyes: 'tis no imagination or idea of an outward light or glory, or any beauty of form or countenance, or a visible luster or brightness of any object. . . . When the mind has a lively discovery of spiritual things, and is greatly affected with the power of divine light, it may, and probably very commonly doth, much affect the imagination: so that impressions of an outward beauty or brightness may accompany those spiritual discoveries. . . . And we can't determine but that the devil, who transforms himself into an angel of light, may cause imaginations of an outward beauty, or visible glory, and of sounds and speeches, and other such things; but these are things of a vastly inferior nature to spiritual light.

3. This spiritual light is not the suggesting of any new truths, or propositions not contained in the Word of God. This suggesting of new truths or doctrines to the mind, independent of any antecedent revelation of those propositions, either in word or writing, is inspiration; such as the prophets and apostles had, and such as some enthusiasts pretend to. But this spiritual light that I am speaking of is quite a different thing from inspiration: it reveals no new doctrine, it suggests no new proposition to the mind, it teaches no new thing of God, or Christ, or another world, not taught in the Bible; but only gives a due apprehension of those things that are taught in the Word of God.

4. 'Tis not every affecting view that men have of the things of religion that is this spiritual and divine light. Men by mere principles of nature are capable of being affected with things that have a special relation to religion, as well as other things. A person by mere nature, for instance, may be liable to be affected with the story of Jesus Christ, and the sufferings he underwent, as well as by any other tragical story: he may be the more affected with it from the interest he conceives mankind to have in it: yea, he may be affected with it without believing it; as well as a man may be affected with what he reads in a romance, or sees acted in a stage play. He may be affected with a lively and eloquent description of many pleasant things that attend the state of the blessed in heaven; as well as his imagination be entertained by a romantic description of the pleasantness of fairy land, or the like. . . . We read in Scripture of many that were greatly affected with things of a religious nature, who yet are there represented as wholly graceless, and many of them very ill men. . . .

But I proceed to show, *second*, positively, what this spiritual and divine light is.

And it may be thus described: a true sense of the divine excellency of the things revealed in the Word of God, and a conviction of the truth and reality of them, thence arising.

This spiritual light primarily consists in the former of these, viz., a real sense and apprehension of the divine excellency of things revealed in the Word of God. A spiritual and saving conviction of the truth and reality of these things arises from such a sight of their divine excellency and glory; so that this conviction of their truth is an effect and natural consequence of this sight of their divine glory. There is therefore in this spiritual light,

1. A true sense of the divine and superlative excellency of the things of religion; a real sense of the excellency of God, and Jesus Christ, and of the work of redemption, and the ways and works of God revealed in the gospel. There is a divine and superlative glory in these things; an excellency that is of a vastly higher kind, and more sublime nature, than in other things; a glory greatly distinguishing them from all that is earthly and temporal. He that is spiritually enlightened truly apprehends and sees it, or has a sense of it. He don't [doesn't] merely rationally believe that God is glorious, but he has a sense of the gloriousness of God in his heart. There is not only a rational belief that God is holy, and that holiness is a good thing; but there is a sense of the loveliness of God's holiness. There is not only a speculatively judging that God is gracious, but a sense how amiable God is upon that account; or a sense of the beauty of this divine attribute.

There is a twofold understanding or knowledge of good that God has made the mind of man capable of. The first, that which is merely speculative or notional: as when a person only speculatively judges that anything is, which by the agreement of mankind, is called good or excellent, viz., that which is most to general advantage, and between which and a reward there is a suitableness; and the like. And the other is that which consists in the sense of the heart: as when there is a sense of the beauty, amiableness, or sweetness of a thing; so that the heart is sensible of pleasure and delight in the presence of the idea of it. In the former is exercised merely the speculative faculty, or the understanding strictly so-called, or as spoken of in distinction from the will or disposition of the soul. In the latter the will, or inclination, or heart, are mainly concerned.

Thus there is a difference between having an opinion that God is holy and gracious, and having a sense of the loveliness and beauty of that holiness and grace. There is a difference between having a rational judgment that honey is sweet, and having a sense of its sweetness. A man may have the former, that knows not how honey tastes; but a man can't have the latter, unless he has an idea of the taste of honey in his mind. . . . When the heart is sensible of the beauty and amiableness of a thing, it necessarily feels pleasure in the apprehension. It is implied in a person's being heartily sensible of the loveliness of a thing, that the idea of it is sweet and pleasant to his soul; which is a far different thing from having a rational opinion that it is excellent.

2. There arises from this sense of divine excellency of things contained in the Word of God, a conviction of the truth and reality of them: and that either indirectly, or directly.

(i) First, indirectly, and that two ways:

1. As the prejudices that are in the heart, against the truth of divine things, are hereby removed; so that the mind becomes susceptive of the due force of rational arguments for their truth. . . .

2. It not only removes the hindrances of reason, but positively helps reason. It makes even the speculative notions the more lively. It engages the attention of the mind, with the more fixedness and intenseness to that kind of objects; which causes it to have a clearer view of them, and enables it more clearly to see their mutual relations, and occasions it to take more notice of them. The ideas themselves that otherwise are dim, and obscure, are by this means impressed with the greater strength, and have a light cast upon them; so that the mind can better judge of them. As he that beholds the objects on the face of the earth, when the light of the sun is cast upon them, is under greater advantage to discern them in their true forms, and mutual relations, than he that sees them in a dim starlight or twilight. . . .

(ii) Second, a true sense of the divine excellency of the things of God's Word doth more directly and immediately convince of the truth of them; and that because the excellency of these things is so superlative. There is a beauty in them that is so divine and godlike, that is greatly and evidently distinguishing of them from things merely human, or that men are the inventors and authors of; a glory that is so high and great, that when clearly seen, commands assent to their divinity, and reality. . . . This evidence, that they, that are spiritually enlightened, have of the truth of the things of religion, is a kind of intuitive and immediate evidence. They believe the doctrines of God's Word to be divine, because they see divinity in them, i.e., they see a divine, and transcendent, and most evidently distinguishing glory in them; such a glory as, if clearly seen, don't [doesn't] leave room to doubt of their being of God, and not of men. . . .

II. I proceed now to the second thing proposed, viz., to show how this light is immediately given by God, and not obtained by natural means. And here,

First. 'Tis not intended that the natural faculties are not made use of in it. The natural faculties are the subject of this light: and they are the subject in such a manner that they are not merely passive, but active in it; the acts and exercises of man's understanding are concerned and made use of in it. God, in letting in this light into the soul, deals with man according to his nature, or as a rational creature; and makes use of his human faculties. But yet this light is not the less immediately from God for that; though the faculties are made use of, 'tis as the subject and not as the cause; and that acting of the faculties in it is not the cause, but is either implied in the thing itself (in the light that is imparted), or is the consequence of it. As the use that we make of our eyes in beholding various objects, when the sun arises, is not the cause of the light that discovers those objects to us.

Second. 'Tis not intended that outward means have no concern in this affair. As I have observed already, 'tis not in this affair, as it is in inspiration, where new truths are suggested: for here is by this light only given a due apprehension of the same truths that are revealed in the Word of God; and therefore it is not given without the Word. . . .

Third. When it is said that this light is given immediately by God, and not obtained by natural means, hereby is intended, that 'tis given by God without making use of any means that operate by their own power, or a natural force. God makes use of means; but 'tis not as mediate causes to produce this effect. There are not truly any second causes of it; but it is produced by God immediately. The Word of God is no proper cause of this effect: it don't [doesn't] operate by any natural force in it. The Word of God is only made use of to convey to the mind the subject matter of this saving instruction: and this indeed it doth convey to us by natural force or influence. It conveys to our minds these and those doctrines; it is the cause of the notion of them in our heads, but not of the sense of the divine excellency of them in our hearts. Indeed a person can't have spiritual light without the Word. But that don't [doesn't] argue that the Word properly causes that light. The mind can't see the excellency of any doctrine, unless that doctrine be first in the mind; but the seeing the excellency of the doctrine may be immediately from the Spirit of God; though the conveying of the doctrine or proposition itself may be by the Word. . . . I come now,

III. [in the third place,] to show the truth of the doctrine; that is, to show that there is such a thing as that spiritual light that has been described, thus immediately let into the mind by God. And here I would show briefly that this doctrine is both scriptural and rational.

First, 'tis scriptural. My text is not only full to the purpose, but 'tis a doctrine that the Scripture abounds in. We are there abundantly taught that the saints differ from the ungodly in this, that they have the knowledge of God, and a sight of God, and of Jesus Christ. . . .

And this light and knowledge is always spoken of as immediately given of God. Matthew 11:25–27, "At that time Jesus answered and said, I thank thee, O Father, Lord of heaven and earth, because thou hast hid these things from the wise and prudent, and hast revealed them unto babes: even so, Father; for so it seemed good in thy sight. All things are delivered unto me of my Father, and no man knoweth the Son but the Father; neither knoweth any man the Father, save the Son, and he to whomsoever the Son will reveal him." Here this effect is ascribed alone to the arbitrary operation, and gift of God, bestowing this knowledge on whom he will, and distinguishing those with it, that have the least natural advantage or means for knowledge, even babes, when it is denied to the wise and prudent. . . .

And that a true and saving belief of the truth of religion is that which arises from such a discovery is also what the Scripture teaches. As John 6:40, "And this is the will of him that sent me, that every one that seeth the Son, and believeth on him, may have everlasting life." Where it is plain that a true faith is what arises from a spiritual sight of Christ. . . .

The apostle Peter mentions it as what gave them (the apostles) good and well-grounded assurance of the truth of the gospel, that they had seen the divine glory of Christ. Second Peter 1:16, "For we have not followed cunningly devised fables, when we made known unto you the power and coming of our Lord Jesus Christ, but were eyewitnesses of his majesty." The Apostle has respect to that visible glory of Christ which they saw in his transfiguration: that glory was so divine, having such an ineffable appearance and semblance of divine holiness, majesty, and grace, that it evidently denoted him to be a divine person. But if a sight of Christ's outward glory might give a rational assurance of his divinity, why may not an apprehension of his spiritual glory do so too? Doubtless Christ's spiritual glory is in itself as distinguishing, and as plainly showing his divinity, as his outward glory; and a great deal more: for his spiritual glory is that wherein his divinity consists; and the outward glory of his transfiguration showed him to be divine, only as it was a remarkable image or representation of that spiritual glory. . . . But this brings me to what was proposed next, viz., to show that,

Second, this doctrine is rational.

1. 'Tis rational to suppose that there is really such an excellency in divine things, that is so transcendent and exceedingly different from what is in other things, that if it were seen would most evidently distinguish them. We can't rationally doubt but that things that are divine, that appertain to the Supreme Being, are vastly different from things that are human; that there is that God-like, high, and glorious excellency in

them, that does most remarkably difference them from the things that are of men. . . .

If Christ should now appear to anyone as he did on the Mount at his transfiguration; or if he should appear to the world in the glory that he now appears in in heaven, as he will do at the day of judgment; without doubt, the glory and majesty that he would appear in would be such as would satisfy everyone that he was a divine person, and that religion was true: and it would be a most reasonable and well-grounded conviction too. And why may there not be that stamp of divinity, or divine glory on the Word of God, on the scheme and doctrine of the gospel, that may be in like manner distinguishing and as rationally convincing, provided it be but seen? . . .

2. If there be such a distinguishing excellency in divine things, 'tis rational to suppose that there may be such a thing as seeing it. What should hinder but that it may be seen? 'Tis no argument that there is no such thing as a distinguishing excellency, or that, if there be, that it can't be seen, that some don't see it; though they may be discerning men in temporal matters. It is not rational to suppose, if there be any such excellency in divine things, that wicked men should see it. 'Tis not rational to suppose that those whose minds are full of spiritual pollution, and under the power of filthy lusts, should have any relish or sense of divine beauty, or excellency, or that their minds should be susceptive of that light that is in its own nature so pure and heavenly. . . .

3. 'Tis rational to suppose that this knowledge should be given immediately by God, and not be obtained by natural means. Upon what account should it seem unreasonable that there should be any immediate communication between God and the creature? 'Tis strange that men should make any matter of difficulty of it. Why should not he that made all things still have something immediately to do with the things that he has made? . . . And if it be rational to suppose that God immediately communicates himself to man in any affair, it is in this. 'Tis rational to suppose that God would reserve that knowledge and wisdom, that is of such a divine and excellent nature, to be bestowed immediately by himself, and that it should not be left in the power of second causes. Spiritual wisdom and grace is the highest and most excellent gift that ever God bestows on any creature: in this the highest excellency and perfection of a rational creature consists. 'Tis also immensely the most important of all divine gifts: 'tis that wherein man's happiness consists, and on which his everlasting welfare depends. . . . There is no gift or benefit that is in itself so nearly related to the divine nature, there is nothing the creature receives that is so much of God, of his nature, so much a participation of the Deity: 'tis a kind of emanation of God's beauty, and is related to God as the light is to the sun. . . .

'Tis rational to suppose that it should be beyond a man's power to obtain this knowledge, and light, by the mere strength of natural reason; for 'tis not a thing that belongs to reason, to see the beauty and loveliness of spiritual things; it is not a speculative thing, but depends on the sense of the heart. Reason indeed is necessary in order to it, as 'tis by reason only that we are become the subjects of the means of it. . . . But if we take reason strictly, not for the faculty of mental perception in general, but for ratiocination, or a power of inferring by arguments; I say if we take reason thus, the perceiving of spiritual beauty and excellency no more belongs to reason than it belongs to the sense of feeling to perceive colors, or to the power of seeing to perceive the sweetness of food. It is out of reason's province to perceive the beauty or loveliness of anything: such a perception don't [doesn't] belong to that faculty. Reason's work is to perceive truth, and not excellency. . . .

[Improvement]

I will conclude with a very brief improvement of what has been said.

I. This doctrine may lead us to reflect on the goodness of God, that has so ordered it, that a saving evidence of the truth of the gospel is such, as is attainable by persons of mean capacities, and advantages, as well as those that are of the greatest parts and learning. If the evidence of the gospel depended only on history, and such reasonings as learned men only are capable of, it would be above the reach of far the greatest part of mankind. But persons, with but an ordinary degree of knowledge, are capable, without a long and subtle train of reasoning, to see the divine excellency of the things of religion: they are capable of being taught by the Spirit of God, as well as learned men. . . .

II. This doctrine may well put us upon examining ourselves, whether we have ever had this divine light, that has been described, let into our souls. If there be such a thing indeed, and it ben't only a notion, or whimsy of persons of weak and distempered brains, then doubtless 'tis a thing of great importance, whether we have thus been taught by the Spirit of God; whether the light of the glorious gospel of Christ, who is the image of God, hath shined into us, giving us the light of the knowledge of the glory of God in the face of Jesus Christ; whether we have seen the Son, and believed on him, or have that faith of gospel doctrines which arises from a spiritual sight of Christ.

III. All may hence be exhorted, earnestly to seek this spiritual light. To influence and move to it, the following things may be considered.

First. This is the most excellent and divine wisdom that any creature is capable of. 'Tis more excellent than any human learning; 'tis far more excellent than all the knowledge of the greatest philosophers, or states-men. Yea, the least glimpse of the glory of God in the face of Christ doth more exalt and ennoble the soul than all the knowledge of those that have the greatest speculative understanding in divinity, without grace. . . .

Second. This knowledge is that which is above all others sweet and joyful. Men have a great deal of pleasure in human knowledge, in stud-ies of natural things; but this is nothing to that joy which arises from this divine light shining into the soul. This light gives a view of those things that are immensely the most exquisitely beautiful, and capable of delighting the eye of the understanding. This spiritual light is the dawning of the light of glory in the heart. There is nothing so powerful as this to support persons in affliction, and to give the mind peace and brightness, in this stormy and dark world.

Third. This light is such as effectually influences the inclination, and changes the nature of the soul. It assimilates the nature to the divine nature, and changes the soul into an image of the same glory that is beheld. Second Corinthians 3:18, "But we all with open face, beholding as in a glass the glory of the Lord, are changed into the same image, from glory to glory, even as by the Spirit of the Lord." This knowledge will wean from the world, and raise the inclination to heavenly things. It will turn the heart to God as the fountain of good, and to choose him for the only portion. This light, and this only, will bring the soul to a saving close with Christ. It conforms the heart to the gospel, mortifies its enmity and opposition against the scheme of salvation therein revealed: it causes the heart to embrace the joyful tidings, and entirely to adhere to, and acquiesce in the revelation of Christ as our Savior: it causes the whole soul to accord and symphonize with it, admitting it with entire credit and respect, cleaving to it with full inclination and affection. And it effectually disposes the soul to give up itself entirely to Christ.

Fourth. This light, and this only, has its fruit in an universal holiness of life. No merely notional or speculative understanding of the doctrines of religion will ever bring to this. But this light, as it reaches the bottom of the heart, and changes the nature, so it will effectually dispose to an universal obedience. It shows God's worthiness to be obeyed and served. It draws forth the heart in a sincere love to God, which is the only principle of a true, gracious, and universal obedience. And it convinces of the reality of those glorious rewards that God has promised to them that obey him.

From Jonathan Edwards, *A Divine and Supernatural Light*. . . . (Boston: S. Kneeland and T. Green, 1734).

Jonathan Edwards

RELIGIOUS AFFECTIONS (1746)

After the *Confessions* of Augustine, Edwards's *Treatise Concerning Religious Affections* ranks as the most widely studied account of the psychology of Christian spirituality, or the science of the soul's transformation by God's grace. Written in 1746, it represents the culmination of a decade of reflection on the thousands of conversions Edwards witnessed in the Awakening. Since the publication of his *Divine and Supernatural Light*, Edwards had penned several other works in the science of revival. His *Faithful Narrative* is best known. But he also published a book of the sermons he preached in the revival (1738), his commencement address at Yale titled *The Distinguishing Marks of a Work of the Spirit of God* upon the soul (1741), as well as a major treatise written at the apex of the Awakening, *Some Thoughts Concerning the Present Revival of Religion in New-England, and the Way in Which It Ought to Be Acknowledged and Promoted* (1742).

Religious Affections recapitulates the themes of these earlier works, driving home the crucial difference Edwards saw between "true religion," or vital spirituality, and its damnable counterfeits. In fact, he began the book on this theme: "There is no question whatsoever, that is of greater importance to mankind, and that it more concerns every individual person to be well resolved in, than this, what are the distinguishing qualifications of those that are in favor with God, and entitled to his eternal rewards? Or which comes to the same thing, What is the nature of true religion?" His answer? "True religion, in great part, consists in holy affections." And what did he mean by the term *affections*? "I answer, the affections are no other than the more vigorous and sensible exercises of the inclination and will of the soul." They are the longings, aspirations, drives, and well-considered passions that comprise a person's spiritual and moral orientation.

Edwards devoted the bulk of *Affections* to developing criteria for distinguishing converted, or truly holy, religious affections from affections that had not been subject to spiritual transformation. He listed twelve "negative signs," red herrings of Christian piety—things such as emotionalism, bodily quirks, and false spiritual confidences—uncertain indicators of regenerate spirituality. Then he fleshed out his "positive signs," twelve reliable indicators that one's affections were for real—things such as confidence in the gospel, a deep reverence for the Bible, and a delight in the beauty and the holiness of God.

What follows is an excerpt of Edwards's twelfth positive sign, "the chief of all the signs of grace," he said, the sign of "Christian practice." If the Holy Spirit inhabited one's soul, Edwards believed, one should bear the fruit of the Spirit in daily life. Of course, there were other, interior ways in which one's life should be transformed. But for an objective, stable measure of one's spiritual condition, one could not do better than to look for Christian charity in action. As Edwards summarizes below, "Holy affections . . . have that influence and power upon him who is the subject of 'em, that they cause that a practice, which is universally conformed to, and directed by Christian rules, should be the practice and business of his life." The proof of Christian faith, in other words, was in the living. Holy affections always showed themselves in concrete acts of love.

XII. Gracious and holy affections have their exercise and fruit in Christian practice. I mean, they have that influence and power upon him who is the subject of 'em, that they cause that a practice, which is universally conformed to, and directed by Christian rules, should be the practice and business of his life.

This implies three things: (1) That his behavior or practice in the world be universally conformed to, and directed by Christian rules. (2) That he makes a business of such a holy practice above all things; that it be a business which he is chiefly engaged in, and devoted to, and pursues with highest earnestness and diligence: so that he may be said to make this practice of religion eminently his work and business. And (3) That he persists in it to the end of life: so that it may be said, not only to be his business at certain seasons, the business of Sabbath days, or certain extraordinary times, or the business of a month, or a year, or of seven years, or his business under certain circumstances; but the business of his life; it being that business which he perseveres in through all changes, and under all trials, as long as he lives.

The necessity of each of these, in all true Christians, is most clearly and fully taught in the Word of God. . . .

Now from all that has been said, I think it to be abundantly manifest that Christian practice is the most proper evidence of the gracious sincerity of professors, to themselves and others; and the chief of all the marks of grace, the sign of signs, and evidence of evidences, that which seals and crowns all other signs. I had rather have the testimony of my conscience, that I have such a saying of my supreme Judge on my side, as that, "He that hath my commandments and keepeth them, he it is that loveth me" (John 14:21); than the judgment, and fullest approbation, of all the wise, sound, and experienced divines that have lived this thousand years, on the most exact and critical examination of my experiences, as to the manner of my conversion. Not that there are no other good evidences of a state of grace but this. There may be other exercises of grace, besides these efficient exercises, which the saints may have in contemplation, that may be very satisfying to them: but yet this is the chief and most proper evidence. There may be several good evidences that a tree is a fig tree; but the highest and most proper evidence of it is that it actually bears figs. 'Tis possible that a man may have a good assurance of a state of grace, at his first conversion, before he has had opportunity to gain assurance, by this great evidence I am speaking of. If a man hears that a great treasure is offered him, in a distant place, on condition that he will prize it so much, as to be willing to leave what he possesses at home, and go a journey for it, over the rocks and mountains that are in the way, to the place where it is: 'tis possible the man may be well assured that he values the treasure to the degree spoken of, as soon as the offer is made him; he may feel a willingness to go for the treasure, within him, beyond all doubt: but yet, this don't [doesn't] hinder but that his actual going for it is the highest and most proper evidence of his being willing, not only to others, but to himself. But then as an evidence to himself, his outward actions, and the motions of his body in his journey, are not considered alone, exclusive of the actions of his mind, and a consciousness within himself, of the thing that moves him, and the end he goes for; otherwise, his bodily motion is no evidence to him of his prizing the treasure. In such a manner is Christian practice the most proper evidence of a saving value of the pearl of great price, and treasure hid in the field.

Christian practice is the sign of signs, in this sense that it is the great evidence, which confirms and crowns all other signs of godliness. There is no one grace of the Spirit of God, but that Christian practice is the most proper evidence of the truth of it. As it is with the members of our bodies, and all our utensils, the proper proof of the soundness and goodness of 'em is in the use of 'em; so it is with our graces (which are given to be used in practice, as much as our hands and feet, or the tools with which we work, or the arms with which we fight) the proper trial and proof of them is in their exercise in practice. Most of the things we use are serviceable to us, and so have their serviceableness proved, in some pressure, straining, agitation, or collision. So it is with a bow, a sword, an ax, a saw, a cord, a chain, a staff, a foot, a tooth, etc. And they that are so weak, as not to bear the strain or pressure we need to put them to, are good for nothing. So it is with all the virtues of the mind. The proper trial and proof of them is in being exercised under those temptations and trials that God brings us under, in the course of his providence, and in being put to such service as strains hard upon the principles of nature. . . .

And as the fruit of holy practice is the chief evidence of the truth of grace; so the degree in which experiences have influence on a person's practice is the surest evidence of the degree of that which is spiritual and divine in his experiences. Whatever pretenses persons may make to great discoveries, great love and joys, they are no further to be regarded, than they have influence on their practice. Not but that allowances must be made for the natural temper. But that don't [doesn't] hinder, but that the degree of grace is justly measured, by the degree of the effect in practice. . . .

Thus I have endeavored to represent the evidence there is that Christian practice is the chief of all the signs of saving grace. And before I conclude this discourse, I would say something briefly, in answer to two objections, that may possibly be made by some, against what has been said upon this head.

Object. I. Some may be ready to say, this seems to be contrary to that opinion, so much received among good people; that professors should judge of their state, chiefly by their inward experience, and that spiritual experiences are the main evidence of true grace.

I answer, 'tis doubtless a true opinion, and justly much received among good people, that professors should chiefly judge of their state by their experience. But it is a great mistake that what has been said is at all contrary to that opinion. The chief sign of grace to the consciences of Christians, being Christian practice, in the sense that has been explained, and according to what has been shewn to be the true notion of Christian practice, is not at all inconsistent with Christian experience being the chief evidence of grace. Christian or holy practice is spiritual practice; and that is not the motion of a body that knows not how, nor when, nor wherefore it moves: but spiritual practice in man is the practice of a spirit and body jointly, or the practice of a spirit, animating, commanding, and actuating a body, to which it is united, and over which it has power given it by the Creator. And therefore the main thing in this holy practice

41

is the holy acts of the mind, directing and governing the motions of the body. And the motions of the body are to be looked upon as belonging to Christian practice, only secondarily, and as they are dependent and consequent on the acts of the soul. The exercises of grace that Christians find, or are conscious to, within themselves, are what they experience within themselves; and herein therefore lies Christian experience: and this Christian experience consists as much in those operative exercises of grace in the will that are immediately concerned in the management of the behavior of the body, as in other exercises. These inward exercises are not the less a part of Christian experience, because they have outward behavior immediately connected with them. A strong act of love to God is not the less a part of spiritual experience, because it is the act that immediately produces and effects some self-denying and expensive outward action, which is much to the honor and glory of God. . . .

And not only does the most important and distinguishing part of Christian experience lie in spiritual practice; but such is the nature of that sort of exercises of grace, wherein spiritual practice consists, that nothing is so properly called by the name of experimental religion. For that experience which is in these exercises of grace, that are found, and prove effectual, at the very point of trial, wherein God proves which we will actually cleave to, whether Christ or our lusts, are as has been shown already, the proper *experiment* of the truth and power of our godliness; wherein its victorious power and efficacy, in producing its proper effect, and reaching its end, is found by experience. This is properly Christian experience, wherein the saints have opportunity to see, by actual *experience* and *trial*, whether they have a heart to do the will of God, and to forsake other things for Christ, or no. As that is called experimental philosophy, which brings opinions and notions to the test of fact; so is that properly called experimental religion, which brings religious affections and intentions to the like test.

There is a sort of external religious practice, wherein is no inward experience; which no account is made of in the sight of God; but it is esteemed good for nothing. And there is what is called experience, that is without practice, being neither accompanied, nor followed with a Christian behavior; and this is worse than nothing. Many persons seem to have very wrong notions of Christian experience, and spiritual light and discoveries. Whenever a person finds within him, an heart to treat God as God, at the time that he has the trial, and finds his disposition effectual in the experiment, that is the most proper and most distinguishing experience. And to have at such a time that sense of divine things, that apprehension of the truth, importance and excellency of the things of religion, which then sways and prevails, and governs his heart and hands; this is the most excellent spiritual light, and these are the most distinguishing discoveries. Religion consists much in holy affection; but those exercises of affection which are most distinguishing of true religion are these practical exercises. Friendship between earthly friends consists much in affection; but yet those strong exercises of affection, that actually carry them through fire and water for each other, are the highest evidences of true friendship. . . .

Object. II. Some also may be ready to object against what has been said of Christian practice being the chief evidence of the truth of grace, that this is a legal doctrine; and that this making practice a thing of such great importance in religion magnifies works, and tends to lead men to make too much of their own doings, to the diminution of the glory of free grace, and does not seem well to consist with that great gospel doctrine of justification by faith alone.

But this objection is altogether without reason. Which way is it inconsistent with the freeness of God's grace, that holy practice should be a sign of God's grace? 'Tis our works being the price of God's favor, and not their being the sign of it, that is the thing which is inconsistent with the freeness of that favor. Surely the beggar's looking on the money he has in his hands, as a sign of the kindness of him who gave it to him, is in no respect inconsistent with the freeness of that kindness. 'Tis his having money in his hand as the price of a benefit that is the thing which is inconsistent with the free kindness of the giver. The notion of the freeness of the grace of God to sinners, as that is revealed and taught in the gospel, is not that no holy and amiable qualifications or actions in us shall be a fruit, and so a sign of that grace; but that it is not the worthiness or loveliness of any qualification or action of ours which recommends us to that grace; that kindness is shown to the unworthy and unlovely; that there is great excellency in the benefit bestowed, and no excellency in the subject as the price of it; that goodness goes forth and flows out, from the fullness of God's nature, the fullness of the Fountain of Good, without any amiableness in the object to draw it. And this is the notion of justification without works (as this doctrine is taught in the Scripture) that it is not the worthiness or loveliness of our works, or anything in us, which is in any wise accepted with God, as a balance for the guilt of sin, or a recommendation of sinners to his acceptance as heirs of life. Thus we are justified only by the righteousness of Christ, and not by our righteousness. And when works are opposed to faith in this affair, and it is said that we are justified by faith and not by works; thereby is meant that it is not the worthiness or amiableness of our works, or anything in us, which recommends us to an interest in Christ and his benefits; but that we have this interest only in faith, or by our souls receiving Christ, or adhering to, and closing with him. But that the worthiness or amiableness of nothing in us recommends and brings us to an interest in Christ is no argument that nothing in us is a sign of an interest in Christ.

If the doctrines of free grace, and justification by faith alone, be inconsistent with the importance of holy practice as a sign of grace; then they are equally inconsistent with the importance of anything whatsoever in us as a sign of grace, and holiness, or any grace that is in us, or any of our experiences of religion: for 'tis as contrary to the doctrines of free grace and justification by faith alone that any of these should be the righteousness which we are justified by, as that holy practice should be so. 'Tis with holy works, as it is with holy qualifications: 'tis inconsistent with the freeness of gospel grace that a title to salvation should be given to men for the loveliness of any of their holy qualifications, as much as that it should be given for the holiness of their works. It is inconsistent with the gospel doctrine of free grace that an interest in Christ and his benefits should be given for the loveliness of a man's true holiness, for the amiableness of his renewed, sanctified, heavenly heart, his love to God, and being like God, or his experience of joy in the Holy Ghost, self-emptiness, a spirit to exalt Christ above all, and to give all glory to him, and a heart devoted unto him: I say, it is inconsistent with the gospel doctrine of free grace that a title to Christ's benefits should be given out of regard to the loveliness of any of these, or that any of these should be our righteousness in the affair of justification. And yet this don't [doesn't] hinder the importance of these things as evidences of an interest in Christ. Just so it is with respect to holy actions and works. To make light of works, because we ben't justified by works, is the same thing in effect, as to make light of all religion, all grace and holiness, yea, true evangelical holiness, and all gracious experience: for all is included, when the Scripture says, we are not justified by works: for by works in this case is meant all our own righteousness, religion, or holiness, and everything that is in us, all the good we do, and all the good which we are conscious of, all external acts, and all internal acts and exercises of grace, and all experiences, and all those holy and heavenly things wherein the life and power, and the very essence of religion do consist, all those great things which Christ and his apostles mainly insisted on in their preaching, and endeavored to promote, as of the greatest consequence in the hearts and lives of men, and all good dispositions, exercises, and qualifications of every kind whatsoever; and even faith itself, considered as a part of our holiness. For we are justified by none of these things: and if we were, we should, in a Scripture sense, be justified by works. And therefore if it ben't legal, and contrary to the evangelical doctrine of justification without works, to insist on any of these, as of great importance, as evidences of an interest in Christ; then no more is it thus, to insist on the importance of holy practice. . . .

'Tis greatly to the hurt of religion, for persons to make light of, and insist little on, those things which the Scriptures insist most upon, as of the most importance in the evidence of our interest in Christ (under a notion that to lay weight on these things is legal, and an old covenant way); and so to neglect the exercises, and effectual operations of grace in practice, and insist almost wholly on discoveries, and the method and manner of the immanent exercises of conscience and grace in contemplation; depending on an ability to make nice distinctions in these matters, and a faculty of accurate discerning in them, from philosophy or experience. It is in vain to seek for any better, or any further signs, than those that the Scriptures have most expressly mentioned, and most frequently insisted on, as signs of godliness. . . . If we had got into the way of looking chiefly at those things, which Christ and his apostles and prophets chiefly insisted on, and so in judging of ourselves and others, chiefly regarding practical exercises and effects of grace, not neglecting other things; it would be of manifold happy consequence; it would above all things tend to the conviction of deluded hypocrites, and to prevent the delusion of those whose hearts were never brought to a thorough compliance with the strait and narrow way which leads to life; it would tend to deliver us from innumerable perplexities, arising from the various inconsistent schemes that are about methods and steps of experience; it would greatly tend to prevent professors neglecting strictness of life, and tend to promote their engagedness and earnestness in their Christian walk; and it would become fashionable for men to shew their Christianity, more by an amiable distinguished behavior than by an abundant and excessive declaring their experiences; and we should get into the way of appearing lively in religion, more by being lively in the service of God and our generation than by the liveliness and forwardness of our tongues, and making a business of proclaiming on the house tops, with our mouths, the holy and eminent acts and exercises of our own hearts; and Christians that are intimate friends would talk together of their experiences and comforts, in a manner better becoming Christian humility and modesty, and more to each other's profit; their tongues not running before, but rather going behind their hands and feet, after the prudent example of the blessed Apostle, 2 Corinthians 12:6; and many occasions of spiritual pride would be cut off; and so a great door shut against the devil; and a great many of the main stumbling blocks against experimental and powerful religion would be removed; and religion would be declared and manifested in such a way that instead of hardening spectators, and exceedingly promoting infidelity and atheism, would above all things tend to convince men that there is a reality in religion, and greatly awaken them, and win them, by convincing their consciences of the importance and excellency of religion. Thus the light of professors would so shine before men that others seeing their good works would glorify their Father which is in heaven.

From Jonathan Edwards, *A Treatise Concerning Religious Affections* (Boston: S. Kneeland and T. Green, 1746).

Jonathan Edwards

AN ACCOUNT OF THE LIFE
OF THE LATE REVEREND
MR. DAVID BRAINERD (1749)

As Jonathan Edwards wrote in reference to Scripture, "There are two ways of representing and recommending true religion and virtue to the world, which God hath made use of: the one is by doctrine and precept; the other is by instance and example." More than any of his writings, Edwards's *Life of David Brainerd* traversed the latter of these two ways, becoming his best-selling book as a result. During New England's Great Awakening, Edwards published several works, all of which defined true faith and sought to encourage it in others. But nowhere else did he labor so hard to flesh out a model of faith, depicting a full-bodied example of regenerate spirituality (though he did use spiritual models in two other major treatises).

David Brainerd (1718–47) was an orphan by the age of fourteen. He was expelled from Yale College at the age of twenty-three—for insulting one of his teachers—and was taken from this world at the tender age of twenty-nine. But during his final years of life, he exhibited the sort of truly converted spirituality Edwards had been championing for years. In November of 1742, he earned a commission to serve as a missionary to Native American Indians (from the Society in Scotland for Propagating Christian Knowledge). He prepared with the Rev. John Sergeant, another Edwards protégé, at the Indian mission in Stockbridge, Massachusetts. He crossed the Hudson soon thereafter, commenced his work in Kaunaumeek (NY), and then moved south to work with the Delawares of central Pennsylvania. Ordained in 1744 by the New York Presbytery, he spent the final years of his ministry in New Jersey. He founded an Indian congregation in the village of Crossweeksung, moved this church to nearby Cranberry in 1746, and, by the time he had to leave this group in 1747, the congregation boasted eighty-five communicants (forty-three adults and forty-two children).

Never a very healthy man, Brainerd contracted tuberculosis, lived for a while with Jonathan Dickinson in Elizabethtown, New Jersey, and thus is sometimes labeled Princeton's first student. (The College of New Jersey, later Princeton University, began in the Dickinson parsonage in 1746.) In the spring of 1747, Brainerd journeyed to New England. He convalesced in the Edwards parsonage in Northampton, Massachusetts, and developed an intimate friendship with Jerusha, Edwards's daughter. He succumbed to tuberculosis in a bedroom at the parsonage on October 9, 1747. (Jerusha died at age eighteen just four months later. She is buried next to Brainerd in the Northampton cemetery.)

From a worldly point of view, Brainerd did not know much success. He lived a short, grueling life without renown or temporal gain. As Edwards himself confesses below, he also wrestled with personal demons. He was "prone to melancholy" and "excessive in his labors." He neglected to take "due care to proportion his fatigues to his strength." But through the leaves of Edwards's *Life*, Brainerd quickly became a hero to the evangelical world. Thousands traveled in spiritual pilgrimage to Brainerd's humble grave. Many more undertook to follow Brainerd into Protestant missions, honoring him as a patron saint of the gospel cause.

Edwards implied that Brainerd ranked among "the best saints in this world," and in the midst of the spiritual turmoil of the era's Great Awakening, Edwards could think of no one better to frame as a picture of Protestant piety. Brainerd demonstrated a knack for limning the crucial differences between authentic and hypocritical revival-era faith. In the words of Edwards himself, he "had that talent at describing the various workings of . . . imaginary enthusiastical religion, evincing the falseness and vanity of it, and demonstrating the great difference between this and true spiritual devotion, which I scarcely ever knew equalled in any other person." Despite his "imperfections," Brainerd also set a striking example of deep Christian devotion, "of true and eminent Christian piety in heart and practice; tending greatly to confirm the reality of vital religion and the power of godliness, most worthy of imitation, and many ways tending to the spiritual benefit of the careful observer." Countless observers, then and since, have found these words of Edwards true. As much as any that he proclaimed, they shaped the popular perception of Edwardsean spirituality during the heyday of New England's New Divinity.

☙

Author's Preface

There are two ways of representing and recommending true religion and virtue to the world, which God hath made use of: the one is by doctrine and precept; the other is by instance and example: Both are abundantly used in the holy Scriptures. Not only are the grounds, nature, design, and importance of religion clearly exhibited in the doctrines of Scripture, and its exercise and practice plainly delineated and abundantly enjoined and enforced in its commands and counsels: but there we have many excellent examples of religion, in its power and practice, set before us, in the histories both of the Old Testament and New. Jesus Christ, the great prophet of God, when he came into the world to be "the light of the world" [John 8:12; 9:5; Matt. 5:14], to teach and enforce true religion, in a greater degree than ever had been before, he made use of both these methods: In his doctrine he declared the mind and will of God, and the nature and properties of that virtue which becomes creatures of our make and in our circumstances, more clearly and fully than ever it had been before, and more powerfully enforced it by what he declared of the obligations and inducements to holiness; and he also in his own practice gave a most perfect example of the virtue he taught. He exhibited to the world such an illustrious pattern of humility, divine love, discreet zeal, self-denial, obedience, patience, resignation, fortitude, meekness, forgive-ness, compassion, benevolence, and universal holiness, as neither men nor angels ever saw before. God also in his Providence has been wont to make use of both these methods to hold forth light to mankind, and inducement to their duty, in all ages: He has from time to time raised up eminent teachers to exhibit and bear testimony to the truth in their doctrine, and oppose the errors, darkness, and wickedness of the world; and also has, from age to age, raised up some eminent persons that have set bright examples of that religion that is taught and prescribed in the Word of God; whole examples have in divine providence been set forth to public view. These have a great tendency to engage the attention of men to the doctrines and rules that are taught, and greatly to confirm and enforce them; and especially when these bright examples have been exhibited in the same persons that have been eminent teachers, so that the world has had opportunity to see such a confirmation of the truth, efficacy, and amiableness of the religion taught, in the practice of the same persons that have most clearly and forceably taught it; and above all, when these bright examples have been set by eminent teachers in a variety of unusual circumstances of remarkable trial; and God has withal remarkably distinguished them with wonderful success of their instructions and labors, consisting in glorious events that have been in many respects new and strange.

Such an instance we have in the excellent person whose Life is published in the following pages. His example is attended with a great variety of circumstances, tending to engage the attention of religious people, especially in these parts of the world: He was one of distinguished natural abilities; as all are sensible that had acquaintance with him: He was a minister of the Gospel, and one who was called to unusual services in that work, whose ministry was attended with very remarkable and unusual events, an account of which has already been given to the public; one whose course of religion began before the late times of extraordinary religious commotion, but yet one that lived in those times, and went through them, and was very much in the way of the various extraordinary effects and unusual appearances of that day, and was not an idle spectator, but had a near concern in many things that passed at that time; one that had a very extensive acquaintance with those that have been the subjects of the late religious operations, in many of these British colonies, in places far distant one from another, in people of many different nations, of different educations, manners, and customs; one who had peculiar opportunity of acquaintance with the false appearances and counterfeits of religion: one who himself was the instrument of a most remarkable awakening, and an exceeding wonderful and abiding alteration and moral transformation of such subjects as do peculiarly render the change rare and astonishing.

In the following account, the reader will have opportunity to see, not only what were the external circumstances and remarkable incidents of the life of this person, and how he spent his time from day to day, as to his external behavior; but also what passed in his own heart, the wonderful change that he experienced in his mind and disposition, the manner in which that change was brought to pass, how it continued, what were its consequences in his inward frames, thoughts, affections, and secret exercises, through many vicissitudes and trials, from thenceforth for more than eight years, till his death; and also to see how all ended at last, in his sentiments, frame, and behavior, during a long illness, and what were the effects of his religion in dying circumstances, or in the last stages of his dying illness. The account being written, the reader may have opportunity at his leisure to compare the various parts of the story, and deliberately to view and weigh the whole, and consider how far what is related is agreeable to the dictates of right reason and the holy Word of God.

I am far from supposing that Mr. Brainerd's inward exercise, and experiences, or his external conduct, were free from imperfection: The example of Jesus Christ is the only example that ever was set in the human nature that was altogether perfect; which therefore is a rule to try all other examples by; and the dispositions, frames, and practices of others must be commended and followed no further, than they were followers of Christ.

There is one thing in Mr. Brainerd, easily discernible by the following account of his life, that may be called an imperfection in him, which though not properly an imperfection of a moral nature, yet may possibly be made an objection against the extraordinary appearances of religion and devotion in him, by such as seek for objections against every thing that can be produced in favor of true vital religion; and that is, that he was one who by his constitution and natural temper was so prone to melancholy and dejection of spirit. There are some who think that all serious strict religion is a melancholy thing, and that what is called Christian experience is little else besides melancholy vapors disturbing the brain, and exciting enthusiastical imaginations. But that Mr. Brainerd's temper or constitution inclined him to despondency is no just ground to suspect his extraordinary devotion as being only the fruit of a warm imagination. I doubt not but that all who have well observed mankind will readily grant this, that it is not all those who by their natural constitution or temper are most disposed to dejection, that are the persons who are the most susceptive of lively and strong impressions on their imagination, or the most subject to those vehement impetuous affections, which are the fruits of such impressions; but that many who are of a very gay and sanguine natural temper are vastly more so, and if their affections are turned into a religious channel, are much more exposed to enthusiasm than many of the former. And as to Mr. Brainerd in particular, notwithstanding his inclination to despondency, he was evidently one of that sort of persons who usually are the furthest from a teeming imagination; being one of a penetrating genius, of clear thought, of close reasoning, and a very exact judgment and knowledge of things in divinity, but especially in things appertaining to inward experimental religion; most accurately distinguishing between real solid piety and enthusiasm, between those affections that are rational and scriptural, having their foundation in light and judgment, and those that are founded in whimsical conceits, strong impressions on the imagination, and those vehement emotions of the animal spirits that arise from them. He was exceeding sensible of men's exposedness to these things, how much they had prevailed, and what multitudes had been deceived by them, of the pernicious consequences of them, and the fearful mischief they had done in the Christian world. He greatly abhorred such a sort of religion, and was abundant in bearing testimony against it, living and dying; and was quick to discern when any thing of that nature arose, though in its first buddings, and appearing under the most fair and plausible disguises; and had that talent at describing the various workings of this imaginary enthusiastical religion, evincing the falseness and vanity of it, and demonstrating the great difference between this and true spiritual devotion, which I scarcely ever knew equalled in any other person. And his judiciousness did not only appear in distinguishing among the experiences of others, but also among the various exercises of his own mind; and particularly in discerning what within himself was to be laid to the score of melancholy; in which he exceeded all melancholy persons that ever I was acquainted with (though I have been in the way of acquaintance with very many); which was doubtless owing to a peculiar strength in his judgment: 'Tis a rare thing indeed that melancholy people are well sensible of their own disease, and fully convinced that such and such things are to be ascribed to it, as are indeed its genuine operations and fruits. Mr. Brainerd did not obtain that degree of skill, which he had in this matter, at once, but gained it gradually; as the reader may discern by the following account of his life. In the former part of his religious course, he imputed much of that kind of gloominess of mind and those dark thoughts to spiritual desertion, which in the latter part of his life, he was abundantly sensible, were owing to the disease of melancholy; accordingly he often expressly speaks of them in his diary as arising from this cause; and he was often in conversation speaking of the difference between melancholy and godly sorrow, true humiliation and spiritual desertion, and the great danger of mistaking the one for the other, and the very hurtful nature of melancholy, discoursing with great judgment upon it, and doubtless much more judiciously for what he knew by his own experience.

But besides what may be argued from Mr. Brainerd's strength of judgment, 'tis apparent in fact that he was not a person of a warm imagination. His inward experiences, either in his convictions or his conversion, and his religious views and impressions through the course of his life to his death (of which he has left a very particular account) none of them consisted in, or were excited by, strong and lively images formed in his imagination; there is nothing at all appears of it in his diary, from beginning to end: Yea, he told me on his deathbed that, although once when he was very young in years and in experience, he was deceived into a high opinion of such things, looking on them as superior attainments in religion, beyond what he had ever arrived to, and was ambitious of them and earnestly sought them, yet he never could obtain them; and that he never in his life had a strong impression on his imagination, of any visage, outward form, external glory, or any other thing of that nature; which kind of impressions abound among the wild enthusiastic people of the late and present day.

As Mr. Brainerd's religious impressions, views, and affections in their nature were vastly different from enthusiasm, so were their effects in him as contrary as possible to the ordinary effect of that. Nothing so puffs men up as enthusiasm, with a high conceit of their own wisdom, holiness, eminency, and sufficiency, and makes them so bold, forward, assuming, and arrogant: But the reader will see that Mr. Brainerd's religion constantly disposed him to a most mean thought of himself, an abasing sense of his own exceeding sinfulness, deficiency, unprofitableness, and ignorance; looking on himself as worse than others; disposing him to universal benevolence, meekness, and in honor to prefer others, and to treat all with kindness and respect. And when melancholy prevailed, though the effects of it were very prejudicial to him, yet it had not those effects of enthusiasm; but operated by dark and discouraging thoughts of himself, as ignorant, wicked, and wholly unfit for the work of the ministry, or even to be seen among mankind, etc. Indeed at the time forementioned, when he had not learned well to distinguish between enthusiasm and solid religion, he joining and keeping company with some that were tinged with no small degree of the former, for a season partook with them in a degree of their dispositions and behaviors; though as was observed before, he could not obtain those things wherein their enthusiasm itself consisted, and so could not become like them in that respect, however he erroneously desired and sought it. But certainly it is not at all to be wondered at that a youth and a young convert, one that had his heart so swallowed up in religion, and so earnestly desired the flourishing of it, but had had so little opportunity for reading, observation, and experience, should for a while be dazzled and deceived with the glaring appearances of that mistaken devotion and zeal; especially considering what the extraordinary circumstances of that day were. He told me on his deathbed that while he was in these circumstances he was out of his element, and did violence to himself, while complying, in his conduct, with persons of a fierce and imprudent zeal, from his great veneration of some that he looked upon much better than himself. So that it would be very unreasonable that his error at that time should nevertheless be esteemed a just ground of prejudice against the whole of his religion, and his character in general; especially considering how greatly his mind was soon changed, and how exceedingly he afterwards lamented his error, and abhorred himself for his imprudent zeal and misconduct at that time, even to the breaking of his heart, and almost to the overbearing and breaking the strength of his nature; and how much of a Christian spirit he shewed, in his condemning himself for that misconduct, as the reader will see.

What has been now mentioned of Mr. Brainerd is so far from being just ground of prejudice against what is related in the following account of his life that, if duly considered, it will render the history the more serviceable. For by his thus joining for a season with enthusiasts, he had a more full and intimate acquaintance with what belonged to that sort of religion, and so was under better advantages to judge of the difference between that, and the other, which he finally approved and strove to his utmost to promote, in opposition to it: And hereby the reader has the more to demonstrate to him that Mr. Brainerd in his testimony against it and the spirit and behavior of those that are influenced by it speaks from impartial conviction, and not from prejudice; because therein he openly condemns his own former opinion and conduct, on account of which he had greatly suffered from his opposers, and for which some continued to reproach him as long as he lived.

Another imperfection in Mr. Brainerd, which may be observed in the following account of his life, was his being *excessive in his labors*; not taking due care to proportion his fatigues to his strength. Indeed the case was very often so, and such the seeming calls of providence, that it was extremely difficult for him to avoid doing more than his strength would well admit of; yea, his circumstances, and the business of his mission among the Indians, were such that great fatigues and hardships were altogether inevitable. However, he was finally convinced that he had erred in this matter, and that he ought to have taken more thorough care, and been more resolute to withstand temptations to such degrees of labor as injured his health; and accordingly warned his brother, who succeeds him in his mission, to be careful to avoid this error.

Besides the imperfections already mentioned, it is readily allowed that there were some imperfections that ran through his whole life, and were mixed with all his religious affections and exercises, some mixture of what was natural with that which was spiritual; as it evermore is in the best saints in this world. Doubtless there was some influence that natural temper had in the religious exercises and experiences of Mr. Brainerd, as there most apparently was in the exercise of devout David, and the apostles Peter, John, and Paul: There was undoubtedly very often some influence of his natural disposition to dejection in his religious mourning, some mixture of melancholy with truly godly sorrow and real Christian humility, and some mixture of the natural fire of youth with his holy zeal for God, and some influence of natural principles mixed with grace in various other respects, as it ever was and ever will be with the saints while on this side [of] heaven. Perhaps none were more sensible of Mr. Brainerd's imperfections than he himself; or could distinguish more accurately than he, between what was natural and what was spiritual. 'Tis easy for the judicious reader to observe that his graces ripened, and the religious exercises of his heart became more and more pure, and he more and more distinguishing in his judgment, the longer he lived: He had much to teach and purify him, and he failed not to make his advantage thereby.

But notwithstanding all these imperfections, I am persuaded, every pious and judicious reader will acknowledge that what is here set before him is indeed a remarkable instance of true and eminent Christian piety in heart and practice; tending greatly to confirm the reality of vital religion and the power of godliness, most worthy of imitation, and many ways tending to the spiritual benefit of the careful observer.

'Tis fit, the reader should be aware, that what Mr. Brainerd wrote in his diary, out of which the following account of his life is chiefly taken, was written only for his own private use, and not to get honor and applause in the world, nor with any design that the world should ever see it, either while he lived or after his death, excepting some few things that he wrote in a dying state, after he had been persuaded (with difficulty) not entirely to suppress all his private writings. He showed himself almost invincibly averse to the publishing of any part of his diary after his death; and when he was thought to be dying at Boston, gave the most strict peremptory orders to the contrary: but being by some of his friends there prevailed upon to withdraw so strict and absolute a prohibition, he was pleased finally to yield so far as that his papers should be left in my hands, that I might dispose of them as I thought would be most for God's glory and the interest of religion. But a few days before his death, he ordered some part of his diary to be destroyed (as will afterwards be observed) which renders the account of his life the less complete. And there are some parts of his diary are here left out for brevity's sake that would (I am sensible) have been a great advantage to the history if they had been inserted; particularly the account of his wonderful successes among the Indians; which for substance is the same in his private diary with that which has already been made public in the *Journal* he kept by order of the Society in Scotland for their information. That account, I am of opinion, would be more entertaining and more profitable, if it were published as it is written in his diary, in connection with his secret religion and the inward exercises of his mind, and also with the preceding and following parts of the story of his life. But because that account has been published already, and because the adding it here would make the book much more bulky and more costly, which might tend to discourage the purchase and perusal of it, and so render it less extensively useful, I have therefore omitted that part. However, this defect may in a great measure be made up to the reader by his purchasing his public *Journal* and reading it in its place, with this history of his life; which undoubtedly would be well worth the while for every reader, and would richly recompense the additional cost of the purchase. I hope therefore that those of my readers who are not furnished with that book will, for their own profit and entertainment, and that they may have the story of this excellent person more complete, procure one of those books; without which he must have a very imperfect view of the most important part of his life, and (on some accounts) of the most remarkable and wonderful things in it. I should also observe that besides that book, and antecedent to it, there is a *Narrative* relating to the Indian affairs, annexed to Mr. Pemberton's Sermon at Mr. Brainerd's ordination; which likewise may the more profitably be read in conjunction with his diary previous to November 5, 1744.

But it is time to end this preface, that the reader may be no longer detained from the history itself. . . .

From Jonathan Edwards, *An Account of the Life of the Late Reverend Mr. David Brainerd. . . .* (Boston: D. Henchman, 1749).

Jonathan Edwards

FREEDOM OF THE WILL (1754)

More than any other treatise, Jonathan Edwards's *Freedom of the Will* became the engine of the Edwardsean tradition. As one can see repeatedly within the selections printed below, its definition of the will ("that by which the mind chooses anything") and distinction between a non-elect sinner's "natural ability" (constitutional capacity) to repent and turn from sin and his or her "moral inability" (ineradicable unwillingness) to do the very same served as what some have called the movement's shibboleths.

Edwards repudiated the notion that the will acts independently of the rest of the soul's faculties. For him, it simply chooses that toward which the soul inclines ("the will always is as the greatest apparent good is"). In fallen sinners, whose souls now suffer from disoriented desires, the will chooses what amounts to opposition to God's rule, though it does so by a moral, not a natural, necessity. Sinners choose to sin voluntarily. They do whatever they want within their sphere of moral control. The problem is that they do not *want* to do what God requires of them. Their affections are misdirected. They prefer to live for themselves and will continue in their sin until their preferences are reoriented supernaturally.

As seen in the text below, Edwards explains his crucial distinction between a sinner's natural ability and his or her moral inability to repent and turn to God by means of analogy. He speaks of two fictional prisoners: one who repents of his offense but remains in chains, behind bars, and thus is *teased* with an offer of pardon if he rises up and begs for it at the feet of his sovereign king; the other is "haughty, ungrateful," and "willful." He is given the same offer *and* released from his constraints.

But though he is naturally (physically) able to meet the terms of his parole, the second prisoner proves "so stout and stomachful, and full of haughty malignity, that he can't be willing to accept the offer: his rooted strong pride and malice have perfect power over him, and . . . bind him, by binding his heart."

Edwards and the Edwardseans proclaimed incessantly that those who failed to respond favorably when the gospel message was preached were like the second, not the first, of these two prisoners. They had the capacity to convert. Nothing material stood in their way. However, their hearts were hard, recalcitrant, and too proud to submit to God. Thus, the moral of their story was that unyielding, obdurate sinners had only themselves to blame for their sin. Nothing hindered them from repenting but their own free wills. Indeed, *this* was the central message of the New England Theology. This was also a major theme of the Second Great Awakening.

ぐう

Part I. Section 4. Of the Distinction of Natural and Moral Necessity, and Inability

The phrase "moral necessity" is used variously: sometimes 'tis used for a necessity of moral obligation. So we say, a man is under necessity, when he is under bonds of duty and conscience, which he can't be discharged from. So the word "necessity" is often used for great obligation in point of interest. Sometimes by "moral necessity" is meant that apparent connection of things, which is the ground of moral evidence; and so is distinguished from absolute necessity, or that sure connection of things, that is a foundation for infallible certainty. In this sense, "moral necessity" signifies much the same as that high degree of probability, which is ordinarily sufficient to satisfy, and be relied upon by mankind, in their conduct and behavior in the world, as they would consult their own safety and interest, and treat others properly as members of society. And sometimes by "moral necessity" is meant that necessity of connection and consequence, which arises from such *moral causes*, as the strength of inclination, or motives, and the connection which there is in many cases between these, and such certain volitions and actions. And it is in this sense that I use the phrase "moral necessity" in the following discourse.

By "natural necessity," as applied to men, I mean such necessity as men are under through the force of natural causes; as distinguished from what are called moral causes, such as habits and dispositions of the heart, and moral motives and inducements. Thus men placed in certain circumstances are the subjects of particular sensations by necessity: they feel pain when their bodies are wounded; they see the objects presented before them in a clear light, when their eyes are opened: so they assent to the truth of certain propositions, as soon as the terms are understood; as that two and two make four, that black is not white, that two parallel lines can never cross one another: so by a natural necessity men's bodies move downwards, when there is nothing to support them.

But here several things may be noted concerning these two kinds of necessity.

1. Moral necessity may be as absolute, as natural necessity. That is, the effect may be as perfectly connected with its moral cause, as a naturally necessary effect is with its natural cause. Whether the will in every case is necessarily determined by the strongest motive, or whether the will ever makes any resistance to such a motive, or can ever oppose the strongest present inclination, or not; if that matter should be controverted, yet I suppose none will deny, but that, in some cases, a previous bias and inclination, or the motive presented, may be so powerful, that the act of the will may be certainly and indissolubly connected therewith. . . . As therefore it must be allowed that there may be such a thing as a sure and perfect connection between moral causes and effects; so this only is what I call by the name of "moral necessity."

2. When I use this distinction of moral and natural necessity, I would not be understood to suppose, that if anything comes to pass by the former kind of necessity, the nature of things is not concerned in it, as well as in the latter. I don't mean to determine that when a moral habit or motive is so strong, that the act of the will infallibly follows, this is not owing to the nature of things. But these are the names that these two kinds of necessity have usually been called by; and they must be distinguished by some names or other; for there is a distinction or difference between them that is very important in its consequences. . . .

I suppose that necessity which is called natural, in distinction from moral necessity, is so called, because "mere nature," as the word is vulgarly used, is concerned, without anything of choice. The word "nature" is often used in opposition to "choice"; not because nature has indeed never any hand in our choice; but this probably comes to pass by means that we first get our notion of nature from that discernible and obvious course of events, which we observe in many things that our choice has no concert in; and especially in the material world; which, in very many parts of it, we easily perceive to be in a settled course; the stated order and manner of succession being very apparent. But where we don't readily discern the rule and connection (though there be a connection, according to an established law, truly taking place), we signify the manner of event by some other name. Even in many things which are seen in the material and inanimate world, which don't discernibly and obviously come to pass according to any settled course, men don't call the manner of the event by the name of nature, but by such names as "accident," "chance," "contingence," etc. So men make a distinction between "nature" and "choice"; as though they were completely and universally distinct. Whereas, I suppose none will deny but that choice, in many cases, arises from nature, as truly as other events. But the dependence and connection between acts of volition or choice, and their causes, according to established laws, is not so sensible and obvious. And we observe that choice is as it were a new principle of motion and action, different from that established law and order of things which is most obvious, that is seen especially in corporeal and sensible things; and also that choice often interposes, interrupts, and alters the chain of events in these external objects, and causes 'em to proceed otherwise than they would do, if let alone, and left to go on according to the laws of motion among themselves. . . .

3. It must be observed that in what has been explained, as signified by the name of "moral necessity," the word "necessity" is not used according to the original design and meaning of the word: for, as was observed before, such terms "necessary," "impossible," "irresistible," etc. in common speech, and their most proper sense, are always relative; having reference to some supposable voluntary opposition or endeavor that is insufficient. But no such opposition, or contrary will and endeavor, is supposable in the case of moral necessity; which is a certainty of the inclination and will itself; which does not admit of the supposition of a will to oppose and resist it. For 'tis absurd to suppose the same individual will to oppose itself, in its present act; or the present choice to be opposite to, and resisting present choice: as absurd as it is to talk of two contrary motions, in the same moving body, at the same time. And therefore the very case supposed never admits of any trial, whether an opposing or resisting will can overcome this necessity.

What has been said of natural and moral necessity may serve to explain what is intended by natural and moral *inability*. We are said to be *naturally* unable to do a thing, when we can't do it if we will, because what is most commonly called nature don't [doesn't] allow of it, or because of some impeding defect or obstacle that is extrinsic to the will; either in the faculty of understanding, constitution of body, or external objects. *Moral* inability consists not in any of these things; but either in the want of inclination; or the strength of a contrary inclination; or the want of sufficient motives in view, to induce and excite the act of the will, or the strength of apparent motives to the contrary. Or both these may be resolved into one; and it may be said in one word that moral inability consists in the opposition or want of inclination. . . .

To give some instances of this moral inability: A woman of great honor and chastity may have a moral inability to prostitute herself to her slave. A child of great love and duty to his parents may be unable to be willing to kill his father. A very lascivious man, in case of certain opportunities and temptations, and in the absence of such and such restraints, may be unable to forbear gratifying his lust. A drunkard, under such and such circumstances, may be unable to forbear taking of strong drink. A very malicious man may be unable to exert benevolent acts to an enemy, or to desire his prosperity: yea, some may be so under the power of a vile disposition that they may be unable to love those who are most worthy of their esteem and affection. A strong habit of virtue and great degree of holiness may cause a moral inability to love wickedness in general, may render a man unable to take complacence in wicked persons or things; or to choose a wicked life, and prefer it to a virtuous life. And on the other hand, a great degree of habitual wickedness may lay a man under an inability to love and choose holiness; and render him utterly unable to love an infinitely holy Being, or to choose and cleave to him as his chief good.

Here it may be of use to observe this distinction of moral inability, viz., of that which is general and habitual, and that which is particular and occasional. By a *general and habitual* moral inability, I mean an inability in the heart to all exercises or acts of will of that nature or kind, through a fixed and habitual inclination, or an habitual and stated defect, or want of a certain kind of inclination. Thus a very ill-natured man may be unable to exert such acts of benevolence as another, who is full of good nature, commonly exerts; and a man, whose heart is habitually void of gratitude, may be unable to exert such and such grateful acts, through that stated defect of a grateful inclination. By *particular and occasional* moral inability, I mean an inability of the will or heart to a particular act, through the strength or defect of present motives, or of inducements presented to the view of the understanding, on this occasion. If it be so that the will is always determined by the strongest motive, then it must always have an inability, in this latter sense, to act otherwise than it does; it not being possible, in any case, that the will should, at present, go against the motive which has now, all things considered, the greatest strength and advantage to excite and induce it. The former of these kinds of moral inability, consisting in that which is stated habitual and general, is most commonly called by the name of "inability"; because the word "inability," in its most proper and original signification, has respect to some stated defect. And this especially obtains the name of "inability" also upon another account; I before observed that the word "inability," in its original and most common use, is a relative term; and has respect to will and endeavor, as supposable in the case, and as insufficient to bring to pass the thing desired and endeavored. Now there may be more of an appearance and shadow of this, with respect to the acts which arise from a fixed and strong habit, than others that arise only from transient occasions and causes. Indeed will and endeavor against, or diverse from present acts of the will, are in no case supposable, whether those acts be occasional or habitual; for that would be to suppose the will, at present, to be otherwise than, at present, it is. But yet there may be will and endeavor against future acts of the will, or volitions that are likely to take place, as viewed at a distance. 'Tis no contradiction to suppose that the acts of the will at one time may be against the acts of the will at another time; and there may be desires and endeavors to prevent or excite future acts of the will; but such desires and endeavors are, in many cases, rendered insufficient and vain, through fixedness of habit: when the occasion returns, the strength of habit overcomes, and baffles all such opposition. In this respect, a man may be in miserable slavery and bondage to a strong habit. But it may be comparatively easy to make an alteration with respect to such future acts as are only occasional and transient; because the occasion or transient cause, if foreseen, may often easily be prevented or avoided. On this account, the moral inability that attends fixed habits, especially obtains the name of "inability." And then, as the will may remotely and indirectly resist itself, and do it in vain, in the case of strong habits; so reason may resist present acts of the will, and its resistance be insufficient; and this is more commonly the case also, when the acts arise from strong habit.

But it must be observed concern[ing] moral inability, in each kind of it, that the word "inability" is used in a sense very diverse from its original import. The word signifies only a natural inability, in the proper use of it; and is applied to such cases only wherein a present will or inclination to the thing, with respect to which a person is said to be unable, is supposable. It can't be truly said, according to the ordinary use of language, that a malicious man, let him be never so malicious, can't hold his hand from striking, or that he is not able to shew his neighbor kindness; or that a drunkard, let his appetite be never so strong, can't keep the cup from his mouth. In the strictest propriety of speech, a man has a thing in his power, if he has it in his choice, or at his election: and a man can't be truly said to be unable to do a thing, when he can do it if he will. 'Tis improperly said that a person can't perform those external actions, which are dependent on the act of the will, and which would be easily performed, if the act of the will were present. And if it be improperly said that he cannot perform those external voluntary actions, which depend on the will, 'tis in some respect more improperly said that he is unable to exert the acts of the will themselves; because it is more evidently false, with respect to these, that he can't if he will: for to say so is a downright contradiction: it is to say, he *can't* will, if he *does* will. And in this case, not only is it true that it is easy for a man to do the thing if he will, but the very willing is the doing; when once he has willed, the thing is performed; and nothing else remains to be done. Therefore, in these things to ascribe a nonperformance to the want of power or ability is not just; because the thing wanting is not a being *able*, but a being *willing*. There are faculties of mind, and capacity of nature, and everything else, sufficient, but a disposition: nothing is wanting but a will.

Part I. Section 5. Concerning the Notion of Liberty and of Moral Agency

The plain and obvious meaning of the words "freedom" and "liberty," in common speech, is power, opportunity, or advantage that anyone has to do as he pleases. Or in other words, his being free from hindrance or impediment in the way of doing, or conducting in any respect, as he wills. . . . And the contrary to liberty, whatever name we call that by, is a person's being hindered or unable to conduct as he will, or being necessitated to do otherwise.

If this which I have mentioned be the meaning of the word "liberty," in the ordinary use of language; as I trust that none that has ever learned to talk, and is unprejudiced, will deny; then it will follow that in propriety of speech, neither liberty, nor its contrary, can properly be ascribed to any being or thing, but that which has such a faculty, power, or property, as is called "will." For that which is possessed of no such thing as will can't have any power or opportunity of doing according to its will, nor be necessitated to act contrary to its will, nor be restrained from acting agreeably to it. And therefore to talk of liberty, or the contrary, as belonging to the very will itself, is not to speak good sense; if we judge of sense, and nonsense, by the original and proper signification of words. For the will itself is not an agent that has a will: the power of choosing, itself, has not a power of choosing. That which has the power of volition or choice is the man or the soul, and not the power of volition itself. And he that has the liberty of doing according to his will is the agent or doer who is possessed of the will; and not the will which he is possessed of. We say with propriety that a bird let loose has power and liberty to fly; but not that the bird's power of flying has a power and liberty of flying. To be free is the property of an agent, who is possessed of powers and faculties, as much as to be cunning, valiant, bountiful, or zealous. But these qualities are the properties of men or persons; and not the properties of properties. . . .

But one thing more I would observe concerning what is vulgarly called liberty; namely, that power and opportunity for one to do and conduct as he will, or according to his choice, is all that is meant by it; without taking into the meaning of the word, anything of the cause or original of that choice; or at all considering how the person came to have such a volition; whether it was caused by some external motive, or internal habitual bias; whether it was determined by some internal antecedent volition, or whether it happened without a cause; whether it was necessarily connected with something foregoing, or not connected. Let the person come by his volition or choice how he will, yet, if he is able, and there is nothing in the way to hinder his pursuing and executing his will, the man is fully and perfectly free, according to the primary and common notion of freedom.

What has been said may be sufficient to shew what is meant by liberty, according to the common notions of mankind, and in the usual and primary acceptation of the word: but the word, as used by Arminians, Pelagians, and others, who oppose the Calvinists, has an entirely different signification. These several things belong to their notion of liberty: 1. That it consists in a self-determining power in the will, or a certain sovereignty the will has over itself, and its own acts, whereby it determines its own volitions; so as not to be dependent in its determinations on any cause without itself, nor determined by anything prior to its own acts. 2. Indifference belongs to liberty in their notion of it, or that the mind, previous to the act of volition be, *in equilibrio*. 3. Contingence is another thing that belongs and is essential to it; not in the common acceptation of the word, as that has been already explained, but as opposed to all necessity, or any fixed and certain connection with some previous ground or reason of its existence. They suppose the essence of liberty so much to consist in these things that unless the will of man be free in this sense, he has no real freedom, how much soever he may be at liberty to act according to his will. . . .

Part IV. Section 4. It Is Agreeable to Common Sense, and the Natural Notions of Mankind, to Suppose Moral Necessity to Be Consistent with Praise and Blame, Reward and Punishment

. . . 1. This will appear if we consider what the vulgar notion of blameworthiness is. The idea which the common people through all ages and nations have of faultiness, I suppose to be plainly this; a person's being or doing wrong, with his own will and pleasure; containing these two things: 1. His doing wrong, when he does as he pleases. 2. His pleasure's being wrong. Or in other words, perhaps more intelligibly expressing their notion; a person's having his heart wrong, and doing wrong from his heart. And this is the sum total of the matter. . . .

. . . 'Tis manifest, they are some of the first notions that appear in children; who discover as soon as they can think, or speak, or act at all as rational creatures, a sense of desert. And certainly, in forming their notion of it, they make no use of metaphysics. All the ground they go upon consists in these two things; *experience*, and a *natural sensation* of a certain fitness or agreeableness which there is in uniting such moral evil as is above described, viz., a *being or doing wrong with the will*, and resentment in others, and pain inflicted on the person in whom this moral evil is. Which *natural sense* is what we call by the name of "conscience." . . .

The common people, in their notion of a faulty or praiseworthy deed or work done by anyone, do suppose that the man does it in the exercise of *liberty*. But then their notion of liberty is only a person's having opportunity of doing as he pleases. They have no notion of liberty consisting in the will's first acting, and so causing its own acts; and determining, and so causing its own determinations; or choosing, and so causing its own choice. Such a notion of liberty is what none have, but those that have darkened their own minds with confused metaphysical speculation, and abstruse and ambiguous terms. If a man is not restrained from acting as his will determines, or constrained to act otherwise; then he has liberty, according to common notions of liberty, without taking into the idea that grand contradiction of all the determinations of a man's free will being the effects of the determinations of his free will. Nor have men commonly any notion of freedom consisting in indifference. For if so, then it would be agreeable to their notion that the greater indifference men act with, the more freedom they act with; whereas the reverse is true. He that in acting proceeds with the fullest inclination does what he does with the greatest freedom, according to common sense. And so far is it from being agreeable to common sense, that such liberty as consists in indifference is requisite to praise or blame, that on the contrary, the dictate of every man's natural sense through the world is, that the further he is from being indifferent in his acting good or evil, and the more he does either with full and strong inclination, the more is he esteemed or abhorred, commended or condemned.

2. If it were inconsistent with the common sense of mankind that men should be either to be blamed or commended in any volitions they have or fail of, in case of moral necessity or impossibility; then it would surely also be agreeable to the same sense and reason of mankind that the nearer the case approaches to such a moral necessity or impossibility, either through a strong antecedent moral propensity on the one hand, . . . or a great antecedent opposition and difficulty on the other, the nearer does it approach to a being neither blamable nor commendable; so that acts exerted with such preceding propensity would be worthy of proportion-

ably less praise; and when omitted, the act being attended with such difficulty, the omission would be worthy of the less blame. . . .

But 'tis apparent that the reverse of these things is true. If there be an approach to a moral necessity in a man's exertion of good acts of will, they being the exercise of a strong propensity to good, and a very powerful love to virtue; 'tis so far from being the dictate of common sense that he is less virtuous, and the less to be esteemed, loved, and praised; that 'tis agreeable to the natural notions of all mankind that he is so much the better man, worthy of greater respect, and higher commendation. And the stronger the inclination is, and the nearer it approaches to necessity in that respect, or to impossibility of neglecting the virtuous act, or of doing a vicious one; still the more virtuous, and worthy of higher commendation. And on the other hand, if a man exerts evil acts of mind; as for instance, acts of pride or malice, from a rooted and strong habit or principle of haughtiness and maliciousness, and a violent propensity of heart to such acts; according to the natural sense of all men, he is so far from being the less hateful and blamable on that account, that he is so much the more worthy to be detested and condemned by all that observe him.

Moreover, 'tis manifest that it is no part of the notion which mankind commonly have of a blamable or praiseworthy act of the will, that it is an act which is not determined by an antecedent bias or motive, but by the sovereign power of the will itself; because if so, the greater hand such causes have in determining any acts of the will, so much the less virtuous or vicious would they be accounted; and the less hand, the more virtuous or vicious. Whereas the reverse is true: men don't think a good act to be the less praiseworthy, for the agent's being much determined in it by a good inclination or a good motive; but the more. And if good inclination or motive has but little influence in determining the agent, they don't think his act so much the more virtuous, but the less. And so concerning evil acts, which are determined by evil motives or inclinations. . . .

And these dictates of men's minds are so natural and necessary that it may be very much doubted whether the Arminians themselves have ever got rid of 'em: yea, their greatest doctors, that have gone furthest in defense of their metaphysical notions of liberty, and have brought their arguments to their greatest strength, and as they suppose to a demonstration, against the consistence of virtue and vice with any necessity: 'tis to be questioned, whether there is so much as one of them, but that if he suffered very much from the injurious acts of a man under the power of an invincible haughtiness and malignancy of temper, would not, from the forementioned natural sense of mind, resent it far otherwise, than if as great sufferings came upon him from the wind that blows, and fire that burns by natural necessity; and otherwise than he would, if he suffered as much from the conduct of a man perfectly delirious; yea, though he first brought his distraction upon him some way by his own fault.

Some seem to disdain the distinction that we make between *natural* and *moral* necessity, as though it were altogether impertinent in this controversy: "That which is necessary (say they) is necessary; it is that which must be, and can't be prevented. And that which is impossible is impossible, and can't be done: and therefore none can be to blame for not doing it." And such comparisons are made use of, as the commanding of a man to walk who has lost his legs, and condemning and punishing him for not obeying; inviting and calling upon a man, who is shut up in a strong prison, to come forth, etc. But in these things Arminians are very unreasonable. Let common sense determine whether there be not a great difference between those two cases; the one, that of a man who has offended his prince, and is cast into prison; and after he has lain there a while, the king comes to him, calls him to come forth to him; and tells him that if he will do so, and will fall down before him, and humbly beg his pardon, he shall be forgiven, and set at liberty, and also be greatly enriched, and advanced to honor: the prisoner heartily repents of the folly and wickedness of his offense against his prince, is thoroughly disposed to abase himself, and accept of the king's offer; but is confined by strong walls, with gates of brass, and bars of iron. The other case is that of a man who is of a very unreasonable spirit, of a haughty, ungrateful, willful disposition; and moreover, has been brought up in traitorous principles; and has his heart possessed with an extreme and inveterate enmity to his lawful sovereign; and for his rebellion is cast into prison, and lies long there, loaden with heavy chains, and in miserable circumstances. At length the compassionate prince comes to the prison, orders his chains to be knocked off, and his prison doors to be set wide open; calls to him, and tells him, if he will come forth to him, and fall down before him, acknowledge that he has treated him unworthily, and ask his forgiveness; he shall be forgiven, set at liberty, and set in a place of great dignity and profit in his court. But he is so stout and stomachful, and full of haughty malignity, that he can't be willing to accept the offer: his rooted strong pride and malice have perfect power over him, and as it were bind him, by binding his heart: the opposition of his heart has the mastery over him, having an influence on his mind far superior to the king's grace and condescension, and to all his kind offers and promises. Now, is it agreeable to common sense, to assert and stand to it, that there is no difference between these two cases, as to any worthiness of blame in the prisoners; because, forsooth, there is a necessity in both, and the required act in each case is impossible? 'Tis true, a man's evil dispositions may be as strong and immovable as the bars of a castle. But who can't see that when a man, in the latter case, is said to be "unable" to obey the command, the expression is used improperly, and not in the sense it has originally and in common speech? And that it may properly be said to be in the rebel's power to come out of prison, seeing he can easily do it if he pleases; though by reason of his vile temper of heart which is fixed and rooted, 'tis impossible that it should please him?

Upon the whole, I presume there is no person of good understanding, who impartially considers the things which have been observed, but will allow that 'tis not evident from the dictates of the common sense, or natural notions of mankind, that moral necessity is inconsistent with praise and blame. And therefore, if the Arminians would prove any such inconsistency, it must be by some philosophical and metaphysical arguments, and not common sense. . . .

Corol. From things which have been observed, it will follow, that it is agreeable to common sense to suppose, that the glorified saints have not their freedom at all diminished, in any respect; and that God himself has the highest possible freedom, according to the true and proper meaning of the term; and that he is in the highest possible respect an agent, and active in the exercise of his infinite holiness; though he acts therein in the highest degree necessarily: and his actions of this kind are in the highest, most absolutely perfect manner virtuous and praiseworthy; and are so, for that very reason, because they are most perfectly necessary.

From Jonathan Edwards, *A Careful and Strict Enquiry into the Modern Prevailing Notions of that Freedom of Will, Which Is Supposed to Be Essential to Moral Agency, Vertue and Vice, Reward and Punishment, Praise and Blame* (Boston: S. Kneeland, 1754).

PART 2

The Emergence of a Movement

Early New Divinity Thought

Jonathan Edwards made no effort of his own to create a particular "school" of New England theology; his complaint all along had been that the emergence of schools of thought apart from the original New England Way had been accompanied by dangerous innovations and theological drift. Yet the Great Awakening had forced the choosing of sides, and those who found themselves on the side of the revivals found themselves looking to Edwards. As early as 1741, he was the principal voice defending the revivals in western Massachusetts, and after his Yale commencement address, he began to attract students, recent college graduates aspiring to the ministry who, in what had become a conventional pattern, studied under some notable minister prior to undergoing the rigors of ordination. Joseph Bellamy, who arrived in Northampton to study under Edwards as early as 1736, was among the first of these students. Samuel Hopkins, who arrived to study under Edwards in the winter of 1741–42, joined Bellamy as Edwards's two most famous pupils, and the two most influential in codifying, interpreting, reshaping, and promoting Edwards's thinking as a distinctive "school." The New England Theology had no other Edwards but Edwards, but his prophets were Joseph Bellamy and Samuel Hopkins.

In a flurry of books, published dialogues, sermons, and treatises, Bellamy and Hopkins laid out four prime concerns, each of which was connected to some facet of Edwards's writings but together built logically on one another to the point where they rapidly assumed a systematic outline. The first of these was the legitimacy and desirability of revivals, which needed little more from Hopkins and Bellamy than a reiteration of Edwards. But once revival assumed a central place in their thinking, this raised questions about whether the church should attempt self-consciously to admit only the revived to membership and the sacraments. This was the same question that had driven Edwards to repudiate Solomon Stoddard's practice of open communion (and cause a fatal breach between Edwards and the congregation in Northampton). But in shouting down the critics, Bellamy and Hopkins staked out a concept of the New England church that was starkly separatistic and come-outer, even to the point of downplaying the significance of infant baptism. Neither Bellamy nor Hopkins actually went so far as to sever all communion with the established Congregational churches of Massachusetts and Connecticut. Bellamy, in fact, remained the pastor of the Connecticut parish of Bethlehem for fifty years. But their ministries were marked by separatist practices and conflicts. Bellamy joined the itinerants during the Great Awakening and preached in almost two hundred communities in New England and New York, while the less-eloquent Hopkins was forced out of his first parish in Housatonic in 1769 and nearly preached away the congregation of his second parish in Newport, Rhode Island, except for a devoted handful of pious admirers like Sarah Osborn.

Allied to the assumption that the church must be reserved solely for the pure was a psychological assumption born out of Edwards's contention in *Freedom of the Will* that sinners possessed all the natural ability required to repent. It was the lack, and only the lack, of moral ability that prevented them from repenting at once and that lay behind the excuse of inability put forward by people of "half-way" commitments who argued that, since conversion was a result of the sovereign movement of God, they were unable to repent on their own and had to wait or to "use the means" of preaching and sacraments until grace descended on them. The argument from natural ability shredded this excuse. Hopkins and Bellamy denounced the elaborate timetables and checklists that well-intentioned New England clergy devised to aid their parishioners' slow progress toward grace as mere delaying tactics employed by sinners to put off the repentance that their natural ability placed within their reach at once. This set the stage for a third principle, an ethical demand that amounted almost to moral perfectionism. If the natural ability to repent lay fully within the grasp of every sinner, then the same natural ability ought to put consistent obedience to the precepts of the Bible fully within the grasp of every saint.

By this point, Hopkins and Bellamy had levered themselves far enough from the standard forms of New England Congregationalism that they had difficulty squaring their ideas with the official Calvinist orthodoxy New Englanders had inherited from Geneva, the Synod of Dordt, the

Westminster Confession, and even their own Cambridge Platform of 1648. In regard to the five cardinal "points" of Calvinist orthodoxy, Hopkins's and Bellamy's preaching needed careful explaining to connect with four of them, while the notion of a natural ability in all sinners seemed to cut directly across the fifth, the limitation of the efficacy of the atonement only to the elect. But like Edwards, Hopkins and Bellamy saw themselves as restorers of pure Calvinism—"consistent Calvinism"—and by the time questions about limitations of the atonement were put to them, they had generated enough intellectual momentum to wave them away.

It may not seem likely that these tinkerings with New England Calvinism, even when justified by Edwards, would have attracted many converts. But between 1758 and 1800, they gave life to a theological movement all its own, known eventually as simply the New Divinity. Partly, this sprang from Bellamy's extraordinary success as a teacher of theological students. Upward of sixty of them passed through the barn he refurbished in Bethlehem as a one-man seminary, including John Smalley, Samuel Spring, Levi Hart, and Jonathan Edwards the Younger, to name only the most famous. These students became the most vivid and demanding voices for a "consistent Calvinism" in the post-Awakening and post-Revolutionary decades. They, in turn, trained ministerial students of their own: Hart trained Charles Backus, and Backus trained fifty others; Asa Burton trained another sixty; and Nathanael Emmons (who was trained by Smalley) set the record by training eighty-seven ministers during his fifty-five-year career. This revolutionary cadre of New Divinity ministers carried revival fire—and Edwardsean doctrine—into more than one hundred towns in New England. By the time of Bellamy's death in 1790, Jonathan Edwards the Younger was able to argue that the energies of the New Divinity were close to tipping the hand of New England Calvinism in their favor: "I believe a majority of the ministers mean to embrace the system of my father and Dr. Bellamy," he told one of his father's longtime Scottish friends. What was surprising was not just Edwards the Younger's optimistic estimate of the New Divinity's success but the closeness with which he articulated the concerns, explicit and implicit, of Jonathan Edwards.

Joseph Bellamy

TRUE RELIGION DELINEATED (1750)

Joseph Bellamy (1719–90) graduated from Yale in 1735 and was "fitted" for ordination by study under Edwards. The New Haven Association licensed him to preach at the unlikely age of eighteen and then ordained him in 1740 as the pastor of the newly organized parish of Bethlehem, Connecticut. Like Edwards, he plunged fully into itinerant preaching during the Great Awakening; like Edwards as well, he gradually was disenchanted by the emergence of unrestrained Antinomian radicals and by the piety of converts whose fervor proved embarrassingly short-lived and insincere.

The problem of discerning the truly converted from the apparently converted in the revivals led Bellamy to begin work on what would prove his most important book and the foundational theological text of the New Divinity, *True Religion Delineated*, which was published in Boston in 1750, with a glowing preface from Jonathan Edwards. *True Religion Delineated* set the bar for measuring genuine piety extraordinarily high: Converts could count themselves saints only if they were "in a conformity to the *law* of God" and "in a compliance with the *gospel* of Christ." That, in turn, was measured by Bellamy in terms of how thoroughly converts manifested (1) a profound knowledge of God, "a sense of his glory and beauty in being what he is" and not a convenient self-deception, (2) esteem, "a sense of the infinite dignity, greatness, glory, excellency, and beauty of the most high God [which] begets in us high and exalted thoughts of him, and makes us admire, wonder, and adore," (3) benevolence, which Bellamy described as *"earnest longings* that God would glorify himself, and honour his great name; and bring all the world into an entire subjection to him," and (4) a delight

73

in God, a "pleasure, sweetness, and satisfaction, which we take in any thing that is very dear to us" and which harks back to Edwards's "sense of the heart."

If this asked a great deal of the converted, Bellamy argued that it was nothing less than God—understood for who God really was—demanded. God was "disposed to take state to himself, and honour, and majesty, the kingdom, the power, and the glory and he sets up himself as the most high God, supreme Lord, and sovereign Governor of the whole world, and bids all worlds adore him, and be in a most perfect subjection to him, and that with all their hearts."

જ/ડ

Discourse I

Showing the Nature of the Divine Law, and Wherein Consists a Real Conformity to It

True religion consists in a conformity to the *law* of God, and in a compliance with the *gospel* of Christ. The religion of innocent man consisted only in a conformity to the law—the law of nature, with the addition of one positive precept: he had no need of gospel-grace. But when man lost his innocency, and became guilty and depraved; when he fell under the wrath of God and power of sin, he needed a Redeemer and a Sanctifier; and in the gospel, a Redeemer and a Sanctifier are provided, and a way for our obtaining pardoning mercy and sanctifying grace is opened: a compliance with which does now, therefore, become part of the religion of a fallen creature. Now, if we can but rightly understand the *law,* and rightly understand the *gospel,* we may easily see wherein a conformity to the one, and a compliance with the other, does consist; and so what *true religion* is.

For the present, let us take the law under consideration. And it will be proper to inquire into these following particulars: 1. What duty does God require of us in his law? 2. From what motives must that duty be done? 3. What is that precise measure of duty which God requires in his law?

. . . I. I am to show *what is implied in love to* GOD. . . . 1. *A true knowledge of God* is *implied*; for this lays the foundation of love. . . . For now we begin to perceive the grounds and reasons of that infinite esteem he has of himself, and infinite complacency in himself, and why he commands all the world to love and adore him. And the same grounds and reasons which move him thus to love himself, and command all the world to do so too, enkindle the divine flame in our hearts. When we see God, in a measure, such as he sees himself to be, and have a sense of his glory and beauty in being what he is, in a measure, as he himself has, then we begin to love him with the same kind of love, and from the same motives, as he himself does; only in an infinitely inferior degree. This sight and sense of God discovers the grounds of love to him. We see why he requires us to love him, and why we ought to love him—how right and fit it is; and so we cannot but love him.

This true knowledge of God supposes that, in a measure, we see God to be just such a one as he is; and, in a measure, have a sense of his infinite glory and beauty in being such. For if our apprehensions of God are not right, it is not *God* we love, but only a false image of him framed in our own fancy. And if we have not a sense of his glory and beauty in being what he is, it is impossible we should truly love and esteem him for being such. To love God for being what he is, and yet not to have any sense of his glory and beauty in being such, implies a contradiction; for it supposes we have a sense of his glory and beauty when we have not: a sense of the beauty and amiableness of any object being always necessarily implied in love to it. . . . Mere speculation, where there is no sense of beauty, will no sooner fill the heart with love than a looking-glass will be filled with love by the image of a beautiful countenance, which looks into it: and a mere speculative knowledge of God will not, cannot, beget a sense of his beauty in being what he is when there is naturally no disposition in our hearts to account him glorious in being such, but wholly to the contrary. . . . Wicked men and devils may know what God is, but none but holy beings have *any sense* of his infinite glory and beauty in being such. . . .

2. Another thing implied in love to God is *esteem*. Esteem, strictly speaking, is that high and exalted thought of and value for any thing, which arises from a sight and sense of its own intrinsic worth, excellency, and beauty. So, a sense of the infinite dignity, greatness, glory, excellency, and beauty of the most high God begets in us high and exalted thoughts of him, and makes us admire, wonder, and adore. . . . This high esteem of God disposes and inclines the heart to acquiesce, yea, to exult, in all the high prerogatives God assumes to himself.

God, from a consciousness of his own infinite excellency, his entire right to, and absolute authority over, all things, is disposed to take state to himself, and honour, and majesty, the kingdom, the power, and the glory and he sets up himself as the most high God, supreme Lord, and sovereign Governor of the whole world, and bids all worlds adore him, and be in a most perfect subjection to him, and that with all their hearts; and esteems the wretch, who does not account this his highest happiness, worthy of eternal damnation. God thinks it infinitely becomes him to set up himself for a GOD, and to command all the world to adore him, upon pain of eternal damnation. He thinks himself fit to govern the world, and that the throne is his proper place, and that all love, honour, and obedience are his due. . . .

And a sight and sense of the supreme, infinite Glory and excellency of the divine nature will not only make us glad that he is GOD, and KING, and GOVERNOR but also exceedingly glad that we live under his government and are to be his subjects and servants, and to be at his disposal. It will show us the grounds and reasons of his law; how infinitely right and fit it is that we should love him with all our hearts, and obey him in every thing; how infinitely unfit and wrong the least sin is, and how just the threatened punishment: and, at the same time, it will help us to see that all the nations of the earth are as a drop of the bucket or small dust of the balance, before him; and that we ourselves are nothing, and less than nothing, in his sight. So that a right sight and sense of the supreme, infinite glory of God will make us esteem him, so as to be glad that he is on the throne, and we at his footstool; that he is king, and we his subjects; that he rules and reigns, and that we are absolutely in subjection, and absolutely at his disposal. In a word, we shall be glad to see him take all that honour to himself which he does, and shall be heartily reconciled to his government, and cordially willing to take our own proper places; and hereby a foundation will begin to be laid in our hearts for all things to come to rights.

3. Another thing implied in love to God may be called *Benevolence*. When we are acquainted with any person, and he appears very excellent in our eyes, and we highly esteem him, it is natural now heartily to wish him well; we are concerned for his interest; we are glad to see it go well with him, and sorry to see it go ill with him; and ready at all times cheerfully to do what we can to promote his welfare. . . . When God is seen in his infinite dignity, greatness, glory, and excellency, as the most high God, supreme Lord, and sovereign governor of the whole world, and a sense of his infinite worthiness is hereby raised in our hearts, this enkindles a holy benevolence, the natural language of which is, "Let God be glorified," Psalm 96:7–8. "And be thou exalted, O God, above the heavens: let thy glory be above all the earth," Psalm 57:5, 11.

This holy disposition sometimes expresses itself in *earnest longings* that God would glorify himself, and honour his great name; and bring all the world into an entire subjection to him. . . .

Again, this divine Benevolence, or wishing that God may be glorified, sometimes expresses itself in earnest Longings that all Worlds might join together to bless and praise the name of the Lord; and it appears infinitely fit and right, and so infinitely beautiful and ravishing, that the whole intelligent creation should for ever join in the most solemn adoration: yea, and that sun, moon, stars; earth, air, sea; birds, beasts, fishes; mountains and hills, and all things, should, in their way, display the divine perfections, and praise the name of the Lord, because his name alone is excellent, and his glory is exalted above the heavens.

Lastly, from this divine Benevolence arises a free and genuine Disposition to consecrate and give up ourselves entirely to the Lord for ever—to walk in all his ways, and keep all his commands, seeking his glory: For if we desire that God may be glorified, we shall naturally be disposed to seek his glory. A sight and sense of the infinite dignity, greatness, glory, and excellency of God, the great creator, preserver, and governor of the world, who has entire right unto, and an absolute authority over, all things, makes it appear infinitely fit that all things should be for him, and him alone; and that we should be entirely for him, and wholly devoted to him; and that it is infinitely wrong to live to ourselves, and make our own interest our last end. . . .

All rational Creatures, acting as such, are always influenced by Motives in their whole conduct. Those things are always the most powerful motives, which appear to us most worthy of our choice. The principal motive to an action is always the ultimate end of the action: Hence, if God, his honour, and interest, appear to us as the supreme good, and most worthy of our choice, then God, his honour, and interest, will be the principal motive and ultimate end of all we do. . . . To love GOD so as to serve *him* is what the law requires; to love *self* so as to serve *self* is *rebellion* against the majesty of heaven. And the same infinite obligations which we are under to love God above ourselves; even the same infinite obligations are we under to live to God ultimately, and not to ourselves. And therefore it is as great a sin to live to ourselves ultimately as it is to love ourselves supremely.

4. And lastly. *Delight* in God is also implied in Love to him. By Delight we commonly mean that pleasure, sweetness, and satisfaction, which we take in any thing that is very dear to us. When a man appears very excellent to us, and we esteem him, and wish him all good, we also, at the same time, feel a delight in him, and a sweetness in his company and conversation; we long to see him when absent; we rejoice in his presence; the enjoyment of him tends to make us happy; So, when a holy soul beholds God in the infinite moral excellency and beauty of his nature, and loves him supremely, and is devoted to him entirely, now also he delights in him superlatively. His delight and complacency is as great as his esteem, and arises from a sense of the same moral excellency and beauty. From this delight in God arise longings after a further acquaintance with him, and greater nearness to him.

. . . Finally, from this delight in God arises a holy disposition to renounce all other things, and live wholly upon him, and take up everlasting content in him, and in him alone. . . . The vain man takes content in vain company; the worldly man takes content in riches; the ambitious man in honour and applause; the philosopher in philosophical speculations; the legal hypocrite in his round of duties; the evangelical hypocrite in his experiences, his discoveries, his joys, his raptures, and confident expectation of heaven: but the true lover of God takes his content in God himself. . . .

And now, that this is a right representation of the nature of that love which is required in the first and great commandment of the law, upon which chiefly all the law and the prophets hang, is manifest, not only from the reason of the thing, and from what has been already said, but also from this, that such a love to God as this *lays a sure and firm foundation for all holy obedience*. That love to God is of the right kind, which will effectually influence us to keep his commands. . . . If we loved him only from self-love, from the fear of hell, or from the hopes of heaven, we might, at the same time, hate his law: but if we love him for being what he is, we cannot but love to be like him; which is what his law requires. To suppose that a man loves God supremely for what he is, and yet does not love to be like him, is an evident contradiction. It is to suppose a thing supremely loved; and yet, at the same time, not loved at all: so that, to a demonstration, this is the very kind of love which the Lord our God requires of us. So, saints in heaven love God perfectly, and so the good man on earth begins, in a weak and feeble Manner, to love God: for there is but one kind of love required in the law; and so but one kind of love which is of the right Sort: for no Kind of Love can be of the right sort, but that very kind of Love which the Law requires. There is, therefore, no difference between their love in heaven, and ours here upon earth, but only in Degree.

From Joseph Bellamy, *True Religion Delineated; or, Experimental Religion, As distinguished from Formality on the one Hand, and Enthusiasm on the other* (Boston: S. Kneeland, 1750), 1–15.

Joseph Bellamy

A DIALOGUE BETWEEN A MINISTER AND HIS PARISHIONER CONCERNING THE HALF-WAY COVENANT (1769)

The instability of converts who thought they had religion but had only delusions troubled Joseph Bellamy, but just as troubling to Bellamy was the serenity of church members who gave no thought to conversion because they looked on the ordinances of the church—preaching and the sacraments—as safe conducts to salvation. From the 1660s onward, the New England churches had struggled with the dilemma of having been founded in order to call out visible saints *from* society, while still functioning as the state churches *in* society. One compromise after another had been worked out, and by the time of the Great Awakening, most of the New England churches had adopted a practice of "owning the covenant," which allowed those who could not (or cared not to) claim they had undergone complete spiritual regeneration access for themselves and their children to baptism and a second-class church membership. This ended up creating two worlds within New England parishes: the general population of the parish, those who were baptized and could have their children baptized but who could not come to communion, and a smaller group of those who had undergone conversion and who constituted the literal "membership" of the church. This smacked of double-dealing in the life of New England Congregationalism, but it worked on the pastoral level in at least two senses: It kept the broad population within the orbit and oversight of the church, and it satisfied serious parish ministers who had qualms about trying to discern who was really of the elect and who was not.

Bellamy had no such qualms, and the Great Awakening seemed to afford all the evidence anyone needed of how direct and unquestioning the renovating work of God could be in a parishioner's soul. In 1762, Bellamy published a criticism of "owning the covenant" in *A Dialogue on the Christian Sacraments*, and then in 1769, he wrote a scorching attack on the practice as little better than a "half-way covenant" that did nothing to promote true religion and only coddled sinners in the belief that they were doing something that pleased God. The nickname—*half-way covenant*—stuck to the practice, to the mortification of Old Light Congregationalists for whom the half-way covenant was an important tool for parish nurture. In reply, Bellamy published a series of four dialogues on the half-way covenant in 1769 in which he asserted that mere baptism earned one the right to exactly nothing if it did not lead to complete conversion. "One baptised in infancy, who in the sight of God practically renounces his baptism when adult, as all do who reject Christ and continue impenitent, is not considered by God as entitled to blessings of the new covenant, but as under the curse of the law." This would, in the long run, serve to comb out the half-hearts from the New England churches and restore the church to its original mission of serving the elect. But Bellamy hoped it would have the short-run value of shocking his readers into realizing that they had been trifling with their God and needed to seek God in earnest, without any half-way compromises.

PARISHIONER. Sir, I am dissatisfied with a part of your public conduct, and am come to open my mind freely to you, if you will be so kind as to allow me an opportunity.

MINISTER. Sir, I am now at leisure, and at your service, and your honest frankness gives me pleasure. Between you and me alone, to let me know the objections you have against any part of my conduct is to act a friendly part. It is more kind and christian-like than to keep your thoughts to yourself, to engender a secret disaffection in your heart. And you may be quite assured that not only now, but in all future times, I shall with pleasure listen to any objections against my public administrations proposed in a friendly, candid manner; and will be ready to be set right, wherein I am wrong; or to let you know the reasons of my conduct. . . .

PAR. I have lately moved into the parish; I had owned the covenant in the town I came from; my other children have been baptised; we have now another child for baptism, and I hear you refuse to baptise the children of any but those who are in full communion. This gives me pain.

MIN. I cannot give you pain, without feeling pain myself. But you would not desire that I should go counter to the will of my LORD and

MASTER, while acting in his name, as his minister; nor would this be a likely means to obtain a blessing for your child. And if I am warranted by the Gospel of Christ to baptise your child, you are very sensible my reputation, and every worldly interest, will join to prompt me to your opinion, if you can point out one text of Scripture to justify that common practice.

P. I have not studied the point. I cannot mention any texts of Scripture; but it is the custom where I was born and brought up; and I knew not but that it was the custom every where, until I moved into this parish.

M. No, sir, it is not the custom every where; it was not the custom where I was born and brought up: and there are many churches in the country that are not in the practice. At the first settling of New-England, there was, so far as I know, not one church that allowed baptism to the children of any but those whose parents were one or both in full communion. . . . It is not practised at all in the church of Scotland, as I have been informed by a rev. gentleman of an established reputation, who has lately been invited, and who has removed from thence, to the Presidency of New-Jersey College. . . .

P. It was the common opinion that none ought to join in full communion, and come to the Lord's table, but those that were godly, that had on a *wedding garment, lest coming unworthily, they eat and drink damnation to themselves.* But it was thought that graceless persons might own the covenant, and have their children baptised; and this was my opinion, and I acted on these principles. . . .

M. If the covenant owned is the covenant of grace, and if the parent acts understandingly and honestly in the affair, he is a good man, he has a right before God to baptism for his children, and an equal right to the Lord's supper. . . . But if the covenant owned is not the covenant of grace, those who have owned it have in the sight of God no right to either of those ordinances, which are seals of the covenant, and of no other: no more right than if they had given their assent to any chapter in the apocrypha. Did you never hear it observed and talked of that those who own the covenant make as full and large a profession as they who join in full communion?

P. Yes. And my former minister read the same covenant to such as owned the covenant, and he did to those that joined in full communion, word for word, only one did not promise to come up to all ordinances, and the other did. And I must confess this sometimes stumbled me.

M. If you please, sir, I will repeat the covenant we use when any join in full communion, the same that was read to me by my minister, when I joined to the church about three and thirty years ago. A brief summary of it is this: "You do now in the presence of the dread Majesty of heaven and earth, and before angels and men, in the sincerity of your soul, avouch

81

the Lord Jehovah to be your sovereign Lord and supreme Good, through Jesus Christ; and solemnly devote and give up yourselves to his fear and service, to walk in all his ways, and keep all his commands, seeking his glory," etc. And is this more full and express than your former minister used when persons owned the covenant?

P. I think not; it is very much like it.

M. So far as I am acquainted, the forms in use all over the country, a very few instances excepted, are very much alike. The only difference of any consequence lies in practice: I think it my duty, in private as well as public, to explain the covenant, and to see to it that persons understand it before they make it, and know what they are about to do, and are sufficiently instructed that it is a wicked thing to *lie to God with their mouths, and flatter him with their lips.*

P. Very well, sir, no doubt this is a minister's duty. But, alas! for me, I never knew what I was about, nor considered the import of the words I publicly gave my consent unto. I knew myself to be unconverted. I meant to own the covenant, as the phrase is, and have my children baptised; but I had no design to profess godliness, or to pretend a real compliance with the covenant of grace. This godly people may do: but it had been great hypocrisy in me to do it. To lie to men is bad, but to lie to God is worse. I supposed that owning the covenant was what the unconverted might do.

M. How can a man that knows himself to be unconverted, dead in sin, and destitute of the grace of God, stand up before the whole congregation, and say, "I do now in the presence of the dread Majesty of heaven and earth, and before angels and men, avouch the Lord Jehovah to be my sovereign Lord and supreme Good through Jesus Christ, and solemnly devote and give up myself to his fear and service, to walk in all his ways, and keep all his commands, seeking his glory"?

P. I freely own I knew not what I did, when I owned the covenant. But you hinted just now that this is not the custom in all the churches where the half-way practice takes place.

M. I have heard of a few churches where the ministers of late have drawn up a new form for those who own the covenant, essentially different from that which is used when any one is admitted to full communion: which new form designedly leaves out the covenant of grace and contains a profession, which unconverted men may make, and yet speak true. And this, with greater propriety, may be called the half-way covenant, although indeed it does not go half-way, and gives no right to those ordinances which are seals of the covenant of grace. Besides, God never did propose any covenant to mankind but which required real holiness on man's part; and any covenant short of this is a mere human device. . . . And it is acknowledged on all hands, Antinomians excepted, that repentance toward God, and faith toward Christ are required in the covenant of grace, as revealed in the Gospel. These ungracious covenants, therefore, are not from heaven, but of men.

P. My conscience is convinced. I am obligated to give up the half-way covenant; but it is with no small reluctance: for what will become of my child? must it remain unbaptised? I cannot bear the thought. What shall I do? . . . Is it lawful for me to join in full communion, when I know I have no grace? can I answer it to God?

M. You remember when the King came in to view the guests, he saw a man among them *not having on a wedding garment,* to whom he said, *friend, how camest thou in hither, not having on a wedding garment? and he was speechless.* To make a false and lying profession is inexcusable wickedness. It is true, there will be tares along with the wheat, but it is the devil sows them there, and not the servants. And if false brethren come into the church, they creep in unawares; they have no right to be there.

P. But does not my own baptism render me a church member, and entitle my child baptism, although I am destitute of faith and repentance?

M. . . . One baptised in infancy, who in the sight of God practically renounces his baptism when adult, as all do who reject Christ and continue impenitent, is not considered by God as entitled to blessings of the new covenant, but as under the curse of the law. . . . And what right hath this man to the seals of the covenant of grace, in the sight of God, who is by Christ himself declared to be under condemnation and wrath?

P. Well, if I have no right to baptism for my poor child, I must be silent. But I wish it might be baptised.

M. Will you allow me to examine the earnest desire of baptism which you express?

P. I ought to be willing. I ought to know the motives that influence me: for God knows them, whether I do or not.

M. I am glad to see your mind so serious and candid. If this temper should continue, I should hope all your doubts would be removed. For I can tell you seriously, I am willing to baptise your child, provided you do understandingly and with all your heart desire it.

P. And do I not? I should be a cruel parent if I did not.

M. . . . Do you love God to that degree, as thus to give him your child for ever? if so, why do not you give yourself to God, first of all? you love your child, but you love yourself better. First of all then cease to be cruel to your own soul; no longer practically renounce your own baptism, by turning your back on God and the Redeemer; but act up to its genuine import; give yourself to God, through Jesus Christ his Son, that you may become the temple of the Holy Ghost; and thus ratify what your parents did for you, when they dedicated you to God in baptism. This is that owning of the covenant which God requires at your hands. Then bring your dear child, and consecrate to God in sincerity and truth. This is the way, the right way for a blessing. But if, instead of this, you are moved only by custom, by a sense of worldly honour, by pride and shame; and desire that holy ordinance to be administered to your child from unholy motives, as Simon Magus desired the miraculous gifts of the Holy Ghost to answer his carnal ends; God knows it, and all the world will know it at the day of judgment. Pray, how was it when your other children were baptised? and how is it in general to all appearance when people own the covenant and get their children baptised? are they brought up for God; or only to serve divers lusts and pleasures? Look through the country wherever you are acquainted; the youth learn to dress, to sing, to dance; but do their parents appear to understand that they have devoted them to God? and is this evidently their great concern to bring them up for God? . . .

P. I must grant that it is absurd and inconsistent for a parent to pretend to have a heart to give his child to God, and yet have no heart to give himself to him. But I do desire to give myself to God.

M. Pray, sir, what then hinders you from giving yourself to him? . . . And if you would now in fact make this choice, it would put an end to your present difficulties about your child. Nothing, therefore, can hinder the baptism of your child, but your continuing to reject God and the Redeemer, by which you practically renounce your own baptism, and forfeit all the blessings of the covenant.

P. Shocking affair! my child unbaptised! none to blame but its own parents! what shall I do?

M. Is not God your Creator? are you not his by an original, absolute, entire right? is he not infinitely worthy of your supreme love? were you not in your infancy dedicated to him in baptism and have you turned your back upon him to this very hour; and practically renounced your baptism in his sight? so that, dying in this state, your baptism will be of no advantage to you; . . . and do you now inquire, what shall you do? ah, my dear sir! the answer is plain. *Repent and be converted, that your sins may be blotted out.* And thus at last comply with the import of your baptism, and become a disciple of Christ.

P. . . . I thank you, sir, for your fidelity, and ask your prayers: for the present, adieu!

M. I thank you for your kind visit. I ask the favour of another hour, when you are at leisure. I am always at your service; and might I be a means of your salvation, it would give me joy, while I live, and after I am dead, through eternal ages. I only add, if you will read what the late learned pious President Edwards wrote on the qualifications for Christian communion, printed at Boston; and the Rev. Mr. Green's pieces on the same subject, printed at New York: you may in them see the truth confirmed, and objections answered more largely. . . .

From Joseph Bellamy, "The Halfway Covenant: A Dialogue between a Minister and his Parishioner," in *The Works of the Rev. Joseph Bellamy, D.D., Late of Bethlem, Connecticut*, with "Funeral Sermon, with an Appendix" by Noah Benedict, vol. 3 (New York: Stephen Dodge, 1811–12), 391–445.

Samuel Hopkins

AN INQUIRY CONCERNING THE PROMISES
OF THE GOSPEL (1765)

Samuel Hopkins (1721–1803) was eighteen years old, and in his third year at Yale, when he heard George Whitefield preach in New Haven. Hopkins was deeply impressed by Whitefield, but he was put to the spiritual test by a fellow student, the sophomore David Brainerd, who vigorously exhorted Hopkins to be sure of his own spiritual condition. The Yale authorities soon came to regret any encouragements they had given Whitefield and the Awakeners, and Brainerd was disciplined and expelled from Yale. But it was too late to rescind Yale's invitation to Jonathan Edwards to preach the commencement sermon *Distinguishing Marks of a Work of the Spirit of God* in 1741, and Hopkins was so enthused by Edwards's defense of the Awakening that he "concluded to go and live with Mr. Edwards" after graduation and study under Edwards for ordination. When Hopkins arrived in Northampton in December 1741, Edwards recruited him almost at once to begin a circuit of itinerant preaching in western Massachusetts, and in 1744, he was ordained minister of the newly organized parish of Great Barrington, Massachusetts.

Hopkins was probably the least celebrated, and least talented, among the New Divinity as a preacher, but he more than made up for that in theological acumen, and it was in Hopkins's hands, even more than in Bellamy's, that the New Divinity took shape. In fact, the New Divinity's identity as a movement of its own really dates to the sensation aroused by the publication in 1765 of Hopkins's *Inquiry Concerning the Promises of the Gospel*. Originally composed as a reply to the publication of two sermons by the liberal Boston minister Jonathan Mayhew, *Striving to*

Enter in at the Strait Gate (1761), Hopkins's *Inquiry* indicted the New England tradition for watering down the depravity of original sin, turning conversion into a genteel embrace of polite morals, and making God into an indulgent uncle rather than a righteous Father. People needed to understand that "corruption or viciousness of heart" is "great and universal"—so great, in fact, that "the sinner will not repent, or have any right exercises towards God and his law, until his heart is in some degree renewed and set right." The use of "means" was no more acceptable to Hopkins than it had been to Bellamy. Given the profound moral warpage of human depravity, one might as well expect a handless climber to scale rock faces as to expect a sinner to repent, or even to know what repentance is. Depravity is so deeply laid that its ill effects can only be overcome "when God gives a new heart in regeneration," because only then is "a foundation . . . laid in the mind for a discerning of the truths of the gospel in their real beauty and excellency (to which the unregenerate heart, or the mind under the dominion of lust, is wholly blind)." This meant that there can be no gradual ramping up to a new heart through the use of means. Instead, "this change" is "wrought by the Spirit of God, immediately and instantaneously." No one should fool themselves into believing that there are "promises of regenerating grace made to the exercises and doings of the unregenerate." There is only one option: "Men are required to repent and believe, and turn to God, on pain of eternal damnation, and are declared to be in a state of condemnation until they do so."

Section VII

A short and plain State of the Case.

. . . Man is not only by sin plunged into a state of infinite guilt, from which he cannot be delivered, consistent with the law and moral government he is under, unless he is interested in, or united to, the Mediator, but he has also by his apostasy lost the moral image of God, or all true holiness; and consequently is wholly corrupt, and under the dominion of appetites and inclinations directly contrary to God and his law. . . . This corruption or viciousness of heart being so great and universal, the sinner will not repent, or have any right exercises towards God and his law, until his heart is in some degree renewed and set right. In this state the gospel finds man; in which pardon and salvation, through a Mediator, are freely offered to his acceptance, and all are invited to come to Christ, believe on him and trust in him, for all they want; being assured that, on this condition, Christ, with all his benefits, shall be theirs.

But as the way in which this salvation is given is in a peculiar manner adapted to do honor to the law which the sinner has broken, and vindicate the divine character, to which he is a perfect enemy; and as the Savior himself, in all he has done in the character of a Mediator, has, above all others, condemned sin, and manifested his love of righteousness and hatred of iniquity; and as the salvation itself which he gives consists summarily in deliverance from sin, and the exercise and enjoyment of true holiness—the sinner is in a peculiar manner an enemy to the gospel, to the Mediator, viewed in his true character, to the way in which he saves sinners, and to the salvation itself. And he always continues so while an enemy to holiness, and an impenitent; or until his heart is changed, and he comes to a new temper and disposition.

. . . As men do in their natural state, with their whole hearts, reject the good things offered in the gospel, and their doing so is wholly owing to an inexcusable wickedness of heart, God is not obliged, in reason or justice, to remove this voluntary, wicked, inexcusable opposition, and bring them to a willing compliance with his proposals. Neither has he obliged himself to do this for any, by promises to any thing which they shall do, as the condition of it. Therefore, whenever, and in whatever instance, God takes away the heart of stone and gives a new heart, he acts as being unobliged, or sovereignly, and bestows an unpromised favor. . . . But when God gives a new heart in regeneration, a foundation is laid in the mind for a discerning of the truths of the gospel in their real beauty and excellency (to which the unregenerate heart, or the mind under the dominion of lust, is wholly blind) and for those right exercises, in which faith or Christian holiness consists. And all the promises of the gospel are made to these exercises of the mind, in which the mind discerns divine truth in some measure as it is, and heartily embraces the gospel. And the first exercise of this kind entitles the person to all divine promises; to pardon of sin and eternal life, and to all those divine influences by which he shall persevere in faith and holiness, until he shall be perfectly delivered from all sin, and awake complete in God's likeness.

There must, therefore, be a distinction kept up between regeneration, which is the work of God in giving a new heart, and in which men are perfectly passive, and active conversion in which men, being regenerated, turn from sin to God. . . .

This change, therefore, called regeneration, by which a new heart is given, as the foundation of all true discerning of the things of God's moral kingdom, and of all right exercises of heart; this change, I say, wrought by the Spirit of God, immediately and instantaneously, and altogether imperceptibly to the person who is the subject of it—it being impossible that he should know what God has done for him but by a consciousness of his own views and exercises, which are the fruit and consequence of the divine operation—these views and exercises of the regenerate, in which they turn from sin to God, or embrace the gospel, are often in scripture spoken of as included in that change which is called *a being born again*; as all the change which is perceptible, and in which man is active, consists in this. And this is sometimes called, by divines, *active conversion*, to distinguish it from regeneration, or that change in which men are passive.

. . . The unregenerate sinner may be in a sort convinced in his judgment and conscience that he has by his sin exposed himself to eternal destruction; that he can be delivered from this evil and obtain salvation only by Jesus Christ, by coming to him and believing on him, and that in order to this he must have a new heart given him by God. And he may have such a sense of his danger and misery and of the awful consequence of sin as to fill his mind with great uneasiness and distress. This may, while it continues, deaden him to all carnal gratifications, and make him afraid to indulge himself in any overt acts of known sin, and lead him to make deliverance from future misery his great concern, and earnestly to seek this in the use of all means; being all attention to the great concerns of his soul, and a future world. But all this does not alter the reigning temper and disposition of the heart. There may be yet no more true hatred of sin than before, and a reigning enmity against the divine character, and law, and against the gospel; and the heart may therefore be as far from repentance and acceptance of offered salvation by Jesus Christ as ever, and really reject and abhor the good things offered in the gospel, and so be far from truly desiring and asking for them. And this is certainly the case with every unregenerate person, whatever concern and exercises he may have about the salvation of his soul, and whatever he may pretend and think of himself. If he thinks better of himself, as thousands do, it is all delusion. . . .

Section VIII

. . . There are no promises of regenerating grace made to the exercises and doings of the unregenerate. . . . In Scripture men are required to repent and believe, and turn to God, on pain of eternal damnation, and are declared to be in a state of condemnation until they do so. . . . To be condemned, and under God's wrath, and to be interested in the promises of God's favor and eternal life at the same time is a contradiction, and absolutely impossible. But if the promises of the gospel are made to the doings of unregenerate sinners, then they have a title to God's favor and eternal salvation, antecedent to faith, or while they are unbelievers; and, therefore, while they are condemned and under the doom of eternal damnation. They are therefore, at the same time, interested in all the divine promises, under God's favor and smiles, and accepted of him to a title to life; and yet under all the curses written in God's book, in a state of condemnation, and under the wrath of God. We cannot avoid this glaring absurdity and contradiction, without concluding that there are no promises of saving mercy made to sinners, upon any condition short of faith in Jesus Christ. . . .

. . . To suppose the unregenerate are not at heart enemies to the way of salvation by Christ, and that any of the exercises of their hearts about this salvation are not consistent with enmity against, and opposition to it, is to take away all distinction between the regenerate and unregenerate. . . . It is therefore observable that men, in arguing that there are promises to the doings of the unregenerate, do always overlook the true character of such, and of their exercises; yea, suppose them to be in a degree friendly to Christ and the salvation by him. In order to prove that there are promises to the unregenerate, they dress them up in the character which belongs only to the regenerate; so that, by stripping them of this disguise, the boasted arguments vanish into nothing but weakness and absurdity, and the truth arises into view, and becomes clear beyond dispute. . . .

If it should here be said that though unregenerate sinners are not willing to accept of salvation which is freely offered, and that this is both their sin and calamity, yet God may offer them regenerating grace, and promise to bring them to a willingness to accept of salvation, by giving them a new heart, upon terms which they, while unregenerate, may come up to; and so regeneration, and consequently the whole of salvation, may be connected with this condition, which really is something short of a hearty acceptance of salvation—for this is one thing promised to be given, and is implied in regeneration—I answer: If we suppose the grace of regeneration or a new heart, which implies a heart to accept of and trust in Christ for salvation, to be offered and promised to the unregenerate, on some condition which they are to come up to and perform while unregenerate, yet still this is an offer of that to which their hearts are as much averse as to salvation itself; they are as far from accepting of such an offer as they are from accepting of salvation, and reject and despise it as much. The grace of regeneration, or a new heart, is as contrary to the unregenerate heart as salvation or holiness itself; the unregenerate do oppose and reject this with their whole hearts; for it is supposed their hearts are now in direct opposition to the new heart offered, otherwise they would stand in no need of a new heart. . . . Therefore, God in the gospel makes no offers and promises of salvation, or of any thing connected with it, to the exercises and doings of the unregenerate.

From Samuel Hopkins, "An Inquiry Concerning the Promises of the Gospel," in *The Works of Samuel Hopkins, D.D.*, ed. Edwards Amasa Park, vol. 3 (Boston: Doctrinal Tract and Book Society, 1854), 183–275.

Samuel Hopkins

AN INQUIRY INTO THE NATURE
OF TRUE HOLINESS (1773)

If Samuel Hopkins had startled people in 1765 by declaring just how deep depravity was, he surprised them even more in 1773 when he published *An Inquiry into the Nature of True Holiness*. Jonathan Edwards had argued (in the unpublished dissertation *The Nature of True Virtue*, which Hopkins saw through the press in 1765) that virtue was not duty but beauty, which is put into actual exercise by "benevolence to being in general." This benevolence was first directed to God, but it also had to include everything God had made, "all beings which exist, capable of good, or that can be, in any sense and degree, objects of good will." That this asked individuals to take in a great deal did not bother Hopkins at all. "Any kind of good will, or any thing which has the appearance of benevolence, which is limited to particular objects, and will not extend to all towards which good will can be exercised, is not universal benevolence, but is essentially different from it, and quite of another nature." Anything less than that was irrevocably tainted with the opposite of benevolence, self-love, "the source of all the profaneness and impiety in the world, and of all pride and ambition among men, which is nothing but selfishness acted out in this particular way."

Hopkins's equation of virtue with benevolence was not only all-embracing but also radically self-denying. Benevolence "comprehends all the love to God, our neighbor, and ourselves, required in the law of God," and where benevolence fell short of the mark, then "all outward expressions of piety in words and actions are emptiness and hypocrisy." Benevolence, to be genuine, had to be *disinterested*. Hence, any professed love for God that contained the slightest measure of self-seeking or self-preservation was ethically worthless, a judgment Hopkins hoped would attach itself obviously to the "use of means." Every hope for self had to drop from the hands, and at once. Similarly, any love for others that was less than purely disinterested was just as suspect and had to be jettisoned just as absolutely.

&

Section III

What is that Love in which all true Holiness consists?

Though it is certain from the Holy Scriptures that all true holiness consists in love, yet all love is not holiness. . . . It is necessary, therefore, that we should carefully inquire into the nature and kind of holy love, in order to find the true and proper distinction and difference between that and the love in which there is no holiness.

Love has been usually distinguished into love of benevolence, or good will, love of complacence, or delight, love of esteem, and love of gratitude. The love of benevolence is good will to beings capable of good, or happiness, and consists in desiring and pursuing their good, or rejoicing in their possessing it. By benevolence is, I suppose, most commonly meant that good will which is exercised towards other beings, in distinction from self-love. But good will is as really implied in self-love as in the love of others; for they who love themselves only, exercise good will towards themselves.

Complacence is . . . the pleasure and delight we take in the person and character of an intelligent being, as beautiful and excellent. . . . And, complacence being understood in this sense, it may be observed that benevolence and complacence have not always the same object. We may exercise good will to a person whose whole character is very disagreeable and displeasing to us, so that he may, at the same time, be the object of our benevolence and of our displacence and aversion, because, though capable of happiness, his present character is disagreeable and hateful.

The love of esteem is nothing distinct from benevolence and complacence exercised towards a worthy, excellent object—at least in our apprehension. The love of gratitude is that affection which we exercise towards another, considered as a benefactor, for his good will exercised towards ourselves or others. This includes in it both benevolence and complacence, and is nothing distinct from this, as might be easily shown were there need of it, and will, perhaps, be more particularly attended to in the sequel.

. . . This universal benevolence, with all that affection or love which is included in it, and inseparable from it, is the holy love which God's law requires, and is the whole of true holiness. This love is distinguished from all other kinds of love both in its nature and object. The object is—

1. Universal being, including God and all intelligent creatures. Benevolence, or universal goodness, has for its object all beings which exist, capable of good, or that can be, in any sense and degree, objects of good will. Any kind of good will, or any thing which has the appearance of benevolence, which is limited to particular objects, and will not extend to all towards which good will can be exercised, is not universal benevolence, but is essentially different from it, and quite of another nature. That good will which will extend only to a limited number, or a certain kind or circle of beings, by the supposition is not universal good will; it falls, as it were, infinitely short of it in this respect, and is so far from uniting its subject to universal existence that it is circumscribed by very narrow bounds, and is consistent with ill will and opposition to general existence. . . .

Section IV

Self-love is no Part of that Love in which holiness consists, but of a Nature quite different and opposite.

Self-love has been represented by many, not only as a branch of holiness, but that in which it radically consists, making it the spring of all our actions. Some have thought it not only no part of holiness, but opposed to it. Others have taken a medium between these two, and represented self-love to be in its nature innocent and good, but not holy love, unless love to God and our neighbor be joined with it, to regulate and govern it. In order to determine which of these opinions is right, we must understand what is intended by self-love. . . . There are three things especially, often called by that name, and their not being distinguished has occasioned great confusion and error in treating this subject.

1. A general appetite to good, and aversion to evil, considered merely as such, or a perception of pain or pleasure, is called self-love. . . .

2. By self-love is sometimes meant selfishness, or those exercises in which a person loves himself only, which wholly confine him to his own personal interest; he taking no pleasure in any thing else, but placing all his good and happiness here. . . .

3. By self-love may be understood the love a person has for himself as part of the whole, which is implied in universal benevolence. . . . Thus selfishness may extend to a whole community, and each individual member of it, because the selfish man considers their welfare as connected

with his own. . . . In this respect there is in selfishness a resemblance to what is found in benevolence, which, though it consists in disinterested good will to the whole, is, as observed above, nevertheless exercised by the benevolent person to individuals, and more strongly to those who are more nearly connected with him, and more particularly to himself. . . . This selfish affection, though extended to the whole community with which the selfish man is connected, is at bottom nothing but love to himself. This is the foundation and centre of his love. He in reality loves nothing but himself, and regards others wholly for his own sake. Therefore, when he considers their welfare as inconsistent with his own, or any way opposing or impeding his interest, his heart will turn against them and hate them, whatever be their connection or relation.

This brings into view another thing, in which these two sorts of love of self differ and oppose each other. He whose regard to himself and his own interest does not arise from selfishness, but general benevolence, is ready to give up his own personal good for the sake of the whole: he desires no good for himself unless consistent with the common good. Whatever supposed good of his own or of another interferes with the greatest general good is no good to him, but the object of his aversion in this view of it; so that all his own particular interest is subordinate to that of the whole. This is necessary when regard to ourselves is but a branch of general good will. Thus the interest of the benevolent man is the common interest, and he has no other. In a word, he subjects and devotes himself and all things to the glory of God, and the happiness and glory of his church and kingdom—which is the greatest universal good, and includes the highest good of the creature—he having no other interest but this.

. . . It has been said, though *inordinate* self-love is sinful, it is not so in itself, but when joined with love to God and our neighbor, and subordinate to the general good, it is a virtuous, holy affection. . . . Nothing but universal benevolence can be obedience to this command; and so far as this takes place it is obeyed, and self-love is opposed and mortified. This benevolence, as has been shown, implies a proper regard to ourselves, and an equal regard to our neighbor—having all that impartiality, and love to our neighbor and ourselves, which this law requires. . . .

Universal good will comprehends all the love to God, our neighbor, and ourselves, required in the law of God, and therefore must be the whole of holy obedience. Every pious sentiment and affection is comprised in this, and all piety in words and practice is but an expression of this love. Where this love is not, all outward expressions of piety in words and actions are emptiness and hypocrisy. Let any serious person think what are the particular branches of true piety; let him view each one by itself; and, when he has discovered the nature and essence of it, he will find that disinterested friendly affection is its distinguishing characteristic. For instance, let fear and reverence of the divine Majesty be considered in this view. What but love and friendly affection distinguishes this from the fear and dread of devils? All the holiness in pious fear, by which it is distinguished from the fear of the wicked, consists in love. Leave all disinterested friendly affection to the divine Being out of fear, and all holiness is excluded.

Again: if we consider what is contained in true gratitude to God, we shall find disinterested kind affection the only thing wherein it differs from the affection of the most wicked creature. Where there is no good will there is nothing in what is called gratitude better than that which the legion of devils exercised when they were so far gratified by Christ as to be suffered to destroy the herd of swine. But so far as good will is exercised, the goodness of God to us and others will excite holy gratitude, which is nothing else but good will to God and our neighbor, in which we ourselves are included, and correspondent affection excited and acted out in the view of the good will and kindness of God.

And universal good will implies the whole of that affection and duty we owe to our neighbor. It all consists in the exercise and expression of this, and those affections that are implied in it. The exercise and practice of righteousness or justice towards our neighbor implies a benevolent regard to him and his interest. Where this is not there is no exercise and practice of justice in the heart, whatever is the external conduct; for justice consists in doing to our neighbor as we would he should do to us, or, in other words, loving our neighbor as ourselves. . . . In short, there is not any one virtue, or branch of godliness, humanity, or sobriety, not any duty we owe to God, our neighbor, or ourselves, that is not comprehended in universal benevolence, and is not necessarily exercised and practiced so far as this affection takes place in the heart. And where there is no defect in the latter, the former are found in their fulness and perfection; for the whole is nothing but benevolence acted out in its proper nature and perfection, or, love to God and our neighbor made perfect in all its genuine exercises and expressions.

. . . Self-love is, in its whole nature and in every degree of it, enmity against God. It is not subject to the law of God, nor indeed can be, and is the only affection that can oppose it. It cannot be reconciled to any of God's conduct, rightly understood, but is, in its very nature, rebellion against it; which is all an expression of that love which is most contrary to self-love. This is, therefore, the fruitful source of every exercise and act of impiety and rebellion against God, and contempt of him, that ever was or can be.

Self-love, exercised and indulged, blinds the heart to every true moral excellence and beauty: this does not suit the taste of the selfish heart, but gives it disgust. Self-love is the foundation and reason of all that blindness to spiritual things—to God, his glorious character, works, and kingdom—which the Scripture represents wicked men to have, and is, therefore, the source of all the errors which men imbibe, as well as all the open idolatry in the heathen world, and false religion under the light of the gospel. All this is agreeable to that self-love which opposes God's true character; and under the influence of this men go off from the truth, and believe, love, and practice a lie—being itself the greatest practical lie in nature, as it sets up that which is comparatively nothing above universal existence. Self-love is the source of all the profaneness and impiety in the world, and of all pride and ambition among men, which is nothing but selfishness acted out in this particular way. This is at the bottom of all the worldliness and sensuality that men run into, as it blinds their eyes to all true good, contracts their hearts, and sinks them down, so that they look upon worldly enjoyments to be the greatest good, and that in which their true interest lies. This is the spring of all the hatred and ill will, strife and contention among men; for this leads men to hate and oppose all those whom they view in the way of their own selfish interest. This is the source of all falsehood, injustice, and oppression under the sun, in which men are, through their selfishness, seeking, by undue methods, to invade the right and property of others. Self-love produces all the violent passions, envy, wrath, clamor, and evil speaking, of which men are guilty. Take away selfishness, and all these would cease immediately. And if there be any other sin, any thing which is contrary to the divine law, it is briefly comprehended in this fruitful source of all iniquity, *self-love*.

And hence we may see that holy love is wholly a disinterested affection, and in what sense it is so. Self-love is wholly an interested affection, as self is the only object of it. Holy love has no regard to self, as self, but is a regard to the greatest general good and interest, the glory of God in the highest glory of his kingdom, and the greatest good of the creation. So far as a man exercises holy love, he has no other interest but this, as all is devoted to this, and given up for the sake of it. And, in this sense, all his love is disinterested, as it seeks not any self-interest but the contrary. He who exercises this disinterested love has pleasure indeed, and is pursuing an interest and happiness, though it is not a selfish interest, but that in the pursuit of which he renounces what self-love seeks. . . . He, who, in the exercise of holy love, pursues the glory of God and the highest interest and happiness of his kingdom, which includes the greatest good of his fellow-creatures, pursues the best, the most important interest, and has the most noble, refined pleasure in the exercise of this affection; yet in all this he is wholly disinterested, as he opposes selfishness and all regard to self, which is not implied in being thus devoted to the greatest general good, and forsakes the whole interest which self-love seeks, for the kingdom of God's sake.

From Samuel Hopkins, "An Inquiry into the Nature of True Holiness," in *The Works of Samuel Hopkins, D.D.*, ed. Edwards Amasa Park, vol. 3 (Boston: Doctrinal Tract and Book Society, 1854), 5–141.

Sarah Osborn

MEMOIRS OF THE LIFE
OF MRS. SARAH OSBORN (1799)

Samuel Hopkins aroused opposition not only from other Congregational clergy but also within his own parish, and repeated attempts were
made by disgruntled villagers in Great Barrington to evict him from the
pastorate or to starve him out by failing to pay his salary. In 1769, an
ecclesiastical council of the lay and clergy leaders of the neighboring
parishes gave Hopkins leave to quit Great Barrington. Hopkins already
had received offers from four other churches (he was even a candidate,
briefly, for the Old South Church in Boston), and in 1770, he accepted
the call of the First Congregational Church in Newport, Rhode Island.

No one could have been more pleased with Hopkins's move to Newport than Sarah Osborn (1714–96), a fervently evangelical member of
the First Church, where she had organized a Religious Female Society
in 1741, a lay society that numbered as many as five hundred members
at its height. Osborn is significant for two reasons: Her society under-
scores the role played by self-organized lay societies in the evangelical
Awakenings on both sides of the Atlantic, and she herself is a marker
of the importance in the Awakening of women, who found that the
marginalization of the Awakeners by the religious establishment put
them on the same ground with the marginal roles assigned to women
in eighteenth-century society.

Born in London in 1714, Osborn migrated to Boston and then to
Rhode Island and was admitted to membership in Newport's First Church
in 1737. She embraced the Great Awakening in the 1740s, and, along
with Susanna Anthony, was one of the prime movers in bringing Hopkins to Newport in 1770. She wrote copiously—biblical commentaries,

devotional works, journals—but all that was published in her lifetime was a fifteen-page tract on Hopkins's favorite theme of discerning true holiness. Hopkins arranged for the publication of extracts from her diary and spiritual autobiography as *Memoirs of the Life of Mrs. Sarah Osborn* in 1799; a collection of her *Familiar Letters* appeared in 1807. Osborn's diaries for the years 1753 to 1784 are in the Library Special Collections of the Newport Historical Society. Her reference to Joseph Bellamy concerns Bellamy's *Theron, Paulinus, and Aspasio, or Letters and Dialogues upon the Nature of Love to God, Faith in Christ, Assurance of a Title to Eternal Life* (1759).

☙

In the year 1741, a religious, female society was formed under the care of Mrs. Osborn, they having chosen her to be their head. . . . Mrs. Osborn was continued and considered the head of this society from that time to her decease, which was above fifty years; and it still subsists, and there are above thirty members of it who are now living. It has consisted of a much greater number of members. About thirty years ago, above sixty persons were members of it. But the war, and other evils which have since that time taken place, have diminished it.

This society have met constantly once every week, during this whole time of above half a century, excepting a few interruptions, by some extraordinary occurrences. They also have observed four whole quarterly days in every year, as days of fasting and prayer, concerning their sins, and seeking God for spiritual blessings on themselves, on the church of Christ, and on all nations. They also have been wont to spend the afternoon of every first Thursday of each month in prayer together; and the afternoon of every Saturday before the monthly administration of the Lord's Supper. They have a box, which stands in the room where they meet, into which money is put by each one, as she is able and inclined. And at the end of the year, or any other time, when they think proper, the box is by their consent opened, and the money contained in it counted, and generally given for the support of the gospel.

They did agree upon a number of articles and rules, which were committed to writing, to be observed by the society and by each individual, and to be signed by every member, and by every one who should afterwards be admitted. The substance of these is as follows:

At the weekly meeting of the society, when the appointed hour arrives, and a number are convened, the exercise shall begin by reading in some profitable book, till all have come in who are expected. Then a prayer shall be made by one of the members; and after that, a chapter in the Bible shall be read, and religious conversation be attended to, as time shall allow. The meeting to be concluded by another prayer. Four quarterly days in the year, in January, April, July, and October, beginning on the first day of every January, to be observed as days of solemn fasting and prayer. We promise not to ridicule or divulge the supposed or apparent infirmities of any fellow member; but to keep secret all things relating to the society, the discovery of which might tend to do hurt to the society or any individual. We resolve to be charitably watchful over each other, to advise, caution, and admonish, where we judge there is occasion, and that it may be useful. And we promise not to resent; but kindly and thankfully receive such friendly advice or reproof from any one of our members. We will endeavor that our discourse, while together shall be on the serious and important subjects of religion: And when separate, that our speech and behavior shall be such as become christians, that we may be holy in all conversation.

If any member commit any scandalous sin, or walk unruly, and after proper reproof continue manifestly impenitent, she shall be excluded from us, until she give evidence of her repentance. Each one shall pay her proportion to defray the necessary expenses for wood, or any thing else, unless excused by the society.

When any person shall manifest to any one of us a desire to join the society, it shall be mentioned in one of our meetings, that all may have opportunity, who desire it, to satisfy themselves, respecting the character and conversation of the person offering to join. And if at the meeting on the next week, there be no objection to her being admitted, she may apply to the head of the society, who will read our articles to her, and if she is willing, and do sign them, she shall be considered as a member of the society, regularly admitted.

As to any other matters, which we shall hereafter find conducive to the benefit and good regulation of our society, we engage to leave to the discretion and decision of a major part of us, to whose determination we promise quietly to agree and submit.

This society has evidently been of great advantage to many if not all the members of it, to the church and congregation to which most of the members have belonged, and to the interest of religion in general especially in Newport, by their prayers and apparent sincerity and engagedness in religion, and exemplary conduct.

Mrs. Osborn was . . . distinguished in her usefulness in this station and capacity, by her prayers, her conversation, advice, judgment, prudence, and example; by which she was a principal medium of the long and happy existence and union of the society. Her influence apparently reached to every member, and her steady, prudent zeal and activity, and her amiable character, were very much the means of their continuance and edification. The society continued to meet in the room in which she lived, till her bodily infirmities were so increased that she was no longer able to sustain their company, and the exercises of the meeting. They then withdrew into another room in her house, where she was tenderly remembered in their prayers; and she was present in spirit with them, and partook largely with them in their exercises and enjoyments.

Monday morning, July 12.—I was engaged last week in reading and thinking on Mr. [Joseph] Bellamy's *Theron, Paulinus, and Aspasio.* An answer to Mr. Harvey's Dialogues. And heartily do I wish that all who are setting their face towards Zion, could and would, divested of all prejudice, for or against either of these authors, weigh Paulinus' strong, clear, and beautiful arguments. O that I may ever love the glorious God for what he is in himself, because he is a perfect glorious Being; just and holy, as well as merciful. O God, I beseech thee, show me thy glory. Let me with open face behold, as in a glass, the glory of the Lord, till I be transformed into the same image. O God, let me ever reach above the publican's standard. O, may I love thee for thyself, as well as what thou art to me. Lord, inspire me with a generous love, I beseech thee, to thee, and thy righteous law, which is holy, just, and good, though the whole human race had been condemned, and eternally banished from thy glorious presence for transgressing it. Shall that beautiful transcript of the divine image be esteemed a tyrant! Severe, hard, and cruel, because it requires me to love the Lord my God with all my heart and soul and strength and mind; and my neighbor as myself? O God, forbid. Slay every degree of enmity that rises up against this righteous law, and calls it cruel. O may I ever [manuscript unclear] for my continual deviations from and violations of thy holy law, and acknowledge I deserve eternal damnation for every breach of it: While I adore the infinite wisdom which has magnified the law and made it honorable in the death of the Son of God; while I adore the grace which has said, There is no condemnation to them who are in Christ Jesus, who walk not after the flesh, but after the Spirit. O, may my evidences be ever clear. Let me never build upon a persuasion that Christ, grace, and pardon are mine, without knowing that I have received him, and do rest upon him alone; am conformed to his image, in the temper of my mind, and tenor of my life. Amidst all my deficiencies, yet I do love righteousness and hate iniquity. Yea, I do delight in the law of God after the inner man. I do esteem it beautiful, holy, just, and good; yea, good for me. I do hate myself for my nonconformity. I do loathe, judge, and condemn myself for this. O thanks be to God that I can, notwithstanding, be cleared in an honorable way from the curse of the law; that God can be just, and yet the justifier of her who believes in Jesus.

[N.B. Mrs. Osborn wrote several volumes on the scriptures; not as a critical commentator; but in a devotional way, improving the passage upon which she meditated in application to herself, and so as to excite devout thoughts and exercises in addressing God, and hearing him speak to her in his word. In this way she wrote on the book of Genesis, and on the gospels of Matthew, Mark, and Luke. The following are copied as specimens of her writings of this kind, to give an idea of the manner in which she meditated and wrote on the scriptures, which she found entertaining and profitable to her: Which may perhaps excite some others to improve the Bible in the same manner, to their own advantage.]

Wednesday morning, October 7, 1767
Matthew 16:13, etc.

MY glorious Lord, dost thou inquire, Whom do men say that I, the Son of man am? There are indeed various opinions of thee this day. Some believe thee to be only as a great prophet, who did not exist till time began, etc. But dost thou ask me, who I think thou art? Lord, I know thou art Christ, the Son of the living God. Yea, from everlasting to everlasting thou art God, that great I AM, who art still the same.

Let me hear thee pronounce the blessing on me; for flesh and blood did not reveal this to me; but thy Father who is in heaven, by his Spirit, for the salvation of my poor soul.

And on thee, as an eternal rock, are all my hopes of safety forever built: And I do believe the gates of hell shall not finally prevail against me, after ten thousand attempts to overthrow my faith, yet this rock is my defense.

I humbly bless thee for assurance from thy word, that what thy Peter and other apostles by their writings bound on earth is bound in heaven; and what they have loosed on earth is loosed in heaven.

Is it thy will that I should keep secret the discoveries thou makest to me of thyself? Then show it to me clearly. Let me not be at a loss to know what is duty in this point: That I may neither withhold, nor reveal, contrary to thy blessed will; but always do the things that please thee, and by which thou wilt be glorified in me, and by others too.

My dear Redeemer, since thou hast suffered, according to thy word, let me never be offended in a crucified Jesus, or any doctrines of his cross; or sufferings to be endured for thy sake. Lord, let me never favor the things that be of men; flesh pleasing things; and hereby merit thy sharp rebukes: But teach me to acquiesce in all the will of God; all that is brought to pass by the determinate counsel and foreknowledge of God, however contrary to flesh and blood. Lord, teach me effectually, to believe at all times, that infinite wisdom knows best what is most for his own glory, and does all things well.

And in whatever thou art pleased to call me to selfdenial, I pray thee, grant me strength from heaven, that in every thing, without reserve, I may cheerfully take up my cross, and follow thee, never attempting to save my life in a sinful way; but joyfully lose it, rather than sin against thee, lose thee, and lose my own soul. What shall all the world profit me, while bemoaning a lost God, a lost Christ, a lost heaven, and a lost soul! Oh, in those circumstances, what would not a man give in exchange for his soul! But alas! Nothing is to be had as an equivalent; nor will God accept of any thing in exchange for the redemption of the soul, when the only Savior he has provided for its redemption is denied and rejected:—For when the Son of man shall come in the glory of his Father, with his holy angels, to reward every man according to his works, it will be forever too late for those out of him to find mercy.

O Lord, set home by thine almighty power, these alarming considerations upon my own soul, for quickening, I pray thee, that I may give all diligence in making my calling and election sure here, and at last have a reward of pure free grace, according to my works, though not for them.

After Mrs. Osborn had laid by her pen for a number of years, through the defect of her eye sight, and debility of body and mind, her thoughts unaccountably turned upon meditating on divine subjects, in verse or rhyme. This increased upon her, so that she made verses on a number of subjects; and her memory retained them, while they were not written, so that she could rehearse them distinctly, when she pleased; which she did to some of her intimate friends. They were pleased with them, not for their elegance and poetry; for to this she made no pretension, but for the sentiments, as expressed by *her*, and flowing from her heart, without any speculative study: And some of them were written from her mouth.

Her mind became more and more engaged in this way, which she found to be entertaining and profitable to herself. At length she thought of attempting to resume her pen, and write her verses on several subjects, though she knew she was not a poet, and had never before attempted any thing of the kind. She found herself able to write, beyond any thing she, or her friends, had ever expected, and wrote so much on a number of subjects, many of which she had before composed in her mind, and retained in her memory that, if collected together, they would make a considerable volume.

As this was, in several respects, an extraordinary event, and these writings express the devout exercises of her heart, in a manner different from her diary, the following is here inserted as a specimen of the whole.

The Employment and Society of Heaven

WHAT goodness this, which God extends
To us, who once were not his friends!
Compassion had on whom he would,
Though we did evil as we could.

Infinite love! 'Tis all divine;
God's wisdom form'd the vast design;
His pow'r has kept and brought us in,
Through all the assaults of hell and sin.

And now we shall forever gaze
On God, and his perfections praise;
We shall be like him more and more
Th' Incomprehensible adore.

No hateful sin, or weariness,
Shall cause us any more distress.
To do God's will with Seraph's joy
Shall ever be our sweet employ,

Ye dear companions here at rest,
With love sincere in every breast,
We now will cordially embrace,
Without a blush in any face.

No more misunderstandings here;
No misconstruction now we fear;
No censures hard, those bitter roots,
Which cast out love and blast its fruits.

No envy now, or selfishness,
Will e'er again our souls possess;
Benevolence shall sweetly flow:
We felt too little when below,

No prejudice shall make us stand
Aloof, as in that foreign land;
Because when there we could not see,
We in essentials did agree,

We surely did, since we are here,
Where none but friends to Christ appear;
And now our God hath brought us home,
We ever will rejoice as one,

O here's no trace of discontent;
Not one who murmurs in his tent:
Nor are there any fiery darts,
Ever to break or vex our hearts.

O precious blood, that once was spilt,
To cleanse our souls from all their guilt;
By which we are, indeed made free,
Our souls from sin at liberty.

O this gives joy its fullest tide,
That our Redeemer's glorify'd;

With satisfaction views the whole,
The fruitful travail of his soul.

Ye who are now before our eyes,
Who were on earth our enemies,
We bless the Lord that you're forgiv'n,
And are arrived safe in heav'n.

For this we gave the Lord no rest,
And he has answer'd our request;
For which we magnify his grace,
And join with you to sing his praise.

Ye worthy friends, who did relieve
Our pinching wants, ye now receive
The great reward Christ promis'd you;
Ten thousand thanks to God most true.

Now grateful love our souls doth cheer,
That we enjoy your presence here:
You did it for King Jesus' sake,
And of his joy you do partake.

Ye sweet acquaintance, christian friends,
Partakers of our joys and pains,
How oft by you did God afford
Relief to us from his own word!

Your tender sympathy and love
Did oft to us as cordials prove;
By sweet reproofs, and fervent prayer,
Ye kindly did our burdens bear.

In fore temptations, sharp and long,
You faithful held the Lord, and strong:
The great atonement all complete,
The promises most sure and sweet.

Ten thousand welcomes to this state,
Each other we congratulate,
And now our work shall all be praise
Through an eternity of days.

Though bonds of nature now do cease,
Our happiness it does increase,
To see our godly parents here,
And relatives to Christ most dear,

Can we review God's providence,
And yet retain no grateful sense
Of all your love and tender care,
Us for this heaven to prepare?

Do we not know you? Yes, we do,
No ignorance hides you from our view:
The leaks in mem'ry are all stopp'd
Since we our imperfections dropp'd.

What multitudes are there which rise
To fill our souls with sweet surprise?
It is the charming infant race,
Brought here thro' rich and sovereign grace.

These little ones were born again,
And did believe in Christ, 'tis plain:
God's Spirit wrought the work; but how
On earth we could not fully know,

Glory to God, that now we see
Nothing's too hard for Deity:
These were the lambs, whom Christ caress'd,
Took in his holy arms and bless'd,

Thanks be to him his word was giv'n
"Of such the kingdom is of heav'n,"
Now they behold his glory too:
Sweet babes we do rejoice with you.

New wonders still! Lo here are they,
Unjustly brought from Africa!
They've heard the gospel's joyful sound,
Though lost indeed they now are found,

Those we see here who once have been
Made slaves to man by horrid sin.
Now through rich grace in Christ are free,
Forever set at liberty.

Thanks be to God, though not to man,
'Twas he who laid this glorious plan
From evil great, this good to bring
All glory to our God and King.

Hail Ministers of Jesus' name,
Who this salvation did proclaim;

Our very souls do live anew
That we in heaven do meet with you,

You have receiv'd the sweet, "Well done":
And your eternal joy's begun;
Rich and complete is your reward,
And we forever bless the Lord.

What saints are these with crowns we see,
Of joy and immortality?
Gladly we find they are the same
Who out of tribulation came.

The holy prophets who did die
Because they truth did prophesy.
Apostles bless'd, and Martyrs, slain
Because Christ's truth they did maintain.

We know that these the world did hate;
But Christ has made them rich and great.
He promis'd them this great reward,
And we adore the faithful Lord.

New scenes arise. Let us attend:
Here's Abram's seed, God's ancient friend.
We see God's covenant was sure,
And did from age to age endure,

All these have had repentance giv'n,
The true Messiah own'd from heav'n,
His promises they did embrace,
And now behold his glorious face.

That very blood by them was spilt,
Which truly wash'd away their guilt,
Glory to God! we see the Jew:
We, Gentiles, do rejoice with you.

Transporting scene! All is delight!
Throngs numberless are in our sight,
Of every kindred, tongue, and size,
To overwhelm us with surprise.

When Christ a thousand years did reign,
Ten thousands then were born again;
Who now, through rich and sovereign grace,
Are here to fill this holy place.

Language is pure and all refin'd;
Quickly we know each other's mind,
All here is concord; all at peace,
And happiness does still increase,

These holy angels all have skill
To know and do Jehovah's will:
They joy'd at our Redeemer's birth,
And minister'd to him on earth.

The Angels, who excel in strength;
Who were our guardians all the length,
Of the afflictive, tiresome road,
And bare us safe to his abode.

Is this the heav'n of which we heard!
Are these the mansions Christ prepar'd!
How low have our conceptions been,
In a blind world of night and sin.

O come, yet lower let us fall,
Before our God, our all in all.
Sing praises to the worthy Lamb:
Ever adore the great I AM.

Amen, Hallelujah.

From Samuel Hopkins, ed., *Memoirs of the Life of Mrs. Sarah Osborn, Who Died at New-port, Rhode Island, on the Second Day of August, 1796. In the Eighty Third Year of Her Age* (Worcester, MA: Leonard Worcester, 1799), 70–380.

Nathan Strong

ON THE EVIDENCE OF FORGIVENESS (1798)

Joseph Bellamy's extraordinary preoccupation with "fitting" candidates for the ministry underlay the emergence, after 1770, of a second generation of New Divinity ministers that included John Smalley, Nathanael Emmons, Jonathan Edwards the Younger, and Nathan Strong. Of these, Strong (1748–1816) had the most public profile, first from his position as the minister of the First Church in Hartford, Connecticut, from 1774 until his death on Christmas Day in 1816, and then for his leading role in Revolutionary and Federalist politics and the organization of the Connecticut Missionary Society in 1798 and the *Connecticut Evangelical Magazine* in 1800. His two volumes of *Sermons on Various Subjects,* published in 1798 and 1800, reiterated the familiar demands of Bellamy and Samuel Hopkins for the most rigorous brand of moral practice. "CHRISTIAN sincerity requires an evidence which rises above formality," Strong insisted. Anyone who had genuinely experienced "a supreme love of GOD" would not let it manifest itself in lukewarmness. Only a "supreme love of GOD and all holy objects" really qualified as "a moral life."

The New Divinity rode this rigorism so single-mindedly that it pushed them into conflict with what had been a central belief of Calvinist orthodoxy since the sixteenth century and, for that matter, the Protestant Reformation itself: the understanding that the righteousness that saves a sinner comes not from the sinner but from a transfer (or imputation) of the merits of Christ to the repentant believer. As early as *True Religion Delineated*, Bellamy suspected that this could lead to the conclusion that the work of salvation required nothing at all from a sinner, and that was as sure a discouragement to revival as Arminianism. The New Divinity's second generation felt less hesitation in jettisoning imputation as the

109

basis for a sinner's salvation, and Strong went as far as to describe as "a very false idea" the idea "that the personal righteousness of CHRIST is made our personal righteousness." The rejection of imputation was the first noticeable departure of the New Divinity from tenets more fundamental to Calvinism than just disagreements about congregational polity. But it was a departure widely shared throughout the evangelical Awakenings in America and Europe and became a feature of the preaching of John Wesley and the Methodists, as well as the Moravians.

ᚱᚱᚱ

There are two sacred passages, written by the apostles Paul and James, which may appear contradictory, if we do not attend to the very different subjects they were considering.

> Paul saith, Therefore we conclude, that a man is justified by faith without the deeds of the law.
> James saith, *Ye see then how that by works a man is justified; and not by faith only.*

. . . Faith is an exercise of a holy heart; and a holy heart will always show itself in a pure practice, in a visible observance of the moral law, and of special gospel institutions. We therefore find all moral duties to GOD and man commanded in the gospel; and all immoralities are considered as sufficient evidence against Christian sincerity. A holy life; a pure practice; actions denoting reverence and a love of God; justice and mercy to men; personal purity and sanctification; and a dedication of all our active powers to the glory of GOD and the good of mankind, both for time and eternity, are enumerated as the proper life of Christians, and the only evidence of their sincerity. There are the most express laws, enjoining Christians to reject from their communion and the fellowship of their holy body, all, who by their practice, do not appear to love the holy commandments of JESUS CHRIST. The unjust, the dishonest, the profane, the impure of every description, the disturbers of society by their willful injury of men's reputation and interests, the intemperate destroyers of GOD and his institutions, and those who by any willful crime injure society and their neighbour can give no evidence they are Christians indeed. The law of CHRIST considers all such as insincere persons, until by reformation, they give evidence of their repentance and faith.
. . . THE question arises, is that, which is commonly called a moral life, sufficient evidence of forgiveness and of being a Christian indeed?
CHRIST tells us, *Wherefore by their fruits ye shall know them.* The fruits of a good and holy heart are proper evidence of sincerity and for-

giveness. And what are these fruits? The description, *a moral life,* may be extended to include everything expressive of the heart; but it is not commonly thus used. A supreme love of GOD and all holy objects is the Christian sincerity to which forgiveness is promised, and this will always express itself in ways beyond what is commonly meant by a moral life. A man may treat his neighbour morally, while it is very apparent that he does not love him, and delight in his prosperity. All mankind see the difference between formal complaisance and the respect of fervent love; between formal obedience and a sincere one; between an action delightful in itself and one that is done to serve another purpose and in which the heart takes no pleasure. There are innumerable cases in which the heart is most perfectly expressed, by things which cannot be described, and duties which can never be reduced to a written rule. The sensibilities of the heart appear in ways which words cannot picture. They are conceived, that are felt, but never described in language. We always expect to find this evidence of sincerity, in forming the friendships of the world; and a want of it at once excites our distrust.

CHRISTIAN sincerity requires an evidence which rises above formality. If men feel a supreme love of GOD, of his character and government, of his law and doctrines; there will be a natural expression of this love. They will be ready to express, in language which will be intelligible to all who have felt the same, their happiness in beholding and serving GOD. Their communion will be sweet in frequent conversation, instruction, advice, and prayer to the glorious object of their common adoration; and the whole scene of their Christian connection and obedience will be raised above formality. By a mutual engagedness to glorify GOD, to advance the kingdom of CHRIST, and save the souls of others, they will give evidence of their own sincerity and faith—that the glory of GOD is near their hearts—and that they think and act to promote it. Their thoughts will appear to be on the things of GOD and another world. This will banish the frivolous discourse and those foolish actions, in which many are constantly engaged, thereby proving that they never think of their own solemn destination, and the account they have to give before GOD. On the evidence which hath been mentioned, the communion of CHRIST's people in this world ought to be founded; and no part of it can be omitted, without substituting the form without the power of godliness. True obedience is of the heart. Whatever expresses this describes the man as he will be finally judged by the Christian law. Those who are afraid to have the heart searched think differently from JESUS CHRIST. They discover insincerity, a want of conformity to GOD, and of preparation for *the day when he shall judge the secrets of men by JESUS CHRIST.*

. . . Men may fall into great and strange delusions. There have been many persons of most immoral life, who appeared to think their salvation secure, from an apprehension of inward illumination and the grace of GOD reigning in their hearts. This is most dangerous delusion and is turning the grace of GOD into licentiousness. There can be no forgiveness without a good heart. There may be a moral practice where the heart is not satisfied, for a practice visibly right may arise from unholy motives; but an immoral practice never can come from a good heart. It is impossible there should be a holy motive to a bad deed. Men may think their motives to be holy, and thence form a false opinion of their bad actions; but in all such cases, the judgment is vitiated through a depravity of heart. An habitual bad practice proves a bad heart.

. . . THERE is a very false idea, entertained by some of being cloathed with CHRIST's righteousness, and depending on this as evidence of their forgiveness. The apostle speaks of not having his own righteousness, which is of the law, but that which is through the faith of CHRIST. So we are said to be justified by the righteousness of faith; and exhorted to put on CHRIST. From such descriptions as these hath arisen the expression of being cloathed with CHRIST's righteousness. They mean that we are justified, by the grace of GOD, through and for the sake of CHRIST's righteousness. Being cloathed with CHRIST's righteousness is being forgiven and accepted by GOD, for the sake of what he hath done and suffered. But it does not mean that the personal righteousness of CHRIST is made our personal righteousness. Although our own personal righteousness or sanctification cannot purchase any favor at the hand of a holy GOD; it is necessary to prepare us for the enjoyment of GOD; and it is necessary to receive the benefits of sovereign mercy; and it is also necessary as evidence that the fruits of CHRIST's righteousness are imparted to us. Our own personal holiness is the only evidence that we are forgiven through the righteousness of CHRIST. Being cloathed with humility and other graces of the Christian temper is the proper evidence that we are cloathed with forgiveness and the promises of eternal glory.

. . . There is no evidence that our faith is sincere, and we are forgiven; but a dedication of ourselves, both body and spirit to the Lord. We must be wholly his or we do not belong to him, for we cannot serve two masters. The works which will justify and prove our faith to be good include the temper—the moral state of the heart—and all the actions of living in the world. This is glorifying him in our body and in our spirit, which are his, and the only evidence of our eternal redemption. AMEN.

From Nathan Strong, "On the Evidence of Forgiveness," in *Sermons on Various Subjects, Doctrinal, Experimental, and Practical*, vol. 1 (Hartford, CT: Oliver D. and I. Cooke, 1798), 311–34.

Nathanael Emmons

THE DECEITFULNESS OF THE HUMAN HEART (1842)

None of the New Divinity preachers had quite the color, the charming eccentricity, or the deadpan sense of humor possessed by Nathanael Emmons (1745–1840). Born in 1745 in East Haddam, Connecticut, he entered Yale in 1763, where a borrowed copy of Edwards's *Freedom of the Will* set him on the path "of metaphysical theology." After graduating in 1767, he studied theology, first under Nathan Strong, then under Joseph Bellamy's pupil John Smalley, who "gradually opened what was then called New Divinity" to Emmons and made Emmons "a thorough convert to his scheme of sentiments." Emmons spent nearly four years candidating in various parishes before the rural parish of Franklin, Massachusetts, would take him, but from the date of his ordination in 1773 until his retirement in 1827, Emmons made the parish of Franklin his world and pushed the theology of the New Divinity to its outer limits.

Like Bellamy, he saw no other antidote to moral laxity—in either its wildfire antinomian forms or its rationalistic Unitarian forms—except the most self-abnegating moral rigorism. But in a significant departure from another aspect of conventional Calvinism, Emmons allowed no one to hide from knowledge of his or her sinfulness by pleading that he or she was possessed of a sinful nature that lay behind human consciousness, controlling human thought and action and requiring a prior renovation by God before he or she could find the wherewithal to repent. There was no essential nature, only conscious acts, and "sinners in general . . . are as conscious of their own hearts as saints are of theirs." As such, sinners knew full well that they were sinners, but they tried to dodge the obligation to deal with their sins by blaming their sinfulness on their nature and pleading that, until God changed their nature, they could only render what limited obedience their natures permitted—use the means, pray, read the Bible, and hope for grace. Emmons swept this away: "If you love God for what he is in himself, or on account of his intrinsic and supreme excellence, you have true love to him." But the love "that sinners ever exercise towards God" is "only for his love to themselves," and they are merely fooling themselves to imagine that this love makes them one jot more acceptable in God's eyes. "Sinners are never under genuine convictions until they see the desperate wickedness and deceitfulness of their hearts," and it was the ease with which that deceitfulness could be seen, and the directness with which it could be remedied by immediate and self-denying repentance, that Emmons excelled in exposing.

☙

. . . Sinners in general . . . are as conscious of their own hearts as saints are of theirs. They know that they have hearts, which are distinct from perception, reason, conscience, and all their intellectual powers and faculties. But this knowledge of their hearts is not that which is intended in the text. For in this sense they may perfectly know their own hearts, while they remain entirely ignorant of them in other important respects. This leads me to observe,

1. That their knowing their hearts . . . implies the knowledge of their selfishness. It is this alone that distinguishes their hearts from the hearts of saints. Those who bear the moral image of God have hearts of universal and disinterested benevolence. But the hearts of sinners are wholly selfish. Saints love those who do not love them; but sinners love those only who do love them; and all the criminality of their hearts consists in their partial, interested affections. . . . They imagine they have both love to God and man which does not arise from mercenary motives. But they cannot be said to know their own hearts, until they know that all their desires and affections are of a selfish nature, and actually flow from love to themselves.

2. The knowledge of their hearts implies the knowledge of their desperate, incurable wickedness. Their hearts are selfish, and so selfish, that no means or mere secondary causes can cure them.

. . . They may one day, or one hour, love what saints love, and the next day, or the next hour, hate what saints continue to love. They never know how they shall feel in respect to any object in any future time. Their hearts can put on the appearance of all holy affections at one time, and at another time put on the appearance of all unholy and selfish affections. As their hearts appear better at one time than at another, so they are very apt to think that they are better than they are. For though their affections vary so often, yet they never alter their nature; though

114

they are always selfish, yet they often appear disinterested; and though they are always enmity to God, yet they appear very often to be friendly to God, and to all other beings. The mutability of their hearts renders them deceitful above all things. And this deceitfulness of their hearts is that which renders it so extremely difficult for them to know that they are totally and desperately wicked.

. . . We learn from what has been said that there is but one way for men to know their own hearts. They cannot know them from the mere consciousness of having free, voluntary exercises. All men, good and bad, are conscious of what passes in their own minds. When they love or hate, choose or refuse, they are conscious of having these exercises of heart, whether they are or are not conscious of the moral nature of them. Nor can they know whether their moral exercises are right or wrong, good or evil, merely from knowing that they have all the various species of affection which are common to mankind in general; such as love and hatred, joy and sorrow, hope and fear, submission, patience, and confidence. All men exercise love and hatred, joy and sorrow, hope and fear, submission, patience, and confidence at certain times and under certain circumstances. This variety of affections forms no essential distinction between saints and sinners, and therefore affords no criterion by which men may determine whether their hearts are good or evil. Nor can they determine this point by merely having the same species of religious affections which are common to good and bad men. Sinners may love God, or love Christ, or love heaven, as well as love any other objects; and they may exercise every species of religious affections that saints exercise. Sinners may counterfeit every religious exercise. How is it possible, then, you will ask, for men to know whether their religious exercises are true or false? There is one way, and but one, to determine this great point; and that is to inquire why they love or hate, rejoice or mourn, hope or fear, or why they exercise submission, patience, and confidence. If you love God, inquire why you love him. If you love Christ, inquire why you love him. If you love heaven, inquire why you love that glorious place. If you exercise submission, inquire why you exercise it. If you exercise patience, inquire why you exercise it. If you exercise confidence, inquire why you exercise it. If you love God for what he is in himself, or on account of his intrinsic and supreme excellence, you have true love to him, which is essentially different from the love that sinners ever exercise towards God; for they love him only for his love to themselves. If you love Christ for the supreme excellence of his divine nature and holy conduct, you have true love to him, which is essentially different from the mercenary love of sinners. If you love heaven, because it is a holy as well as happy place, your love is holy, and essentially different from the selfish love of sinners in desiring heaven only as a place of happiness. If you exercise submission to God, because you choose that he should dispose of you for his glory through every period of your existence, you exercise true submission, which is essentially different from the submission of sinners, in case they know or believe that he will certainly save them. If you exercise patience, because you are willing that God should afflict you as long as he sees best to afflict you, you exercise true patience, which is essentially different from the patience which arises from mere necessity, which is all the patience that sinners ever exercise. If you trust in God because you choose to trust in him rather than trust in yourselves, or in any of your fellow-creatures, you place a confidence in him which sinners durst not do. Thus all men may know their own hearts, notwithstanding their extreme mutability and deceitfulness.

. . . We learn from what has been said that sinners are never under genuine convictions until they see the desperate wickedness and deceitfulness of their hearts. There is a very great difference between awakenings and convictions. Sinners are often awakened to see their danger, while they are entirely ignorant of the plague of their own hearts, or that incorrigible obstinacy which is incurable and desperate, and which no means nor moral motives will remove. Accordingly we find awakened sinners anxiously inquiring what they shall do in order to obtain regenerating grace. They think their hearts are already so good that they are willing to do all that is reasonable for them to do in their present situation. They are willing to read and pray, seek and strive, to enter into the strait gate, which is all they suppose God can reasonably require. And they have courage to seek and strive, because they imagine they are sincerely doing their duty, and their hearts are growing better; for they have stronger and stronger desires to be saved. But when the Spirit of God sets home the commandment upon their hearts, which requires disinterested love and forbids all selfish views, desires, and exercises, they are convinced that all their seekings and strivings, hopes and fears, have been entirely selfish and sinful; and instead of recommending them to God have only exposed them to his greater displeasure. Then sin revives, and their hopes die. Then they see that their selfish hearts have deceived them, and that their selfishness is desperate and incurable. They despair of men and means. They realize that they are out of reach of all secondary causes, and that they are entirely in the sovereign hand of God, who alone is able to save or destroy, and who will either save them or leave them to perish with their eyes wide open. They are not prepared to see and feel the grace of God in renewing their hearts and breaking the cords of their iniquity, until they have such genuine convictions of the nature and criminality of their selfish hearts. But sinners under mere awakenings are in the most dangerous situation. It is then their hearts become deceitful above all things, and powerfully persuade them that they are not so guilty as others, and that God will hear their cries for mercy, and graciously pardon and save them, because they have become better than they once were, and better than others now are. It is always owing to the deceitfulness and blindness of the heart that sinners ever gain and cherish a false hope.

. . . Saints fear that sinners never will be awakened; and if they are awakened, that they never will be converted. They know that while they continue under the entire dominion of a heart full of selfishness and deception, they will love to deceive themselves and to be deceived, and will resist every thing that is said to them or done for them to undeceive them. Though at one time and another they may put on promising appearances occasioned by the change of circumstances, yet they know not what they may be, or what they may do in time to come. For there is no deception in respect to sentiment or practice that they are not liable to believe and pursue. They see their feet stand on slippery places, and are fearful they will soon slide into destruction. In this light they view sober, regular sinners; and in this light they view the vain, trifling, and profane. And it would be well, indeed, if Christians were more concerned about sinners than they are; and they would be more concerned about them if they were more concerned about themselves. Let all search and try their hearts; for it is vain to try to conceal them. God says he knows them: for it is vain to try to conceal them. God says he knows them: "I the Lord search the heart, I try the reins, even to give every man according to his ways, and according to the fruit of his doings."

From Nathanael Emmons, "The Deceitfulness of the Human Heart," in *The Works of Nathanael Emmons, D.D.*, vol. 4, ed. Jacob Ide (Boston: Crocker & Brewster, 1842), 553–67.

Nathanael Emmons

THE DUTY OF SINNERS TO MAKE THEMSELVES A NEW HEART (1812)

Nathanael Emmons's announcement that sinners require no "new natural power or faculty of the soul" to render them "capable of understanding and doing their duty" did not endear him to either Old Calvinists—referring to mainstream New England Calvinists who endorsed the orthodoxy of the Cambridge or Saybrook Platforms but not the revivals—or their fellow Calvinists of the German Reformed, Dutch Reformed, or Scots-Irish Presbyterian churches of the mid-Atlantic. But it had a clear connection to Jonathan Edwards's teaching about the "natural ability" that made sinners accountable for their sins. For Emmons, the denial of a "new taste, disposition, or principle, which is prior to, and the foundation of all holy exercises"—a "dormant, inactive principle in the mind, which is often supposed to be the foundation of all virtuous or holy exercises"—was the best means to reinforce that sinners "are as completely moral agents as saints, and as completely capable, in point of natural ability, of understanding and obeying the will of God." Repentance toward God, therefore, "must consist in free, holy, voluntary exercises, and not in any thing whatever which is supposed to be prior to them, or the foundation of them."

This threw the onus of moral responsibility entirely, as Edwards had designed, on the sinner. If "a new heart wholly consists in new holy affections," of which the sinner is consciously aware, and if the sinner possesses the natural ability required for these holy affections, "then all the sinner has to do to make him a new heart is to exercise benevolence instead of selfishness, or to put forth holy instead of unholy exercises." Total depravity is not about a depraved nature but about the depraved consistency with which sinners choose to sin. What this also meant, though, was that "if the making of a new heart consists in the exercising of holy instead of unholy affections, then sinners are not *passive*, but *active* in regeneration." They have the natural ability to make new hearts for themselves, and so, in the strictest sense, "regeneration is not a miraculous or supernatural work" that sinners wait for but a goal that they have the natural ability to seize for themselves.

But having natural ability, as Edwards had demonstrated, is not the same thing as having the moral ability to use it. The moment Emmons tears away the sinner's self-delusions and forces the realization that "if it be their duty, in the first instance, to make them a new heart, then, according to their own plea" that becomes the moment when "they have no excuse for neglecting any other act of obedience to the divine commands." And it is at that moment that, unlike the Arminian who believes that sinners simply make moral and natural choices together, sinners discover that they have no equivalent moral ability to repent. The abyss yawns before them, and they cannot stop. "As soon as this commandment comes, sin revives, and they die. They find that they cannot love God, simply because they hate him, and that they hate him without a cause; which is their criminality, not their excuse."

What Emmons hoped to induce—as Joseph Bellamy had in his denial of the efficacy of the half-way covenant and Samuel Hopkins had in his demand for disinterested benevolence—was an existential flood of angst in a sinner, trapped between a natural ability that allowed full moral accountability and a moral inability that prevented him or her from ever squaring those accounts. It was in the frenzy of that trap that the New Divinity hoped for the sovereign intervention of God, while also hoping that the depth of this paradox would drive a sinner into submission.

. . . There is no ground to suppose that it means any new natural power or faculty of the soul, which is necessary to render sinners capable of understanding and doing their duty. They are as completely moral agents as saints, and as completely capable, in point of natural ability, of understanding and obeying the will of God. . . . Since God appeals to sinners as moral agents, we cannot suppose that the new heart which he requires them to make is any natural power or faculty of mind, which they do not need, and which, if they did need, they could be under no obligation to obtain.

Nor can a new heart mean any new natural appetite, instinct, or passion. Whatever belongs to our mere animal nature belongs to sinners as well as to saints. And when sinners become saints, they experience no change in their natural appetites, or animal propensities; but a new heart commonly serves to weaken and restrain, instead of increasing or strengthening such sensibilities as are destitute of every mortal quality.

Nor can a new heart mean any dormant, inactive principle in the mind, which is often supposed to be the foundation of all virtuous or holy exercises. Such a principle appears to be a mere creature of the imagination; but supposing it really exists, what valuable purpose can it serve? Can a dormant principle, which is destitute of all perception and sensibility, produce love, penitence, faith, hope, joy, and the whole train of Christian graces? We may as easily conceive that all holy affections should spring from that piece of flesh which is literally called the heart, as to conceive that they should spring from any principle, devoid of activity. A new heart, therefore, cannot mean a new principle, taste, relish, or disposition, which is prior to or the foundation of, all holy affections or gracious exercises.

This leads me to say positively, that a new heart consists in gracious exercises themselves; which are called new, because they never existed in the sinner before he became a new creature, or turned from sin to holiness. This will appear to be a just and scriptural explanation of a new heart, from various considerations.

In the first place, the new heart must be something which is morally good, and directly opposite to the old heart, which is morally evil. But there is nothing belonging to the mind that is either morally good, or morally evil, which does not consist in free, voluntary exercises. Supposing there is a dormant principle in the soul, which lies at the bottom of all voluntary exercises, yet so long as it lies dormant and inactive, there can be no moral quality belonging to it. And, indeed, if it should really produce moral exercises, still all moral good or evil would lie in the exercises themselves, and not in the principle. There can be no moral good or moral evil in any thing belonging to the mind, which has no perception and activity. Accordingly, we never praise or blame any person for any property he possesses, or any motive he puts forth, or any thing in him or about him in which he is totally inactive and involuntary. The new heart, therefore, which must be allowed to be morally good, must consist in free, holy, voluntary exercises, and not in any thing whatever which is supposed to be prior to them, or the foundation of them.

This will further appear, if we consider, in the next place, that the divine law requires nothing but love, which is a free, voluntary exercise. The first and great commandment requires us to love God with all our heart; and the second commandment requires us to love our neighbor as ourselves. . . . It is absurd to suppose that God would require any thing of us in which we are altogether passive, because this would be to require us to do nothing. Hence the new heart required in the text must consist in activity, or the free, voluntary exercise of true benevolence, which comprises every holy and virtuous affection.

. . . If a new heart consisted in a new principle or natural faculty, it would be difficult to see how a sinner could make him a new heart, without exerting almighty power or performing an act of creation; which is absolutely impossible. But if, as we have seen, a new heart wholly consists in new holy affections, then all the sinner has to do to make him a new heart is to exercise benevolence instead of selfishness, or to put forth holy instead of unholy exercises.

. . . God explicitly commands sinners to make them a new heart; and he implicitly requires the same thing in every other command he has given them in his word. When God commands them to love him with all their hearts, and their neighbors as themselves; or when he commands them to repent, to believe, to submit, to pray, to rejoice, or to do anything else; he implicitly commands them to make them a new heart, or to exercise holy instead of unholy affections. And for sinners to exercise holy affections is to exercise the new affections in which a new heart consists. Thus it appears that sinners, notwithstanding their total depravity, are capable of making a new heart, and are commanded to make a new heart; and of consequence that it is their first and indispensable duty to make them a new heart.

. . . If the making of a new heart consists in the exercising of holy instead of unholy affections, then sinners are not *passive*, but *active* in regeneration. It has been the common opinion of Calvinists that a new heart consists in a new taste, disposition, or principle, which is prior to, and the foundation of all holy exercises. And this idea of a new heart has led them to suppose that sinners are entirely passive in regeneration. But if a new heart consists in new holy exercises, then sinners may be as active in regeneration as in conversion. Though it be true that the divine agency is concerned in the renovation of the heart, yet this does by no means destroy the activity of sinners. Their activity in all cases is owing to a divine operation upon their minds. In God they live, and move, and have their being. They are not sufficient of themselves to think any thing as of themselves, but their sufficiency is of God. He always works in them both to will and to do, in all their free and voluntary exercises. . . . It is generally allowed that sanctification is the work of God's Spirit, and at the same time it is supposed that saints are active in the growth of grace, or perseverance in holiness. Indeed, it is expressly said that God, who begins, carries on the good work in the hearts of believers. But if saints can act freely under a divine influence in sanctification, why cannot sinners act freely under a divine influence in regeneration?

. . . If sinners are free and voluntary in making them a new heart, then regeneration is not a miraculous or supernatural work. . . . Since in regeneration God does not create any new nature, disposition, or principle of action, but only works in men holy and benevolent exercises, in which they are completely free and active, there is a plain absurdity in calling the renovation of the heart a miraculous or supernatural change. This is

121

carrying the *passivity* of the creature in regeneration to an extravagant height, and so as to destroy all obligation of sinners to do the least duty, until a miracle has been wrought upon them. How this is consistent with that distinction between natural and moral inability, which has been so clearly stated and strongly supported by a very acute and eminent divine, I can by no means conceive.

. . . If it be a duty which God enjoins upon sinners, and which they are able to perform, to make them a new heart, then there is no more difficulty in preaching the gospel to sinners than to saints. Those ministers who hold to passive regeneration, and maintain that sinners neither can, nor ought to make them a new heart, always find great difficulties in applying their discourses to the unregenerate. . . . Such a want of conformity to the divine standard of preaching is undoubtedly owing, in all cases, to a belief that sinners are passive in regeneration, and cannot make them a new heart. Let ministers, therefore, only renounce the false notion of passivity in regeneration, and they will find no more difficulty in exhorting sinners, than in exhorting saints, to do their duty. They will see the same propriety in exhorting sinners to make them a new heart, or to repent and believe immediately, as in exhorting saints to grow in grace, and to perfect holiness in the fear of God.

. . . Since it is the duty of sinners to make them a new heart, they have no excuse for the neglect of any other duty. When they are urged to love God, repent of sin, believe the gospel, make a public profession of religion, or to do anything in a holy and acceptable manner, they are always ready to excuse themselves for their negligence, by pleading their inability to change their hearts. This they say is the work of God; and until he pleases to appear for them, and take away their stony hearts and give them hearts of flesh, they cannot internally obey any of his commands, and therefore must be excused for all their delays, neglects, and deficiencies in duty. But if it be their duty, in the first instance, to make them a new heart, then, according to their own plea, they have no excuse for neglecting any other act of obedience to the divine commands. If it were their duty to *begin,* they acknowledge it would be their duty to *persevere* in obedience; and by acknowledging this, they virtually give up every excuse, and become self-condemned for all their internal as well as external transgressions of the divine law. . . . As soon as this commandment comes, sin revives, and they die. They find that they cannot love God, simply because they hate him, and that they hate him without a cause; which is their criminality, not their excuse.

From Nathanael Emmons, "The Duty of Sinners to Make Themselves a New Heart," in *The Works of Nathanael Emmons, D.D.,* vol. 3, ed. Jacob Ide (Boston: Congregational Board of Publication, 1860), 104–6, 109–11, 113.

Jonathan Edwards the Younger

REMARKS ON THE IMPROVEMENTS MADE IN THEOLOGY BY HIS FATHER, PRESIDENT EDWARDS (1842)

The second Jonathan Edwards (1745–1801)—referred to variously as Jonathan Edwards the Younger or Jonathan Edwards junior or simply *Doctor* Edwards to distinguish him from his father, *President* Edwards— was Jonathan Edwards's second son and ninth child, born in 1745 while the elder Edwards was still pastor of the church in Northampton. He was six years old when the Edwards family moved to Stockbridge, and he grew up among the Mahican children, speaking Mahican better than he spoke English. He graduated from Princeton in 1765 and was schooled for ordination under Joseph Bellamy. From there, Edwards the Younger embarked on a career eerily reminiscent of that of his father. Like Edwards senior, Edwards the Younger was licensed to preach in 1766 but was briefly recalled to Princeton for two years as a tutor; like his father again, Edwards the Younger was ordained in 1769 to a lengthy pastorate of the White Haven church, which had been founded as a split-off from the First Church in New Haven by New Light dissidents during the Awakening and legally organized as a separate society in 1759. But Edwards the Younger was, if anything, even more ready for theological combat than his father. The White Haven church suffered a split of its own, and when his father's old enemy James Dana became pastor of First Church, Edwards the Younger refused to join Dana at communion. By 1795, Edwards the Younger's relations with his own parish had deteriorated so badly that an ecclesiastical council had to authorize a separation. Edwards took up a new parish in Colebrook, Connecticut (in the heart of New Divinity country in Litchfield County), but in 1799, he followed his father's example again by accepting a college presidency—this time, Union College in Schenectady, New York. Like his father one last time, he presided over Union College only briefly, dying at age fifty-seven from complications of an "intermittent fever."

Appropriately for a man who stood so completely in his father's shadow, Edwards was the first to give the New Divinity a history. When Sereno Edwards Dwight, Edwards the Younger's great-nephew, produced his *Memoir of the Life of President Edwards* (1829) and a new ten-volume edition of Edwards's works, *The Works of President Edwards: With a Memoir of His Life* (1829–30), Dwight included "with peculiar pleasure" an essay by Edwards the Younger on "Clearer Statements of Theological Truth, Made by President Edwards, and Those Who Have Followed His Course of Thought." This was retitled and reprinted by Tryon Edwards in 1842 for a two-volume edition of Edwards the Younger's *Works*. Neither Sereno Edwards Dwight nor Tryon Edwards offered any background to the essay. But it offers a valuable précis of the elder Edwards's principal publications, deftly connecting Edwards and his followers at every point in order to blend Edwards and the New Divinity into a seamless whole. The only point at which Edwards the Younger surrenders this effort concerns the atonement, where he simply remarks that "the followers of Mr. Edwards have thrown new and important light upon *The Doctrine of Atonement*" and leaves it to readers to note that on this point Edwards himself quietly vanishes.

෴

1. The important question, concerning the *ultimate end of the creation,* is a question upon which Mr. Edwards has shed much light. For ages it had been disputed, whether the end of creation was *the happiness of creatures* themselves, or *the declarative glory of the Creator.* Nor did it appear that the dispute was likely to be brought to an issue. On the one hand, it was urged that reason declared in favor of the former hypothesis. It was said that, as God is a benevolent being, he doubtless acted under the influence of his own infinite benevolence in the creation; and that he could not but form creatures for the purpose of making them happy. Many passages of Scripture also were quoted in support of this opinion. On the other hand, numerous and very explicit declarations of Scripture were produced to prove that God made all things for his own glory. Mr. Edwards was the first who clearly showed that both these were the ultimate end of the creation, that they are only one end, and that they are really one and the same thing. According to him, the declarative glory of God is the creation, taken, not distributively, but collectively, as a system raised to a high degree of happiness. The creation, thus raised

and preserved, is the declarative glory of God. In other words, it is the exhibition of his *essential* glory.

2. On the great subject of *Liberty and Necessity*, Mr. Edwards made very important improvements. Before him, the *Calvinists* were nearly driven out of the field by the *Arminians, Pelagians, and Socinians.* . . . They were pressed and embarrassed by the objection—*That the sense in which they interpreted the sacred writings was inconsistent with human liberty, moral agency, accountableness, praise, and blame.* It was consequently inconsistent with all command and exhortation, with all reward and punishment. . . . How absurd, it was urged, that a man totally dead would be called upon to arise and perform the duties of the living and sound—that we should need a divine influence to give us a new heart, and yet be commanded to make us a new heart, and a right spirit—that a man has no power to come to Christ, and yet be commanded to come to him on pain of damnation! The Calvinists themselves began to be ashamed of their own case and to give it up, so far at least as relates to liberty and necessity. . . . But Mr. Edwards put an end to this seeming triumph of those, who were thus hostile to that system of doctrines. This he accomplished by pointing out the difference between *natural* and *moral* necessity and inability, by showing the absurdity, the manifold contradictions, the inconceivableness, and the impossibility of a *self-determining power*, and by proving that *the essence* of the virtue and vice, existing in the disposition of the heart and the acts of the will, lies not in their *cause*, but in their *nature*. Therefore, though we are *not* the efficient causes of our own acts of will, yet they may be either virtuous or vicious; and also that *liberty of contingence*, as it is an exemption from all previous certainty, implies that free actions have no cause, and come into existence by mere chance. But if we admit that any event may come into existence by chance, and without a cause, the existence of the world may be accounted for in this same way; and atheism is established. Mr. Edwards and his followers have further illustrated this subject by showing that *free action* consists in *volition* itself, and that *liberty* consists in *spontaneity*. Wherever, therefore, there is volition, there is free action; wherever there is spontaneity there is liberty; however and by whomsoever that liberty and spontaneity are caused. . . . The power of self-determination, alone, cannot answer the purpose of them who undertake its defense; for self-determination must be free from all control and previous certainty, as to its operations, otherwise it must be subject to what its advocates denominate a fatal necessity, and therefore must act by contingence and mere chance. But even the defenders of self-determination themselves are not willing to allow the principle that our actions, in order to be free, must happen *by chance*. Thus Mr. Edwards and his followers understand that the whole controversy concerning liberty and necessity depends on the explanation

125

of the word *liberty*, or the sense in which that word is used. They find that all the senses in which the word has been used, with respect to the mind and its acts, may be reduced to these two:

1. Either *an entire exemption from previous certainty*, or the certain futurity of the acts which it will perform; or,

2. *Spontaneity.* Those who use it in the former sense cannot avoid the consequence that, in order to act freely, we must act by chance, which is absurd, and what no man will dare to avow. If then liberty means an exemption from an influence, to which the will is or can be opposed, every *volition* is free, whatever may be the manner of its coming into existence. If, furthermore, God, by his grace, create in man a clean heart and holy volitions, such volitions being, by the very signification of the term itself, *voluntary*, and in no sense opposed to the divine influence which causes them, they are evidently as free as they could have been, if they had come into existence by mere chance and without cause. We have, of course, no need of being the efficient causes of those acts, which our wills perform, to render them either virtuous or vicious. As to the liberty, then, of self-determination or contingence, it implies, as already observed, that actions, in order to be free, must have no cause; but are brought into existence by chance. Thus have they illustrated the real and wide difference between *natural* and *moral* necessity. They have proved that this difference consists, not *in the degree of previous certainty* that an action will be performed—but in the fact, that *natural necessity* admits an entire *opposition* of the will, while *moral necessity* implies, and, in all cases, secures the *consent* of the will. It follows that all necessity of the will, and of its acts, is of the *moral* kind; and that *natural* necessity cannot possibly affect the will or any of its exercises. It likewise follows that if liberty, as applied to a moral agent, mean an exemption from all *previous certainty* that an action will be performed, then no action of man or any other creature can be free; for on this supposition, every action must come to pass without divine prescience, by mere chance, and consequently without a cause. Now, therefore, the Calvinists find themselves placed upon firm and high ground. They fear not the attacks of their opponents. They face them on the ground of reason, as well as of Scripture. They act not merely on the defensive. . . . But all this is peculiar to America; except that a few European writers have adopted, from American authors, the sentiments here stated. Even the famous Assembly of Divines had very imperfect views of this subject. This they prove, when they say, "Our first parents, *being left to the freedom of their own will*, fell from the state wherein they were created"; and "God foreordained whatsoever comes to pass, so as *the contingency* of second causes is not taken away, but rather established." These divines unquestionably meant that our first parents, in the in-

stance, at least, of their fall, acted from self-determination, and by mere contingence or chance. But there is no more reason to believe or even suppose this than there is to suppose it true of every sinner, in every sin which he commits.

3. Mr. Edwards very happily illustrated and explained *The Nature of True Virtue, or Holiness*. What is the nature of true virtue, or holiness?—In what does it consist?—and, Whence arises our obligation to be truly virtuous or holy?—are questions which moral writers have agitated in all past ages. Some have placed virtue in *self-love*; some in *acting agreeable to the fitness of things*; some in *following conscience*, or *moral sense*; some in *following truth*; and some in *acting agreeably to the will of God*. Those who place or found virtue in *fitness,* and those who found it in *truth,* do but use one synonymous word for another. For they doubtless mean *moral* fitness and *moral* truth; these are no other than *virtuous* fitness and *virtuous* truth. No one would pretend that it is a virtuous action to give a man poison, because it is a *fit* or direct mode of destroying his life. No person will pretend that the crucifying of Christ was virtuous, because it was *true*, compared with the ancient prophecies. To found virtue *in acting agreeably to conscience*, or *moral sense*, justifies the persecutions of Christians by Saul of Tarsus, as well as a great proportion of heathenish idolatry. If we found virtue in the *will of God*, the question arises, Whether the will of God be our rule, because it is in fact what it is, *wise, good*, and *benevolent*, or whether it be our rule, merely *because it is his will*, without any consideration of its nature and tendency; and whether it would be a rule equally binding, as to observance, if it were foolish and malicious? Mr. Edwards teaches that virtue consists in *benevolence*. He proves that every *voluntary action*, which, in its general tendency and ultimate consequences, leads to *happiness*, is virtuous; and that every such action, which has not this tendency, and does not lead to this consequence, is vicious. By happiness, in this case, he does not mean the happiness of *the agent* only or principally, but happiness in general, happiness *on the large scale*. Virtuous or holy benevolence embraces both the agent himself and others—all intelligences, wherever found, who are capable of a rational and moral blessedness. All actions, proceeding from such a principle, he holds to be *fit*, or *agreeable to the fitness of things*—agreeable equally to *reason*, and, *to a well-informed conscience*, or *moral sense*, and to *moral truth*—and agreeable especially to *the will of God*, who "is love," or benevolence. In this scheme of virtue or holiness, Mr. Edwards appears to have been original. Much indeed has been said, by most moral writers, in favor of benevolence. Many things they had published, which imply, in their consequences, Mr. Edwards' scheme of virtue. But no one before him had traced these consequences to their

proper issue. No one had formed a system of virtue, and of morals, built on that foundation.

4. Mr. Edwards has thrown much light on the inquiry concerning *The Origin of Moral Evil*. This question, comprehending the influence which the Deity had in the event of moral evil, has always been esteemed most difficult and intricate. That God is *the author of sin* has been constantly objected to the Calvinists, as the consequence of their principles, by their opponents. To avoid this objection, some have holden that God is the author of the sinful act, which the sinner commits, but that the sinner himself is the author of its *sinfulness*. But how we shall abstract the sinfulness of a malicious act from the malicious act itself; and how God can be the author of a malicious *act*, and not be the author of the *malice*, which is the sinfulness of that act; is hard to be conceived. Mr. Edwards rejects, with abhorrence, the idea that God either is, or can be, the agent, or actor, of sin. He illustrates and explains this difficult subject by showing that God may dispose things in such a manner, that sin will certainly take place in consequence of such a disposal. In maintaining this, he only adheres to his own important doctrine of *moral necessity*. The divine disposal, by which sin certainly comes into existence, is only establishing a certainty of its future existence. If that *certainty*, which is no other than moral necessity, be not inconsistent with human liberty; then surely the cause of that certainty, which is no other than *the divine disposal*, cannot be inconsistent with such liberty.

5. The followers of Mr. Edwards have thrown new and important light upon *The Doctrine of Atonement*. It has been commonly represented that the atonement which Christ made was *the payment of a debt* due from his people. By this payment, they were purchased from slavery and condemnation. Hence arose this question, If the sinner's *debt* be paid, how does it appear that there is any *pardon* or *grace* in his deliverance? The followers of Mr. Edwards have proved that the atonement does not consist in the payment of a debt, properly so called. It consists rather in doing that, which, for the purpose of establishing the authority of the divine law, and of supporting in due tone the divine government, is equivalent to the punishment of the sinner according to the letter of the law. Now, therefore, God, without the prostration of his authority and government, can pardon and save those who believe. As what was done to support the divine government was not done *by the sinner*, so it does not at all diminish the free grace of his pardon and salvation.

6. With respect to *The Imputation of Adam's Sin*, and *The Imputation of Christ's Righteousness*, their statements also have been more accurate. The common doctrine had been that *Adam's* sin is so *transferred* to his posterity, that it properly becomes *their* sin. The righteousness *of Christ*, likewise, is so *transferred* or *made over* to the believer, that it properly

becomes his righteousness. To the believer it is reckoned in the divine account. On this the question arises, How can the righteousness or good conduct of one person be the righteousness or good conduct of another? If, in truth, it cannot be the conduct of that other; how can God, who is omniscient, and cannot mistake, reckon, judge, or think it to be the conduct of that other? The followers of Mr. Edwards find relief from this difficulty by proving that *to impute righteousness* is, in the language of Scripture, *to justify*; and that *to impute the righteousness of Christ* is to justify *on account of* Christ's righteousness. The *imputation* of righteousness can, therefore, be no *transfer* of righteousness.

They are *the beneficial consequences of righteousness*, which are transferred. Not therefore *the righteousness* of Christ *itself*, but its beneficial consequences and advantages, are transferred to the believer. In the same manner they reason with respect to the imputation of *Adam's* sin. The baneful consequences of Adam's sin, which came upon *himself*, came also upon *his posterity*.

These consequences were, that, after his first transgression, God left him *to an habitual disposition to sin*, to *a series of actual transgressions*, and to *a liableness to the curse of the law, denounced against such transgression*. The same consequences took place with regard to Adam's *posterity*. By divine constitution, they, as descending from Adam, become, like himself, the subjects of an habitual disposition to sin. This disposition is commonly called *original depravity*. Under its influence they sin, as soon as, in a moral point of view, they act at all. This depravity, this disposition to sin, leads them naturally to a series of actual transgressions, and exposes them to the whole curse of the law.

On this subject two questions have been much agitated in the Christian world: 1. Do the posterity of Adam, unless saved by Christ, suffer final damnation on account of Adam's sin? and, if this be asserted, how can it be reconciled with justice? 2. How shall we reconcile it with justice that Adam's posterity should be doomed, in consequence of his sin, to come into the world, with an habitual disposition themselves to sin? On the former of these questions, the common doctrine has been that Adam's posterity, unless saved by Christ, are damned on account of Adam's sin, and that this is just, because his sin is imputed or transferred to them. By imputation, *his* sin becomes *their* sin. When the justice of such a transfer is demanded, it is said that the constitution, which God has established, makes the transfer just. To this it may be replied, that in the same way it may be proved to be just, to damn a man without any sin at all, either personal or imputed. We need only resolve it into a sovereign constitution of God. From this difficulty the followers of Mr. Edwards relieve themselves by holding that, though Adam was so constituted the federal head of his posterity, that in consequence of his sin they all sin or become sinners, yet they are damned on account of *their own personal sin merely*, and not on account of *Adam's sin*, as though they were individually guilty of his identical transgression. This leads us to the second question stated above, viz., How shall we reconcile it with perfect justice that Adam's posterity should, by a divine constitution, be depraved and sinful, or become sinners, in consequence of Adam's apostasy? But this question involves no difficulty, beside that which attends the doctrine of divine decrees. And this is satisfactory; because for God to decree that an event shall take place is, in other words, the same thing as if he make a constitution, under the operation of which that event shall take place. If God has decreed whatever comes to pass, he decreed the fall of Adam. It is obvious that, in equal consistency with justice, he may decree any other sin. Consequently he may decree that every man shall sin; and this too, as soon as he shall become capable of moral action. Now if God could, consistently with justice, establish, decree, or make a constitution, according to which this depravity, this sinfulness of disposition, should exist, *without* any respect to Adam's sin, he might evidently, with the same justice, decree that it should take place *in consequence* of Adam's sin. If God might consistently with justice decree that the Jews should crucify Christ, without the treachery of Judas preceding, he might with the same justice decree that they should do the same evil deed, in consequence of that treachery. Thus the whole difficulty, attending the connexion between Adam and his posterity, is resolved into the doctrine of the divine decrees; and the followers of Mr. Edwards feel themselves placed upon strong ground, ground upon which they are willing, at any time, to meet their opponents. They conceive, furthermore, that, by resolving several complicated difficulties into one simple vindicable principle, a very considerable improvement is made in the representations of theological truth. Since the discovery and elucidation of the distinction between natural and moral necessity, and inability; and since the effectual confutation of that doctrine, which founds moral liberty on self-determination; they do not feel themselves pressed with the objections, which are made to divine and absolute decrees.

7. With respect to *The State of the Unregenerate, The Use of Means*, and *The Exhortations, which ought to be addressed to the Impenitent*, the disciples of Mr. Edwards, founding themselves on the great principles of moral agency, established in *Freedom of the Will*, have since his day made considerable improvement upon former views. . . . Dr. Hopkins . . . published several pieces on *The Character of the Unregenerate*, on *Using the Means of Grace*; and on *The Exhortations, which ought to be addressed to the Unregenerate*. He clearly showed that, although they are dead in depravity and sin, yet, as this lays them under a mere *moral inability* to the exercise and practice of true holiness—and as such ex-

ercise and practice are their unquestionable duty—to *this* duty they are to be exhorted. To this duty only, and to those things which imply it, the inspired writers constantly exhort the unregenerate. Every thing short of this duty is sin. . . .

8. Mr. Edwards greatly illustrated *The Nature of Experimental Religion*. He pointed out, more clearly than had been done before, the distinguishing marks of genuine Christian experience, and those religious affections and exercises, which are peculiar to the true Christian. The accounts of Christian affection and experience which had before been given, both by American and European writers, were general, indiscriminate, and confused. . . . They did not show *how far* the unregenerate sinner can proceed in religious exercises, and yet fall short of saving grace. But this whole subject, and the necessary distinctions with respect to it, are set in a striking light by Mr. Edwards, in his treatise concerning *Religious Affections*.

9. Mr. Edwards has thrown much light upon the subject of affection as disinterested. The word *disinterested* is, indeed, capable of such a sense, as affords a ground of argument against disinterested affections; and scarcely perhaps is an instance of its use to be found, in which it does not admit of an equivocation. . . . The plain meaning is that his regard for him is *direct* and benevolent *not selfish*, nor arising from selfish motives. In this sense, Mr. Edwards maintained that our religious affections, if genuine, are disinterested; that our love to God arises chiefly—not from the motive that God has bestowed, or is about to bestow, on us favors, whether temporal or eternal, but—from his own infinite excellence and glory. . . .

10. He has thrown great light on the important doctrine of *Regeneration*. Most writers before him treat this subject very loosely. . . . They represent the man before regeneration as dead, and no more capable of spiritual action than a man naturally dead is capable of performing those deeds, which require natural life and strength. From their description, a person is led to conceive that the former is as excusable, in his omission of those holy exercises, which constitute the Christian character and life, as the latter is, in the neglect of those labors, which cannot be performed without natural life. . . . But according to Mr. Edwards, and those who adopt his views of the subject, regeneration consists in *the communication of a new spiritual sense or taste*. In other words, a new heart is given. This communication is made, this work is accomplished, by the Spirit of God. It is their opinion that *the intellect*, and *the sensitive faculties*, are not the *immediate* subject of any change in regeneration. They believe, however, that, in consequence of the change which the renewed heart experiences, and of its reconciliation to God, light breaks in upon the understanding. The subject of regeneration sees, therefore,

the glory of God's character, and the glory of all divine truth. . . . None of
the *awakenings, fears, and convictions*, which precede the new heart, are,
according to this scheme, any part of regeneration; though they are, in
some sense, a preparation for it, as all doctrinal knowledge is. The sinner,
before regeneration, is allowed to be totally dead to the exercises and
duties of the spiritual life. He is nevertheless accounted a moral agent.
He is therefore entirely blamable in his impenitence, his unbelief, and
his alienation from God. He is therefore, with perfect propriety, exhorted
to repent, to become reconciled to God in Christ, and to arise from
his spiritual death, that "Christ may give him light." According to this
system, regeneration is produced, neither by moral suasion, i.e., by the
arguments and motives of the gospel, nor by any supernatural, spiritual
light; but by the immediate agency of the Holy Spirit. Yet the light and
knowledge of the gospel are, by divine constitution, usually necessary
to regeneration, as the blowing of the rams' horns was necessary to the
falling of the walls of Jericho; and the moving of the stone from the
mouth of the sepulchre was necessary to the raising of Lazarus.

From Jonathan Edwards the Younger, "Remarks on the Improvements Made in Theology
by His Father, President Edwards," in *The Works of Jonathan Edwards, D.D., Late President of Union College*, vol. 1, ed. Tryon Edwards (Andover, MA: Allen, Morrill & Wardwell, 1842), 481–92.

PART 3

The Moral Government of God

Edwardseans and the Atonement

Calvinist orthodoxy, and before it, the first generation of Protestant Reformers, taught that the atonement was a judicial transaction: Sinners had offended God by breaking his law, and as a judge, he was bound to punish them with death; however, he accepted the death of his Son as a real and legitimate substitute for the death of sinners, and in that transaction, the merits of Christ were imputed to the elect (so that they became righteous), and their sins were imputed to Christ (so that he died their death). By this means, God could be perfectly just and yet still welcome sinners into his fellowship. Their forgiveness and their standing as righteous persons were wholly dependent on the merits Christ had transferred from his account to theirs.

The judicial model of justification had immediate connections to the nature of the atonement, since a justification accomplished by the merits of Christ could be applied only to those whom Christ consciously intended them for, the elect. Lavishing them on the non-elect would entirely defeat the purpose of election itself, just as spreading them around to the entire world would subvert the foundations of morality. Hence, reasoned Calvinist orthodoxy, the atonement must be considered limited or at least intentional in scope. However, like justification, this structured the atonement as a transaction in which a believer had no real role. While this could be tolerated in the larger context of divine providence when speaking about predestination, it was harder to encourage the faithful to devout spiritual practice while at the same time assuring them that their practice would make no ultimate difference in what made them right with God. For that reason, many of the evangelical movements of the eighteenth century either softened or abandoned the limited atonement model.

Just how deeply the tendency to adjust doctrine to experience ran in the eighteenth century Awakenings can be seen in how Samuel Hopkins and Joseph Bellamy followed the pattern of expanding the boundaries of the atonement. If only the elect could be atoned for, sinners would have an excuse not to repent; if the elect were justified before God by someone else's merits, they would never use their natural ability to obey him. The only logical alternatives would be mechanism or Arminianism. The sad state of New England Congregationalism before the Great Awakening only confirmed Hopkins's and Bellamy's suspicions that a governmental model of the atonement needed to be confected to fit the demands of true revival and pure Christianity. In this pattern, God was thought of primarily as a governor, with sin defined as a sort of *lèse-majesté*. To assert his moral authority in the face of human sinfulness, God determined to use the death of Christ as a means of showing "the infinite hatefulness and ill-desert of sin." That death did not provide a literal application of Christ's merits to the elect; rather, it created a theater in which God showed his anger and power against sin. Sinners—and this meant all sinners—could now see in the death of Christ the real fearsomeness of God's wrath against sin, take note, and repent. No longer could they plead a lack of certainty about their status as the elect as a sort of excuse. God had the authority to forgive anyone, on those terms, and everyone had an immediate obligation to repent. The death of Christ did not, therefore, literally provide an atonement for the limited number of the elect as much as it provided an opportunity for God to save anyone he wished without any doubts being raised about his moral government of the universe.

Stephen West

THE SCRIPTURE DOCTRINE OF ATONEMENT, PROPOSED TO CAREFUL EXAMINATION (1785)

Stephen West (1735–1819) was a native of western Connecticut and graduated from Yale in 1755. Having "embraced substantially the Arminian system," he was the first choice of the anti-Edwards factions in western Massachusetts to succeed Jonathan Edwards at the Indian mission at Stockbridge after Edwards's departure for Princeton in 1758. To their horror, Samuel Hopkins inveigled West into "frequent theological discussions," and West ended up as thoroughgoing a convert to Edwardseanism as Hopkins. West wrote a lengthy and admiring essay of his own on Edwards's notion of free will in 1772 and, like both Hopkins and Edwards, plunged himself into theological controversy over the terms of church membership and communion. Apart from a series of published sermons, West's other major theological writing was his *Scripture Doctrine of the Atonement, Proposed to Careful Examination* (1785), which was the earliest fully developed statement of a governmental theory of the atonement from a New Divinity parson. West's fundamental concept of the atonement began with an understanding of God as a law-giving magistrate who had certain requirements and expectations to fulfill as a lawgiver. "It is essential to the goodness of a Governor, or King, to guard the rights, secure the peace, and promote the prosperity of his subjects. . . . Should a ruler suffer crimes to go unpunished; the laws, however good and righteous in themselves, would presently lose their authority; and government fall into contempt." It was necessary, therefore, in any scheme for pardoning sinners, that the act of pardon appear based on real power and not mere incapacity. "Should God pardon *absolutely* or without adopting measures, at the same time, to convince his creatures of his infinite hatred of iniquity; his regards to the good of the great community over which he presides would necessarily appear to his creatures to be defective." What kept God's pardon of sinners from looking this way was the death he had decreed for Jesus Christ, "the death of Christ as being designed more immediately and directly to make a visible discovery of the anger of God against sin." No one viewing that death could doubt afterward that God hated sin and had the power to punish it. With that guaranteed, God was then justified in forgiving any repentant sinner who asked for it.

ᘓᘔ

Chapter II

An inquiry into the original ground of the necessity of the atonement, in order to the forgiveness of sin.

The original design of God, in the creation of the world, will naturally lead us to suppose that a disposition to exhibit his character in its true colours was the cause of his requiring an atonement for sin, before he would exercise pardoning mercy. Since this was God's original End in creation, this must, also, be the governing principle in all his future administration. Of course, therefore, the true reason why God required an atonement for sin was that *the real disposition of his own infinite mind, toward such an object, might appear; even though he pardoned and saved the sinner.*

. . . It is reasonable to suppose that God required an atonement for sin, that his creatures might be sensible of the abhorrence he has of it, notwithstanding the forgiveness he is pleased to exercise toward the sinner. . . . And that, in order to this, there was originally in the nature of things a necessity of an atonement, before mercy could be exercised in the pardon of the sinner; will appear from the following considerations, viz.

I. Should God pardon *absolutely* or without adopting measures, at the same time, to convince his creatures of his infinite hatred of iniquity; his regards to the good of the great community over which he presides would necessarily appear to his creatures to be defective.

It is essential to the goodness of a Governor, or King, to guard the rights, secure the peace, and promote the prosperity of his subjects. . . . Should a ruler suffer crimes to go unpunished; the laws, however good and righteous in themselves, would presently lose their authority; and government fall into contempt. Laws have no force, any further than they are carried into execution; and authority loses its respect whenever it ceases to be exercised. Whenever the supreme Magistrate neglects the execution of the laws, he loses the confidence of the people; and his regard to the public welfare becomes suspected. No one can confide in his public spirit, when he suffers the disturbers of the peace to go unpunished: For ideas of true regard to public good, as necessarily connect punishments with crimes, as rewards with virtue.

. . . Should God pardon the sinner, without taking effectual measures to minister conviction of his hatred of his sins, the evidence of his love to the public good would necessarily be defective. This, of course, would be a mode of administration exceedingly inconsistent with his original design in the creation and government of the world. For,

II. If God should pardon sin without an atonement, he could not be believed to hate iniquity. . . . If God should pardon the sinner, without taking some sufficient and effectual method, at the same time, to discover his infinite hatred of iniquity; if he should treat the clean and the unclean, the virtuous and the vicious, alike; we should have no means left whereby to determine that he held their characters in any different estimation; and, either approved, or disapproved the one, more than the other. Therefore, such a mode of providence would be inconsistent with the End which God had in view, both in the creation and government of the world; which was to manifest his own glory, and to display his own glory, and to display own infinitely holy and virtuous character.

III. THE government of God could not be respectable, should he pardon the sinner, without discovering, at the same time, his infinite hatred of his sins; and the perfect abhorrence he hath of his character. . . . No one can *respect* a government which provides no punishment for the wicked. And, whatever punishments be provided by *law*, if the executive authority neglect the execution, the government must, of necessity, fall into contempt. No sooner, therefore, will God cease to discover his hatred of the rebellion and wickedness of his creatures than he loses his authority, and renders his benevolence and good-will justly suspicious. But if the treatment God gives his creatures, in the good and the evil he confers upon them, be sure indications of the views he entertains of their characters; for him to pardon the sinner without an atonement or without taking some effectual measures to discover his hatred of his sins; must necessarily injure his character, weaken his authority, and bring his government into contempt.

. . . The honour of the divine law, agreeably to the true spirit and import of it, is fully preserved in the government of God, when his displeasure against sin is made to appear, to equal advantage, as it doth in the execution of the penalties of the law; *in whatever way it be done*. . . . Not only so, but it will, on these principles, be essential to the divine glory that the moral government of God should be as *full and sensible an expression* of his abhorrence of *every impure character* among his creatures, as of his approbation of the conduct of *all such* as never rebelled against him.

. . . Seeing therefore the existence of moral evil naturally furnished occasion for a display of God's *hatred of iniquity,* and evidently called for it, this would lead us to view the death of Christ as being designed more immediately and directly to make a visible discovery of the anger of God against sin.

. . . It appears from the nature of God's design in creation, and from the ground on which an atonement became necessary, that the great end of the coming and death of Christ was not to give evidence of the equity and righteousness of the moral law; but rather to exhibit in its proper colours, the disposition of the divine mind toward us for breaking it. The *righteousness of the law,* merely as a *rule,* and the *disposition of the divine mind* toward creatures who violate it are distinct objects which are to be separately considered. The objects are as perfectly different from each other, as the *divine Mind itself* and any of those *media* or objects through which it is seen. And in regard of these two different objects, when viewed in a separate light, it is to be remembered that, in real importance, the *former* is infinitely exceeded by the *latter.* However truly, therefore, a testimony to the righteousness of God's law *as a rule of life* might be contained in the design of the coming and death of Christ; a discovery of the divine disposition toward men for *violating* it was what, nevertheless, made an infinitely greater part of the design of Christ's work than the other.

To suppose that the principal design of the coming of Christ was to exhibit evidence to the consciences of men, of the righteousness and equity of the divine law, either as a *rule* of government for God, or of conduct for us; for aught we can see, would be rather a reproach than an honour to the divine character. . . . It is easy to see that conviction of the righteousness of the law might be wrought in the consciences of men, in a way infinitely less expensive than by the coming and death of the Son of God: Yea, were there no other ground of conviction in the case, this remarkable event would be far from affording it. For so long as we judge a rule itself to be *bad,* no *conduct* of any one formed upon it will make us believe it to be *good.* While we dispute the righteousness of the rule *given,* we dispute the righteousness of him who *gave it.* And in that case, his *obeying it himself* will no more convince us of its equity than his administering government *over us* in conformity to it. . . . But when men had *violated* the law, there needed visible demonstration of the existence of that displeasure in the divine mind, with which the sinner is *threatened,* in order to convince the creature that the law is indeed a transcript of the divine perfection; and that it truly expresseth the mind and will of God. Otherwise the exercise of pardoning mercy would render it doubtful whether the moral law expressed the divine character, and is really *in every part* equitable, even in the view of God. The exercise of mercy, therefore, without a sensible exhibition of that divine wrath which is threatened in the Law would give abundant occasion to call in question the perfect real conformity of the divine will, to that moral law which he has given us. This consequently could in no wise be for the glory of God.

From Stephen West, *The Scripture Doctrine of Atonement, Proposed to Careful Examination* (New Haven: Meigs, Bowen & Dana, 1785), 10–34.

Jonathan Edwards the Younger

THREE SERMONS ON THE NECESSITY OF THE ATONEMENT, AND ITS CONSISTENCY WITH FREE GRACE IN FORGIVENESS (1785)

In the same year that Stephen West published his *Scripture Doctrine of the Atonement*, Jonathan Edwards the Younger joined him in articulating the New Divinity's governmental model of the atonement in a series of three sermons preached before the legislature of Connecticut at the opening of their fall session. Edwards's opening premise in analyzing the atonement was that "it cannot be reconciled with the wisdom and goodness of God to make intelligent creatures and leave them at random, without moral law and government." This was, of course, what Arminians had accused Calvinists of promoting by limiting salvation and the atonement only to the elect, and the difficulty in that accusation "exceedingly perplexed and embarrassed" Edwards. "It is impossible for God himself to uphold his moral government, over intelligent creatures, when once his law hath fallen into contempt," he conceded. "He may indeed govern them by *irresistible force*, as he governs the material world," and this was also what Arminians had accused Calvinism of teaching. "But he cannot govern them *by law*, by rewards and punishments." Hence, an atonement was necessary, but an atonement of such a nature "equivalent to the punishment of the sinner according to the literal threatening of the law"—not literally imputing merit to the sinner but preparing "the way . . . for the dispensation of pardon." The most obvious example of the folly of powerless government was standing before them in 1785 in the form of the Articles of Confederation, and it would not have been difficult for the Connecticut legislature's collective mind to wander from theology to politics when Edwards reminded them that "in every instance in human governments, in which just laws are not strictly executed, the government is so far weakened, and the character of the rulers either legislative or executive suffers, either in point of ability or in point of integrity."

If our forgiveness be purchased, and the price of it be already paid, it seems to be a matter of debt, and not of grace. This difficulty hath occasioned some to reject the doctrine of Christ's redemption, satisfaction, or atonement. Others, who have not been driven to that extremity by this difficulty, yet have been exceedingly perplexed and embarrassed. Of these last, I freely confess myself to have been one. Having from my youth devoted myself to the study of theoretic and practical theology, this has to me been one of the GORDIAN KNOTS in that science. . . .

[I.] *Are we forgiven through the redemption or atonement of Jesus Christ only*? I say, *redemption or atonement*, because, in my view, they mutually imply each other. That we *are* forgiven through the atonement of Christ, and *can* be forgiven in *no other way*, the scriptures very clearly teach. . . .

II. *Our next inquiry is, what is the reason or ground of this mode of forgiveness? Or why is an atonement necessary in order to the pardon of the sinner?* . . . This, I suppose, would have been necessary, *to maintain the authority of the divine law*. If that be not maintained, but the law fall into contempt, the contempt will fall equally on the legislator himself; his authority will be despised, and his government weakened. And as the contempt shall increase, which may be expected to increase, in proportion to the neglect of executing the law; the divine government will approach nearer and nearer to a dissolution, till at length it will be totally *annihilated*.

. . . It cannot be reconciled with the wisdom and goodness of God to make intelligent creatures and leave them at random, without moral law and government. This is the dictate of reason from the nature of things. Besides the nature of things, we have in the present instance *fact*, to assist our Reasoning. God hath *in fact* given a moral law and established a moral government over his intelligent creatures. So that we have clear proof, that infinite wisdom and goodness judged it to be necessary, to put intelligent creatures under moral law and government. But in order to a moral law, there must be a penalty; otherwise it would be mere advice, but no law. . . . Hence, to execute the threatening of the divine law is necessary to preserve the dignity and authority of the law, and of the author of it, and to the very existence of the divine moral government. It is no impeachment of the divine power and wisdom, to say, that it is impossible for God himself to uphold his moral government, over intelligent creatures, when once his law hath fallen into contempt. He may indeed govern them by *irresistible force*, as he governs the material world: but he cannot govern them *by law*, by rewards and punishments.

If God maintain the authority of his law, by the infliction of the penalty, it will appear that he acts consistently in the legislative and executive parts of his government. But if he were not to inflict the penalty, he would act and appear to act, an inconsistent part; or to be inconsistent with himself. If the authority of the divine law be supported by the punishment of transgressors, it will most powerfully tend to restrain all intelligent creatures from sin. But if the authority of the law be not supported, it will rather encourage and invite to sin than restrain from it.

For these reasons, which are indeed all implied in supporting the dignity and authority of the divine law, it would have been necessary, had no atonement for sin been made, that the penalty of the law be inflicted on transgressors.

If in this view of the matter, it should be said . . . Why could not the Deity in a sovereign way, without any atonement, have pardoned all mankind? I presume it will be granted, for the reasons before assigned, that such a proceeding as this would be inconsistent with the dignity and authority of the divine law and government. And the same consequence *in a degree* follows from *every instance* of pardon in this mode. It is true the ends of human governments are tolerably answered, though in some instances the guilty are suffered to pass with impunity. But as imperfection attends all human affairs; so it attends human governments in this very particular, that there are *reasons of state* which require, or the public good requires, that gross criminals, in some instances, be dismissed with impunity, and without atonement. . . . But as not any of these is supposable in the divine government, there is no arguing conclusively, from pardons in human governments, to pardons in the divine.

It may be added that in every instance in human governments, in which just laws are strictly executed, the government is so far weakened, and the character of the rulers either legislative or executive suffers, either in point of ability or in point of integrity. If it be granted that the law is just, and condemns sin to no greater punishment than it deserves, and if God were to pardon it without atonement, it would seem that he did not hate sin in every instance, nor treat it as being what it really is, infinitely vile.

For these reasons . . . the very idea of an atonement or satisfaction for sin is something which, to the purposes of supporting the authority of the divine law, and the dignity and consistency of the divine government, is equivalent to the punishment of the sinner according to the literal threatening of the law. That which answers these purposes being done, whatever it be, atonement is made, and the way is prepared for the dispensation of pardon. In any such case, *God can be just and the justifier of the sinner.* And that that which is sufficient to answer these purposes has been done for us according to the gospel plan, I presume none can deny who believe that the eternal word was made flesh, and dwelt among us, and that he the only begotten and well beloved Son of God. . . .

From Jonathan Edwards the Younger, "Three Sermons on the Necessity of the Atonement, and Its Consistency with Free Grace in Forgiveness," in *The Works of Jonathan Edwards, D.D., Late President of Union College,* vol. 2, ed. Tryon Edwards (Andover, MA: Allen, Morrill & Wardwell, 1842), 11–52.

John Smalley

THE SUFFICIENCY OF THE ATONEMENT OF CHRIST FOR THE SALVATION OF ALL MEN (1814)

John Smalley (1734–1820) was a boy of six years when he heard George Whitefield preach in 1740, and the impression never left him. His parish minister, Eleazar Wheelock, was an ardent proponent of both Whitefield and Edwards and "fitted" Smalley for entrance into Yale in 1752. After graduation, Smalley studied under Joseph Bellamy and in 1758 was ordained pastor of the parish of New Britain, Connecticut, where he stayed for the next half century. He published surprisingly little until his retirement, when two anthologies of his sermons were issued. But they were quite possibly the gems of the New Divinity sermon literature, not only for their scope but also for their literary flair. Although he was anything but an elegant preacher in terms of style—"he was accustomed to preach with his manuscript before him, and read as doggedly as most of his contemporaries"—his preaching struck such a remarkable balance of theological technicality and pithy explanation "that few congregations were more regular and punctual than his, in their attendance on the services of the sanctuary."

In Smalley's definition of moral rigorism, "sin is always so written with a pen of iron, and the point of a diamond, that the moral evil of it can never literally be blotted out, or taken away, when once it has been committed." For God to forgive it by transferring the merits of Christ to a sinner, and forgiving the sinner on that basis, was exactly such an attempt to pretend that sin had not been inscribed into the sinner's actual moral character. "The sins of believers are not so taken away by the sufferings of Christ, but that they have occasion enough still to work out their own salvation with fear and trembling: and are still dependant on

God, for his working in them both to will and to do, of his good pleasure; that they should not think, Christ has so done all for them in this matter, that there is nothing left for them to do." Likewise, for God to limit the application of the atonement only to the elect put an excuse into the hands of every sinner. Would not a limited atonement, Smalley asked, "be a great stumbling block and discouragement to many sinners, and have a tendency to prevent their seeking and obtaining salvation? If it were true, must it not be known, or believed, what persons are of the number of the elect, for whom Christ died, before either they, or their preachers could see, that the calls of the gospel were to them? Or before it could be thought, on sufficient ground, that there was a natural possibility of their being saved?"

But in wiping away the notion that the atonement was limited judicially, Smalley did not want anyone to conclude that he was suggesting that everyone could be saved. Ironically, Smalley believed in a limited atonement as thoroughly as any other Calvinist, except that his notion of limitation was not judicial but magisterial, based solely on a sovereign decision by God to impart grace. "In regard to giving mankind the knowledge of the gospel way of peace, a genuine conviction of their totally sinful and lost condition, and saving them by the washing of regeneration, God hath mercy on whom he will have mercy; and whom he will, he leaves in ignorance, unbelief, impenitence, and hardness of heart. In these respects, he has an indisputable right to deal with all, according to his sovereign, wise, and holy pleasure." The atonement might be unlimited, in that God had set out a repentance-inducing example to all in the death of Christ, but the actual repenting would occur as God willed, on a one-by-one basis.

John 1:29

Behold the Lamb of God which taketh away the sin of the world!

These are the words of John the Baptist; the harbinger of the promised Messiah; the day-star, which ushered in the rising Sun of Righteousness. . . .

How are we to understand that this precious Lamb of God's providing, *taketh away sin?* . . . Certainly, he neither does, nor could, take away the criminality of it, or its just desert of punishment. Sin is always so written with a pen of iron, and the point of a diamond, that the moral evil of it can never literally be blotted out, or taken away, when once it has been committed. Of this we have plain proof, from the concurrent testimony of scripture and reason. Penitent sinners, sinners that have an interest in Christ by faith, pardoned and justified sinners, account themselves sinners still; and they are so considered in the word of God, and are so treated in his providence. They confess their sins, they are reproved for their sins; as sinners they are punished in this world, and all the hope given them of escaping punishment in the world to come is grounded on the free grace of God, as well as on the atoning merits of Christ. Not only are we to ascribe the gift of a Saviour, and of a Sanctifier, to the free grace of God; but also the justification of any of mankind, after they have been created unto good works, by the renewing of the Holy Ghost, and after they are entitled to the rewards of the Mediator's perfect righteousness, is a matter of grace, and not of debt, or desert. Thus, I think, the holy scriptures plainly teach; and in the nature of things, I apprehend it must be so; notwithstanding good Calvinistic divines, in former times, have taught differently. It appears evidently impossible that the Creator, and rightful Proprietor of all things, and Lord of all, should be indebted for any services or offerings, as men are, for value received. And thus it is written, by the apostle to the Romans: "Who hath first given to him, and it shall be recompensed unto him again? For of him, and through him, and to him, are all things." It was an exhortation of the pious Psalmist; "Let Israel hope in the Lord: for with the Lord there is *mercy*, and with him is plenteous redemption." And unless it had been believed, that in God there is *infinite mercy*, as well as that plenteous provision had been made for the remission of sins, neither all the house of Israel, nor even the man after God's own heart himself, could have had sufficient ground thus to hope; or to expect forgiveness, or any loving kindness from him. . . .

Can these assertions and representations possibly be consistent with the opinion entertained by some, that no provision is made, by the obedience and death of Christ, for the salvation of only a part of the ruined race of man?

We may be asked, If full satisfaction has been made by the atonement of Christ, for the sins of all men, why are not all saved?

But to this the sufficient answer is, So it seemeth good in the sight of God. In regard to giving mankind the knowledge of the gospel way of peace, a genuine conviction of their totally sinful and lost condition, and saving them by the washing of regeneration, God hath mercy on whom he will have mercy; and whom he will, he leaves in ignorance, unbelief, impenitence, and hardness of heart. In these respects, he has an indisputable right to deal with all, according to his sovereign, wise, and holy pleasure. No one has any right or reason to say unto him, Why doest thou thus? There is no more difficulty in comprehending this than there is in seeing why any rational creatures were at first left to transgress, or not perfectly to obey, the holy and righteous law of their Creator. He had certainly power enough to have preserved them all from apostacy; and it is certain that his thus preserving them would not have been inconsistent with his justice or truth. But we find he hath seen fit, no doubt, for wise and sufficiently important ends, to leave some of the once holy and happy angels of heaven, and our innocent first parents in paradise, to fall into a state of sin and misery. And he may have as good reasons undoubtedly, for not recovering all mankind to holiness and happiness; not withstanding he might do so, through the mediation and atonement of the infinitely meritorious Son of his love, without any dishonor to his violated law, or inconsistency with maintaining the essential truth of his threatenings, to every soul of man that doeth evil: the literal execution of the threatened penalty for every transgression and disobedience—"The soul that sinneth, it shall die," having been fully answered by the sufferings of Christ, who hath tasted death for every man.

It hath been objected, against the sufficiency of the death of Christ, to atone for the sins of all men, that if the merit of it had been thus universally extensive, justice would have required the salvation of all.

But this objection is grounded on a wrong idea of the merit of Christ's obedience unto death in the room of men. It supposes it to be like the payment of a debt, or the making of a purchase between man and man. Whereas, crimes are not to be thus cancelled; nor can any be thus purchased of God, as hath been before observed. There are two different kinds of merit; which have been distinguished, by calling one a merit of condignity, and the other a merit of congruity. The former giving one a just claim to a reward; the latter being only such as renders the bestowment of a free favor consistent with justice. And it is self-evident that no good can be merited at the hand of God, in any other than the latter sense. For as is asked by the apostle to the Romans, "Who hath first given unto him, and it shall be recompensed again? For of him, and through him, and to him, are all things." A merit of condignity is supposable, only when something is given, or some services are rendered by one to another to which he had no rightful claim. . . .

1. Undoubtedly, many who have embraced and taught that doctrine were, and are, good men; and, in other respects, good, sound, and orthodox divines. But, nevertheless, may not a belief of it be a great stumbling block and discouragement to many sinners, and have a tendency to prevent their seeking and obtaining salvation? If it were true, must it not be known, or believed, what persons are of the number of the elect, for whom Christ died, before either they, or their preachers could see, that the calls of the gospel were to them? Or before it could be thought, on sufficient ground, that there was a natural possibility of their being saved?

2. It may be seen, from what has been said, that the sins of believers are not so taken away by the sufferings of Christ, but that they have occasion enough still to work out their own salvation with fear and

trembling: and are still dependant on God, for his working in them both to will and to do, of his good pleasure; that they should not think, Christ has so done all for them in this matter, that there is nothing left for them to do; nor so as to supersede the necessity they are in, of the pardoning mercy of God the Father; or of the assisting and sanctifying influence of God the Holy Ghost. Yet,

3. The best Christians should hence be led to live by the faith of the Son of God, the second person in the Trinity, the lives which they now live in the flesh. They should look daily unto him who patiently suffered the contradiction of sinners against himself, and who endured the cross, despising the shame; as their great infallible example; and should rely alone upon what he hath done and suffered, as the meritorious ground of the pardon and acceptance with God.

For these purposes, we should never forget the exhortation which yet speaketh unto believers, "Behold the Lamb of God." We cannot now behold him, with our bodily eyes, as those might to whom it was first spoken. Nor should we think of literally eating his flesh and drinking his blood, as the Papists vainly dream, who have invented the gross absurdity of transubstantiation: nor, like them, should we make images or pictures of him, to bow before them, and worship them. But believers may yet behold him, with the eye of faith, in his heavenly discourses, in his parables, and in the miracles recorded of him, and there learn his amiable moral character, and his power to save: and may see him, and have communion with him in his holy ordinances, especially in the sacrament of his Supper, instituted to keep in remembrance his painful and ignominious sufferings, for our salvation.

4. From our subject, those who are most vile in their own sight may learn not to sink into despondency, as if for them there was no hope. "This is a faithful saying, and worthy of all acceptation, that Christ Jesus came into the world to save sinners," even the chief of sinners: and faithful also is the saying that "the blood of Jesus Christ, God's only begotten Son, cleanseth from all sin."

5. And finally; Let those who are deeply burdened with indwelling sin, as well as with outward sorrow, and who long for deliverance from the body of this death, hear his gracious call and merciful promise; "Come unto me, all ye that labor and are heavy laden and I will give you rest. Take my yoke upon you and learn of me, for I am meek and lowly in heart; and ye shall find rest unto your souls."

From John Smalley, "The Sufficiency of the Atonement of Christ for the Salvation of All Men," in *Sermons on Various Subjects, Doctrinal and Practical* (Middletown, CT: Hart & Lincoln, 1814), 267–79.

PART 4

Edwardsean Ethics

Antislavery and Missions

The intense commitment of the New Divinity to the most *ultra* forms of "consistent Calvinism" (to use Nathanael Emmons's phrase) would seem to imply that there was little to hope for from the Edwardseans in terms of practical ethics. But it was exactly an ethical crisis to which the New Divinity strategy of preaching down moral ability but preaching up natural ability had been tending all along. However much the idea of moral inability satisfied the Calvinist requirement to immobilize mere human initiative before a sovereign God, the idea of natural ability presented the same person with the requirement to do everything within his or her power to repent and practice holiness. The fact that the New Divinity made no serious attempt to reconcile these contrary demands only made their psychological pressure on the individual greater. Behind this stood Jonathan Edwards's own example in his edition of the missionary journal of David Brainerd and Samuel Hopkins's imperative to practice disinterested benevolence for the glory of God and the improvement of humanity, both of which made the New Divinity ripe for a commitment to the most exacting demands of missionary work.

The first result was manifest in the waves of New Divinity revivals that washed over western New England after 1810 in what became known as the Second Great Awakening. But the dynamic that erupted in this second set of parish revivals was not contained by the bounds of New England. In the three decades following the American Revolution, American commerce had successfully established itself in China, the Pacific islands, southeast Asia, India, and western Africa, alongside political enclaves established in the same places by European colonization. The opening up of Americans' world horizons beckoned to the Edwardseans. Hopkins began agitating for an African mission as early as 1771, and in 1798, Edwards the Younger and Nathan Strong drafted a constitution for the Connecticut Missionary Society and in 1800 launched a missions magazine, the *Connecticut Evangelical Magazine*. In 1799, Emmons and his circle of Massachusetts New Divinity parsons founded the Massachusetts Missionary Society and began publishing their own periodical, the *Massachusetts Missionary Magazine*. In 1810, the American Board of Commissioners for Foreign Missions was founded, top-heavy with Edwardseans in its leadership, and by 1812, the ABCFM's first contingent of New England missionaries had embarked for India.

Africa offered almost as tempting a target as British-ruled India for mission work. The principal mover of the ABCFM, Samuel John Mills (1783–1818), saw his calling as "the elevation of the colored people in this country and the regeneration of the Continent of Africa." The juxtaposition of evangelizing both Africa and the 1.2 million African-born or African-descended slaves in the United States was no accident. When Hopkins was finally able to organize a missionary society in Rhode Island in 1801 (and serve as its first president), the purpose written into its constitution was "to assist Africans in coming to a knowledge of the truth," not only in Africa itself but "in any part of the State where there may be an opportunity for it." After all, enslavement described precisely the sort of natural inability that Calvinism's critics had long tagged Calvinist theology with promoting, and to the extent that slavery literally involved the forcible repression of Christianity among the slaves by their masters, it was bound to arouse the animus of the New Divinity. Oddly, Edwards himself had been a slave owner. But as early as 1741, Edwards was already criticizing the New England–based slave trade, and during Edwards's pastorate in Northampton, six African slaves were admitted to full communicant membership. It was Hopkins who, characteristically, applied the full logic of Edwardseanism to slavery and in 1771 began preaching against the slave trade as a violation of the principle of disinterested benevolence. Two years later, he began directly attacking slavery itself and was joined in his protest by Edwards the Younger in New Haven and two years after that by another Edwardsean, Levi Hart, in eastern Connecticut. Radical opposition to slavery eventually became an issue of its own for the New Divinity, and in 1859, the most radical blow yet struck against American slavery would come from a man nurtured under a New Divinity pastorate in Torrington, Connecticut: John Brown.

Samuel Hopkins

A DIALOGUE CONCERNING THE SLAVERY OF THE AFRICANS, SHOWING IT TO BE THE DUTY AND INTEREST OF THE AMERICAN COLONIES TO EMANCIPATE ALL THEIR AFRICAN SLAVES (1776)

When Samuel Hopkins moved from Great Barrington to the First Church in Newport, Rhode Island, in 1770, he was moving into the very epicenter of the North American slave trade. Newport was the principal port of registry for the approximately 150 American-owned slave ships involved in the triangular trade between western Africa, the West Indies and the American South, and New England. Hopkins began preaching against the slave trade, and then slavery as an institution, almost from his arrival in Newport, which won him a substantial following among Newport's African American community and considerable hostility from the slave ship owners, who mostly belonged to Ezra Stiles's rival Second Congregational Church.

Slavery, as Hopkins beheld it, was an offense against benevolence, the fruits of a "most criminal, contracted selfishness." Once slavery was established in Hopkins's mind as a sinful trespass against disinterested benevolence, he saw no other solution than total and immediate emancipation. If slavery "be all wrong, and real oppression of the poor, helpless blacks," then slave owners have incurred all the guilt that belongs to slaveholding "and make ourselves, in a measure at least, answerable for the whole." The only proper solution, then, was "freeing all our slaves," and at once, as a "matter" that (like any other form of natural ability) "admits of no delay." Slavery was, in fact, a living exercise in the imposition of natural inability. Did the slaves have "any access to the gospel? Have they any instruction more than if they were beasts?" Evidently not. "So far from this that their masters guard against their

151

having any instruction to their utmost; and if any one would attempt any such thing, it would be at the risk of his life."

☙

A. Sir, what do you think of the motion made by some among us to free all our African slaves? They say that our holding these blacks in slavery as we do is an open violation of the law of God, and is so great an instance of unrighteousness and cruelty that we cannot expect deliverance from present calamities, and success in our struggle for liberty in the American colonies, until we repent, and make all the restitution in our power. For my part, I think they carry things much too far on this head; and if any thing might be done for the freedom of our slaves, this is not a proper time to attend to it while we are in such a state of war and distress, and affairs of much greater importance demand all our attention, and the utmost exertion of the public.

B. Sir, I am glad you have introduced this subject, especially as you own a number of these slaves. I shall attend to it with pleasure, and offer my sentiments upon it freely, expecting you will as freely propose the objections you shall have against any thing I shall advance. And I take leave here to observe, that if the slavery in which we hold the blacks is wrong, it is a very great and public sin, and, therefore, a sin which God is now testifying against in the calamities he has brought upon us; consequently, must be reformed before we can reasonably expect deliverance, or even sincerely ask for it. It would be worse than madness, then, to put off attention to this matter, under the notion of attending to more important affairs. This is acting like the mariner, who, when his ship is filling with water, neglects to stop the leak, or ply the pump, that he may mend his sails. There are, at the lowest computation, 800,000 slaves in British America, including the West India islands, and a greater part of these are in the colonies on the continent; and if this is, in every instance, wrong, unrighteousness, and oppression, it must be a very great and crying sin, there being nothing of the kind equal to it on the face of the earth. There are but few of these slaves, indeed, in New England, compared with the vast numbers in the islands and the southern colonies; and they are treated much better on the continent, and especially among us, than they are in the West Indies. But, if it be all wrong, and real oppression of the poor, helpless blacks we, by refusing to break this yoke and let these injured captives go free, do practically justify and support this slavery in general, and make ourselves, in a measure at least, answerable for the whole: and we have no way to exculpate ourselves from the guilt of the whole, and bear proper testimony against this great evil, but by freeing all our slaves. Surely, then, this matter admits of no delay, but demands our first and most serious attention and speedy reformation.

A. I acknowledge the slave trade, as it has been carried on with the Africans, cannot be justified; but I am not yet convinced that it is wrong to keep those in perpetual bondage who by this trade have been transported from Africa to us, and are become our slaves. If I viewed this in the light you do, I should agree with you that it is of the highest importance that they should all be made free without delay; as we could not expect the favor of Heaven, or with any consistency ask it, so long as they are held in bondage.

B. I am glad you have attended to the affair so much as to be convinced of the unrighteousness of the slave trade. Indeed, this conviction has been so spread of late that it has reached almost all men on the continent, except some of those who are too deeply interested in it to admit the light which condemns it; and it has now but few advocates, I believe, being generally condemned and exploded. And the members of the continental congress have done themselves much honor in advising the American colonies to drop this trade entirely, and resolving not to buy another slave that shall be imported from Africa.

But I think it of importance that this trade should not only be condemned as wrong, but attentively considered in its real nature, and all its shocking attendants and circumstances, which will lead us to think of it with a detestation and horror which this scene of inhumanity, oppression, and cruelty—exceeding every thing of the kind that has ever been perpetrated by the sons of men—is suited to excite; and awaken us to a proper indignation against the authors of this violence and outrage done to their fellow-men. . . .

A. Sir, there is one important circumstance in favor of the slave trade, or which will at least serve to counterbalance many of the evils you mention, and that is, we bring these slaves from a heathen land to places of gospel light, and so put them under special advantages to be saved.

B. I know this has been mentioned by many in favor of the slave trade; but when examined, will turn greatly against it. It can hardly be said with truth that the West India islands are places of gospel light. But if they were, are the negroes in the least benefited by it? Have they any access to the gospel? Have they any instruction more than if they were beasts? So far from this that their masters guard against their having any instruction to their utmost; and if any one would attempt any such thing, it would be at the risk of his life. And all the poor creatures learn of Christianity from what they see in those who call themselves Christians, only serves to prejudice them in the highest degree against the Christian religion. For they not only see the abominably wicked lives of most of those who are called Christians, but are constantly oppressed by them, and receive as cruel treatment from them as they could from the worst of beings. And as to those who are brought to the continent, in the southern colonies, and even to New England, so little pains are taken to instruct them, and there is so much to prejudice them against Christianity, that it is a very great wonder and owing to an extraordinary divine interposition, in which we may say God goes out of his common way, that any of them should think favorably of Christianity and cordially embrace it. As to the most of them, no wonder they are unteachable and get no good by the gospel, but they have imbibed the deepest prejudices against it from the treatment they receive from professed Christians; prejudices which most of them are by their circumstances restrained from expressing, while they are fixed in the strongest degree in their minds.

But if this was not the case, and all the slaves brought from Africa were put under the best advantages to become Christians, and they were in circumstances that tended to give them the most favorable idea of Christians and the religion they profess, and though all concerned in this trade, and in slavery in general, should have this wholly in view, viz., their becoming Christians, by which they should be eternally happy, yet this would not justify the slave trade, or continuing them in a state of slavery; for, to take this method to Christianize them would be a direct and gross violation of the laws of Christ. He commands us to go and preach the gospel to all nations, to carry the gospel to them, and not to go and with violence bring them from their native country without saying a word to them, or to the nations from whom they are taken, about the gospel or any thing that relates to it.

If the Europeans and Americans had been as much engaged to Christianize the Africans as they have been to enslave them, and had been at half the cost and pains to introduce the gospel among them that they have to captivate and destroy them, we have all the reason in the world to conclude that extensive country, containing such a vast multitude of inhabitants, would have been full of gospel light, and the many nations there civilized and made happy, and a foundation laid for the salvation of millions of millions, and the happy instruments of it have been rewarded ten thousand fold for all their labor and expense. But now, instead of this, what has been done on that coast by those who pass among the negroes for Christians has only served to produce and spread the greatest and most deep-rooted prejudices against the Christian religion, and bar the way to that which is above all things desirable—their coming to the knowledge of the truth, that they might be saved. So that, while by the murdering or enslaving millions of millions they have brought a curse upon themselves and on all that partake with them, they have injured in the highest degree innumerable nations, and done what they could to prevent their salvation and to fasten them down in ignorance and barbarity to the latest posterity. Who can realize all this and not feel a mixture of grief, pity, indignation, and horror, truly ineffable? And must he not be filled with zeal to do his utmost to put a speedy stop to this seven-headed monster of iniquity, with all the horrid train of evils with which it is attended?

And can any one consider all these things, and yet pretend to justify the slave trade, or the slavery of the Africans in America? Is it not impossible that a real Christian who has attended to all this should have any hand in this trade? And it requires the utmost stretch of charity to suppose that any one ever did or can buy or sell an African slave with a sincere view to make a true Christian of him.

A. You have repeatedly spoken of the attempt that is made to oppress and enslave the American colonies, and the calamities this has introduced, as a judgment which God has brought upon us for enslaving the Africans, and say we have no reason to expect deliverance, but still greater judgments, unless this practice be reformed. But is not this supposition inconsistent with the course of divine Providence since this war began? Have we not been strengthened and succeeded in our opposition to the measures taken against us, even beyond our most sanguine expectations; and a series of events very extraordinary and almost miraculous have taken place in our favor, and so as remarkably to disappoint our opposers and baffle them in all their plots and attempts against us? How is this consistent with the above supposition? If these calamities were brought on us for our sin in enslaving the Africans, and an expression of God's displeasure with us on that account, would he in such a signal manner appear on our side and favor, protect, and prosper us, even so that those of our enemies who are considerate and attentive have been obliged to acknowledge God was for us; I say, could this be, while we persist in that practice so offensive to him?

B. When I speak of our being under the divine judgments for this sin of enslaving the Africans, I do not mean to exclude other public crying sins found among us, such as impiety and profaneness, formality and indifference, in the service and cause of Christ and his religion, and the various ways of open opposition to it—intemperance and prodigality, and other instances of unrighteousness, etc., the fruits of a most criminal, contracted selfishness, which is the source of the high-handed oppression we are considering. But that this is a sin most particularly pointed out, and so contrary to our holy religion in every view of it, and such an open violation of all the laws of righteousness, humanity, and charity, and so contrary to our professions and exertions in the cause of liberty, that we have no reason to expect, nor can sincerely ask deliverance, so long as we continue in a disposition to hold fast this iniquity. . . .

But your objection is worthy of a more particular answer. It has been observed that there has been a general resolution to suppress the slave trade in these colonies, and to import no more slaves from Africa. This is a remarkable instance of our professed regard to justice, and a wise and notable step towards a reformation of this evil, and, as has been observed, a complete reformation will be the unavoidable consequence, if we will be consistent with ourselves. For no reason can be given for suppressing the slave trade which is not equally a reason for freeing all those who have been reduced to a state of slavery by that trade; and that same regard to justice, humanity, and mercy which will induce us to acquiesce in the former will certainly oblige us to practice the latter. Have we not, therefore, reason to think that the righteous and infinitely merciful Governor of the world has been pleased to testify his well-pleasedness with that regard to righteousness and mercy which we professed and appeared to exercise in refusing to import any more slaves, and which is an implicit condemnation of all the slavery practiced among us, by appearing on our side in the remarkable, extraordinary manner you have mentioned, by which wonderful interposition in our favor he has, at the same time, given us the greatest encouragement not to stop what we have begun, but to go on to a thorough reformation, and act consistently with ourselves by breaking every yoke and doing justice to all our oppressed slaves, as well as to repent of and reform all our open, public sins? So that God is hereby showing us what he can do for us, and how happy we may be under his protection, if we will amend our ways and our doings, and loudly calling us to a thorough reformation in this most kind and winning way.

But if we obstinately refuse to reform what we have implicitly declared to be wrong, and engaged to put away the holding the Africans in slavery, which is so particularly pointed out by the evil with which we are threatened, and is such a glaring contradiction to our professed aversion to slavery and struggle for civil liberty, and improve the favor God is showing us as an argument in favor of this iniquity and encouragement to persist in it, as you, sir, have just now done, have we not the greatest reason to fear, yea, may we not with great certainty conclude, God will yet withdraw his kind protection from us, and punish us yet seven times more? This has been God's usual way of dealing with his professing people; and who can say it is not most reasonable and wise? He, then, acts the most friendly part to these colonies and to the masters of slaves, as well as to the slaves themselves, who does his utmost to effect a general emancipation of the Africans among us; and, in this view, I could wish the conversation we have now had on this subject, if nothing better is like to be done, were published and spread through all the colonies, and had the attentive perusal of every American.

From Samuel Hopkins, "A Dialogue Concerning the Slavery of the Africans, Showing It to Be the Duty and Interest of the American States to Emancipate All Their African Slaves," in *The Works of Samuel Hopkins, D.D.*, vol. 2, ed. Edwards Amasa Park (Boston: Doctrinal Tract and Book Society, 1854), 551–88.

Jonathan Edwards the Younger

THE INJUSTICE AND IMPOLICY
OF THE SLAVE TRADE AND OF SLAVERY (1791)

Edwards the Younger followed Samuel Hopkins into opposition to the slave trade in a series of articles in late 1773 that were later worked into the sermon he preached for the founding of the Connecticut Society for the Promotion of Freedom and for the Relief of Persons Unlawfully Holden in Bondage. "His sympathies for the afflicted and suffering were strong, and at times deeply excited." When he moved to Schenectady to become president of Union College in 1799, he was astounded to find that the college church permitted blacks to come "to the Lord's table [only] after the other members," and "to one that had taken the stand that he had in favor of the colored race," the blatant injustice of this segregation "excited feelings that found relief only in tears."

Edwards was, if anything, even more confrontational than Hopkins in his denunciations of slavery. "I conceive it [the slave trade] to be unjust in itself—abominable on account of the cruel manner in which it is conducted—and totally wrong on account of the impolicy of it, or its destructive tendency to the moral and political interests of any country." But the trade and slavery alike were equally infamous. "Who can hesitate to declare this trade and the consequent slavery to be contrary to every principle of justice and humanity, of the law of nature and of the law of God?" Edwards asked. Its infamy lay partly in its practical wrongs. But a far greater infamy arose from the intrinsic evil of slavery itself. The abolition of slavery was an event "necessary and conducive to the interests of humanity and virtue to the support of the rights, and to the advancement of the happiness of mankind."

157

ℰℐ

Matthew 7:12

Therefore all things whatsoever you would that men should do to you, do ye even so to them; for this is the law and the prophets.

. . . Should we be willing that the Africans or any other nation should purchase us, our wives and children, transport us into Africa and there sell us into perpetual and absolute slavery? Should we be willing, that they by large bribes and offers of a gainful traffic should entice our neighbors to kidnap and sell us to them, and that they should hold in perpetual and cruel bondage, not only ourselves, but our posterity through all generations? Yet why is it not as right for them to treat us in this manner as it is for us to treat them in the same manner? Their color indeed is different from ours. But does this give us a right to enslave them? The nations from Germany to Guinea have complexions of every shade from the fairest white to a jetty black: and if a black complexion subject a nation or an individual to slavery, where shall slavery begin, or where shall it end?

I propose to mention a few reasons against the right of the slave trade—and then to consider the principal arguments, which I have ever heard urged in favor of it. What will be said against the slave trade will generally be equally applicable to slavery itself; and if conclusive against the former will be equally conclusive against the latter.

As to the slave trade, I conceive it to be unjust in itself—abominable on account of the cruel manner in which it is conducted—and totally wrong on account of the impolicy of it, or its destructive tendency to the moral and political interests of any country.

I. *It is unjust in itself.* It is unjust in the same sense, and for the same reason, as it is to steal, to rob, or to murder. It is a principle, the truth of which hath in this country been generally, if not universally acknowledged, ever since the commencement of the late war, *that all men are born equally free.* If this be true, the Africans are by nature equally entitled to freedom as we are; and therefore we have no more right to enslave, or to afford aid to enslave them, than they have to do the same to us. They have the same right to their freedom, which they have to their property or to their lives. Therefore to enslave them is as really and in the same sense wrong as to steal from them, to rob or to murder them. . . .

II. *The slave trade is wicked and abominable on account of the cruel manner in which it is carried on.* Beside the stealing or kidnapping of men, women, and children, in the first instance, and the instigation of others to this abominable practice; the inhuman manner in which they are transported to America, and in which they are treated on the passage and in their subsequent slavery, is such as ought forever to deter every man from acting any part in this business, who has any regard to justice or humanity. They are crowded so closely into the holds and between the decks of vessels that they have scarcely room to lie down, and sometimes not room to sit up in an erect posture; the men at the same time fastened together with irons by two and two: and all this in the most sultry climate. The consequence of the whole is that the most dangerous and fatal diseases are soon bred among them, whereby vast numbers of those exported from Africa perish in the voyage: others in dread of that slavery which is before them, and in distress and despair from the loss of their parents, their children, their husbands, their wives, all their dear connections, and their dear native country itself, starve themselves to death or plunge themselves into the ocean. Those who attempt in the former of those ways to escape from their persecutors are tortured by live coals applied to their mouths. Those who attempt an escape in the latter and fail are equally tortured by the most cruel beating, or otherwise as their persecutors please. If any of them make an attempt, as they sometimes do, to recover their liberty, some, and as the circumstances may be, many, are put to immediate death. Others beaten, bruised, cut, and mangled in a most inhuman and shocking manner are in this situation exhibited to the rest, to terrify them from the like attempt in future: and some are delivered up to every species of torment, whether by the application of the whip, or of any other instrument, even of fire itself, as the ingenuity of the ship master and of his crew is able to suggest or their situation will admit; and these torments are purposely continued for several days, before death is permitted to afford relief to these objects of vengeance.

By these means, according to the common computation, twenty-five thousand, which is a fourth part of those who are exported from Africa, and by the concession of all, twenty thousand, annually perish, before they arrive at the places of their destination in America.

But this is by no means the end of the sufferings of this unhappy people. Bred up in a country spontaneously yielding the necessaries and conveniences of savage life, they have never been accustomed to labor: of course they are but ill prepared to go through the fatigue and drudgery to which they are doomed in their state of slavery. Therefore partly by this cause, partly by the scantiness and badness of their food, and partly from dejection of spirits, mortification, and despair, another twenty-five thousand die in the seasoning, as it is called, i.e., within two years after their arrival in America. This I say is the common computation. Or if we will in this particular be as favorable to the trade as in the estimate of the number which perishes on the passage, we may reckon the number which die in the seasoning to be twenty thousand. So that of the hundred thousand annually exported from Africa to America, fifty thousand, as it is commonly computed, or on the most favorable estimate, forty thousand, die before they are seasoned to the country.

Nor is this all. The cruel sufferings of these pitiable beings are not yet at an end. Thenceforward they have to drag out a miserable life in absolute slavery, entirely at the disposal of their masters, by whom not only every venial fault, every mere inadvertence or mistake, but even real virtues, are liable to be construed into the most atrocious crimes, and punished as such, according to their caprice or rage, while they are intoxicated sometimes with liquor, sometimes with passion.

By these masters they are supplied with barely enough to keep them from starving, as the whole expense laid out on a slave for food, clothing, and medicine is commonly computed on an average at thirty shillings sterling annually. At the same time, they are kept at hard labor from five o'clock in the morning, till nine at night, excepting time to eat twice during the day. And they are constantly under the watchful eye of overseers and negro drivers, more tyrannical and cruel than even their masters themselves. From these drivers, for every imagined, as well as real neglect or want of exertion, they receive the lash, the smack of which is all day long in the ears of those who are on the plantation or in the vicinity; and it is used with such dexterity and severity as not only to lacerate the skin, but to tear out small portions of the flesh at almost every stroke.

This is the general treatment of the slaves. But many individuals suffer still more severely. Many, many are knocked down; some have their eyes beaten out; some have an arm or a leg broken, or chopped off; and many, for a very small, or for no crime at all, have been beaten to death merely to gratify the fury of an enraged master or overseer.

Nor ought we, on this occasion, to overlook the wars among the nations of Africa, excited by the trade, or the destruction attendant on those wars. Not to mention the destruction of property, the burning of towns and villages, etc., it hath been determined, by reasonable computation, that there are annually exported from Africa to the various parts of America, one hundred thousand slaves, as was before observed; that of these, six thousand are captives of war; that in the wars in which these are taken, ten persons of the victors and vanquished are killed, to one taken; that, therefore the taking of the six thousand captives is attended with the slaughter of sixty thousand of their countrymen. Now does not justice, does not humanity, shrink from the idea, that in order to procure one slave, to gratify our avarice, we should put to death ten human beings?

Or that, in order to increase our property, and that only in some small degree, we should carry on a trade, or even connive at it, to support which, sixty thousand of our own species are slain in war?

These sixty thousand, added to the forty thousand who perish on the passage and in the seasoning, give us an hundred thousand who are annually destroyed by the trade; and the whole advantage gained by this amazing destruction of human lives is sixty thousand slaves. For you will recollect that the whole number exported from Africa is an hundred thousand; that of these, forty thousand die on the passage and in the seasoning, and sixty thousand are destroyed in the wars. Therefore, while one hundred and sixty thousand are killed in the wars and are exported from Africa, but sixty thousand are added to the stock of slaves.

Now when we consider all this; when we consider the miseries which this unhappy people suffer in their wars, in their captivity, in their voyage to America, and during a wretched life of cruel slavery: and especially when we consider the annual destruction of an hundred thousand lives, in the manner before mentioned; who can hesitate to declare this trade and the consequent slavery to be contrary to every principle of justice and humanity, of the law of nature and of the law of God?

III. *This trade and this slavery are utterly wrong on the ground of their impolicy. In a variety of respects they are exceedingly hurtful to the state which tolerates them.*

1. They are hurtful, as they *deprave the morals* of the people. The incessant and inhuman cruelties practiced in the trade and in the subsequent slavery necessarily tend to harden the human heart against the tender feelings of humanity, in the masters of vessels, in the sailors, in the factors, in the proprietors of slaves, in their children, in the overseers, in the slaves themselves, and in all who habitually see those cruelties. Now the eradication, or even the diminution of compassion, tenderness, and humanity, is certainly a great depravation of heart, and must be followed with correspondent depravity of manners. And measures which lead to such depravity of heart and manners cannot but be extremely hurtful to the state, and consequently are extremely impolitic.

2. The trade is impolitic, as it is so *destructive of the lives of seamen.* The ingenious Mr. Clarkson hath, in a very satisfactory manner, made it appear, that in the slave trade alone, Great Britain loses annually about nineteen hundred seamen; and that this loss is more than double to the loss annually sustained by Great Britain in all her other trade taken together. And, doubtless, we lose as many as Great Britain, in proportion to the number of seamen whom we employ in this trade. Now can it be politic to carry on a trade which is so destructive of that useful part of our citizens, our seamen?

3. African slavery is exceedingly impolitic, as it *discourages industry*. Nothing is more essential to the political prosperity of any state than industry in the citizens. But in proportion as slaves are multiplied, every kind of labor becomes ignominious: and in fact, in those of the United States, in which slaves are the most numerous, gentlemen and ladies of any fashion disdain to employ themselves in business, which in other states is consistent with the dignity of the first families and first offices. In a country filled with negro slaves, labor belongs to them only, and a white man is despised in proportion as he applies to it. Now how destructive to industry in all of the lowest and middle class of citizens, such a situation and the prevalence of such ideas will be, you can easily conceive. The consequence is that some will nearly starve, others will betake themselves to the most dishonest practices, to obtain the means of living.

As slavery produces indolence in the white people, so it produces all those vices which are naturally connected with it; such as intemperance, lewdness, and prodigality. These vices enfeeble both the body and the mind, and unfit men for any vigorous exertions and employments either external or mental; and those who are unfit for such exertions are already a very degenerate race; degenerate, not only in a moral, but a natural sense. They are contemptible too, and will soon be despised even by their negroes themselves.

Slavery tends to lewdness, not only as it produces indolence, but as it affords abundant opportunity for that wickedness, without either the danger and difficulty of an attack on the virtue of a woman of chastity, or the danger of a connection with one of ill fame. And we learn the too frequent influence and effect of such a situation, not only from common fame, but from the multitude of mulattoes in countries where slaves are very numerous.

Slavery has a most direct tendency to haughtiness also, and a domineering spirit and conduct in the proprietors of the slaves, in their children, and in all who have the control of them. A man who has been bred up in domineering over negroes can scarcely avoid contracting such a habit of haughtiness and domination, as will express itself in his general treatment of mankind, whether in his private capacity, or in any office civil or military with which he may be vested. Despotism in economics naturally leads to despotism in politics, and domestic slavery, in a free government is a perfect solecism in human affairs. . . .

From the view we have now taken of this subject, we scruple not to infer that to carry on the slave trade, and to introduce slaves into our country, is not only to be guilty of injustice, robbery, and cruelty toward our fellow men; but it is to injure ourselves and our country, and therefore it is altogether unjustifiable, wicked, and abominable. . . .

If the slave trade be unjust, and as gross a violation of the rights of mankind, as would be, if the Africans should transport us into perpetual slavery in Africa; to unite our influence against it is a duty which we owe to mankind, to ourselves, and to God too . . . and so prepare the way for its total abolition. For until men in general are convinced of the injustice of the trade and of the slavery itself, comparatively little can be done to effect the most important purposes of the institution.

It is not to be doubted that the trade is even now carried on from this state. Vessels are from time to time fitted out for the coast of Africa, to transport the negroes to the West Indies and other parts. Nor will an end be put to this trade, without vigilance and strenuous exertion on the part of this society, or other friends of humanity, nor without a patient enduring of the opposition and odium of all who are concerned in it, of their friends and of all who are of the opinion that it is justifiable. Among these we are doubtless to reckon some of large property and considerable influence. And if the laws and customs of the country equally allowed of it, many, and perhaps as many as now plead for the right of the African slave trade, would plead for the right of kidnapping us, the citizens of the United States, and of selling us into perpetual slavery. . . .

Though we must expect opposition, yet if we be steady and persevering, we need not fear that we shall fail of success. The advantages, which the cause has already gained, are many and great. Thirty years ago, scarcely a man in this country thought either the slave trade or the slavery of negroes to be wrong. But now how many and able advocates in private life, in our legislatures, in Congress, have appeared and have openly and irrefragably pleaded the rights of humanity in this as well as other instances? Nay, the great body of the people from New Hampshire to Virginia inclusively have obtained such light, that in all those states, the further importation of slaves is prohibited by law. In Massachusetts and New Hampshire, slavery is totally abolished.

Nor is the light concerning this subject confined to America. It hath appeared with great clearness in France, and produced remarkable effects in the National Assembly. It hath also shone in bright beams in Great Britain. It flashes with splendor in the writings of Clarkson and in the proceedings of several societies formed to abolish the slave trade. Nor hath it been possible to shut it out of the British parliament. This light is still increasing, and in time will effect a total revolution. And if we judge of the future by the past, within fifty years from this time, it will be as shameful for a man to hold a negro slave as to be guilty of common robbery or theft. But it is our duty to remove the obstacles which intercept the rays of this light, that it may reach not only public bodies, but every individual. And when it shall have obtained a general spread, shall have dispelled all darkness, and slavery shall be no more; it will

163

be an honor to be recorded in history as a society which was formed, and which exerted itself with vigor and fidelity, to bring about an event so necessary and conducive to the interests of humanity and virtue to the support of the rights, and to the advancement of the happiness of mankind.

From Jonathan Edwards the Younger, "The Injustice and Impolicy of the Slave Trade and of Slavery," in *The Works of Jonathan Edwards, D.D., Late President of Union College,* vol. 2, ed. Tryon Edwards (Andover, MA: Allen, Morrill & Wardwell, 1842), 75–97.

Society of Inquiry Respecting Missions

HISTORICAL SKETCH OF THE SOCIETY (1833)

The most celebrated moment in the history of American Protestant missionary work is the so-called haystack prayer meeting in the summer of 1806. Five pious students at Williams College in western Massachusetts were driven by a rainstorm from a maple grove, where they proposed to hold a prayer meeting for the conversion of the heathen, and sought shelter under a haystack, where they joined together in an emotional dedication of their lives to missions work. The haystack prayer meeting is probably of less significance than the petition the Williams students—Samuel John Mills, Adoniram Judson, Samuel Newell, and Samuel Nott—addressed on June 27, 1810, to the General Association of Massachusetts Congregationalists, which led to the founding of the American Board of Commissioners for Foreign Missions. The ABCFM became the model for missions societies across New England and New York, and its principal training ground became Andover Theological Seminary, which had been founded jointly by New Divinity and Old Calvinist Congregationalists in 1808. But it was Samuel Hopkins and the New Divinity who had set the original patterns of interest: Jacob Ide, who in this extract is identified only as "one of the founders of the Society," was a pupil of Nathanael Emmons; Adoniram Judson "was approbated to preach as a Hopkinsian and an Emmonite," while "Mills, [Gordon] Hall, [James] Richards, and [Luther] Rice were," according to one of their colleagues, "Hopkinsian in the type of their theology." William Goodell, of Dartmouth, later became a prominent abolitionist.

☙❧

Historical Sketch of the Society

In June 1807, the Trustees [of Phillips Academy] obtained liberty from the Legislature of Massachusetts to receive and hold donations for the support of a *Theological Institution*, intended to furnish a professional education to youth destined for the Christian ministry. The Institution was opened in October 1808, for the reception of students, and thirty-six received instruction the first year. For several years, the Institution was commonly known by the name of "Divinity College."

On Tuesday evening, January 8, 1811, the following persons, members of Divinity College, united in forming a "Society of Inquiry on the subject of Missions," and adopted a Constitution. The names are arranged in the order in which they signed the Constitution.

SAMUEL NOTT, Wareham, Massachusetts
*SAMUEL JOHN MILLS, Agent to Africa
*JOSHUA DEAN, Locke, New-York
JACOB IDE, Medway, Massachusetts
LUTHER RICE, Washington City
*ROBERT CHAUNCY ROBBINS, Colchester, Conn.
SIMEON WOODRUFF, Strongsville, Ohio
*JAMES RICHARDS, Missionary to Ceylon

The motives which led to the formation of the Society are briefly stated in the preamble of the Constitution, which is as follows: "Feeling the importance of a more extensive acquaintance with the subject of Missions to enable us to ascertain our duty, and prepare us to promote the glory of our Redeemer and the eternal happiness of our fellow-men; we, the undersigned, looking to our Heavenly Father for direction, do form ourselves into a Society, and adopt the following Constitution."

The object of the Society, according to the second article of the Constitution, was "to inquire into the state of the heathen; the duty and importance of missionary labors; the best manner of conducting Missions, and the most eligible places for their establishment; also, to disseminate information relative to these subjects, and to excite the attention of Christians to the importance and duty of Missions."

The germ of this Society can be distinctly seen in the Missionary Society which was formed by Mills, Richards, and two or three others at Williams College, in the fall of 1808. The objects of the two Societies were in some respects the same. The one at Williams College, however, was composed *exclusively* of such as had already devoted their lives to the cause of Missions. Its object was *to effect a Mission to the heathen in the persons of its members.* The Society at Andover seems to have been planned by the same individuals, for the purpose of exciting inquiry, and enlisting others in the same cause.

The following extract of a letter from the Rev. Mr. [Jacob] Ide, one of the founders of the Society, makes some interesting disclosures on this subject. "The causes which led to the formation of the Society are perhaps all comprised in an anxious desire which then existed in the minds of a number of the students, to obtain, and diffuse information on the subject of Missions. When I first entered the Seminary, which was in the winter of 1810, I found that this subject lay, with great weight, upon the minds of a number. They were very anxious to know what was their personal duty. They conversed much on the subject with each other, and with other members of the Seminary who had before thought little upon it. They appeared to be very anxious, that every one should, as soon as practicable, settle this point of duty for himself. *The spirit of Missions was there.* This special influence upon the minds of a goodly number was distinctly perceived, for some time, before this society was formed. I thought at the time, and have often thought since, that God then sent his Spirit into the Seminary, to *convert* the students to the subject of Missions. For seldom have I ever seen a more evident movement of the Spirit upon the minds of sinners, to awaken, to convince, and to convert them, than was manifest in the Seminary, in turning the attention and hearts of the students to the condition of the perishing heathen."

From this extract, as well as from many circumstances which might be mentioned, it is evident that there existed in the Seminary at this time what may be emphatically called a missionary spirit. Several members of the Seminary had come to the solemn resolution of spending their lives in heathen lands. There was, however, no missionary society in this country, to which they could look for assistance and direction. Nothing deterred by seemingly insurmountable obstacles, they applied to their fathers in the church for advice. At a meeting of the Massachusetts Association, held at Bradford, June 27, 1810, the following paper, written by Mr. [Adoniram] Judson, was presented:

The undersigned, members of the Divinity College, respectfully request the attention of their reverend fathers, convened in the General Association at Bradford, to the following statement and inquiries:

They beg leave to state that their minds have been long impressed with the duty and importance of personally attempting a mission to the heathen; that the impressions on their minds have induced a serious, and they trust, a prayerful consideration of the subject in its various attitudes, particularly in relation to the probable success, and the difficulties attending such an attempt; and that after examining all the information which they can obtain, they consider themselves as devoted to this work for life, whenever God in his providence shall open the way.

They now offer the following inquiries, on which they solicit the opinion and advice of this Association. Whether, with their present views and feelings, they ought to renounce the object of Missions as visionary or impracticable; if not, whether they ought to direct their attention to the eastern or the western world; whether they may expect patronage and support from a Missionary Society in this country, or must commit themselves to the direction of a European Society, and what preparatory measures they ought to take previous to actual engagement?

The undersigned, feeling their youth and inexperience, look up to their fathers in the church, and respectfully solicit their advice, direction, and prayers.

ADONIRAM JUDSON,
SAMUEL NOTT,
SAMUEL J. MILLS,
SAMUEL NEWELL

This document occasioned the appointment of the American Board of Commissioners for Foreign Missions.

The same spirit which prompted this application to the Massachusetts Association of ministers, a few months afterwards led to the formation of the Society of Inquiry; although, as Messrs. Newell and Judson had now completed their course at the Seminary, they did not become members of the Society until a later period. . . .

The following list is designed to include the names of all members of the Society of Inquiry, who have ever gone on Foreign Missions. The column next to the names shows the college at which the individuals graduated, and the year of their graduation. The other column of figures shows the year of their leaving the Seminary. The remaining column indicates the mission to which they respectively belonged. An asterisk (*) prefixed to a name shows that the individual died in the field of his missionary labors.

Abbreviations

A.C.—Amherst College	B.U.—Brown University	H.C.—Hamilton College
M.C.—Middlebury College	U.V.—University of Vermont	Y.C.—Yale College
B.C.—Bowdoin College	D.C.—Dartmouth College	H.U.—Harvard University
U.C.—Union College	W.C.—Williams College	

Missionaries in Foreign Lands

Names	Graduated	Left the Seminary	Missions
*Gordon Hall	W.C. 1808	1810	Bombay
Adoniram Judson	B.U. 1807	1810	Burmah

Names	Graduated	Left the Seminary	Missions
*Samuel Newell	H.U. 1807	1810	Bombay
Samuel Nott	U.C. 1808	1810	Bombay
Luther Rice	W.C. 1810	1811	India
*Samuel John Mills	W.C. 1809	1812	Agent to Africa
*James Richards	W.C. 1809	1812	Ceylon
*Edward Warren	M.C. 1808	1812	Ceylon
Benj. Clark Meigs	Y.C. 1809	1813	Ceylon
*Joseph R. Andrus	M.C. 1812	1814	Agent to Africa
Horatio Bardwell	———	1814	Bombay
Daniel Poor	D.C. 1811	1814	Ceylon
Allen Graves	M.C. 1812	1815	Bombay
*John Nichols	D.C. 1813	1816	Bombay
*Levi Parsons	M.C. 1814	1817	Palestine
*Pliny Fisk	M.C. 1814	1818	Palestine
Levi Spaulding	D.C. 1815	1818	Ceylon
Miron Winslow	M.C. 1815	1818	Ceylon
Hiram Bingham	M.C. 1816	1819	Sandwich Isl.
Jonas King	W.C. 1816	1819	Syria and Greece
Asa Thurston	Y.C. 1816	1819	Sandwich Isl.
Isaac Bird	Y.C. 1816	1820	Syria
William Goodell	D.C. 1817	1820	Syria and Constantinople
Daniel Temple	D.C. 1817	1820	Malta
John Clark Brigham	W.C. 1819	1822	South America
William Richards	W.C. 1819	1822	Sandwich Isl.
*Edmund Frost	M.C. 1820	1823	Bombay
*Elnathan Gridley	Y.C. 1819	1823	Asia Minor
Josiah Brewer	Y.C. 1821	1824	Smyrna
Cyrus Stone	D.C. 1822	1825	Bombay
Eli Smith	Y.C. 1821	1826	Western Asia
David Oliver Allen	A.C. 1823	1827	Bombay
Eph. Weston Clark	D.C. 1824	1827	Sandwich Isl.
Jona. Smith Green	———	1827	Sandwich Isl.
H. Gray Otis Dwight	H.C. 1825	1828	Constantinople
Judah Isaac Abraham	———	1829	To the Jews
E. Coleman Bridgman	A.C. 1826	1829	China
John Taylor Jones	A.C. 1825	1829	Burmah
John S. Emerson	D.C. 1826	1830	Sandwich Isl.
Wm. Gottlieb Schauffler	———	1830	Jews in Turkey
David Belden Lyman	W.C. 1828	1831	Sandwich Isl.
Ephraim Spaulding	M.C. 1828	1831	Sandwich Isl.
John Diell	H.C. 1826	1832	Sandwich Isl.
Henry Lyman+	A.C. 1829	1832	
Samuel Munson+	B.C. 1829	1832	

Names	Graduated	Left the Seminary	Missions
Benj. Wyman Parker	A.C. 1829	1832	Sandwich Isl.
Elias Riggs	A.C. 1829	1832	Greece
Ira Tracy+	D.C. 1829	1832	

+ Designated to Southeastern Asia

Missionaries to the American Indians

Names	Graduated	Left the Seminary	Missions
Alfred Wright	W.C. 1812	1814	Arkansas Choctaws
Cyrus Kingsbury	B.U. 1812	1815	Choctaws
*Alfred Finney	D.C. 1815	1816	Arkansas Choctaws
Cyrus Byington	———	1819	Choctaws
*Samuel Moseley	M.C. 1818	1821	Choctaws
S. Austin Worcester	U.V. 1819	1823	Cherokees
*Harrison Allen	B.C. 1824	1828	Choctaws
Cutting Marsh	D.C. 1826	1829	Green Bay
W. Thurston Boutwell	D.C. 1828	1831	Ojibeways
Sherman Hall	D.C. 1828	1831	Ojibeways
Asher Wright	———	1831	Indians in N.Y.
Asher Bliss	A.C. 1829	1832	Indians in N.Y.

Of the preceding 60 individuals, 13 are graduates of Dartmouth College; 10 of Middlebury; 9 of Williams; 7 of Amherst; 6 of Yale; 2 of Brown University; 2 of Bowdoin College; 2 of Hamilton; 1 of Harvard University; 1 of Vermont University; 1 of Union College; and 6 are not graduates of any college.

From *Memoirs of American Missionaries, Formerly Connected with the Society of Inquiry Respecting Missions, in the Andover Theological Seminary—Embracing a History of the Society, Etc., with an Introductory Essay, by Leonard Woods, D.D.* (Boston: Peirce and Parker, 1833), 13–41.

PART 5

The Exercisers
and the Tasters

The single greatest ambiguity left by Jonathan Edwards in *Freedom of the Will* concerned the operation of motives, which were key to his description of what caused the will to act. If motives were understood to be influences or objects of perception external to a perceiver, then it became necessary to divide the chain of actions that resulted in a volition into three parts: the motive, the perception, and the volition itself. This posed no strain on the imaginations of most New England divines, since it reflected an understanding of the structure of the human mind as old as St. Augustine, in which a sinful self intervened between a motive and a volition to corrupt the volition. The key factor, then, that rendered certain volitions sinful was the miasma of depravity within the perceiving self that distorted and misshaped the impulses sent by the perceiving self to the will.

This assumed that perception was performed by some form of spiritual substance, whether as a mind or a nature or a soul, and that this spiritual substance occupied space within the human confines of the body's material substance and apart from all other material substances in the exterior world. But that assumption posed two problems to the New England divines of the eighteenth century. First, the scientific revolution that began with Galileo and Newton had been calling into question the idea of spiritual substance ever since the mid-1600s, and that skepticism had reached a crest in the mid-1700s in the raw epiphenomenalism of David Hume and the even more raw materials of Julien la Mettrie. Second, the instinct of Edwardsean thinking to heighten the accountability that grew from one's natural ability and to diminish the excuses sinners could make because of inability gave the New Divinity a substantial incentive to minimize any effort to locate sin in some form of intervening substance—a sinful *nature,* a depraved *soul*—and to move it entirely into the operation of the will, where it could be attacked as a failure of a sinner's natural ability.

On the other hand, the elimination of a depraved spiritual substance as the *fons et origo* of sin forced the Edwardseans to adopt a notion of the self that was entirely too close to Humean epiphenomenalism and too far from their moorings to classical Augustinian and Calvinist thought to gain any kind of uniform assent from the New Divinity. And so there arose a major split in Edwardsean thinking between the advocates of what became called the "taste scheme," which located sin in a depraved spiritual taste, or nature, and the "exercise scheme," which minimalized all talk of a nature and confined sin firmly to the workings, or exercises, of the will. It alarmed the Tasters to hear New Divinity divines speaking (as Samuel Hopkins complained) of "the *new* notion of no spiritual substance." But Edwards had already foreshadowed this in *Original Sin* by making depravity a matter of God's immediate communication of a sinful status rather than a communicable quality passed down through inherited natures. The Edwardsean imperative to concentrate human sin in a place where it could be held accountable—the will—rather than in a substance where sinners could plead that sin was an inheritance they could not help gave the Exercisers all the reason they felt they needed to argue that "there is nothing which can, with any propriety, be termed either a good or a bad state of mind . . . beside volition, or voluntary exertion."

Nathanael Emmons

MAN'S ACTIVITY
AND DEPENDENCE ILLUSTRATED
AND RECONCILED (1842)

Nathanael Emmons was the king of the Exercisers. It was "the doctrine of Edwards," Emmons insisted, that "*all moral agency consists in choosing*," and not in a "taste" underlying and manipulating human choice. The moment sin was located in a depraved nature or sinful disposition, sinners had a natural inability they could plead. "We can frame no higher idea of moral freedom," Emmons preached, "than acting voluntarily, or just as we please, in the view of motives." Anyone who imagines that "the human soul, as well as the human body," inherits some natural depraved quality that "proceeds directly from the parents, who naturally and necessarily convey their own moral image to their children," has given every sinner precisely the excuse he or she craves for not repenting. "Moral depravity," he countered, "consists in the free, voluntary exercises of a moral agent; and of consequence cannot be transmitted by one person to another."

But just as anxious as Emmons was to pinpoint depravity in "free and voluntary" exercises, he was just as eager not to lose a grip on Calvinism in the process. Moral depravity was not a product of a sinful nature, but it was a fact, a fact in which God was ultimately involved. Rather than locating depravity in a spiritual nature below the working consciousness, Emmons described depravity in almost Humean terms as a "connection" that defied all definitions of cause and effect. Adam sinned, and afterward "God constituted such a connection between Adam and his posterity, that if he sinned, they should all become sinners" with the first exercise of their volition. In the progeny of Adam, God intended, "by working in them to will and to do," to produce "those moral exercises in their hearts, in which moral depravity properly and essentially consists." In this way, they become sinners "while they are acted upon by the Deity," but because no nature or taste compels them, "they have no manner of excuse for neglecting to obey any of his commands."

ℴℴ

. . . Every command which God has given to men plainly supposes that they are moral agents, who are capable of acting freely in the view of motives; because a command could have no more influence, or lay no more obligation upon men, than upon stocks or stones, were men incapable of seeing the nature, and of acting under the power, of motives. As all the commands in the Bible, therefore, require men to put forth some motion, some exercise, some exertion, either of body or of mind, or of both; so they necessarily suppose that men are, in the strictest sense of the word, moral agents, and capable of yielding active, voluntary, rational obedience to the will of God. But yet the prayers of all good men equally suppose that they must be acted upon by a divine operation, in all their virtuous exercises and actions. For when they pray for themselves that God would give them joy, peace, love, faith, submission, or strengthen and increase these and all other Christian graces; their prayers presuppose the necessity of a divine operation upon their hearts, in all their gracious exercises and exertions.

. . . But still we find many who consider this Scriptural doctrine as a gross absurdity, or at least, as the Gordian knot in divinity, which, instead of untying, they violently cut asunder; and so make a sacrifice either of activity, or of dependence. Some give up activity for the sake of dependence; some give up dependence for the sake of activity; and some first give up one and then the other, for the sake of maintaining both. The fatalists give up activity for the sake of dependence. They suppose men are totally dependent and constantly acted upon, as mere machines, and of consequence are not free agents. The Arminians, on the other hand, give up dependence for the sake of activity. They suppose men live a self-determining power, or a power to originate their own volitions, and are capable of acting independently of any divine operation upon their hearts. But many of the Calvinists endeavor to steer a middle course between these two extremes, and first give up activity and then dependence, in order to maintain both. They hold that men are active both before and after regeneration, but passive in regeneration itself. These three classes of men, however they may differ in other respects, seem to agree in this, that no man can act freely and virtuously while he is acted upon by a divine operation; and accordingly unite in pronouncing the doctrine, which we have been laboring to establish, inconsistent and absurd. . . .

Some may suppose that human dependence and activity cannot be reconciled, because they are unwilling to see the consistency of a doctrine which throws them absolutely into the hands of God. . . . Some may suppose that dependence cannot be reconciled with activity, because they are conscious of being active, but not of being dependent. . . . They appeal to common sense as an infallible proof that men act freely and voluntarily, without feeling the least compulsion or influence from the hand of God. It is undoubtedly true that we are all conscious of activity, and intuitively know that we are free moral agents. But to what does this dictate of common sense amount? Does it prove that we are not dependent upon the Supreme Being for all our moral exercises? Most certainly it does not. For supposing God does really work in us both to will and to do, we cannot be conscious of his agency, but only of our own, in willing and doing. Though in God we live, and move, and have our being, yet we are never conscious of his almighty hand, which upholds us in existence every moment.

. . . Many, by reasoning unjustly on this subject, persuade themselves that they cannot act while they are acted upon. They reason, from matter to mind, which is by no means conclusive. Since matter is incapable of acting while it is acted upon, they conclude the mind must also be incapable of action while it is acted upon. They suppose, if we are as dependent upon God for all our voluntary exercises, as a clock or watch is dependent upon weights or springs for all its motions, then we are as incapable of moral agency as these, or any other mere machines. But the fallacy of this mode of reasoning may be easily exposed. The fallacy lies here. It takes for granted that the only reason why a clock, or a watch, or any other machine, is not a moral agent, is simply because it is acted upon or depends upon some power out of itself for all its motions. But is this true? Let us make the trial. Suppose a clock which has hitherto been dependent and moved by weights and wheels should this moment become independent and move of itself. Is this clock now any more a moral agent than it was before? Are its motions now any more moral exercises, or any more worthy of praise or blame, than they were before? By no means. But why not? Because, notwithstanding it is now independent, and moves of itself, yet being still matter, and not mind, it moves without perception, reason, conscience, and volition, which are attributes essential to a moral agent. The reason why a clock, or watch, or any other machine, is incapable of moral agency is not because it is either dependent or independent; but simply because it is senseless matter, and totally destitute of all the principles of moral action. As neither dependence nor independence can make a machine a mind, so neither dependence nor independence can make a mind a machine.

. . . Some involve themselves in confusion by reasoning too far upon this subject. They carry reason out of its province, and employ it in deciding that which it has no power nor authority to decide. Many complain that they have often attempted to reconcile dependence with activity, but after all their efforts, have been obliged to give up the subject, as surpassing the reach of their comprehension. And to keep themselves in countenance, they bring in Mr. Locke, that oracle of reason, who ingenuously owns that he could never reconcile prescience in the Deity with human liberty; or, in other words, man's dependence with moral freedom. This however will not appear strange, if we consider that it belongs not to the office of reason to reconcile these two points. Though activity and dependence are perfectly consistent, yet they are totally distinct; and of course fall under the notice of distinct faculties of the mind. Dependence falls under the cognizance of reason; but activity falls under the cognizance of common sense. It is the part of reason to demonstrate our dependence upon God, in whom we live, and move, and have our being. But it is the part of common sense to afford us an intuitive knowledge of our activity and moral freedom. We must therefore consult both reason and common sense, in order to discover the consistency between activity and dependence. . . .

Having endeavored to reconcile man's activity and dependence . . . I proceed to draw a number of inferences from the subject. . . .

If it be true that men act, while they are acted upon by a divine operation, then their actions are their own, and not the actions of God. The divine agency is not human agency, nor human agency the divine agency. Though God does work in men to repent, to believe and to obey, yet God does not repent, nor believe, nor obey, but the persons themselves, on whom he operates. When God works in men to will and to do, he does not act in their stead, but they act for themselves; and therefore what they do is entirely distinct from what he does. Whether they act virtuously or viciously, their actions are their own, and the praise or the blame is their own, as much as if they acted independently.

. . . If men always act under a divine operation, then they always act of *necessity,* though not of *compulsion.* The Deity, by working in them to will and to do, lays them under an absolute necessity of acting freely; but this is directly opposed to compulsion. God may cause men to move, without making them willing to move; but he cannot cause them to act, without making them willing to act. Action always implies choice; and choice always implies motive. It is out of the power of the Deity, therefore, to oblige men to act, without making them willing to act in the view of motives. Accordingly, when he works in us both to will and to do, he first exhibits motives before our minds, and then excites us to act voluntarily in the view of the motives exhibited. And in thus acting voluntarily in the view of the motives presented to us, we exercise the most perfect liberty or moral freedom. For we can frame no higher idea of moral freedom than acting voluntarily, or just as we please, in the view of motives. This however is perfectly consistent with moral necessity. Suppose a man at leisure desires to read, and some person presents him a Bible and a novel. Though he knows the contents of each of these books, yet it depends upon a divine operation on his mind, which of them he shall choose to read; for the bare perception of motive is incapable of producing volition. If in this case God works in him to will to read the Bible, it is his own choice in the view of the object chosen. He is not compelled to read the Bible, though he is necessarily obliged to read it. He acts under a moral necessity, but not under a natural compulsion.

. . . Since God can work in men both to will and to do of his good pleasure, it is as easy to account for the first offence of Adam as for any other sin . . . and to suppose that God wrought in Adam both to will and to do in his first transgression. As Adam acted freely while he was acted upon before he fell, so he acted freely while he was acted upon at the moment of his fall. His first sin was a free, voluntary exercise, produced by a divine operation in the view of motives. Satan placed certain motives before his mind, which, by a divine energy, took hold of his heart and led him into sin.

. . . If God can work in moral agents both to will and to do of his good pleasure, then we may easily account for the moral depravity of infants. . . . Some suppose that the human soul, as well as the human body, proceeds directly from the parents, who naturally and necessarily convey their own moral image to their children. And upon this principle, they suppose that after our first parents became corrupt, they conveyed a corrupt nature to their children, and they again to theirs; and so a corrupt nature has ever since the fall been transmitted from parents to children, and will continue to be transmitted in the same manner to the latest posterity. This solution, however, by no means gives satisfaction. . . . For moral depravity consists in the free, voluntary exercises of a moral agent; and of consequence cannot be transmitted by one person to another. Adam's moral impurity or defilement was his own voluntary wickedness, which could not, by any divine constitution or appointment, become the moral impurity or defilement of his natural offspring, either in whole or in part. . . . But though we cannot suppose that infants derive their moral corruption from Adam, nor from their own mortal bodies, yet we can easily conceive of their becoming depraved in consequence of the first apostasy. God constituted such a connection between Adam and his posterity, that if he sinned, they should all become sinners. Accordingly, in consequence of Adam's first transgression, God now brings his posterity into the world in a state of moral depravity. But how? The answer is easy. When God forms the souls of infants, he forms them with moral powers, and makes them men in miniature. And being men in miniature, he works in them as he does in other men, both to will and to do of his good pleasure; or produces those moral exercises in their hearts, in which moral depravity properly and essentially consists. Moral depravity can take place nowhere but in moral agents; and moral agents can never act but only as they are acted upon by a divine operation. It is just as easy, therefore, to account for moral depravity in infancy, as in any other period of life.

. . . It appears from God's working in all men both to will and to do that he governs the moral as well as the natural world. This is denied by many who believe in divine providence. Though they acknowledge that God has a controlling influence over all the material and animal creation, yet they suppose that it is out of his power to govern the free and voluntary actions of moral agents. But if he works in all men both to will and to do of his good pleasure, then he governs the moral as well as the natural world, and both by a positive agency, and not a bare permission. It is impossible for the Deity to govern any of his creatures or works by permission, because his permission would be nothing short of annihilation. . . . The Deity, therefore, is so far from permitting moral agents to act independently of himself that, on the other hand, he puts forth a positive influence to make them act, in every instance of their conduct, just as he pleases.

. . . If sinners are able to act freely while they are acted upon by the Deity, then they have no manner of excuse for neglecting to obey any of his commands. . . . They can act as freely as if they were not dependent; and they are as able to obey the divine commands as if they could act of themselves. They can love God, repent of sin, believe in Christ, and perform every religious duty, as well as they can think, or speak, or walk. They have no cloak for the least sin, whether internal or external.

From Nathanael Emmons, "Man's Activity and Dependence Illustrated and Reconciled," in *The Works of Nathanael Emmons, D.D.*, vol. 4, ed. Jacob Ide (Boston: Crocker & Brewster, 1842), 339–62.

Asa Burton

ESSAY XXX (1824)

Unlike many of the New Divinity, Asa Burton (1752–1836) was a graduate of Dartmouth. But he studied for ordination under Levi Hart, and once he was ordained in 1779 as pastor of Thetford, Vermont, "he ceased not to preach and to exhort with all tenderness and fidelity." Within two years, he had sparked a revival in Thetford, followed by another in 1794, with "frequent and considerable additions to the church." The reputation he acquired through the revivals in Thetford also brought him theological students, and over the fifty-six years of his pastorate in Thetford, he rivaled Nathanael Emmons by training "nearly sixty young men in the preparation for the ministry."

The theology he taught them, however, differed sharply from that of Emmons on the question of spiritual substance. When the curriculum he developed for ministerial training was finally published in 1824 as his *Essays*, it became clear that Burton had not only broken with Emmons on the primacy of taste, or nature, to the will but was in fact breaking apart the unity of the faculties Jonathan Edwards had tried to weld in *Freedom of the Will* and *Religious Affections*. Burton suspected that Emmons and the Exercisers were reducing the mind to "nothing more than a composition of thoughts or ideas, feelings and volitions." This flew in the face of every worthwhile intuition people have about their mental life, because it was evident to Burton that everyone inferred the existence of "the faculty called the understanding" and a separate "faculty termed the will, which chooses or rejects." Having reerected the partitions between understanding and will that Edwards had sought to remove, Burton went on to affirm the existence of a faculty of taste, the "feeling faculty," or "the heart." By this means, Burton separated the heart from the will and, by defining it as a feeling faculty, introduced for the first time in Edwardsean thinking the Romantic concept of an emotive heart that overrules both mind and will.

ℰℐ

A Summary View of the System, Advanced and Illustrated in These Essays

Every science is founded on what are generally called *first principles*. And as far as persons differ in their views of these, they will embrace different systems. And yet first principles are commonly self evident propositions. . . .

If we can ascertain the first principles of Theology and Ethics, and reason correctly from them, different persons will harmonize in sentiments. To proceed directly to the subject before us, it may be asserted,

1. That happiness is an *absolute good,* and this is one first principle in Ethics. As happiness is considered a good in itself by all rational beings; and as no one can give a reason why he thus esteems it, the proposition is self evident. And,

2. That pain or misery is an absolute evil is another self evident truth. All fear and dread pain, and no one can give a reason why he does. . . . Some pretend to make a distinction between *pleasure* and *happiness*. But when nothing more is taken into view than their *simple nature,* who can show a difference between them? Happiness, pleasure, in their simple nature, are nothing but agreeable, pleasant *sensations*. A pleasant sensation, emotion, or feeling is happiness, and it is pleasure. . . . No objects or sources of enjoyment can afford as durable, satisfying happiness, as full as our capacities will admit, but those which are infinite and eternal. The happiness derived from such objects may be styled true, real, and substantial; while pleasures given us by fading, fleeting, and uncertain objects can never fill or satisfy the mind.

. . . As societies are composed of individuals, and as the greatest happiness an individual *can* enjoy is *his* highest good; so the sum total of the perfect happiness of the individuals constituting a society is the highest, the greatest good, which can exist in it. This is so evident, no one can consistently deny it. . . . But here let it be observed that to the existence of happiness a

3. Proposition must be admitted as self evident, which is this, that a feeling faculty capable of pleasant and painful sensations existing in a rational mind is absolutely necessary.

This cannot be proved, because it is self evident. But it can be explained and illustrated, and made clear to every person. Can a stone, a tree, or any part of the inanimate creation enjoy, or be the subjects of happiness? And why not? Because they are not endued with a feeling faculty, are incapable of all pleasant and painful emotions. And as such a faculty is necessary to happiness, to the existence of the greatest good, so but one faculty of this nature is necessary in the same individual. We therefore find that man is endued with only one feeling faculty. The understanding can see, or perceive objects, their properties, qualities, relations, and connexions; and the will can choose, and execute the pleasure of the heart; but neither of them is the subject of pleasant or painful emotions. All pleasant and painful sensations must exist antecedent to volition. Were not this a fact, volitions could never have any existence in the mind, as it is hoped has been fully proved. These explanations show, it is self evident that a feeling faculty is requisite to the existence of happiness.

. . . The will, if not requisite to the being of happiness, is surely necessary to the increase of it. For objects, when perceived, may please, or appear agreeable; yet to a full enjoyment of them we must have possession of them. By the will, producing external actions, we get possession of the objects of our desire; and by it we select the pleasing, and reject the painful. By this faculty we use the means adapted to the attainment of sources of happiness. . . . Do not these remarks make it evident that not only a faculty for pleasure and pain, but also a faculty to *perceive* objects, and a faculty to *choose*, and *refuse*, and perform actions, and *liberty*, or freedom from restraint, are each of them essential to the existence of happiness? And a being, endued with these faculties, is an entire moral agent. Such a being man is; for he is possessed of these faculties. And do we know, or can we invent, any other or more properties necessary to constitute a complete moral agent, or requisite to as great a measure of happiness as our nature will admit? We now see what things are essential to the highest felicity, or misery of man, according to the nature or inclination of his heart. And these truths are so evident that when clearly stated, and explained, who can deny them, or withhold his assent from them?

. . . It must be granted that happiness is the only final good, which renders existence desirable. This being granted, there is no greater good, which can be sought. And when happiness is obtained, we have then arrived at an ultimate end, to the last exertion in our pursuit; and here, in the enjoyment of this good, we rest satisfied. And as this is an absolute good, and the greatest good, we ought to delight and rejoice in it, wherever we see it existing. But here an important inquiry presents itself; whether our own personal happiness, or the happiness of other rational beings, ought to be our ultimate end of pursuit. In attempting to reflect some light on this subject, a distinction ought to be made between an *end* and the reason or *motive* which influences us in seeking it. Every one does not at once discern this distinction. Yet it is very important to distinguish properly between the *nature* of *selfishness*, and that of *benevolence*.

Here then it may be observed that our personal individual happiness ought not to, neither can be, the ultimate object or *end* of our pursuit.

. . . Hence, if a person's heart is wholly destitute of every benevolent feeling; if the happiness of other beings is not any source of pleasure to him, he will never seek their felicity. He will never aim at any higher objects than those which gratify his personal self gratification. All his pursuits will ultimately centre in personal self gratification. This is the true idea of selfishness. Hence the objects on their own account agreeable, and those he uses as means to his ends, he will engross and monopolize to himself as far as he is able. He would possess all the riches and honor of this world, were it in his power. If other beings are by this means deprived of happiness, and rendered unhappy, this will give him no uneasiness, unless their misery should in some way lessen his happiness. Because he has no feeling for their happiness on its own account, and because their pains will afford him no uneasiness, if his own pleasure is not affected or lessened by it. In unrenewed men, each individual appetite of the heart never aims at any other or higher end than its own gratification. . . . If natural affection governs, and he desires the happiness of his wife, or his children, in the enjoyment of worldly prosperity and greatness, as far as they enjoy those blessings his desires are gratified, and he aims at no higher end. . . . Selfishness then is predicable of each appetite, belonging to the heart of unrenewed men. For under the government of each appetite his end is to obtain the object or objects, which on their own account afford to each full gratification.

. . . But benevolence delights in the happiness of others, or of rational beings. And as the greatest sum of happiness is the highest good of the universe, this is the end in which a benevolent heart delights on its own account, and which it seeks as its ultimate end. And from this it is evident that the only direct way for a benevolent person to promote his own happiness is to increase the felicity of intelligent beings. Their happiness is an object of pursuit, and of delight. This object is his ultimate end, and the pleasure it affords gives the influence of a motive, which stimulates him to promote the blessedness of God's holy kingdom to his utmost ability. . . . The greatest happiness of rational existence *ought* to be the ultimate end of moral agents.

. . . Here is a proper place . . . to observe *that in God all good, both absolute and relative, exists in an infinite fulness.* . . . God is a being of infinite majesty, excellency, greatness, and glory. He ought, therefore, to be loved supremely, worshipped and served perfectly, by all his intelligent subjects, for his intrinsic excellency and beauty. . . . Also it follows that the work of redemption, which Christ is accomplishing, is, in all its parts, glorious and excellent. For its ultimate tendency, in all its parts, is to produce the greatest sum of happiness. And the sum of all the gospel requires is love to God and our neighbor. Hence it harmonizes with the moral law, and tends ultimately to the same end. The gospel contains a glorious system of relative good and is a ministration of life.

. . . Some make *utility* the standard, by which we are to determine what is good and evil. This is a foundation on which some have erected a system of Ethics, if understood aright. Does not the term utility, as commonly used, have reference to some ultimate end? And do we not call things useful or hurtful, according to their ultimate tendency? So it seems. For those who proceed on the plan of utility seem to consider the public good as the ultimate end to be sought, according to their system; and hence consider every thing as useful or hurtful as it tends to promote or destroy this end, the public good. If by the public good they mean the greatest happiness of a community, or society of beings; and if in such society they mean to include God as the supreme head, and all created beings as his subjects, forming one entire whole, or society of beings; and then say the greatest sum of happiness they can enjoy is their highest good; and all things are useful or hurtful, as they tend to this end ultimately; then they agree with the system, which has been exhibited. Then the real difference between us would consist in the use of different terms. By the terms utility and *inutility* they would mean what has been called all along relative good and evil. And if this be not their meaning, and their system is essentially different from ours, as has been explained; then it must be considered as erroneous, like the system of the fitness and unfitness of things.

Before this essay is closed . . . one sentiment, which has already been advanced respecting moral agency, ought to be deeply impressed on every mind. Because it might silence some objections often made against the Calvinistic views of depravity. . . . All created beings had a beginning. And as the Creator is perfectly wise and good, he would give existence to as many things as are necessary to the highest good, and no more. On this principle, it is generally granted, it was requisite to the general good a race of beings should be created, endued with all the properties essential to moral agency. In order to the existence of such a class of creatures, they must be endued with a *feeling* faculty, or capacity for pleasure and pain. For, if they have not this property, they are not, neither can be, agents.

It has been made evident that such a faculty constitutes agency; and is the primary and only active principle in moral agents. Divest them of it, and mankind would remain as inactive as the inanimate creation is. Hence, if moral agents are created, they must be endued with that faculty, which is denominated taste. And this faculty must have a *nature*; by which I mean, it must be *pleased*, or the contrary, with the divine character, and with the whole system of moral or divine objects, whenever they are distinctly perceived and known. . . . This feeling faculty, if it exists, will be pleased or disgusted in view of God's character and will influence man to pursue a line of conduct, which will ultimately tend to promote or destroy the happiness of God's kingdom; and this tendency is what is meant by its nature. And if created, it must have such a *nature*, and its nature must be *holy* or *sinful*. For such a nature as described is necessarily good or evil, sinful or holy, according to its tendency.

. . . These observations are made, because some suppose moral agents may be created without any nature, either good or evil, and may have objects in view, and even contemplate the divine character, and remain in a state of *perfect indifference*; and be inclined no way, to good or evil, or even to remain as they are. . . . Such a view of a moral agent is inconsistent with analogy, with experience, with facts, and the word of God; and it is as unphilosophical as to say, God has created trees to bring forth particular kinds of fruit, but he has not given them a nature to bear *any kind* of fruit. It is a matter of indifference with them what kind of fruit they bear, or whether they bring forth fruit of any kind; and of course they never will or can be fruit trees.

As it is now evident, if moral agents are created, they must be endued with a feeling, active faculty, and this faculty must have a nature good or evil; so we find from revelation that when God created Adam he did endue him with this active faculty, which made him an agent; and this faculty had a good, a *holy nature*. . . . Many are pleased with God's creating Adam with a holy nature; yet they cannot peaceably endure the idea of necessary holiness, or sin. Though they are more satisfied with the former than with the latter. Yet the nature of everything, if it exist, must be good or evil. As no fault can be found with God, in creating Adam at first as he did, unless it is because he was necessarily holy; the next inquiry is whether blame can be imputed to him for suffering, or permitting Adam to eat of the forbidden fruit? And then in consequence of this to take from him the holy nature, or benevolent appetite, with which he had been created? That such a change did take place, that holy Adam became a sinner, is generally granted. As God might have prevented it, the question is whether it was wise and holy for him to permit this change to take place.

. . . Some consider the doctrine of total depravity, as explained and defended by reputed and orthodox divines, to be *physical*. And being physical in its nature, the opponents consider it as destroying agency and blameworthiness. Viewing the doctrine in this light, they pronounce it very alarming and appalling. It is not designed here to inquire, whether some have, or have not, so explained it as to imply a *physical* defect; or in what precise sense opponents use the word physical. They scorn to consider *any* defect in the soul, which incapacitates it for holy exercises, to be a *physical* defect. They therefore, in opposition to this, represent our race as born with capacities, which are inclined neither to vice nor virtue, or as destitute of, any *moral nature*; and are, like clean paper, liable to receive impressions, which are holy or sinful according to the influence motives have upon them. In connexion with this sentiment, they affirm men are the efficient causes of all their exercises and actions of a moral class. Is the doctrine of depravity, which has been expressly or implicitly exhibited in these essays, so appalling as represented?

. . . Adam, by eating the prohibited fruit, forfeited into the hand of his benefactor that moral image in which he was created, and which was his glory, and it was taken from him. From that day he had no propensity or love in his heart towards his Maker. All his other appetites remained unaffected and unaltered, as principles of action. Here it may be asked, was he not as really a moral agent after his fall as before? Had he not active principles in his heart, which constituted him a complete agent for action? And when this moral image or benevolent appetite is restored to man in regeneration, is he any more an agent for action than he was previous to this change? If any man is born blind, or after his birth becomes blind, is he not still a man, as really as those who have eyes? And if eyes are given him, is he on this account any more a man than before? All that can be said of the blind man he is, not in all respects so perfect, as those who have all their senses entire. He labors under a defect or imperfection; still he is a man. Adam by eating was deprived of one *sense*, or appetite, with which his Maker had adorned him; yet he was an agent, and had all the properties or capacities, which constitute a complete moral agent. Hence he had all the qualifications necessary to render him a proper object of praise or blame, according to the moral nature or state of his heart. If opponents consider this loss in Adam *a physical defect*, incapacitating him for holy exercises; yet it does not in the least destroy, or impair the powers requisite to moral agency, or to render him a proper object of blame. Hence what is there alarming or appalling in this description of total depravity? Though man in all respects is not so *perfect* a moral agent, as before this defect existed; yet he is as complete a moral agent as ever. He has the faculty of understanding, and of will; he has a faculty to which active principles belong, and which constitute agency; and he may and will be influenced and governed by motives, and act with aim and design, as Adam did before his fall, and as men do after they are regenerated, and have this moral defect repaired. This defect, which opponents call *physical,* is in fact no more than a *moral defect.* . . . Hence orthodox divines have nothing to fear from the attack, by which they are represented as imputing to man a physical defect, which is in truth no more than a moral defect.

If mankind are born with an *efficient power,* which is not inclined either to vice or virtue, but is in fact indifferent to both; it is believed to be impossible to show how this efficient power can exercise itself, without implying the previous existence of a disposition either to sin or holiness. And if a previous disposition must exist, to put this power into exercise, then all the ends supposed to be answered by it are defeated. But concerning what might have been said to show the absurdity of this scheme, the reader for farther light is referred to essay twenty first. But if, by a self determining power, and an efficient power to produce all our exercises and actions, no more is intended than this, that in order for mankind to be agents, they ought to be endued with a *feeling, active* faculty, by which the whole man is governed, and from which all his exercises and actions proceed, it must be granted that men do possess this faculty or power. Then all the actions and exercises of men may be traced back to this faculty, as the primary active principle from which they proceed, or flow as streams from a fountain. And as they cannot be traced back any farther, or to any previous active principle in men, this faculty, which has been denominated the taste, is the *primary active power,* which constitutes agency, and gives rise to all our voluntary exertions and actions. I say, if such a faculty is what others mean by a self determining, efficient power, it is granted; and some pains have been taken to prove that mankind are in fact endued with it; and that without it they would not be agents, and could not be considered as moral agents.

If opponents admit this, then the dispute is ended, concerning the nature and degree of power requisite to constitute a moral agent, and nothing further need be said on either side.

But if they advance an idea of an efficient power, which has no nature, inclined to neither good nor evil, and is in itself indifferent, they are laboring, it is fully believed, to establish and prove the existence of an *impossibility.* For an active power, or efficiency, must necessarily have a nature to be influenced by motives, to be pleased or the contrary with moral objects. And if it have not such a nature, it is no active power, and can never operate in any other way than an instrument used by some other external and foreign agent.

From Asa Burton, "Essay XXX," in *Essays on Some of the First Principles of Metaphysicks, Ethicks, and Theology* (Portland, ME: A. Shirley, 1824), 350–70.

PART 6

Theology
in New Haven

The most controversial modifications of Edwardsean theology came from the pens of the professors teaching at Jonathan Edwards's alma mater. Beginning in 1795, Edwards's grandson, Timothy Dwight, assumed the presidency of Yale. Concerned with the threat of "infidelity" to the boys now under his charge—when he arrived, they were calling themselves by the names of philosophes such as D'Alembert and Voltaire—Dwight devoted himself to destroying Enlightenment naturalism. He led a revival at the college, quelled his students' fascination with the philosophes and deists, and trained a whole new generation of Edwardsean clergymen before his death in January 1817. So successful were these efforts that, during the early nineteenth century, Dwight and his students supervised the region's Second Great Awakening.

Before his death, Dwight laid plans for a divinity school at Yale, one that, like Andover, would counter the forces of liberalism at Harvard. His favorite student, Nathaniel Taylor, was already ministering in town. Only thirty years old at the time that his beloved mentor died, Taylor had quickly risen to fame as a preacher and Calvinist theologian. He led New Haven's First Church through a season of revival, as well as a major building program that renewed the town's green. So when the divinity school began at Yale in 1822, the Dwight family and Yale's faculty agreed unanimously that Taylor should take its Timothy Dwight Chair in Didactic Theology.

Like Dwight before him, Taylor knew that modern liberal Christianity, especially Unitarianism, was changing the face of Christian education in New England. Its moral critique of Calvinism called for a tightly reasoned response, and Andover's faculty, though orthodox, proved ill equipped for the task. Dwight himself had responded forcefully in the years before his death, fusing American patriotism, Federalist politics, and faith. But by the latter 1810s, when the Federalists declined and when Connecticut's Congregationalists were formally disestablished, it became clear that a much more winsome evangelicalism was needed.

No sooner did Yale inaugurate its program in divinity than Taylor and his colleagues—especially fellow faculty members such as Eleazar Fitch and Taylor's neighbor, Chauncey Goodrich—set to work on the needed revisions. Through their teaching, preaching, and writings, and especially through the pages of New Haven's *Christian Spectator* (later the *Quarterly Christian Spectator*), the New Haven Theologians, often called the Taylorites, repackaged Edwardsean ideas for antebellum America. Focusing mainly on the doctrines of sin and spiritual regeneration, they formed a kinder, gentler evangelical Calvinism. They rebutted the accusations of their Unitarian critics that Calvinists worshiped a heavenly tyrant—one who loved those he predestined but neglected those he did not—thereby undermining the future of liberal, democratic America. Yale emphasized the *moral* nature of God's earthly rule, the power that *everyone* had to be saved, as well as the *voluntary* basis of vice and virtue.

By the late 1820s, the Taylorites had stirred up a hornet's nest of controversy. Denying that humans are born guilty of the sin of Adam and Eve and affirming that people play a role in their own regeneration, they seemed to some Edwardsean siblings to have sold the farm to save the family business. Soon a disgruntled group of pastors came together to oppose them. Worried that Taylor was winning the hearts and minds of far too many ministers, these Tylerites, named after their powerful leader, Bennet Tyler, founded the Doctrinal Tract Society, the *Evangelical Magazine*, an association of clergy soon to be called the Pastoral Union, and a seminary to rival the one in New Haven. Naming their alternate school the Theological Institute of Connecticut (later Hartford Seminary), they opened its doors in tiny East Windsor, Jonathan Edwards's hometown—literally right down the street from Edwards's birthplace. This sally symbolized vividly the power of Edwards's legacy—and the evangelicals' intramural struggle to control it.

Though the Taylorite-Tylerite feud petered out in the 1850s, the schisms it created still reverberate today. It split the General Association of Connecticut Congregationalists, the Presbyterian Church (whose "New School" followed Taylor's teachings), and, during the century that followed, much of the rest of evangelical America. By the time of the Civil War, it had contributed to what proved to be the irreversible fall of the Edwardsean tradition.

Timothy Dwight

SERMON III: COMPARATIVE INFLUENCE
OF ATHEISM AND CHRISTIANITY (1818)

Timothy Dwight (1752–1817) was born in Northampton, Massachusetts, two years after the town ejected Jonathan Edwards from its pulpit. His mother, Mary Edwards Dwight, never got over the town's ill treatment of her world-famous father. She refused to share the Lord's Supper at Northampton's First Church. She raised her son to champion her father's clerical concerns. And when young Timothy came of age, she made sure he would follow in his grandfather's footsteps by sending him to Yale and encouraging his tutelage with her brother, Jonathan Jr., a well-known clergyman and, later, a college president.

Dwight assumed Yale's presidency in 1795, a time when evangelical piety on campus was at an ebb. He worked immediately to shore up his students' confidence in Scripture. He also preached a regular, four-year cycle of sermons in the chapel, giving the boys a solid grounding in traditional Protestant doctrine. Dwight succeeded in promoting revival at Yale. Hundreds of students were converted, many through personal time with him. After he died, his chapel sermons were published in five bound volumes titled *Theology Explained and Defended*. The set was used widely in theological schools for several decades.

The sermon below is characteristic of Dwight's lifelong passion to stand in the way of what he feared might be "the triumph of infidelity" (the title of a poem he published in 1788, one that featured, anonymously, Jonathan Edwards as a hero). Ever concerned about the spread of French-inspired skepticism, especially at the hands of Jeffersonian intellectuals, he argued that atheist views not only were "false, and plainly impossible" but also tore at the moral fabric of the new United States. Christianity was necessary to fortify this fabric. Indeed, truth and public happiness depended on its success.

❦

Psalm 14:1

The fool hath said in his heart, There is no God. They are corrupt; they have done abominable works: there is none that doeth good.

In my last discourse, I considered the objections of Atheists against the being and government of God; and those doctrines concerning the origin and existence of things, which they have substituted for the doctrines of Theism and the Scriptures, on this most important subject. The objections I endeavoured to prove unsound and nugatory, and the doctrines to be mere hypotheses, demonstrably false, and plainly impossible. Hence I concluded them to be the doctrines of the heart, and not of the intellect. Hence also I concluded that he who embraces them is, according to the language of the text, *a fool.* There is no more absolute folly than to believe doctrines because we love them, and to reject doctrines because we hate them; or, in other words, to suffer our inclinations to govern our understanding.

The consequences of these doctrines, or of Atheism generally, are in the text declared in these words, *They are corrupt; they have done abominable works: there is none that doeth good.* In other words, *Atheists are corrupt, they do abominable works: there is none of them that doeth good.* This character of Atheists, seen by the Psalmist, and declared by the Spirit of God, three thousand years ago, has not changed for the better, at any period, down to the present day. They have ever been corrupt; they have ever done abominable works; there has never been among them a single good or virtuous man.

It cannot but be an useful employment to examine this interesting subject, and to learn, from such an examination, the manner in which these false principles, dictated and embraced by a bad heart, contribute, in their turn, as powerful causes, to render that heart still more corrupt; to fill the life with abominable actions; and to prevent every one who embraces these doctrines from assuming the character of virtue.

Before I enter upon the direct discussion of this subject, it will be proper to observe that *Virtue is nothing but voluntary obedience to truth; and Sin, nothing but voluntary obedience to falsehood.* Or, more generally, virtue and sin consist in a disposition or preparation of the heart, flowing out into acts of obedience, in the respective manners which I have mentioned. From these definitions, which, it is presumed, cannot be successfully denied, it is evident that every false doctrine, which is relished by the heart, will, of course, govern its affections and volitions; and will, therefore, control the conduct. Nor is it less evident that, in the present case, the doctrines in question, being embraced only because they are loved, will eminently influence the heart which has dictated them, and eminently affect all the moral conduct.

It will also be clear to all persons, accustomed to the investigation of moral subjects, that *the character of a man must, at least in a great measure, be formed by his views of the several subjects with which he is acquainted.* As these are expanded, magnificent and sublime; or narrow, ordinary, and grovelling; the taste, character, and the conduct will be refined and noble, or gross and contemptible. . . .

When men are educated to contemplation, and science, it may not unnaturally be imagined that *their minds,* allowing for the difference of their endowments, *will*, from the similarity of their pursuits, *be formed into a similarity of character*. This, however is, to a great extent, a mistaken opinion. The very objects with which such men are *equally conversant* may, *from their respective modes of viewing them*, become totally unlike, and even contradictory, in their apprehension. It will not be questioned that the mind of a *Heathen*, studying, with the views of a Heathen, the *polytheism of Greece and Rome*, would be affected very differently from the mind of a Christian, investigating the same subject. The manner in which we regard any object of inquiry may differ from some other manner almost as much as any two objects of inquisition may differ from each other. The views of him, who regards the firmament as a great blue canopy, and the stars as little sparks of light, differ from the views of the Astronomer who considers the firmament as a boundless expansion and the stars as an innumerable multitude of Suns, almost as widely as the two objects of contemplation differ. The manner, therefore, in which human contemplations are directed may be very various, although the objects are the same. In truth it is not the grandeur or diminutiveness of the objects, but the greatness or littleness of the views entertained of them, which affect and form the character.

The taste, or relish, of the mind, particularly, *will*, in a great measure, if not wholly, *be formed by this cause*. The mind, by an early habit accustomed to little views, will soon learn to relish no other. Accustomed from the beginning to a connection with grovelling objects only, it soon ceases to be pleased with any other objects. Accustomed to form diminutive and debased schemes of action, it becomes easily, and finally, disgusted with every thing of an enlarged and superior nature.

As these things are true of all the views entertained by Man: so they are especially true of those, which may be called original, and fundamental;

191

which involve all subordinate ones; which direct every future course of thought; and to which the mind thinks it necessary to reconcile every succeeding purpose, relish, and opinion. If the stem, here, be a mere twig; the branches must be poor and diminutive indeed. Thus, he, the basis of whose religion was an idol, must form a system of theology and ethics, dismally lean and contemptible.

All the motives to human conduct are found, either in the Objects with which we converse; or in the VIEWS, with which we regard them. If the objects, or the views, be low and debased, low and debased motives, only, will arise out of them. But motives originate all our conduct, regulate its progress, and determine its nature. If they be low and debased, the conduct will partake of the same characteristics, and will of course be grovelling, unworthy, and odious.

Thus the objects, with which we are conversant, and the views which we form of them, will determine both the internal and external character of Man. . . .

Thus have I taken a summary, comparative view of these two schemes of existence. In that of the Christian, an intelligent Mind, possessed of boundless power, wisdom, and goodness, existed from everlasting; commanded into being the Universe of Matter, and the Universe of Minds; is present in every place; sees, with an intuitive survey, every thing; controls all things with an almighty and unerring hand; and directs all to the accomplishment of *the* divine and eternal purpose, for which all were made. Over the Universe of Minds, destined to an immortal existence, he exercises a moral and eternal government; and prescribes laws, which require the best conduct, and insure the greatest happiness. To obedience he promises an endless reward; to disobedience he threatens an endless punishment. From this great source, the Christian sees himself derived; to this glorious end, believes himself destined; and in this sublime scheme, is presented with all motives to make him good, and with all means to make him happy.

The Atheist, on the contrary, supposes all things derived from chance, or necessity; originated without design; existing to no purpose, and terminating, whenever they do terminate, by the coercion of Fate, or the sport of Accident, as they began. Himself he regards as a lump of organized Matter; without a Mind; without law or government, except that of Fate or force; without moral action; incapable of obligation or rectitude; united to his fellow-men only by Time and Place; formed only to animal enjoyment; and destined to perish with his kindred brutes. By this scheme, all that is glorious, divine, and lovely, in that of the Christian, is annihilated; and all which, in the natural world, cannot be annihilated, and which possesses an inherent greatness and sublimity, is miserably contracted and degraded. Nothing is left to expand his views, refine his affections, or ennoble his conduct. Motives to virtue, dignity, and usefulness, he obliterates from the creation. In the future World, he finds no such motives; for to him the future world is nothing. His evil passions, in the mean time (for such passions, whencesoever derived, he possesses), are let loose without restraint, to rage and riot without control. Of all motives to do evil, his scheme is prolific; of motives to do good, it is absolutely barren. At the same time, it is founded on mere hypothesis, sustained by no evidence, and believed, against demonstration and impossibility.

Thus it is, I think, unanswerably evident that *he, who hath said, There is no God, is a Fool*; that his Atheism is a scheme dictated only by an evil heart; that *it corrupts*, of course, the whole moral character; that it is productive of all *abominable works*; and that it completely precludes *the performance* of any thing that is *good*.

From Timothy Dwight, "Sermon III: Comparative Influence of Atheism and Christianity," in *Theology, Explained and Defended, in a Series of Sermons*, vol. 1 (Middletown, CT: Charles Lyman, 1818), 17–25.

Nathaniel W. Taylor

CONCIO AD CLERUM (1828)

Timothy Dwight's protégé, Nathaniel W. Taylor (1786–1858), grew up in the town of New Milford, Connecticut. Prepared for college by the New Divinity pastor Azel Backus, he matriculated at Yale in 1800. He was converted in 1806 during a conversation with Dwight and lived in the Dwight family home in 1808 and 1809. He served as Dwight's amanuensis, read theology with him, and accepted a call to the pulpit of New Haven's First Church in 1812 under Dwight's paternal influence.

During the next ten years, Taylor became one of the leading Congregationalists in New England. He led his church through three periods of intense revivalism (1815, 1816, and 1820–21), adding four hundred souls to the rolls within a decade. By the time he started at Yale Divinity School as Dwight Professor (1822), he was the best-known thirty-six-year-old theologian in America. Already active as a writer by the time he went to Yale, Taylor accelerated his scholarship throughout the 1820s. By late in 1828, when the following tract was finished, the so-called Taylorite affair was underway.

The *Concio ad Clerum* ("Charge to the Clergy") is Taylor's best-known publication. Delivered originally as a speech to the annual meeting of Connecticut's Congregational clergymen, it hit on many of Taylor's most controversial themes. Technically, it offered a new defense of original sin. But in the process, Taylor redefined this classic Christian teaching, excluding the notion that all are guilty of Adam's sin in the Garden of Eden. Taylor granted that all are born with ruefully sinful human natures, natures bereft of the Holy Spirit that lead to sin "in all the appropriate circumstances of our being." He denied, however, that humans are born with natures to which God has attached a positive sinful charge, or even guilt for others' sins—a denial intended to keep sinners from blaming God for their moral problems.

The *Concio* redefined the Edwardsean doctrine of the will. Whereas Jonathan Edwards distinguished the unregenerate sinner's "natural ability" from his "moral inability" to repent and believe the gospel, Taylor abandoned the term *inability* altogether. He granted that sin is "certain" in everyone who has not yet been converted, but he insisted that sin is never "necessary." Relatedly, Taylor defended a so-called infralapsarian doctrine of the derivation of sin, resisting the view of some Hopkinsians that sin was planned by God as requisite to human salvation. According to Taylor's view, God knows that to run the best system of moral government he must allow his creatures genuine freedom to dissent. God never actively wills sin. He only permits it to take place. He makes it possible to guarantee our liberty.

As noted above, these teachings sparked a conflagration in the northeast, one that later spread through most of the rest of the nation. During the 1830s and 1840s, it sundered Edwardsean unity. As more people followed Edwards's teachings, Edwards's legacy diversified. This was only to be expected, but it rendered the movement difficult to sustain.

Ephesians 2:3

And were by nature the children of wrath, even as others.

The Bible is a plain book. It speaks, especially on the subject of sin, directly to human consciousness; and tells us beyond mistake, what sin is, and why we sin. In the text, the Apostle asserts the fact of the moral depravity of mankind, and assigns its cause. To be "the children of wrath" is to possess the character which deserves punishment; in other words, it is to be sinners, or to be entirely depraved in respect to moral character. The text then teaches THAT THE ENTIRE MORAL DEPRAVITY OF MANKIND IS BY NATURE.

In illustrating this position, I shall attempt to show, First, In what the moral depravity of man consists; and Secondly, That this depravity is by nature.

1. By the moral depravity of mankind I intend, generally, the entire sinfulness of their moral character—that state of the mind or heart to which guilt and the desert of wrath pertain. I may say then negatively,

This depravity does not consist in any essential attribute or property of the soul—not in *any thing created* in man by his Maker. On this point,

I need only ask—does God create in men a sinful nature, and damn them for the very nature he creates? Believe this, who can.

Nor does the moral depravity of men consist in a sinful nature, which they have corrupted by being one with Adam, and by acting in his act. To believe that I am one and the same being with another who existed thousands of years before I was born, and that by virtue of this identity I truly acted in his act, and am therefore as truly guilty of his sin as himself—to believe this, I must renounce the reason which my Maker has given me; I must believe it also, in face of the oath of God to its falsehood, entered upon the record.

Nor does the moral depravity of men consist in any *constitutional propensities* of their nature. Whoever supposed himself or others to be guilty, for being hungry or thirsty after long abstinence from food or drink; or merely for desiring knowledge, or the esteem of his fellow-men, or any other good, abstractly from any choice to gratify such desires? Who does not know that a perfectly holy man must be subject to all these propensities? The man Christ Jesus was subject to every one of them, for he "was *in all points* tempted like as we are, yet without sin."

Nor does *any* degree of *excitement* in these propensities or desires, not resulting in choice, constitute moral depravity. Suppose them then, in the *providence* of God, excited in any degree, and yet the man to prefer doing the will of God to their gratification; all will admit that it is the noblest act of obedience conceivable in a moral being. All will agree that the man, who always triumphs over excited propensity, who duly subordinates all his desires of inferior good to the will of God is a perfect man. It is the uniform sentiment of inspired truth that this ruling of the spirit, this government of himself, imparts unrivaled glory to his character. We add the express declaration of the Apostle: "*Blessed* is the man that *endureth* temptation."

Nor does the moral depravity of man consist in *any disposition or tendency* to sin, which is *the cause of all sin*. It is important on this point to guard against error from the ambiguity of terms. There is an obvious distinction between a *disposition* or tendency to sin which is prior to *all* sin, and a *sinful* disposition. I am not saying then that there is not, what with entire propriety may be called a disposition or tendency to sin, which is the cause of *all* sin; nor that there is not, as a *consequence* of *this* disposition or tendency, what with equal propriety may be called a *sinful* disposition, which is the true cause of all *other* sin, itself excepted. But I say that that which is the cause of *all* sin is not itself sin. The cause of all sin itself sin! Whence then came the first sin? Do you say, from a previous sin as its cause? Then you say, there is a sin before the first sin. Our first parents and fallen angels were once holy. Tell us now, whence came *their* first sin? Do you still repeat, from a previous sin? And what sort of philosophy, reason, or common sense is this—a sin before the first sin—sin before all sin? Do you say there must be *difficulties* in theology? I ask must there be *nonsense* in theology?

The question then still recurs, what is this moral depravity for *which* man deserves the wrath of God? I answer—it *is man's own act, consisting in a free choice of some object rather than God, as his chief good; or a free preference of the world and of worldly good, to the will and glory of God.*

In support of *these* views of the subject, I now appeal to the testimony of some of the ablest divines, of Apostles, and of common sense.

Says Calvin, speaking of our text, "our nature is there characterized, not as it was created by God, but as it was vitiated in Adam; *because* it would be unreasonable to make God the author of death." Again, "natural depravity is not a substantial property originally innate, but can be imputed to none but man himself." He says of sin expressly, "it is voluntary." "If they are convicted of any fault, the Lord justly reproaches them with their own perverseness." "He who sins necessarily, sins no less voluntarily."

The Westminster divines say that "every sin both original and actual being a transgression of the righteous law of God, etc." I ask, is not transgression action? is it not something done, and done knowingly and voluntarily?

Dr. Bellamy, speaking of the *sinful* propensities of man, says, "They are not created by God with the essence of the soul, but result from its native choice, or rather, more strictly, are themselves its native *choice*. They are not natural in the same sense in which the *faculties* of our souls are; for they are not the workmanship of God, but are our native *choice*, and the *voluntary, free, spontaneous* bent of our hearts."

Says President Edwards, "The inferior principles of self-love and natural appetite which were given only to serve (and which as he also says, 'were in man in innocence'), being alone and left to themselves became reigning principles. Man did set up himself (which by the way was doing something) and the objects of his private affections and appetites as *supreme*, and so they took the place of God. Man's love to his own honour, private interest, and pleasure which was before wholly subordinate unto love to God and regard to his glory (and while thus, he says also, 'all things were in excellent order and in their proper and perfect state'), now disposes him to pursue those objects without regard to God's honour or law." Thus he adds, "It is easy to give an account, how total corruption of heart should follow—without God's putting *any evil* into his heart, or implanting any *bad principle*, or infusing any *corrupt taint*, and *so* becoming the author of depravity." Again, he says, "If the essence of virtuousness or fault does not lie in the nature of the dispositions or *acts of the mind*, then it is certain, it lies no where at all." "That which makes vice hateful is a certain deformity in that *evil will*, which is the soul of all vice." "If a thing be from us, and not from our *choice*, it has not the nature of blame-worthiness or ill-desert."

What says St. Paul? In the context he describes the nature of human depravity, and I request you to mark the agreement between his description and that of the last named author. He says, "ye, who were dead in trespasses and sins, wherein ye *walked*." You see it was a *walking—living* death. Dead as they were, they did something: "Wherein ye walked according to the course of this world." And what is the course of this world? What is it, but as Edwards says, "Men setting up themselves and the objects of their private affections as supreme, so that these things take the place of God?" What is it, but a world loving the creature more than God the Creator, and acting accordingly. Again says this Apostle, "Among whom we all had our conversation"—our deportment and manner of life, "in the lusts of the flesh, fulfilling the desires of the flesh and the mind." Now what is this, but freely and voluntarily yielding to propensities, which men ought to restrain and govern, and to subordinate to the will of God; what is it but propensities rising into a free preference of their objects, and going out into a free purpose of self-gratification? For how can men walk in the lusts of the flesh and fulfill the desires of the flesh and of the mind without preferring the gratification of these lusts and desires to other good? How live and act thus, without choosing to do it? You see then that the sin, which the Apostle describes, consists not merely in external action, not merely in having propensities for natural good, but in acting freely, in yielding to these propensities as a matter of choice and preference.

What saith St. James? "Let no man say when he is tempted, I am tempted of God" (and was there ever a more fatal tempter than God, if he creates sin in us?)—"for God is not tempted of evil neither tempteth he any man; but every man is tempted when he is drawn away of his own lust and enticed. *Then*, when lust, i.e., strong desire (the same word used by Paul when he says 'I have a *desire* to depart, etc.'—and by our Lord when he says 'with *desire* have I *desired* to eat this passover') *then* when lust hath conceived it bringeth forth sin." Now when does lust or strong desire conceive and bring forth sin? When it rises into a preference of its object, and goes out in action to secure its own gratification. Or, if you say the lust is itself the sin (though I think this is ascribing to the Apostle the absurdity of asserting sin before sin), yet be it so. What then is the lust which is sin, but a *preference of its object*, a *stronger* affection for it than for God? Interpret then the language of the Apostle either way, and you come to the same result—that all sin consists in freely preferring some inferior good to God. I might add to these many other passages. I only ask what is the import of the most common terms used by Apostles to describe sin in its true nature? I refer to such as these, *minding the flesh, walking in the flesh, living after the flesh, the flesh lusting against the Spirit*, what is this, but freely, voluntarily setting up the gratification of our natural propensities and appetites as our chief good, fixing our supreme affections upon it—setting the heart, when the living God claims it, upon some inferior good?

I now enquire, what says common sense? Take then any action which common sense in the common use of language calls a *sinful* action—what is the sin of it? As an example, take the act of murder. Now do we mean by this term in common usage to denote simply the external act of killing? Clearly not. This may be by accident, or in obedience to a divine law. Do we mean simply the external act, together with the specific volition to perform the act? Clearly not; for there must be such a volition, though the act were performed in obedience to a divine command. It is only when the circumstances and manner of the action evince a selfish or malicious purpose—a state of mind in which the perpetrator of the deed shows a preference of some private selfish interest to the life of a fellow-being, and to the will of God, that we call it murder. So true is it, that we regard this state of mind as constituting the sin of the action, that could we ascertain independently of external action, the existence of such a preference, we should, as the Bible does, pronounce it murder. This preference then of some private interest, object, or end, rather than God, common sense decides to be the sin of all that we call sinful action, and strictly speaking, the sum total of all sin.

But common sense decides the question in another form. And here we come to what I regard as the turning point of the whole controversy. So far as I know, the only argument in support of the opinion that sin pertains to something which is not preference is based in a supposed decision of common sense. The decision claimed is that all particular or specific sins, as fraud, falsehood, injustice, unbelief, envy, pride, revenge, result from a *wicked heart*—from a *sinful disposition*, as the cause or source of such sinful acts. To this fact, I yield unqualified assent, as "the dictate of the universal sense and reason of mankind," and by this universal judgment, I wish the present question to be decided. Let us then look at the fact in its full force and just application. There is a man then, whose course of life is wholly that of a worldling, his heart and hand shut against human woe living without prayer, without gratitude, unmindful of God, and rejecting the Saviour of men, devising all, purposing all, doing all, for the sake of this world. Why is it? You say, and *all* say, and say *right*, it is owing to his love of the world—to his worldly disposition—to a heart set on the world. Now while all say this, and are right in saying it, we have one simple question to decide, viz., what do all *mean by* it? Every child can answer. Every child knows that the meaning is that this man does freely and voluntarily fix his affections on worldly

199

good, in preference to God; that the man has chosen the world as his chief good, his portion, his God. He knows that this is what is meant by *a worldly heart, a worldly disposition*, which leads to all *other* sins. So when we ascribe the sins of the miser to his *avaricious disposition*, we mean his supreme love of money; or the crimes of the hero or conqueror to his *ambitious disposition*, we mean his supreme love of fame, a state of mind which involves *preference* for its object. And whatever previous tendency, or if you will previous disposition, there is to this state of mind; this state of mind itself and not any previous thing as the cause of it, is the *wicked heart*—the sinful disposition of men. They love the creature more than the Creator, when they can and ought to love the Creator most. This forbidden choice of worldly good, this preference of the low and sordid pleasures of earth to God and his glory—this love of the world which excludes the love of the Father—*this*—*this* is man's depravity. This is that evil treasure of the heart, from which proceed evil things; this is the fountain, the source of all *other* abominations—man's free, voluntary preference of the world as his chief good, amid the revealed glories of a perfect God.

Having attempted to show in what the moral depravity of man consists, I now proceed to show

II. That this depravity is by nature. This I understand the Apostle to assert when he says, "and were by nature the children of wrath."

What then are we to understand, when it is said that mankind are depraved by *nature*? I answer—*that such is their nature, that they will sin and only sin in all the appropriate circumstances of their being*.

To bring this part of the subject distinctly before the mind, it may be well to remark that the question between the Calvinists and the Arminians on the point is this—whether the depravity or sinfulness of mankind is truly and properly ascribed to their *nature* or to their *circumstances of temptation*? And since, as it must be confessed, there can no more be sin without circumstances of temptation, that there can be sin without a nature to be tempted, why ascribe sin exclusively to nature? I answer, it is truly and properly ascribed to *nature*, and *not* to circumstances, because all mankind sin in all the appropriate circumstances of their being. For all the world ascribe an effect to the nature of a thing, when no possible change in its appropriate circumstances will change the effect; or when the effect is uniformly the same in all its appropriate circumstances. To illustrate this by an example: Suppose a tree, which in one soil bears only bad fruit. Change its circumstances, transplant it to another soil, and it bears very good fruit. Now we say, and all would say, the fact that it bore bad fruit was owing to its situation—to its circumstances; for by changing its circumstances, you have changed its fruit. Suppose now another tree, which bears bad fruit place it where you will; change its situation from one soil to another, dig about it and dung it, cultivate it to perfection—do what you will, it still bears bad fruit only. Now every one says, the fact is owing to *the nature* of the tree—the cause is in the tree, in its nature and *not* its circumstances. So of mankind, change their circumstances as you may; place them where you will within the limits of their being; do what you will to prevent the consequence, you have one uniform result, entire moral depravity. No change of condition, no increase of light nor of motives, no instructions nor warnings, no any thing, within the appropriate circumstances of their being, changes the result. Unless there be some interposition, which is not included in these circumstances, unless something be done which is above nature, the case is hopeless. Place a human being any where within the appropriate limits and scenes of his immortal existence, and such is his nature, that he will be a depraved sinner.

When therefore I say that mankind are entirely depraved *by nature*, I do not mean that their nature is *itself* sinful, nor that their nature is the *physical* or *efficient* cause of their sinning; but I mean that their nature is the occasion, or reason of their sinning; that such *is their nature, that in all the appropriate circumstances of their being, they will sin and only sin. . . .*

. . . That sin or guilt pertains exclusively to voluntary action is the true principle of orthodoxy. We have seen that the older orthodox divines assert this principle, and that they abundantly deny that God is the creator or author of sin. By some strange fatality however these writers are not believed by many on these points; and we are told, as the ground for discrediting these unequivocal declarations, that they also constantly affirm that men are *born* with a corrupt and sinful nature, and with guilt upon them. True, very true. But now to the real question—how in the view of these writers does this nature with which they are born become corrupt and sinful? By being so created? No such thing: for this they constantly and vehemently deny; and give as we have seen this reason for denying it—that it would make God the author of sin. How then is it that in their view each has a corrupt and sinful nature when born, and yet that God does not create it? Why, by the *real act* of each—by each one's corrupting his nature, just as Adam did his. But how can this be? They tell us how; viz., that Adam and his posterity were in God's estimation and were thus truly constituted, ONE BEING, one MORAL WHOLE—so that in Adam's act of sin, all his posterity *being* ONE *with him*, also acted as truly as Adam himself; and so, each and all corrupted their nature as freely and voluntarily as Adam corrupted his nature. The question is, not whether this is not very absurd, but what did these men believe and teach? And I say they *did* believe and *did* teach that all Adam's posterity *acted* in his act, "sinned in *him* and fell with *him*," and are considered truly and properly as sinning *in manner and form*, just as Adam sinned; and every one who has read his catechism or his primer must know it. This class of divines then never thought of predicating sin or guilt, except in cases of free voluntary action. So far as *they* are concerned therefore the doctrine of physical depravity is a theological novelty.

The history of this peculiarity shows the same thing. The process has been this. The doctrine of imputation being rejected, as it has been in New England for many years, and with it *our personal identity with Adam*, there was no way left in which we could be viewed as the older divines viewed us; the criminal authors when born, of our own corrupt and sinful nature. Still the doctrine of a corrupt and sinful nature *as such* has been retained by *some*, and thus what the older divines made every man *as one in Adam* the author of, God must now answer for as its author by a creative act. Hence some have so professed and so preached, and have talked much of their own orthodoxy and of the heresy of others, and yet after all the outcry, not a theological writer of eminence has ventured to this hour to publish to the world such a doctrine. The entire annals of orthodoxy do not contain the doctrine that *God creates* a sinful nature in man. Those men who have fought the battles of orthodoxy from the reformation to the present day, and who have been esteemed its successful defenders, have held most firmly and asserted abundantly that all sin or fault must belong *to the acts of the mind*—to the *evil will*, or belong to nothing at all. Brethren, were these men heretics for this? Is the man who believes and teaches the same thing, a heretic? . . .

. . . We see the importance of this view of man's depravity, compared with any other, in its bearing on the preaching of the Gospel. To what purpose do we preach the Gospel to men, if we cannot reach the conscience with *its charge of guilt* and *obligations to duty*? And how I ask can this be done, unless sin and duty be shown to consist simply and wholly in acts and doings which are their own? Can this be done if we tell them and they believe us, that their sin is something which God creates in them; or something done by Adam thousands of years before they existed? I care not what you call it, taste, disposition, volition, exercise, if it be that which *cannot* be unless God creates it, and cannot but be if he exerts power to produce it, can we fasten the arrows of conviction in the conscience, and settle on the spirit the forebodings of a *merited* damnation? Can men be induced to make an effort to avoid sin which is thus produced in them, or to perform duties which must with the same passivity on their part be produced in them? Does God charge on men, as that which deserves his endless indignation, what Himself does? Does God summon men to repentance with commands and entreaties, and at the same time tell them that all efforts at compliance are as useless as the muscular motions of a corpse to get life again? Does this book of

God's inspiration shock and appal the world, with the revelation of such things, respecting God and respecting man? Will the charge of *such sin* on man touch the secret place of tears? Will the exhibition of such a God allure the guilty to confide in his mercy? If so, preach it out—preach it consistently—preach nothing to contradict it—dwell on your message, that God creates men sinners and damns them for being so. Tell them such is *their* nature and such the *mode* of his interposition, that there is no more hope from acting on the part of the sinner than from not acting; tell them they may as well sleep on, and sleep away these hours of mercy, as attempt any thing in the work of their salvation; that all is as hopeless with effort as without it. Spread over this world such a curtain of sackcloth, such a midnight of terror, and how as the appropriate effect would each accountable immortal either sit down in the sullenness of inaction, or take his solitary way to hell in the frenzy of despair!

But such is not the message of wrath and of mercy, by which a revolted world is to be awed and allured back to its Master. The message we are to deliver to men is a message of wrath, because they are the perpetrators of the deed that deserves wrath. It is a message of mercy to men who by acting are to comply with the terms of it, and who can never hope to comply even through God's agency, without putting themselves to the doing of *the very thing* commanded of God. And it is only by delivering such a message that we, Brethren, can be "workers together with God." Let us then go forth with it; and clearing God, throw all the guilt of sin with its desert of wrath upon the sinner's single self. Let us make him see and feel that he can go to hell only as a self-destroyer—that it is this fact that will give those chains their strength to hold him, and those fires the anguish of their burning. Let us if we can make this conviction take hold of his spirit, and ring in his conscience like the note of the second death. If he trembles at the sound in his ears, then let us point him to that mercy which a dying Jesus feels for him, and tell him with the sympathies of men who have been in the same condemnation that he need but to love and trust HIM, and heaven is his inheritance. Without derogating from the work of God's Spirit let us urge him to his duty—*to his duty*—*to his duty*, as a point-blank direction to business now on hand and now to be done. With the authorised assurance that "peradventure God may give him repentance," let us make known to him the high command of God *"strive*, to enter in at the strait gate"—and make him hear every voice of truth and mercy in heaven and on earth, echoing the mandate.

Then shall the ministers of reconciliation be clad with truth as with a garment, and delivering their message not only in its substance but in its true manner and form, shall commend themselves to every man's conscience in the sight of God. Having his strength perfected in their weakness, they shall go forth "as archangels strong," and bidding the wide earth receive God's salvation, the bands of hell shall break, and a redeemed world return to the dominion of its God.

Finally, I cannot conclude without remarking how fearful are the condition and prospects of the sinner. His sin is his own. He yields himself by his own free act, by his own choice, to those propensities of his nature, which under the weight of God's authority he *ought to govern*. The gratification of these he makes his chief good, immortal as he is. For this he lives and acts—this he puts in the place of God—and for this, and for nothing better he tramples on God's authority and incurs his wrath. Glad would he be to escape the guilt of it. Oh—could he persuade himself that the fault is not his own—this would wake up peace in his guilty bosom. Could he believe that God is bound to convert and save him, or even that he could make it certain that God will do it—this would allay his fears—this would stamp a bow on the cloud that thickens, and darkens, and thunders damnation on his guilty path. But his guilt is all his own, and a just God may leave him to his choice. He is going to a wretched eternity, the self-made victim of its woes. Amid sabbaths and bibles, the intercessions of saints, the songs of angels, the intreaties of God's ambassadors, the accents of redeeming love, and the blood that speaketh peace, he presses on to death. God beseeching with tenderness and terror—Jesus telling him he died once and could die again to save him—mercy weeping over him day and night—heaven lifting up its everlasting gates—hell burning, and sending up its smoke of torment, and the weeping and the wailing and the gnashing of teeth, within his hearing—and onward still he goes. See the infatuated immortal! Fellow sinner—IT IS YOU.

Bowels of divine compassion—length, breadth, height, depth of Jesus' love—Spirit of all grace, save him—Oh save him—or he dies forever.

From Nathaniel W. Taylor, *Concio ad Clerum. A Sermon Delivered in the Chapel of Yale College, September 10, 1828* (New Haven: Hezekiah Howe, 1828).

Nathaniel W. Taylor

REVIEW OF SPRING ON THE MEANS
OF REGENERATION (1829)

Nathaniel W. Taylor also redefined the doctrine of spiritual regeneration—the historic centerpiece of the Edwardsean party platform. He did so for largely practical reasons, fearing the spiritual consequences of the New Divinity emphasis on the sinfulness of "unregenerate doings." Taylor agreed with the Hopkinsians that *prior* to regeneration all that one does is radically sinful—even making use (halfheartedly) of the stated means of grace (things such as Bible study, prayer, and corporate worship). But he claimed that *during* regeneration there is a moment when the mind is convinced of the truthfulness of the Bible (by the power of the Holy Spirit), the "selfish principle" is suspended in the souls of anxious seekers, and they cling to the gospel message—using the means—without sin.

Taylor was nothing if not pragmatic. He knew that preaching for conversion while condemning the use of the means was like demanding people to climb a rungless ladder (a notion Harriet Beecher Stowe would later make popular in her novels). His own doctrine of regeneration proved forbiddingly complex, but he kept it to the classroom and the theological quarterlies. In the pulpit, he made things simple, declaring in contrast to the Hopkinsians that God was ready and willing to use the means to effect regeneration.

Taylor developed his singular doctrine in response to Gardner Spring (1785–1873), the pastor of New York City's Brick Church (Presbyterian), best known for the "Spring Resolutions" he presented to the General Assembly of 1861, which supported the federal government and precipitated the sectional schism of Old School Presbyterians. An expatriated New Englander with strong Hopkinsian leanings, Spring had published in 1827 a *Dissertation on the Means of Regeneration*. It took a standard Hopkinsian line. Extending the call for instant conversion while condemning the use of means (that is, by unconverted sinners), it seemed yet again to present a spiritual goal impossible to attain.

Taylor's review of Spring required no fewer than 112 pages in the *Quarterly Christian Spectator*, more than twice the number in Spring's *Dissertation*. Disturbed by Spring's reversion to the high Calvinist logic of "damned if you do and damned if you don't," Taylor chastised him for leaving sinners without legitimate recourse. Distinguishing what he called the proper "using" from the "abusing" of the means of regeneration, and breaking down this "complex act" into its several parts, Taylor found a way to encourage anxious souls to come to Jesus without departing from the system of the Edwardseans.

❧

. . . We begin with some explanatory remarks. That the acts and doings of unregenerate men which are designated by Dr. Spring and many others, as those which constitute *using the means of regeneration* are sinful, we have already expressed our full conviction. That these acts should be accurately described in their principle and their nature, that sinners may have knowledge of their moral quality and condemning power, is also in our view of great practical utility. But the error, the grand error on this subject, as we regard it, is *that these acts and doings which are so obviously sinful, and therefore forbidden by divine authority, should be called using the means of regeneration, and be pronounced* (as indeed using the means of regeneration must be) *of indispensable necessity to regeneration itself.* The truth is, as we shall attempt to show, that according to all correct usage of terms these acts of the sinner are not *using*—they are, . . . *abusing* the means of regeneration.

The question then naturally arises, *what are the acts which constitute using the means of regeneration?* We answer that by *using the means of regeneration* we do not understand any acts, which either precede or are to be distinguished from regeneration itself, when this term is used in its more common popular import; but we understand *those acts which, together with another act, are in the more popular use of language, included under the term regeneration.* Regeneration, considered as a moral change of which man is the subject—giving God the heart—making a new heart—loving God supremely, etc., are terms and phrases which in popular use denote a complex act. Each in popular use denotes what in a more *analytical* mode of speaking may be viewed and described as made up of several particular acts and states of mind, or as a series of such acts and states; which are yet so related and connected that for all ordinary purposes they are sufficiently defined when spoken of in combination and as constituting ONE ACT under *one* name. Indeed it is of this combination or series of mental acts only that moral quality can be predicated; since no one act of the process viewed abstractly from the other acts can be a *moral* act. The act of the will or heart viewed abstractly from the acts of intellect is not moral, nor are the acts of the intellect viewed abstractly from the act of the will or heart. That the preference of God to all other objects of affection may be a moral act, it must be, and in all ordinary speech is assumed to be, an intelligent preference. For the homage of beings who are intelligent as well as voluntary, and who can estimate the comparative worth of objects, is the homage which honors God, and which he claims as a moral governor. Indeed what we are now saying of the words and phrases under consideration is true of all complex words, such as walk, sit, read, write, etc. These words in all ordinary speech and writing are used to denote *one* act, and yet this one act includes a process of mental acts, consisting of the perception and comparison of motives, the estimate of their relative worth, and the choice or willing of the external action. Of course the complex act, denoted by a single word may be, it often is, for necessary purposes, analysed or separated into its several parts, and the complex term is applied to one or more of these parts, as the object of the speaker may require. But we shall have occasion to resume this topic hereafter.

In respect to the mode of divine operation in producing a change of heart, we are averse to indulging in speculation. The Scriptures, however, authorize us to assert generally that *the mode* of divine influence *is consistent with the moral nature of this change as a voluntary act of man; and also that it is through the truth, and implies attention to truth on the part of man.* Any views which contravene in any respect either of these positions, we regard as unscriptural. That the influence of the Divine Spirit in regeneration, accords in *the mode* of it with the laws of moral agency and the nature of moral action, is apparent from the distinct recognition in the Scriptures of this change as the sinner's duty and the sinner's act—as his act done in obedience to the divine will, in view of his obligations and in the exercise of his powers as a moral being. That the change is through the truth, and implies attention to the truth—the sober solemn consideration of the objects which truth discloses, prior to the requisite act of the will or heart will not be doubted by the reader of the sacred volume.

When however we speak of the priority of these mental acts, we refer rather to the order of nature than of time. We are aware that the progress of thought and feeling is often as rapid as that of light, and we no more intend to affirm any *measurable* duration between the first and last act in the series than when we say the sun must exist before it can shine. On this point it is indispensable, if we would not dispute about mere words, to consider the popular looseness of such terms and phrases as *before, after, immediate, as soon as, etc.*; and to remember that the degree of definiteness intended is to be decided not by the mere words, but by the known object of the speaker. Thus in a case in which some unusual precision of thought is required, we should say the sun must have existed *before* it shone; while in another case, in which the same precision of ideas is not required, we should say with equal truth and propriety, the sun shone *as soon as* it existed. In the one case the object would require that the priority be noticed by the form of speaking; in the other it would not. So in the present case, when we speak of the priority of certain mental acts to the act of the will, it is because, as we shall show hereafter, our object requires this precision of thought and expression. At the same time we intend by it no such priority as renders it improper or untrue to speak, according to popular usage and the more ordinary purposes of instruction of the entire series of acts as cotemporaneous, and as constituting ONE ACT under one term, *regeneration*; or to speak of it as one act, the *immediate* performance of which is required of the sinner.

Now from this more popular and comprehensive import of the term *regeneration*, we are obliged by the object in view to depart *when we speak of using the means of regeneration*. As we shall have occasion to illustrate the reason and necessity of this departure in another part of the discussion, we would merely remark here that we suppose the distinction between using the means of regeneration, and regeneration itself, is a theological rather than a scriptural distinction and that it has been made solely for the purpose of obviating, what would otherwise be a very formidable objection to the performance of immediate duty, in view of the doctrine of the sinner's dependence. This objection we suppose to be founded wholly in a false *analytical* view of *the mode* of the sinner's dependence, and that therefore it can be refuted only by a similar method of discussion.

Accordingly when we speak of the means of regeneration we shall use the word regeneration in a more limited import than its ordinary popular import, and shall confine it, chiefly for the sake of convenient phraseology, to the act of the will or heart, in distinction from other mental acts, connected with it; or to that act of the will or heart which consists in preference of God to every other object; or to that disposition of the heart, or governing affection or purpose of the man, which consecrates him to the service and glory of God.

In thus confining the term regeneration to the act of the will or heart, when we speak of using the means of regeneration, we do not intend to decide any minute questions respecting the precise thing done by the agency of the Spirit, nor whether his interposition does or does not influence other acts beside that of the will or heart. All that our present object requires us to say on these topics is that regeneration in the popular import of the term is an event which depends on the interposition of the Holy Spirit; that it so depends on this interposition, that whatsoever part of that process of mental acts and states which, in the popular use of the term, constitute regeneration, is produced by this divine interposition, *some part* of the process is preliminary to such interposition, and preliminary also to that which, in the limited use of the word, may be called regeneration; and that whatever acts be regarded as thus preliminary, they are to be regarded and spoken of either as using the means of grace, or as using the means of regeneration. Allowing these things to be so, we have no controversy here with any who may prefer to include more than the act of the will or heart in the term *regeneration,* when they speak of using the means of regeneration.

Applying the word *regeneration* then in some limited import, not precisely defined, we affirm that *there are and must be certain mental acts and states, which in the order of nature at least, precede regeneration; or which precede,* as we propose to use the term regeneration, *that act of the will or heart,* in which God is preferred to every other object. Of these mental acts and states, our object does not require that we give an accurate analysis. It is sufficient for our purpose to show that there are such acts and states, and that we so far describe them, that it may be understood, what class of mental acts we designate as preliminary to regeneration, and as constituting using the means of regeneration. We proceed to say then that before the act of the will or heart in which the sinner first prefers God to every other object, the object of the preference must be viewed or estimated as the greatest good. Before the object can be viewed as the greatest good, it must be compared with other objects, as both are sources or means of good. Before this act of comparing, there must be an act dictated not by selfishness, but by *self-love,* in which the mind determines to direct its thoughts to the objects for the sake of considering their relative value, of forming a judgment respecting it, and of choosing one or the other as the chief good. . . .

Should any doubt or hesitation in regard to what has just been stated, respecting the process of mental acts, arise in the mind of the reader, it would probably respect the position that the acts of considering and comparing the objects of choice are dictated not by selfishness but by *self-love.* To remove all doubts on this point, we deem it sufficient to say that such an act of consideration as we have described cannot be dictated by selfishness, because the act is not fitted to subserve, but fitted to defeat, a selfish purpose. . . .

This self-love or desire of happiness is the primary cause or reason of all acts of preference or choice which fix supremely on any object. In every moral being who forms a moral character, there must be a first moral act of preference or choice. This must respect some one object, God or mammon: as the chief good, or as an object of supreme affection. Now whence comes such a choice or preference? Not from a previous choice or preference of the same object, for we speak of the first choice of the object. The answer which human consciousness gives is that the being constituted with a capacity for happiness desires to be happy; and knowing that he is capable of deriving happiness from different objects, considers from which the greatest happiness may be derived, and as in this respect he judges or estimates their relative value, so he chooses or prefers the one or the other as his chief good. While this must be the process by which a moral being forms his first moral preference, substantially the same process is indispensable to *a change* of this preference. The change involves the preference of a new object as the chief good; a preference which the former preference has no tendency to produce, but a direct tendency to prevent; a preference therefore not resulting from, or in any way occasioned by a previous preference of any given object, but resulting from those acts, of considering and comparing the sources of happiness, which are dictated by the desire of happiness or self-love.

Nor ought it to be overlooked that this part of our nature is always with us, be our moral character what it may. It always longs for happiness, without including in itself the act of the will or heart fixed on any given source or object, whence we resolve to seek our happiness: for whether by an act of the will or heart we resolve to seek our chief happiness from one object or another, we still desire to be happy. Whenever we do fix upon the object, self-love primarily prompts to the choice (not determines it) and therefore exists prior to the act of will by which we fix our affections on any object as our chief good. To self-love the appeal may always be made, and feelingly made, even in the lowest stages of moral degeneracy, to produce both the conviction and impression that there is greater good in God than in the world. To this part of our nature, all motives designed to change the governing purpose or supreme affection of the heart must always be primarily addressed. They cannot be addressed to a *holy* heart, already existing in sinful man. Nor will it be pretended that God proffers gratification to the selfish principle in man as the means of winning him to holiness, since this would have no other tendency than to prevent the change. The motives fitted to destroy the selfish principle (and such must be all the motives addressed to man to restore him to holiness), can find nothing in that principle but resistance. If therefore there be not in man a constitutional capacity of happiness from some other source than the world, if man cannot be made to *see* and to *feel* that there is to him greater good in God than in any other object, the motives to holiness might as well be addressed to the trees of the forest, as to men. So certain as man is a moral agent and is properly addressed by motives to holiness, so certain is it that he has constitutional susceptibilities to that good which these motives proffer; and that, if he is led at all to prefer this good to every other, he is primarily prompted to the choice by the desire of happiness or self-love. . . .

. . . We have already said that the sinner is the subject of that constitutional desire of happiness, called self-love, to which no moral quality pertains. Let the sinner then, as a being who loves happiness and desires the highest degree of it, under the influence of such a desire, take into solemn consideration the question whether the highest happiness is to be found in God or in the world; let him pursue this inquiry, if need be, till it result in the conviction that such happiness is to be found in God only; and let him follow up this conviction with that intent and engrossing contemplation of the realities which truth discloses, and with that stirring up of his sensibilities in view of them, which shall invest the world, when considered as his only portion, with an aspect of insignificance, of gloom and even of terror, and which shall chill and suspend his present active love of it; and let the contemplation be persevered in till it shall discover a reality and an excellence in the objects of holy affection, which shall put him upon direct and desperate efforts to fix his heart upon them; and let this process of thought, of effort, and of action be entered upon as one which is never to be abandoned, until the end proposed by it is accomplished—until the only living and true God is loved and chosen, as his God forever; and we say that in this way the work of his regeneration, through grace, *may be* accomplished. On this course he may now enter, instead of rejecting or perverting, or abusing or sinfully using, the truths of God another moment. In this way, he may become a child of God, while truth and duty are present in his thoughts. . . .

. . . The tendency of the selfish principle being to subserve and gratify itself in all specific action amounts to a tendency to protect and perpetuate its own existence. Accordingly we shall see that the transition of the mind from the supreme love of the world to the supreme love of God, without the suspension of the entire influence of the former, and of all acts dictated by it, is in the most absolute sense impossible. Before the supreme affections of the heart can be transferred from one object to another, the latter must be made the subject of consideration, and also of comparison with the former, as the means of good; and this must be done with the design of choosing *anew* one or the other as the supreme good. But so long as the selfish principle continues active in the mind, the only possible voluntary acts are those which are designed and fitted to subserve and gratify this principle. . . .

. . . The only supposable acts of a sinner with which his regeneration can be connected involve the suspended influence of the selfish principle; and how impossible it is, that without such a suspension, the heart should be changed. So entirely does this principle, while active in the mind, control and direct the thoughts, and modify and check all the constitutional emotions and feelings in subserviency to itself; so entirely does it employ them on the things of earth and of time; so absolutely does it enlist the whole man to secure its own gratification, protection, and perpetuity that it shuts every avenue of the mind against the sanctifying approach of truth. No dungeon was ever more firmly barred, or more deeply dark, than all the inner chambers of the soul, when under the active tyranny of this principle. How profoundly conscience sleeps! How is every sensibility to the excellence and worth of divine realities hushed! How relentless too in its dominion, and how desperate and triumphant in its resistance of truth and of the God of truth! Were there no other access to the inner man, except through this principle of the heart; were there nothing to which the motives of the gospel could be addressed but the hardihood of this fell spirit—no way to overcome this "strong man" except by direct assault, then for aught we can see, the *moral* transformation of the soul, were hopeless, even to Omnipotence.

We have thus attempted to show that *no acts of the sinner, done while the selfish principle remains active in the heart, constitute using the means of regeneration*; first, as they have no tendency to produce the change; secondly, as they have no necessary or real connexion with it, and thirdly, as they have a direct and fatal influence to prevent it.

We have dwelt longer on this part of the subject, not merely to expose doctrinal error, but chiefly on account of the dangerous practical tendency of inculcating it upon sinners. The position appears to us incontrovertible that so long as the sinner believes that any acts done while the selfish principle remains active in the heart are necessary to his regeneration, he will never be regenerated. . . . While he regards the course proposed, as that which furnishes the only hope of his regeneration, why should he, or rather how can he, adopt any other? We are aware that exhortations to this course have been pronounced important and even indispensable, in order that the sinner may learn in his own experience its utter uselessness, and thus be led to despair of all efforts of his own. Despair of all efforts of his own, when life and death depend, under God, on effort! This would either sink him at once into sullen devotedness to sin, or awaken the frenzy of a "certain fearful looking for of judgment and fiery indignation." Despair of all efforts of his own, even of all efforts to love God, or to think of him! This were death. That he may learn, in his own experience, the uselessness of the course proposed? But why not let him know its uselessness at the outset? Cannot such truth be communicated by instruction; and must a sinner continue in sin, to discover how vain it is to perpetrate iniquity as the means of holiness? Why not then, instead of leaving him to ascertain the uselessness of such a course by experiment, give him instruction according to truth? Why exhort him to the doing of that as the means of an end, which is confessedly useless in respect to that end? He may die and go to judgment in his sins, while making the experiment. Why then put his soul in jeopardy by teaching falsehood? Do you say that you inculcate the necessity of immediate repentance? Be it so. But you also inculcate the *necessity* of previous sin! And if the sinner adopts your instructions on this point, he must regard the sinful acts inculcated as all that are necessary or useful to the end in view. He must believe that these *may be,* and that nothing else will be connected with his regeneration, i.e., to continue in sin, will therefore be all that will be attempted. Neither the practicability of immediate duty nor its obligations will so reach the mind as to prompt corresponding action. The very objects which truth presents, as those on which to fix the thoughts and affections, and which should be his instant and whole concern, will under this relation be thought of. Instead of an active agent summoning his powers of action to the immediate performance of duty, you will see only a statue-like being, waiting in motionless dependence to receive what, in sovereign kindness, may be given; or rather you will see the moral agent active only to prevent his regeneration. Regeneration, conversion, giving God the heart, call it what you will, though always to be ascribed to the interposing grace of God, is ACTION on the part of the sinner; and can never take place, unless the objects of holy affection are brought before the mind as objects on which the affections *are now to be fixed*. But this view of these objects is in absolute contrariety to the views produced by inculcating the necessity of prior sinful action; and the sinner can no more give his heart to God in holy affection while performing such action than were he exclusively occupied in perpetrating any other abomination. It is not then merely the impropriety and error of calling such acts and doing using the means of regeneration, but it is the inculcation of them as such upon sinners, in view of its fatal tendency, which we deplore. We do not say that the auspicious inconsistency of urging the duty of immediate repentance does not often counteract this tendency; nor that sinners do not in their own experience often learn the vanity of such efforts and the falsehood of such teaching, and act under the conviction that present duty must be a present act, but we say that the true uncounteracted tendency of such teaching is fatal—that its appropriate effect is continued sin and final ruin. . . .

From Nathaniel W. Taylor, "Review of Spring on the Means of Regeneration," *Quarterly Christian Spectator* 1 (1829): 1–40, 209–34, 481–508, 692–712.

Nathaniel W. Taylor

LECTURES ON THE MORAL GOVERNMENT
OF GOD (1859)

The theme of God's moral government pervaded Nathaniel W. Taylor's thought, serving to integrate the Taylorites' theological concerns. Practically speaking, this meant that no matter what the subject under discussion, God's sovereign grace was consistently depicted in New Haven—à la Edwards and other Edwardseans—in moral rather than natural or physiological terms. Granting that God always effects what God intends to effect in us, Taylor claimed that he does so morally, by winning over our wills, rather than physically, irresistibly, or coercively.

The selection below comes from the first lecture in Taylor's famous two-volume *Lectures on the Moral Government of God*. Though posthumously published, these lectures date back to Taylor's earliest years as a Yale professor. They were a staple of the curriculum—refined throughout his thirty-five years of teaching at the divinity school—an emblem of the New Haven style of thought. The lecture below provides a taste of the theological repast on which hundreds of students dined while in New Haven. (Taylor taught a total of 815 students while at Yale, sending them by the dozens into the churches of New England and the western frontier.) Full of the Taylorites' signature emphasis on God's moral influence on the actions of his creatures, it makes for a fitting end to the section on New Haven's Edwardseans.

☙

Section 1

What Is a Perfect Moral Government? or Moral Government in the Abstract

LECTURE 1

Can we determine the nature of a perfect Moral Government?—A perfect Moral Government defined.—The definition explained and vindicated in the following particulars:

I. Moral Government is an influence on moral beings.

II. Moral Government implies a moral Governor.

III. Moral Government is designed so to control the action of moral beings as to secure the great end of action on their part.

IV. The influence of a perfect Moral Government is the influence of authority. . . .

By a perfect moral government I intend—
THE INFLUENCE OF THE AUTHORITY, OR OF THE RIGHTFUL AUTHORITY OF A MORAL GOVERNOR ON MORAL BEINGS, DESIGNED SO TO CONTROL THEIR ACTION AS TO SECURE THE GREAT END OF ACTION ON THEIR PART, THROUGH THE MEDIUM OF LAW.

In explaining and justifying this definition, I propose to consider the several parts of it, more or less extensively, as the case may seem to require.

I. *A moral government is an influence on moral beings,* or on *beings capable of moral action.*

While this will be readily admitted, there are some things involved in it, which demand consideration. One is that the influence of moral government being an influence on moral beings and designed to control moral action is as diverse in its nature from the influence of physical causes as moral action is from a physical effect; or as a moral cause is from a physical cause. It is an influence, which is designed and fitted to give, not the necessity, but merely the certainty of its effect; and which leaves the moral liberty of the subject unimpaired. Hence, it is not essential to this influence that it actually secure the kind of action which it is fitted to secure. A perfect moral government may exist with all its influence, and yet be wholly counteracted in its designed effect on its subjects, since it is obvious that such a government may be maintained over subjects in revolt as well as over subjects who are loyal. Rebellion against government cannot exist when there is no government. A perfect moral government then, as a government over moral beings, in respect to any cause of action giving the necessity of action, leaves every subject as free to perform the action which it aims to prevent as to perform that which it aims to secure.

II. A perfect moral government implies *a moral governor.*

215

In this respect a moral government differs from a *moral system* as a species differs from a genus. A moral system *may* be conceived to exist either with or without a moral governor. We can conceive of moral beings, who should act under the direct influence of motives, so far as these reach the mind in the perceived nature, tendencies, and consequences of action, though there were no influence of a superior being sustaining the relation of a ruler or moral governor. The direct influence of motives, as these are thus apprehended by the mind, and that influence which results from the character and relation of a moral governor, though different, may yet coexist; and either may be supposed, to exist without the other. The former without the latter would simply imply a moral system without a moral government. The latter with or without the former would imply a moral system in that particular form which includes a moral government. The peculiar influence therefore, which arises from the character and relation of a moral governor, whether other influences combine with it or not, is the essential constituting influence of moral government. So far as moral beings act under the peculiar influences of a moral governor, so far and no farther do they act under the influence of moral government.

III. The influence of a perfect moral government is *designed so to control the action of moral beings as to secure the great end of action on their part.*

It will be admitted that this influence is designed to control the action of moral beings in relation to some end which depends on their action in a community of such beings, and which is the best end, and in this sense the great end of such action. What, then, is this end? I answer—It is the production of well-being, even the highest well-being of all, and the prevention of misery, even the highest misery of all. A moral being is capable of performing two and only two kinds of moral action, and as a subject of moral government, is under an absolute necessity of performing one or the other in all action. He cannot, as a moral being, be inactive. His nature and relations necessarily exclude alike all inaction and all neutrality of action, or action in which he does not act morally. Again, the nature—the peculiar powers and properties of a moral being—show that he is qualified to perform, what no other being is qualified to perform—that kind of action, which tends to produce the best conceivable end of all action, the highest conceivable well-being of all sentient beings, both of himself and of all others. It is this nature of a moral being, which gives to his existence its peculiar value—its pre-eminent worth, compared with the nature of any other being. It is this, which, as a creature, raises man to companionship with his Creator and with creatures the most exalted, and brings him under obligation to act with them in principle, in purpose and in all subordinate and executive doings, for the accomplishment of the great end of all action here on earth, and amid the scenes of eternity.

Exalted thus by his nature as a moral being, he is by the same nature qualified to act in a manner which tends to defeat the great end of his creation, and to bring on himself and on all other beings, unmingled and perfect misery. And, what adds inconceivable importance to such a being is that he cannot avoid, as we have said, acting in one or the other of these two modes of acting now specified. Even in every subordinate action, he acts from principle, he acts with or in the form of a supreme elective preference. These existing together are often called his action; and its tendency as moral action is the tendency of his action in its principle; or rather, the tendency of the action in principle is its true tendency. To neglect to act in that mode which is fitted to secure the great and true end of all action on his part, viz., the highest well-being of all—is not only to sacrifice and defeat that *end*, but it is necessarily to act in that mode, which in its true tendency is fitted to produce the opposite result—the highest misery of all.

Every thing of real significance in the being of a moral agent, viewed in relation to himself and to other beings, every thing virtuous and praiseworthy in the use of his exalted powers, every thing vicious and blamable in the abuse of them, every thing that is dignified and honorable, every thing that is mean and disgraceful, every thing that affords inward peace and triumph, every thing that brings remorse and despair—every good and every evil to himself and to others—all, all depends on action. The highest happiness and the highest misery of all, all that blesses and all that curses, life and death, are in the power of action. Such issues, according to the true nature and tendencies of things, depend on the action of moral beings.

Here, then, the design of a perfect moral government is manifest. The design of the pendulum of a clock to control and direct its motion, so as to mark the division of time as the true end of the machine, is not more obvious than is the design of a perfect moral government so to control the action of moral beings as to secure the great end of action on their part, viz., the production of the highest well-being of all, and the prevention of the highest misery of all.

IV. The influence of a perfect moral government is *the influence of authority*.

By the influence of authority, I mean that influence which results from that right to command, which is founded in competence and disposition to govern in the best manner, and which imposes an obligation to obey. In other words, it is the influence of a right to command which imposes an obligation to obey, as this right results from competence and disposition to give and maintain the best law. Intelligent voluntary beings never act voluntarily without acting from a regard to their own well-being. Instead, however, of relying wholly, or even partially on their own wisdom or judgment, in respect to the best mode of action, or the mode in which they ought to act, they may rely partially or even wholly on the decision of superior wisdom and superior goodness. It is true that the subjects of a moral government may possess such knowledge of the nature and tendency of action on their part as to know, irrespectively of any decision of the moral governor, that their own highest well-being as well as that of all others can be secured only by conformity to the law of his government. In this way natural good and evil as directly known to result from the nature and tendency of different kinds of action may concur with the influence of authority to secure their conformity to the law. But in that conformity to law which is secured by the single influence of natural good and evil as motives, there is no recognition of the moral governor's authority. The influence of authority is not the direct influence of natural good and evil reaching the mind through the known nature and tendency of action. It is that influence which results from one's having a right to command by virtue of the superior power, wisdom, and goodness, which qualify him to govern in the best manner. So far as this influence reaches moral beings, whether resisted or unresisted by them, they are under the influence of moral government. Where this influence does not exist, there is nothing which can be called moral government. . . .

Some evidently rest the right to govern by law simply on the power to execute its sanctions. This theory obviously places the entire influence of moral government in the influence of natural good and of natural evil, as the one is promised to obedience and the other threatened to disobedience; viewed only as motives to persuade to the one and dissuade from the other. According to this view, might gives right, and the veriest tyrant with power to execute the sanctions of law, combined with the most fell malignity, has a righteous claim for the unqualified submission of his subjects. On this scheme there can be no fixed standard, no permanent and essential elements of right and wrong moral action. All moral distinctions are subverted, and any being having the power would have the right to fill the universe with misery. This monstrous theory of moral government is the legitimate consequence of the selfishness of this selfish world, looking only at natural good and evil in the form of legal reward and penalty, as the only motives to secure obedience and prevent disobedience to law. No account is made of the essential element of a moral government, *the influence of authority*. The right to govern, which results from competence and disposition to govern in the best manner—the right which imposes an obligation to obey, is unknown, and obedience and disobedience to a moral governor as having this right are impossible. . . .

From Nathaniel W. Taylor, *Lectures on the Moral Government of God*, vol. 1 (New York: Clark, Austin, and Smith, 1859), 1–15.

PART 7

Finney and the New Measures

If Samuel Hopkins and Joseph Bellamy represent the first generation of the New England Theology, and Nathanael Emmons, John Smalley, Nathan Strong, and Edwards the Younger represent the second, then its third (and for all practical purposes, last) generation includes Nathaniel W. Taylor, Harriet Beecher Stowe, Lyman Beecher, Edwards Amasa Park, James Harris Fairchild, and, most surprising of all, Charles G. Finney (1792–1875). It is one measure of how much the New England Theology had developed its own intellectual momentum that Finney has only rarely been thought of as part of the Edwardsean lineage. His reputation as a pragmatic and hugely successful preacher of revivals, his biting contempt for conventional Calvinist teachings about the inability of sinners to repent, and even his occasional criticisms of Edwards on free will and original sin seem to give credence to Finney's own claims to be a self-made man in theology, a Jacksonian original. But any close reading of Finney's published sermons, essays, and memoirs quickly reveals how much Finney owed to the New England Theology. And both his associates in the venture that led to the development of Oberlin College and the Old School Presbyterians who were the most resistant to the blandishments of the New England Theology recognized in Finney the offspring of the most radical forms of the New Divinity. James Waddell Alexander (the son of Old School Presbyterianism's banner bearer, Archibald Alexander of Princeton Seminary) thought Finney was simply "an odious caricature of old Hopkinsian divinity." Finney's more sympathetic colleague at Oberlin, Henry Cowles, confidently identified Finney's theology with that "commonly known as . . . the theology expounded by Edwards, Bellamy, and Hopkins."

In fact, to follow the outline of Finney's favorite topics in theology is to revisit most of the ideas originally fashioned by the New Divinity. Finney's notorious announcement, in his *Lectures on Revivals of Religion* (1835), that revivals were "not a miracle, nor dependent on a miracle, in any sense," was Finney's sensational way of restating the obligation imposed by a sinner's natural ability to repent. He never denied the doctrine of election—his *Lectures on Systematic Theology* (2 vols., 1846–47) affirmed that "none but the elect are converted"—nor did he deny that "man alone never does or can convert a sinner." What he wanted to affirm, however, was that sinners "do not become Christian by virtue of any physical change in the substance of either body or soul." He was, in other words, an Exerciser, and it is no coincidence that his most provocative sermon, "Sinners Bound to Change Their Own Hearts" (1836), shared the same ideas as Nathanael Emmons's "Duty of Sinners to Make Themselves a New Heart." Even Finney's doctrine of perfectionism, which became the ethical keystone of the so-called Oberlin Theology, was based on the Hopkinsian idea of pure, disinterested benevolence rather than on the perfectionist teachings of John Wesley. When, in the 1840s, Finney published his first outright criticisms of Edwards, the criticisms were influenced not by a repudiation of Calvinism but by Nathaniel W. Taylor and the New Haven theologians.

James Harris Fairchild

OBERLIN THEOLOGY

James Harris Fairchild (1817–1902) was one of Charles G. Finney's earliest students in the original Oberlin Collegiate Institute, from 1835 to 1838, and he later succeeded Finney both as professor of moral philosophy and as president of Oberlin College. Born in Stockbridge, Massachusetts, Fairchild—along with Asa Mahan, James Thome, Henry Cowles, and John Morgan—was one of the principal architects of the Oberlin Theology. However, when he was invited to contribute an article on the Oberlin Theology to John McClintock and James Strong's *Cyclopaedia of Biblical, Theological, and Ecclesiastical Literature* (1867–87), Fairchild was at pains to stress how much the Oberlin theologians stood on the shoulders of the New England Theology. "The Ethical Philosophy inculcated by Mr. Finney and his associates of later times is essentially that of the elder Edwards," Fairchild explained. Moral action occurs, as it had for Edwards, "under the motives which gather about him." But more like Nathanael Emmons, "sin is a voluntary failure to meet obligation." Rather than locating depravity in a sinful nature, Fairchild and the Oberliners followed Emmons in fixing "righteousness or holiness" in "a voluntary conformity to obligation, such as is always in the power of every moral agent." Similarly, Fairchild defined the atonement in governmental terms, codified Oberlin perfectionism as the full use of natural ability, and singled out benevolence as "the grand element of all virtue." However radical this seemed, Fairchild insisted that it was nothing less than "the theory . . . presented by . . . President Edwards . . . and by his pupil and friend Samuel Hopkins."

❧

Oberlin Theology. An impression has very generally prevailed that the theological views inculcated at Oberlin College by the late Rev. Charles G. Finney and his associates involved a considerable departure from the accepted orthodox faith; and the term Oberlin Theology was for many years supposed to embrace very serious errors, or even "damnable heresies." There has doubtless been much misapprehension on the subject, and while these teachers have held views of their own on some points of metaphysical and ethical theology, and even of practical religion, there has been no such divergence from the accepted doctrines of the Church as to warrant the idea of a new theology.

The type of theology and doctrine inculcated has been the New School Calvinism, of which the characteristic thought is that all responsible character pertains to the will in its voluntary attitude and action, and that each moral agent determines for himself in the exercise of his own freedom under the motives which gather about him whatever is praiseworthy or blameworthy in his character and life—that sin is a voluntary failure to meet obligation and that nothing else is sin, and that righteousness or holiness is a voluntary conformity to obligation, such as is always in the power of every moral agent. Anything desirable or undesirable in the nature or thought or feeling, which lies beyond the range of voluntary action, is not a matter of immediate obligation, and can be neither holiness nor sin. Hence neither sin nor holiness can be transmitted or inherited, or imputed in the sense of reckoned to the account of one in whose will it has not originated, As punishment is or can be inflicted only as an expression of blameworthiness. No one can be liable to punishment for Adam's sin because he cannot be blameworthy for any sin but his own. Just as impossible is it that one should be forgiven any sin but his own.

Repentance is the renunciation of sin, an obligation which presses upon every sinner, and is always within his power. The power to sin involves the power to renounce it, and this voluntary renunciation of sin is the change required as a condition of salvation. The work of the Holy Spirit in the sinner's conversion is a moral work, presenting the motives which induce repentance, and the subsequent work of sanctification and preservation is essentially of the same nature as work accomplished by the Spirit through the truth.

The sovereignty of God works always in harmony with the sinner's freedom and responsibility of the creature, so that one factor in man's salvation must always be his own voluntary consent and co-operation. As the sin of one cannot be imputed to another so neither can righteousness or merit. Hence the atonement cannot involve the transfer either of any guilt to Christ or of his righteousness or merit to us but consists rather in such an exhibition in the Cross of Christ of divine love and faithfulness—of man's sin and ill desert, as to make the remission of penalty safe and right in the case of the penitent sinner. These views, in general, characterize what has been called the Oberlin Theology.

The Ethical Philosophy inculcated by Mr. Finney and his associates of later times is essentially that of the elder Edwards, which made the wellbeing or blessedness of the sentient universe the *summum bonum* or ultimate good, and the voluntary regard for this good—respect for all interests according to their value, which is called benevolence—the grand element of all virtue. This benevolence is the love which is the fulfilling of the law—not a mere Kindly or considerate feeling, or any emotion whatsoever, but an attitude of will giving to every interest its proper place, exercised towards men, being capable of good, beginning with God, whose worth is infinite and coming down to the meanest of his creatures—embracing alike the evil and the good, the just and the unjust. This benevolence is consistent with every natural emotion involving complacency when exercised toward other virtuous beings and displacency when exercised toward the wicked, maintaining the same essential character—regard for the wellbeing of its object.

This voluntary attitude called benevolence is the constant element in all virtuous character, and the source of all virtuous action. It is the root of all the particular virtues and constitutes the virtuous element in them all. Justice and Mercy and obedience and veracity, and the like become virtues by being expressions of benevolence under varying conditions, and they cease to be virtuous when this benevolence fails. All duty finds its binding force and its limitations in benevolence. The duty of benevolence is apprehended intuitively and rationally upon the apprehension of well-being, and can never fail to be duty to Every moral being. This is absolute righteousness. All other duties are seen to be duties from this tendency in the promotion of well-being, and this and executive duties. Hence this schema is distinguished from every system of utilitarianism. Benevolence is seen to be binding from its own inherent nature and not from its tendency, while all executive action prompted by benevolence is binding by reason of its apprehended tendency to promote the good. The term utilitarianism is a misnomer applied to such a system.

The faculty by which the primal duty of benevolence is apprehended is conscience, and its affirmation, in its own sphere, is inevitable and infallible. Every moral being affirms the duty of benevolence by the very necessity of his nature. Hence in reference to primary subjective duty, the deliverance of conscience is forever the same and always right. A being whose conscience failed in this respect would cease to be a moral being. As to all relative duties the judgment must decide what on the whole will tend to promote well-being or the good; then conscience follows the judgment and enjoins the performance of this apprehended duty as an expression of benevolence. But the judgment is fallible, and there may be, and often is, misjudgment on the subject of outward or objective duty, and conscience may thus require us to do what is outwardly wrong. Still one must follow the best judgment we can obtain, and the error is a mistake and not a sin. The moral character is right while the conscience is followed in the maintenance of the benevolent attitude. Blameworthiness can be involved only in a failure in this required ultimate attitude of the will. Hence a moral being always knows his duty—that which is immediately binding upon him, and meeting this duty he is truly conscientious, and at the same time, truly righteous. His mistakes require correction, Enlightenment, not forgiveness.

As benevolence is the whole of virtue, so the refusal to be benevolent is the whole of sin, whatever the motive which incites it. These motives are always the solicitations of impulse, desires, or passion, which turn the will aside from the obligation of benevolence. The sin takes its form from the immediate impulse to which the will subjects itself; but the essence of the sin is the refusal to assume that benevolent attitude of the will which reason or conscience requires. The sinner then is not pursuing his own good as his supreme end. He sacrifices his duty and his good alike in his subjection to an unworthy impulse. He is "Carnally minded"—cares for the flesh, the desires. Benevolence requires him to regard his own well-being as well as that of his neighbor, but he sacrifices both in his voluntary subjection to desire. Every Moral being, in the exercise of his freedom, stands between the Motives which the reason presents which urge to benevolence—regard for the well-being of the universe because of its value, and the motives which the desires or impulses present, urging to gratification immediate or remote, to the neglect of the true good of himself and of the universe at large. The character and action determined by the motives of the reason are right—they meet obligation. Determined by the motives of the flesh, the desires and passions, they are wrong and are in violation of obligation. The righteousness on the one hand and the sinfulness on the other must lie in the voluntary attitude assumed in the acceptance of one or the other class of motives which address the will; and this character, right or wrong, remains while the voluntary attitude remains, whether the circumstances of outward action do or do not. Virtue or righteousness lies in that primary attitude of benevolence; virtuous action is the action which springs from that benevolence. Sin is in the refusal to be benevolent, and sinful action is the expression of the unbenevolent will in the outward life.

It is a peculiarity of the Oberlin Ethical philosophy to regard virtue or righteousness and sin as thus, in their own nature antagonistic to each other, each being contradictory of the other and necessarily exclusive of it. Virtue being benevolence and sin the refusal to be benevolent, they cannot coexist in the same will. The will must be, at any given time, wholly in one attitude or the other. They may alternate, one giving place to the other, but in the unity of action which of necessity belongs to the will they cannot coexist. The supposition of coexistence involves essentially a twofold personality, capable of maintaining at the same instant contradictory ultimate attitudes of will. Hence the sinner, in turning from his sin discards it utterly for the time, and yields his whole will to God; and the good man falling into sin fails utterly in the benevolent attitude of the will, and so far as his moral action is concerned, during that lapse he is wholly wrong. Many of his former experiences and plans and executive purposes may remain unchanged, but the element of righteousness, the benevolent attitude of the will must be wholly wanting.

This view of the moral action as necessarily either right or wrong, and of Moral Character as necessarily, at any time, either one thing or the other, has shaped what has become known as the Oberlin doctrine of sanctification. The view first promulgated at Oberlin by Mr. Finney and others was based upon the common apprehension that some what of sin still remains in the Character and action of the Converted man, coexisting with his obedience. The problem of sanctification then must be to eliminate this remnant of sin and make the obedience entire, complete, and permanent, and it is generally assumed that it would be permanent or that it should become entire. This view led to the idea of a special experience, corresponding with the original Conversion, in which the Christian rises from a partial to a complete obedience. The attainment of this condition is always possible and always obligatory—just as the original conversion was obligatory and possible to the sinner. The only difficulty in the way must be a partial and imperfect faith. On this view there were supposed to be two classes of Christians, the simply Converted rendering a partial consecration and obedience, and the entirely sanctified, whose consecration and obedience were entire. The preaching of this privilege and duty of entire sanctification, as thus apprehended, in the community at Oberlin, led to a very general quickening of the religious life, and to many marked experiences regarded at the time as the special experience called sanctification. But in the fuller development of the conception of moral action as necessarily simple forbidding the consistence of sin and holiness, a restatement of the doctrine of sanctification became necessary. Thus conversion becomes necessarily entire Consecration and obedience and faith, as moral exercises are necessarily complete. The difficulty with the regenerate soul is not that he has only partially surrendered his will, but that he is weak, inexperienced, and temptable, liable at any moment to lapse into sin under the presence of temptation. Sanctification thus becomes a growth, an attainment of experience and strength—not to be found in a special experience, rising from a partial to an entire consecration, but in the attainment of stability and spiritual power by successive enlightenments and baptisms of the Spirit, and by "patient continuance in well-doing." No clear line of division can separate the sanctified and unsanctified Christians. Every believer is sanctified in the sense of being entirely consecrated, and there are as many degrees of enlightenment and strength and stability as there are varying experiences in the Church of God. With this Clearer view of the Nature of Moral action, the inculcation of the attainment of sanctification by one special experience has ceased to be a feature of the religious instruction at Oberlin. Christians are encouraged to expect baptisms of the Spirit to qualify them for duty and to give victory over temptation.

The theoretical and practical views maintained at Oberlin may be gathered from the *Oberlin Evangelist*, published at Oberlin from 1839 to 1862 (24 volumes); the *Oberlin Quarterly Review*, published at Oberlin from 1845 (4 volumes); *Finney's Systematic Theology*, 2 vols., published at Oberlin 1845–46 and republished in London in one volume in 1851; and *Fairchild's Moral Philosophy* (New York: Sheldon & Co., 1869).

From James Harris Fairchild Papers, Oberlin College Archives. Published in revised form in the *Cyclopaedia of Biblical, Theological, and Ecclesiastical Literature*, vol. 7, ed. John McClintock and James Strong (New York: Harper & Brothers, 1877), 277–78.

Charles G. Finney

LECTURES ON REVIVALS
OF RELIGION (1835)

Charles G. Finney was born in the heart of the old Edwardsean country of western Connecticut and was influenced by the preaching of Peter Starr in the New Divinity parish of Warren, Connecticut. Originally trained to be a lawyer, Finney experienced a dramatic conversion in 1821 and was ordained as an evangelist by the New School Presbyterians in Oneida County in western New York. He proved his mettle as a preacher through a succession of revival missions, culminating in 1831 in the great revival he led in Rochester, New York. He briefly led the founding of a New York City mission, the Chatham Street Chapel, but his opposition to slavery aroused bitter antagonism within the New York commercial community. The chapel was mobbed, and in 1834, Finney suffered a breakdown. The new Collegiate Institute in Oberlin, Ohio, invited him to serve as a visiting professor of theology in 1835, and after 1837, Finney made Oberlin his permanent home.

Finney's *Lectures on Revivals of Religion* were originally delivered in New York City and published as a series in the *New York Evangelist* in December 1834 and January 1835. Issued in book form in May 1835, the *Lectures* sold twelve thousand copies at once. Finney's principal task in the *Lectures* was to demolish the notion that sin inhered in a substantial nature and that a divine miracle was required to change that nature. Instead, sin was a characteristic of the human will, and trying to depict revivals as miracles only gave sinners an excuse to dodge their responsibility to submit to God. The *Lectures* recommended the use of the "new measures" Finney had developed in the Upstate New York revivals. These included a more direct, confrontational approach in speaking to congregations, new and more stimulating forms of hymnody, the mobilization of the laity, the use of special-purpose revival meetings, and the calling of sinners to an anxious seat to demonstrate that sinners really did possess natural ability—all of which he justified by the example of Jonathan Edwards.

⧼⧽

Lecture 1: What a Revival of Religion Is

Religion is the work of man. It is something for man to do. It consists in obeying God. It is man's duty. It is true God induces him to do it. He influences him by His Spirit, because of his great wickedness and reluctance to obey. . . . The ground of necessity for such a prayer is that men are wholly indisposed to obey; and unless God interpose the influence of His Spirit, not a man on earth will ever obey the commands of God.

. . . Almost all religion in the world has been produced by revivals. God has found it necessary to take advantage of the excitability there is in mankind, to produce powerful excitements among them, before He can lead them to obey. Men are so sluggish, there are so many things to lead their minds off from religion and to oppose the influence of the Gospel, that it is necessary to raise an excitement among them, till the tide rises so high as to sweep away the opposing obstacles. They must be so aroused that they will break over these counteracting influences, before they will obey God.

. . . There is so little *principle* in the Church, so little firmness and stability of purpose, that unless it is greatly excited, it will go back from the path of duty, and do nothing to promote the glory of God. The state of the world is still such, and probably will be till the millennium is fully come, that religion must be mainly promoted by means of revivals. How long and how often has the experiment been tried, to bring the Church to act steadily for God, without these periodical excitements! Many good men have supposed, and still suppose, that the best way to promote religion is to go along *uniformly*, and gather in the ungodly gradually, and without excitement. But however sound such reasoning may appear in the abstract, *facts* demonstrate its futility. . . . The great political and other worldly excitements that agitate Christendom are all unfriendly to religion, and divert the mind from the interests of the soul. Now, these excitements can only be counteracted by *religious* excitements. And until there is sufficient religious principle in the world to put down irreligious excitements, it is in vain to try to promote religion, except by counteracting excitements. This is true in philosophy, and it is a historical fact. . . .

A Revival Is Not a Miracle

1. A miracle has been generally defined to be a Divine interference, setting aside, or suspending, the laws of nature. A revival is not a miracle in this sense. All the laws of matter and mind remain in force. They are neither suspended nor set aside in a revival.

2. A revival is not a miracle according to another definition of the term "miracle"—something above the powers of nature. There is nothing in religion beyond the ordinary powers of nature. It consists entirely in the *right exercise* of the powers of nature. It is just that, and nothing else. When mankind becomes religious, they are not *enabled* to put forth exertions which they were unable before to put forth. They only exert powers which they had before, in a different way, and use them for the glory of God.

3. A revival is not a miracle, nor dependent on a miracle, in any sense. It is a purely philosophical result of the right use of the constituted means—as much so as any other effect produced by the application of means. . . . There has long been an idea prevalent that promoting religion has something very peculiar in it, not to be judged of by the ordinary rules of cause and effect; in short, that there is no connection of the means with the result, and no tendency in the means to produce the effect. No doctrine is more dangerous than this to the prosperity of the Church, and nothing more absurd.

Suppose a man were to go and preach this doctrine among farmers, regarding their sowing of grain. Let him tell them that God is a Sovereign, and will give them a crop only when it pleases Him, and that for them to plough, and plant, and labour, as if they expected to raise a crop, is very wrong, that it amounts to taking the work out of the hands of God, that it is an interference with His Sovereignty, and that there is no connection between the means and the result on which they can depend. Suppose the farmers should believe such a doctrine? Why, they would starve the world to death.

Just such results would follow on the Church being persuaded that promoting religion is somehow so mysteriously a subject of Divine Sovereignty that there is no natural connection between the means and the end. In fact, what *are* the results? Why, generation after generation has gone to hell, while the Church has been dreaming and waiting for God to save them without the use of the means. . . .

What a Revival Is

It presupposes that the Church is sunk down in a backslidden state and a revival consists in the return of the Church from her backslidings, and in the conversion of sinners.

1. A revival always includes conviction of sin on the part of the Church. Backslidden professors cannot wake up and begin right away in the service of God, without deep searchings of heart. The fountains of sin need to be broken up. In a true revival, Christians are always brought under such conviction; they see their sins in such a light that often they find it impossible to maintain a hope of their acceptance with God. It does not always go to that extent, but there are always, in a genuine revival, deep convictions of sin, and often cases of abandoning all hope.

2. Backslidden Christians will be brought to repentance. A revival is nothing else than a new beginning of obedience to God. Just as in the case of a converted sinner, the first step is a deep repentance, a breaking down of heart, a getting down into the dust before God, with deep humility, and a forsaking of sin. . . .

The Agencies Employed

Ordinarily, there are employed in the work of conversion three agents and one instrument. The agents are God; some person who brings the truth to bear on the mind; and the sinner himself. The instrument is the truth. There are always two agents, God and the sinner, employed and active in every case of genuine conversion.

1. The agency of God is twofold: by His Providence and by His Spirit.

(a) By His providential government He so arranges events as to bring the sinner's mind and the truth in contact. He brings the sinner where the truth reaches his ears or his eyes. . . .

(b) God's special agency by His Holy Spirit. Having direct access to the mind, and knowing infinitely well the whole history and state of each individual sinner, He employs that truth which is best adapted to his particular case, and then drives it home with Divine power. He gives it such vividness, strength, and power that the sinner quails, and throws down his weapons of rebellion, and turns to the Lord. Under His influence the truth burns its way like fire. He makes the truth stand out in such aspects that it crushes the proudest man down with the weight of a mountain. If men were *disposed* to obey God, the truth is given with sufficient clearness in the Bible; and from preaching they could learn all that is necessary for them to know. But because they are wholly *disinclined* to obey it, God makes it clear before their minds, and pours in upon their souls a blaze of convincing light which they cannot withstand; and they yield to it, obey God, and are saved.

2. The agency of men is commonly employed. Men are not mere *instruments* in the hands of God. Truth is the instrument. The preacher is a moral agent in the work: he acts; he is not a mere passive instrument; he is voluntary in promoting the conversion of sinners.

3. The agency of the sinner himself. The conversion of a sinner consists in his obeying the truth. It is therefore impossible it should take place without his agency, for it consists in his acting right. He is influenced to this by the agency of God and by the agency of men. . . . The whole drift of a revival, and everything about it, is designed to present the truth *to* your mind, for your obedience or resistance.

Remarks

. . . Revivals have been greatly hindered by mistaken notions concerning the Sovereignty of God. Many people have supposed God's Sovereignty to be something very different from what it is. They have supposed it to be such an arbitrary disposal of events, and particularly of the gift of His Spirit, as precluded a rational employment of means for promoting a revival. But there is no evidence from the Bible that God exercises any such sovereignty. . . . He exercises a universal superintendence and control. And yet every event in nature has been brought about by means. He administers neither providence nor grace with that sort of sovereignty that dispenses with the use of means. There is no more sovereignty in the one than in the other.

And yet some people are terribly alarmed at all direct efforts to promote a revival, and they cry out: "You are trying to get up a revival in your own strength. Take care, you are interfering with the Sovereignty of God. Better keep along in the usual course, and let God give a revival when He thinks it is best. God is a Sovereign, and it is very wrong for you to attempt to get up a revival, just because *you think* a revival is needed." This is just such preaching as the devil wants. And men cannot do the devil's work more effectually than by preaching up the Sovereignty of God as a reason why we should not put forth efforts to produce a revival.

Lecture II: When a Revival Is to Be Expected

. . . Nothing but a revival of religion can prevent the means of grace from doing a great injury to the ungodly. Without a revival they will grow harder and harder under preaching, and will experience a more horrible damnation than they would if they had never heard the Gospel. Your children and your friends will go down to a much more horrible fate in hell, in consequence of the means of grace, if there are no revivals to convert them to God. Better were it for them if there were no means of grace, no sanctuary, no Bible, no preaching, than to live and die where there is no revival. The Gospel is the savour of death unto death, if it is not made a savour of life unto life. . . .

Most of the time the labours of ministers are, it would seem, directed to other objects. They seem to preach and labour with no particular design to effect the *immediate* conversion of sinners, and then it need not be expected that there will be a revival under their preaching. There never will be a revival till *somebody* makes particular efforts for this end. But when the attention of a minister is directed to the state of the families in his congregation, and when his heart is full of feeling of the necessity of a revival, and he puts forth the proper efforts for this end, then you may be prepared to expect a revival. As I have explained, the connection between the right use of means for a revival, and a revival, is as philosophically sure as between the right use of means to raise grain, and a crop of wheat. I believe, in fact, it is more certain, and that there are fewer instances of failure.

. . . A revival may be expected whenever Christians are found willing to make the sacrifices necessary to carry it on. They must be willing to sacrifice their feelings, their business, their time, to help forward the work. Ministers must be willing to lay out their strength, and to jeopard their health and life. They must be willing to offend the impenitent by plain and faithful dealing, and perhaps offend many members of the Church who will not come up to the work. They must take a decided stand with the revival, be the consequences what they may. They must be prepared to go on with the work even though they should lose the affections of all the impenitent, and of all the cold part of the Church. The minister must be prepared, if it be the will of God, to be driven away from the place. He must be determined to go straight forward, and leave the entire event with God. . . . So the people, also, must be willing to have a revival, let the sacrifice be what it may. It will not do for them to say: "We are willing to attend so many meetings, but we cannot attend any more." Or: "We are willing to have a revival if it will not disturb our arrangements about our business, or prevent our making money." I tell you, such people will never have a revival till they are willing to do anything, and sacrifice anything, that God indicates to be their duty. Christian merchants must feel willing to lock up their stores for six months, if it is necessary to carry on a revival. I do not mean that any such thing is called for, or that it is their duty to do so. But if there should be such a state of feeling as to call for it, then it would be their duty and they ought to be willing to do it. They ought to be willing to do it at the call of God, for He can easily burn down their stores if they do not. In fact, I should not be sorry to see such a revival in New York, as would make every merchant in the city lock up his store till spring, and say that he had sold goods enough and would now give up his whole time to leading sinners to Christ.

. . . Sometimes ministers are not willing to have a revival unless *they* can have the management of it, or unless *their* agency can be conspicuous in promoting it. They wish to prescribe to God what He shall direct and bless, and what men He shall put forward. They will have no new measures. They cannot have any of this "new-light" preaching, or of these *evangelists* that go about the country preaching! They have a good deal to say about God being a Sovereign, and that He will have revivals come in His own way and time. But then He must choose to have it just in their way or they will have nothing to do with it. Such men will sleep on until they are awakened by the judgment trumpet, without a revival, unless they are willing that God should come in His own way—unless they are willing to have anything or anybody employed that will do the most good. . . .

Remarks

. . . You see why you have not a revival. It is only because you do not want one. Because you are neither praying for it, nor feeling anxious for it, nor putting forth efforts for it. I appeal to your own consciences: Are you making these efforts now, to promote a revival? You know, brethren, what the truth is about it. Will you stand up and say that you have made efforts for a revival and have been disappointed—that you have cried to God: "Wilt Thou not revive us?" and that God would not do it?

Lecture XIV: Measures to Promote Revivals

. . . It is manifest that in preaching the Gospel there must be *some* kind of measures adopted. The Gospel must be presented before the minds of the people, and measures must be taken so that they *can* hear it, and be induced to attend to it. This is done by building churches, holding stated or other meetings, and so on. Without some measures, the Gospel can never be made to take effect among men. . . . Our present forms of public worship, and everything so far as *measures* are concerned, have been arrived at *by degrees*, and by a succession of New Measures. . . .

(a) Lay prayers. Much objection was formerly made against allowing any man to pray or to take a part in managing a prayer-meeting, unless he was a clergyman. It used to be said that for a layman to pray in public

was interfering with the dignity of ministers, and was not to be tolerated. A minister in Pennsylvania told me that a few years ago he appointed a prayer-meeting in the Church, and the elders opposed it and "turned it out of house." They said they would not have such work; they had hired a minister to do the praying, and he should do it; and they were not going to have common men praying. . . . What a state of things!

(b) Lay exhortation. This has been made a question of vast importance, one which has agitated all New England and many other parts of the country, whether laymen ought to be allowed to exhort in public meetings. Many ministers have laboured to shut up the mouths of laymen entirely. Such persons overlooked the practice of the primitive Churches. So much opposition was made to this practice, nearly a hundred years ago, that President Edwards had actually to take up the subject, and write a laboured defence of the rights and duties of laymen. But the opposition has not entirely ceased to this day. "What, a man that is not a minister, to talk in public! It will create confusion; it will let down the ministry: what will people think of ministers, if we allow common men to do the same things that *we* do?" Astonishing!

But now all these things are gone by in most places, and laymen can preach and exhort without the least objection. The evils that were feared, from the labours of laymen, have not been realised, and many ministers are glad to induce laymen to exercise their gifts in doing good.

4. *Women's prayer-meetings.* Within the last few years women's prayer-meetings have been extensively opposed. What dreadful things! A minister said that when he first attempted to establish these meetings, he had all the clergy around opposed to him. "Set women to pray? Why, the next thing, I suppose, will be to set them to preach!" Serious apprehensions were entertained for the safety of Zion if women should be allowed to get together to pray, and even now it is not tolerated in some Churches. So it has been in regard to all the active movements of the Church. Missions and Sunday Schools have been opposed, and have gained their present hold only by a succession of struggles and a series of innovations. . . .

5. I will mention several men who, in Divine providence, have been set forward as prominent in *introducing innovations*.

. . . *President Edwards* . . . was famous in his day for new measures. Among other innovation, he refused to baptize the children of impenitent parents. The practice of baptizing the children of the ungodly had been introduced into the New England Churches in the preceding century, and had become nearly universal. President Edwards saw that the practice was wrong, and he refused to do it, and the refusal shook all the Churches of New England. A hundred ministers joined and determined to put him down. He wrote a book on the subject, and defeated them all. It produced one of the greatest excitements there ever was in New

England. Nothing, unless it was the Revolutionary War, ever produced an equal excitement. . . .

. . . *In the present generation*, many things have been introduced which have proved useful, but have been opposed on the ground *that they were innovations*. And as many are still unsettled in regard to them, I have thought it best to make some remarks concerning them. . . . These are all opposed, and are called "new measures."

(a) Anxious meetings. The first that I ever heard of under that name were in New England, where they were appointed for the purpose of holding personal conversation with anxious sinners, and to adapt instruction to the cases of individuals, so as to lead them immediately to Christ. . . .

(1) By spending a few moments in personal conversation, in order to learn the state of mind of each individual, and then, in an address to the whole meeting, to take up their errors and remove their difficulties.

(2) By going round to each, and taking up each individual case, and going over the whole ground with each one separately, and getting them to promise to give their hearts to God. Either way the meetings are important, and have been found most successful in practice. But multitudes have objected against them because they were new. . . .

(c) The anxious seat. By this I mean the appointment of some particular seat in the place of meeting, where the anxious may come and be addressed particularly, and be made subjects of prayer, and sometimes be conversed with individually. Of late, this measure has met with more opposition than any of the others. What is the great objection? I cannot see it. The *design* of the anxious seat is undoubtedly philosophical, and according to the laws of mind. It has two bearings:

(a) When a person is seriously troubled in mind, everybody knows there is a powerful tendency to conceal it. When a person is borne down with a sense of his condition, if you can get him willing to have it known, if you can get him to break away from the chains of pride, you have gained an important point towards his conversion. . . .

(b) Another bearing of the anxious seat is to detect deception and delusion, and thus prevent false hopes. . . . Just so with the awakened sinner. Preach to him, and, at the moment, he thinks he is willing to do anything; he thinks he is determined to serve the Lord; but bring him to the test; call on him to do one thing, to take one step, that shall identify him with the people of God or cross his pride, and his pride comes up, and he refuses; his delusion is brought out, and he finds himself a lost sinner still; whereas, if you had not done it, he might have gone away flattering himself that he was a Christian. If you say to him: "There is the anxious seat, come out and avow your determination to be on the Lord's side," and if he is not willing to do so small a thing as that, then he is not willing to do *anything,* and there he is, brought out before his own conscience. It uncovers the delusion of the human heart, and prevents a great many spurious conversions, by showing those who might otherwise imagine themselves willing to do anything for Christ that in fact they are willing to do *nothing.*

From Charles G. Finney, *Lectures on Revivals of Religion . . . from notes by the Editor of the N.Y. Evangelist, rev. by the Author* (New York: Leavitt, Lord & Co., 1835).

Charles G. Finney

LECTURES ON SYSTEMATIC THEOLOGY (1846–47)

Charles G. Finney began teaching at Oberlin College in May 1835, dividing his time between Oberlin and New York City. This arrangement lasted only until 1837, when Finney left New York for good. Oberlin had been founded as a "colony" by expatriate New Englanders in the old Western Reserve of northern Ohio, and Finney served Oberlin and its college as professor of moral philosophy and theology, president of the college, and pastor of Oberlin's First Congregational Church. He made the *Oberlin Evangelist* his regular printed organ and published the outlines of his early theology lectures in 1840 as *Skeletons of a Course of Theological Lectures*. These were followed in 1846 and 1847 by his two-volume *Lectures on Systematic Theology* (the *Skeletons* and the *Lectures*, taken together, made up a three-volume series). In these lectures, Finney addressed the favorite topics of the New England Theology: the moral government of God, the atonement, regeneration, and the will. But here, for the first time, Finney embarked on serious criticism of Jonathan Edwards. The distinction between natural and moral ability was "nonsensical," argued Finney, and it "has been in the mouth of the Edwardean school of theologians, from Edwards' day to the present." The substance of his criticism, however, was less a repudiation of Edwards's thought than an embrace of Nathaniel W. Taylor's critique of the natural/moral dichotomy. Even in his most substantive departure from Edwards, Finney was still working within the orbit of the New England Theology.

৩৩

Lecture 17: Regeneration

Regeneration is . . . the same thing, in the Bible use of the term, as to have a new heart, to be a new creature, to pass from death unto life. In other words, to be born again is to have a new moral character, to become holy. To regenerate is to make holy. To be born of God, no doubt expresses and includes the Divine agency, but it also includes and expresses that which the Divine agency is employed in effecting, namely, making the sinner holy. Certainly, a sinner is not regenerated whose moral character is unchanged. . . . The term regeneration, or the being born of God, is designed to express primarily and principally the thing done, that is, the making of a sinner holy, and expresses also the fact that God's agency induces the change. Throw out the idea of what is done, that is, the change of moral character in the subject, and he would not be born again, he would not be regenerated, and it could not be truly said, in such a case, that God had regenerated him. . . . It is nonsense to affirm that his moral character is changed without any activity or agency of his own. Passive holiness is impossible. Holiness is obedience to the law of God, the law of love, and of course consists in the activity of the creature. . . . Sinners are required to make to themselves a new heart, which they could not do, if they were not active in this change. If the work is a work of God, in such a sense, that He must first regenerate the heart or soul before the agency of the sinner begins, it were absurd and unjust to require him to make to himself a new heart, until he is first regenerated.

. . . Both conversion and regeneration are sometimes in the Bible ascribed to God, sometimes to man, and sometimes to the subject; which shows clearly that the distinction under examination is arbitrary and theological, rather than biblical. The fact is that both terms imply the simultaneous exercise of both human and Divine agency. . . . The same is true of conversion, or the turning of the sinner to God. God is said to turn him and he is said to turn himself. God draws him, and he follows. In both alike God and man are both active, and their activity is simultaneous. God works or draws, and the sinner yields or turns, or which is the same thing, changes his heart, or, in other words, is born again. . . . The sinner puts forth his activity, and God draws him into life; or rather, God draws, and the sinner comes forth to life. . . . In our investigations henceforth, let it be understood that I use regeneration and conversion as synonymous terms.

What regeneration is not.

It is not a change in the substance of soul or body. If it were, sinners could not be required to effect it. Such a change would not constitute a change of moral character. No such change is needed, as the sinner has all the faculties and natural attributes requisite to render perfect obedience to God. All he needs is to be induced to use these powers and attributes as he ought. The words conversion and regeneration do not imply any change of substance, but only a change of moral state or of moral character. The terms are not used to express a physical, but a moral change. Regeneration does not express or imply the creation of any new faculties or attributes of nature, nor any change whatever in the constitution of body or mind.

. . . Regeneration then is a radical change of the ultimate intention, and, of course, of the end or object of life. We have seen that the choice of an end is efficient in producing executive volitions, or the use of means to obtain its end. A selfish ultimate choice is, therefore, a wicked heart, out of which flows every evil; and a benevolent ultimate choice is a good heart, out of which flows every good and commendable deed.

Regeneration, to have the characteristics ascribed to it in the Bible, must consist in a change in the attitude of the will, or a change in its ultimate choice, intention, or preference; a change from selfishness to benevolence; from choosing self-gratification as the supreme and ultimate end of life, to the supreme and ultimate choice of the highest well-being of God and of the universe; from a state of entire consecration to self-interest, self-indulgence, self-gratification for its own sake or as an end, and as the supreme end of life, to a state of entire consecration to God, and to the interests of His kingdom as the supreme and ultimate end of life. . . .

What is implied in regeneration.

1. The nature of the change shows that it must be instantaneous. It is a change of choice, or of intention. This must be instantaneous. The preparatory work of conviction and enlightening the mind may have been gradual and progressive. But when regeneration occurs, it must be instantaneous.

2. It implies an entire present change of moral character, that is, a change from entire sinfulness to entire holiness. We have seen that it consists in a change from selfishness to benevolence. We have also seen that selfishness and benevolence cannot coexist in the same mind; that selfishness is a state of supreme and entire consecration to self; that benevolence is a state of entire and supreme consecration to God and the good of the universe. Regeneration, then, surely implies an entire change of moral character. . . .

3. The scriptures represent regeneration as the condition of salvation in such a sense, that if the subject should die immediately after regeneration, and without any further change, he would go immediately to heaven.

Lecture 18: Philosophical Theories of Regeneration

The principal theories that have been advocated, so far as my knowledge extends, are the following:

1. The taste scheme. . . . Moral depravity, according to this school, consists in a constitutional relish, taste, or craving for sin. . . . They hold that it does not consist in any voluntary state of mind, but that it lies back of, and controls voluntary action, or the actions of the will. The wicked heart, according to them, consists in an appetency or constitutional taste for sin, and with them, the appetites, passions, and propensities of human nature in its fallen state are in themselves sinful. . . . A change of heart, in the view of this philosophy, must consist in a change of constitution. It must be a physical change, and wrought by a physical as distinguished from a moral agency. . . . It assumes the dogma of original sin, as taught in the Presbyterian Confession of Faith, and attempts to harmonize the philosophy of regeneration with that philosophy of sin, or moral depravity.

2. The divine efficiency scheme or theory. . . . It maintains that the universe exists only by an act of present and perpetual creation. . . . This philosophy denies constitutional moral depravity, or original sin, and maintains that moral character belongs alone to the exercises or choices of the will; that regeneration does not consist in the creation of any new taste, relish, or craving, nor in the implantation or infusion of any new principles in the soul: but that it consists in a choice conformed to the law of God, or in a change from selfishness to disinterested benevolence; that this change is effected by a direct act of divine power or efficiency, as irresistible as any creative act whatever. . . .

3. The susceptibility scheme. This theory represents that the Holy Spirit's influences are both physical and moral; that He, by a direct and physical influence, excites the susceptibilities of the soul and prepares them to be affected by the truth; that He, thereupon, exerts a moral or persuasive influence by presenting the truth, which moral influence induces regeneration. . . . It admits and maintains that regeneration is effected solely by a moral influence, but also that a work preparatory to the efficiency of the moral influence, and indispensable to its efficiency, in producing regeneration, is performed by a direct and physical agency of the Holy Spirit upon the constitutional susceptibilities of the soul, to quicken and wake it up, and predispose it to be deeply and duly affected by the truth. . . .

4. The last theory to be examined is that of a Divine Moral Suasion. This theory teaches . . . that regeneration consists in a change in the ultimate intention or preference of the mind, or in a change from selfishness to disinterested benevolence. . . . This scheme honors the Holy

Spirit without disparaging the truth of God. . . . Sinners must not wait for and expect physical omnipotence to regenerate them. The physical omnipotence of God affords no presumption that all men will be converted; for regeneration is not effected by physical power. God cannot do the sinner's duty, and regenerate him without the right exercise of the sinner's own agency. . . .

Lecture 20: Natural Ability

. . . Edwards considers freedom and ability as identical. He defines freedom or liberty to consist in the power, opportunity, or advantage, that any one has, to do as he pleases. . . . His definition of natural ability, or natural liberty, as he frequently calls it, wholly excludes the power to will, and includes only the power or ability to execute our volitions. Thus it is evident that natural ability, according to him, respects external action only, and has nothing to do with willing. When there is no restraint or hindrance to the execution of volition, when there is nothing interposed to disturb and prevent the natural and established result of our volitions, there is natural ability according to this school. It should be distinctly understood that Edwards, and those of his school, hold that choices, volitions, and all acts of will are determined, not by the sovereign power of the agent, but are caused by the objective motive, and that there is the same connection, or a connection as certain and as unavoidable between motive and choice, as between any physical cause and its effect: "the difference being," according to him, "not in the nature of the connection, but in the terms connected." Hence, according to his view, natural liberty or ability cannot consist in the power of willing or of choice, but must consist in the power to execute our choices or volitions. Consequently, this class of philosophers define free or moral agency to consist in the power to do as one wills, or power to execute one's purposes, choices, or volitions. . . .

If we have not the power to will, we have not power or ability to do anything. All ability or power to do resides in the will, and power to will is the necessary condition of ability to do. In morals and religion, as we shall soon see, the willing is the doing. The power to will is the condition of obligation to do. . . . Edwards himself held that the will is the executive faculty, and that the soul can do nothing except as it wills to do it, and that for this reason a command to do is strictly a command to will. We shall see by and by that he held also that the willing and the doing are identical, so far as moral obligation, morals, and religion are concerned. For the present it is enough to say, whether Edwards or anybody else ever held it or not, that it is absurd and sheer nonsense to talk of an ability to do when there is no ability to will. Every one knows with intuitive certainty that he has no ability to do what he is unable to will to do. It is, therefore, the vilest of folly to talk of a natural ability to do anything whatever, when we exclude from this ability the power to will. If there is no ability to will, there is and can be no ability to do; therefore, the natural ability of the Edwardean school is no ability at all . . . and nothing but an empty name, a metaphysico-theological fiction.

. . . True freedom or liberty of will must consist in the power or ability to will in every instance either in accordance with, or in opposition to, moral obligation. Observe, moral obligation respects acts of will. What freedom or liberty of will can there be in relation to moral obligation unless the will or the agent has power or ability to act in conformity with moral obligation? To talk of a man's being free to will, or having liberty to will, when he has not the power or ability, is to talk nonsense. . . . Edwards I revere; his blunders I deplore. I speak thus of this Treatise on the Will, because, while it abounds with unwarrantable assumptions, distinctions without a difference, and metaphysical subtleties, it has been adopted as the text-book of a multitude of what are called Calvinistic divines for scores of years.

Lecture 21: Gracious Ability

The question is not whether, as a matter of fact, men ever do obey God without the gracious influence of the Holy Spirit. I hold that they do not. So the fact of the Holy Spirit's gracious influence being exerted in every case of human obedience is not a question in debate between those who maintain, and those who deny, the doctrine of gracious ability, in the sense above explained.

. . . Let it be distinctly understood before we close this subject that we do not deny, but strenuously maintain, that the whole plan of salvation, and all the influences, both providential and spiritual, which God exerts in the conversion, sanctification, and salvation of sinners, is grace from first to last. . . . I admit the ability of man, and hold that he is able, but utterly unwilling to obey God. Therefore I consistently hold that all the influences exerted by God to make him willing are of free grace abounding through Christ Jesus.

Lecture 26: Sanctification

Sanctification does not imply any constitutional change, either of soul or body. . . . Sanctification consists in the will's devoting or consecrating

itself and the whole being, all we are and have, so far as powers, susceptibilities, possessions are under the control of the will, to the service of
God, or, which is the same thing, to the highest interests of God and of
being. Sanctification, then, is nothing more nor less than entire obedience, for the time being, to the moral law.

. . . The true question at issue is, Is a state of entire, in the sense of
permanent sanctification, attainable in this life? . . . It is self-evident that
entire obedience to God's law is possible on the ground of natural ability.
To deny this is to deny that a man is able to do as well as he can. The
very language of the law is such as to level its claims to the capacity of
the subject, however great or small that capacity may be. . . . Here then
it is plain that all the law demands is the exercise of whatever strength
we have, in the service of God.

. . . A man may believe in what is really a state of entire sanctification,
and aim at attaining it, although he may not call it by that name. This
I believe to be the real fact with Christians; and they would much more
frequently attain what they aim at, did they know how to appropriate
the grace of Christ to their own circumstances. Mrs. President Edwards,
for example, firmly believed that she could attain a state of entire consecration. She aimed at, and manifestly attained it, and yet, such were
her views of constitutional depravity that she did not call her state one
of entire sanctification. It has been common for Christians to suppose
that a state of entire consecration is attainable; but while they believe in
the sinfulness of their natures, they would not of course call even entire
consecration, entire sanctification. . . . Call it what you please, Christian
perfection, heavenly mindedness, the full assurance of faith or hope, or
a state of entire consecration; by all these I understand the same thing.
And it is certain, that by whatever name it is called, the thing must be
aimed at to be attained. . . .

From Charles G. Finney, *Lectures on Systematic Theology, embracing lectures on Moral Government, together with Atonement, Moral and Physical Depravity, Regeneration, Philosophical
Theories, and Evidences of Regeneration*, 2 vols. (Oberlin, OH: James M. Fitch, 1846–47).

PART 8

Last of the
"Consistent Calvinists"

Edwards Amasa Park

Edwards Amasa Park (1808–1900) did more than any other New Englander to synthesize the history of the Edwardsean tradition. Son of the Rev. Calvin Park (a student and friend of Nathanael Emmons and a professor at Brown University), Edwards Park attended Brown, married Anna Maria Edwards (Jonathan Edwards's great-granddaughter), graduated from Andover in 1831, and then engaged in pastoral ministry in Braintree, Massachusetts. Though heralded for his preaching, Park decided that academic work would better suit his gifts. Therefore, after a time of study with Nathaniel W. Taylor at Yale Divinity School (1834–35), he accepted a post at Amherst College in mental and moral philosophy.

In 1836, Park returned to Andover Seminary to teach as the Bartlet Professor of Sacred Rhetoric. He remained there forty-five years, retiring in 1881. In 1844, he assumed control with B. B. Edwards of the *Bibliotheca Sacra*, an Andover organ that he edited until 1884. In 1847, he succeeded Leonard Woods as the Abbot Professor of Christian Theology, his school's most influential teaching position. In 1853, he became the president of the faculty, a role he played until 1868. In the 1850s and 1860s, Park released a series of studies on the New England Theology. Both of the articles printed below appeared in the early 1850s. He published memoirs of Samuel Hopkins (1852), Moses Stuart (1852), B. B. Edwards (1852–53), Nathanael Emmons (1861), and, later, Leonard Woods (1880). In addition to numerous other pieces treating Edwardsean themes, he published a highly acclaimed anthology of Edwardsean views of atonement, *The Atonement: Discourses and Treatises*, in 1859.

Dubbed the last "consistent Calvinist," Park was the final representative and the first major historian of Edwards's living legacy in New England. For many years, he cared for a cache of Edwards's personal manuscripts, planning but never executing a magnum opus on the man. He defended New England tirelessly, primarily against Princetonians staking a claim to Edwards's legacy and opposed to New England's recontextualization of his views (especially by the Taylorites). Even after his retirement, Park championed Edwards's views at Andover Seminary for years. In the face of his school's marked transition to Progressive Orthodoxy, a more liberal social gospel, higher criticism, and Darwin's evolution, Park stood fast on the old-time gospel of the Edwardsean evangelicals.

Park is sometimes said to have "invented" the New England Theology. In response to Presbyterians—particularly at Princeton—who were alarmed about New England's drift away from high Calvinism, Park appealed to Edwards, it is said, for self-protection. He depicted Edwardseanism as a seamless doctrinal garment, covering all its theologians with the authority of their eponym. In the process, he gave new currency to the title New England Theology, employing it as never before to whitewash local disagreements and to feign a united front within the region.

As the entries below make clear, there is a kernel of truth to this claim. Park frequently plastered over cracks and fissures in the monolith *he* called the New England Theology, explaining them away with his "theology of the feelings" and focusing mainly on his movement's continuities. But as should be clear by this point in the volume, Park did little more to invent the movement than most of his predecessors. Consistent Calvinists had always sought to "improve" on Edwards's teaching for their own, pastoral purposes. None of them simply (slavishly) parroted the pronouncements of the master. Park invented, or recontextualized, his own Edwardseanism, but he did not do so *de novo*. The New England Theologians had been "inventing" their tradition since the days when they studied together in Edwards's manse.

Edwards Amasa Park

THE THEOLOGY OF THE INTELLECT AND THAT OF THE FEELINGS (1850)

First delivered on May 30, 1850, to the Convention of the Congregational Ministers of Massachusetts, "The Theology of the Intellect and That of the Feelings" quickly became the talk of the theological world. On its surface, it simply echoed a common Edwardsean concern, the need to respect both head and heart as one interprets the Word of God. But underneath, it involved what some considered a doctrinal subterfuge, using a theology of the feelings to hide departures from Calvinist orthodoxy.

The theology of the intellect, for Edwards Amasa Park, was that of the reason. Governed by logic and precision, it majored in accuracy, consistency, and scholarly utility. The theology of the feelings was that of the pious, Christian heart. Governed by poetry and passion, it majored in art, sensibility, and liturgical propriety. Of course, these two theologies overlapped each other. But needless consternation arose when people neglected their differences. Indeed, Park contended, many controversies dividing Christian thinkers from one another actually pertained to matters of style rather than substance. Too often polemical precisionists "treated the language of a sensitive heart as if it were the guarded and wary style of the intellect," he claimed. But the theology of the feelings had an integrity of its own. It need not be straightened into the propositional language of the schoolmen. It must not be judged by its conformity to their goals.

Many American theologians proved suspicious of these claims. Professing allegiance to particular confessional traditions, they resisted Park's attempt to undermine their differences or to gloss them over in the name of Christian piety. Princeton's Charles Hodge, especially, took exception to the sermon, engaging Park in a major paper war that lasted a year and a half (culminating in Park's tour de force, "New England Theology," excerpted below). In Hodge's view, Park's distinction between the intellect and the feelings raised a dangerous smoke screen, disguising Park's and others' departures from the Westminster Confession (1648). Whenever Park had trouble assenting to his church's faith tradition, he chalked it up to alleged language of the feelings at Westminster (or in other confessional statements) never intended for a literal subscription. When he affirmed a point of doctrine, he attributed it to the intellect. But it seemed as though, too often, his theologies diverged.

Truth be told, Park did make use of his theology of the feelings to avoid assenting to the doctrines he opposed. As he admits in the excerpt below, "In the Bible there are pleasing hints of many things which were never designed to be doctrines, such as the literal and proper necessity of the will, passive and physical sin, baptismal regeneration, clerical absolution, the literal imputation of guilt to the innocent, transubstantiation, eternal generation and procession." In the leaves of Holy Writ, "these metaphors bloom as the flowers of the field; *there* they toil not neither do they spin." Sadly, however, "the schoolman has transplanted them to the rude exposure of logic; here they are frozen up, their fragrance is gone, their juices evaporated, and their withered leaves are preserved as specimens of that which in its rightful place surpassed the glory of the wisest sage."

Park did not think, however, that the theologies of intellect and feelings disagreed. Rather, he thought they belonged together—much like body and soul—although he differed with the Princetonians over the doctrinal implications of their ultimate integration. For Park, "the theology of the intellect illustrates and vivifies itself by that of feeling." To be sure, "we lose the influence of literal truth upon the sensibilities, if we persevere in refusing it an appropriate image. We must add a body to the soul of a doctrine, whenever we would make it palpable and enlivening." In the best of all theologies, then, intellect and feelings reinforce one another. Ironically, Hodge would eventually come to agree with Park in principle, employing the "two theologies—one of the intellect, and another of the heart"—in the introduction to his *Systematic Theology* (1872–73).

THE STRENGTH OF ISRAEL WILL NOT LIE NOR REPENT: FOR HE IS NOT A MAN THAT HE SHOULD REPENT.

1 Samuel 15:29

AND IT REPENTED THE LORD THAT HE HAD MADE MAN ON THE EARTH, AND IT GRIEVED HIM AT HIS HEART.

Genesis 6:6

I have heard of a father who endeavored to teach his children a system of astronomy in precise philosophical language, and although he uttered nothing but the truth, they learned from him nothing but falsehood. I have also heard of a mother who, with a woman's tact, so exhibited the general features of astronomical science that although her statements were technically erroneous, they still made upon her children a better impression, and one more nearly right than would have been made by a more accurate style. For the same reason many a punctilious divine, preaching the exact truth in its scientific method, has actually imparted to the understanding of his hearers either no idea at all or a wrong one; while many a pulpit orator, using words which tire the patience of a scholastic theologian, and which in their literal import are false, has yet lodged in the hearts of his people the main substance of truth. John Foster says that whenever a man prays aright he forgets the philosophy of prayer; and in more guarded phrase we may say that when men are deeply affected by any theme, they are apt to disturb some of its logical proportions, and when preachers aim to rouse the sympathies of a populace, they often give a brighter coloring or a bolder prominence to some lineaments of a doctrine than can be given to them in a well compacted science.

There are two forms of theology, of which the two passages in my text are selected as individual specimens, the one declaring that God never repents, the other that he does repent. For want of a better name these two forms may be termed the theology of the intellect, and the theology of feeling. Sometimes, indeed, both the mind and the heart are suited by the same modes of thought, but often they require dissimilar methods, and the object of the present discourse is to state some of the differences between the theology of the intellect and that of feeling, and also some of the influences which they exert upon each other.

What, then, are some of the differences between these two kinds of representation?

The theology of the intellect conforms to the laws, subserves the wants and secures the approval of our intuitive and deductive powers. It includes the decisions of the judgment, of the perceptive part of conscience and taste, indeed of all the faculties which are essential to the reasoning process. It is the theology of speculation, and therefore comprehends the truth just as it is, unmodified by excitements of feeling. It is received as accurate not in its spirit only, but in its letter also. Of course it demands evidence, either internal or extraneous, for all its propositions. These propositions, whether or not they be inferences from antecedent, are well fitted to be premises for subsequent trains of proof. This intellectual theology, therefore, prefers general to individual statements, the abstract to the concrete, the literal to the figurative. In the creed of a Trinitarian it affirms that he who united in his person a human body, a human soul, and a divine spirit expired on the cross, but it does not originate the phrase that his soul expired, nor that "God the mighty Maker died." Its aim is not to be impressive, but intelligible and defensible. Hence it insists on the nice proportions of doctrine, and on preciseness both of thought and style. Its words are so exactly defined, its adjustments are so accurate, that no caviller can detect an ambiguous, mystical, or incoherent sentence. It is, therefore, in entire harmony with itself, abhorring a contradiction as nature abhors a vacuum. Left to its own guidance, for example, it would never suggest the unqualified remark that Christ has fully paid the debt of sinners, for it declares that this debt may justly be claimed from them; nor that he has suffered the whole punishment which they deserve, for it teaches that this punishment may still be righteously inflicted on themselves; nor that he has entirely satisfied the law, for it insists that the demands of the law are yet in force. If it should allow those as logical premises, it would also allow the salvation of all men as a logical inference, but it rejects this inference and accordingly, being self consistent, must reject those when viewed as literal premises. It is adapted to the soul in her inquisitive moods, but fails to satisfy her craving for excitement. In order to express the definite idea that we are exposed to evil in consequence of Adam's sin, it does not employ the passionate phrase, "we are guilty of his sin." It searches for the proprieties of representation, for seemliness and decorum. It gives origin to no statements which require apology or essential modification; no metaphor, for example, so bold and so liable to disfigure our idea of the divine equity, as that Heaven imputes the crime of one man to millions of his descendants, and then imputes their myriad sins to him who was harmless and undefiled. As it avoids the dashes of an imaginative style, as it qualifies and subdues the remark which the passions would make still more intense, it seems dry, tame to the mass of men. It awakens but little interest in favor of its old arrangements; its new distinctions are easily introduced, to be as speedily forgotten. As we might infer, it is suited not for eloquent appeals, but for calm controversial treatises and bodies of divinity; not so well for the hymn-book as for the catechism; not so well for the liturgy as for the creed.

In some respects, but not in all, the theology of feeling differs from that of intellect. It is the form of belief which is suggested by, and adapted to the wants of the well-trained heart. It is embraced as involving the substance of truth, although, when literally interpreted, it may or may not be false. It studies not the exact proportions of doctrine, but gives especial prominence to those features of it which are and ought to be most grateful to the sensibilities. It insists not on dialectical argument, but receives whatever the healthy affections crave. It chooses particular

250

rather than general statements; teaching, for example, the divine om-nipotence by an individual instance of it; saying, not that God can do all things which are objects of power, but that He spake and it was done. It sacrifices abstract remarks to visible and tangible images; choosing the lovely phrase that "the children of men put their trust under the shadow of Jehovah's wings," rather than the logical one that his providence com-prehendeth all events. It is satisfied with vague, indefinite representa-tions. It is too buoyant, too earnest for a moral result, to compress itself into sharply-drawn angles. It is often the more forceful because of the looseness of its style, herein being the hiding of its power. It is sublime in its obscure picture of the Sovereign who maketh darkness his pavilion, dark waters and thick clouds of the sky. Instead of measuring the exact dimensions of a spirit, it says, "I could not discern the form thereof: an image was before mine eyes; there was silence and I heard a voice"; and in the haziness of this vision lies its fitness to stir up the soul. Of course, the theology of feeling aims to be impressive, whether it be or not minutely accurate. Often it bursts away from dogmatic restraints, forces its passage through or over rules of logic, and presses forward to expend itself first and foremost in affecting the sensibilities. For this end, instead of being comprehensive, it is elastic; avoiding monotony it is ever pertinent to the occasion; it brings out into bold relief now one feature of a doctrine and then a different feature, and assumes as great a variety of shapes as the wants of the heart are various. . . . In order to make us feel the strength of God's aversion to sin, it declares that he has repented of having made our race, has been grieved at his heart for transgressors, weary of them, vexed with them. But it does not mean that these expressions which, as inflected by times and circumstances, impress a truth upon the soul, be stereotyped into the principle that Jehovah has ever parted with his infinite blessedness; for in order to make us confide in his stability, it denies that he ever repents, and de-clares that he is without even the shadow of turning. It assumes these discordant forms so as to meet the affections in their conflicting moods. Its aim is not to facilitate the inferences of logic, but to arrest attention, to grapple with the wayward desires, to satisfy the longings of the pious heart. And in order to reach all the hiding-places of emotion, it now and then strains a word to its utmost significancy, even into a variance with some other phrase and a disproportion with the remaining parts of the system. We often hear that every great divine, like Jonathan Edwards, will contradict himself. If this be so, it is because he is a reasoner and something more; because he is not a mere mathematician, but gives his feelings a full, an easy, and a various play; because he does not exhibit his faith always in the same form, straight like a needle, sharp-pointed and one-eyed.

The free theology of the feelings is ill fitted for didactic or controversial treatises or doctrinal standards. Martin Luther, the church fathers, who used it so often, became thereby unsafe polemics. Anything, everything, can be proved from them; for they were ever inditing sentences congenial with an excited heart, but false as expressions of deliberate opinion. But this emotive theology is adapted to the persuasive sermon, to the pleadings of the liturgy, to the songs of Zion. By no means can it be termed mere poetry, in the sense of a playful fiction. It is no play, but solemn earnestness. It is no mere fiction, but an outpouring of sentiments too deep, or too mellow, or too impetuous to be suited with the stiff language of the intellect. Neither can its words be called merely figurative, in the sense of arbitrary or unsubstantial. They are the earliest, and if one may use a comparison, the most natural utterances of a soul instinct with religious life. They are forms of language which circumscribe a substance of doctrine, a substance which, fashioned as it may be, the intellect grasps and holds fast; a substance which arrests the more attention and prolongs the deeper interest by the figures which bound it. This form of theology, then, is far from being fitly represented by the term imaginative, still farther by the term fanciful, and farther yet by the word capricious. It goes deeper; it is the theology both of and for our sensitive nature; of and for the normal emotion, affection, passion. It may be called poetry, however, if this word be used, as it should be, to include the constitutional developments of a heart moved to its depths by the truth. And as in its essence it is poetical, with this meaning of the epithet, so it avails itself of a poetic license, and indulges in a style of remark which for sober prose would be unbecoming, or even, when associated in certain ways, irreverent. All warm affection, be it love or hatred, overleaps at times the proprieties of a didactic style. Does not the Bible make this obvious? There are words in the Canticles and in the imprecatory Psalms, which are to be justified as the utterances of a feeling too pure, too unsuspicious, too earnest to guard itself against evil surmises. There are appearances of reasoning in the Bible, which the mere dialectician has denounced as puerile sophisms. But some of them may never have been intended for logical proof; they may have been designed for passionate appeals and figured into the shape of argument, not to convince the reason but to carry the heart by a strong assault, in a day when the kingdom of heaven suffered violence and the violent took it by force. In one of his lofty flights of inspiration, the Psalmist cries, "Awake! why sleepest thou, oh Lord"; and Martin Luther, roused more than man is wont to be by this example, prayed at the Diet of Worms, in language which we fear to repeat, "Hearest thou not, my God; art thou dead?" And a favorite English minstrel sings of the "dying God," of the "sharp distress," the "sore complaints," of God, his "last groans," his "dying blood"; of his throne, also, as once a "burning throne," a "seat of dreadful wrath"; but now "sprinkled over" by "the rich drops" of blood "that calmed his frowning face." It is the very nature of a theology framed for enkindling the imagination and thereby inflaming the heart, to pour itself out, when a striking emergency calls for them, in words that burn; words that excite no congenial glow in technical students, viewing all truth in its dry light, and disdaining all figures which would offend the decorum of a philosophical or didactic style, but words which wake the deepest sympathies of quick-moving, wide-hearted, many-sided men, who look through a superficial impropriety and discern under it a truth which the nice language of prose is too frail to convey into the heart, and breaks down in the attempt. . . .

Having considered some of the differences between the intellectual and the emotive theology, let us now glance, as was proposed, at some of the influences which one exerts on the other.

And *first*, the theology of the intellect illustrates and vivifies itself by that of feeling. As man is compounded of soul and body, and his inward sensibilities are expressed by his outward features, so his faith combines ideas logically accurate with conceptions merely illustrative and impressive. Our tendency to unite corporeal forms with mental views may be a premonition that we are destined to exist hereafter in a union of two natures, one of them being spirit, and the other so expressive of spirit as to be called a spiritual body. We lose the influence of literal truth upon the sensibilities, if we persevere in refusing it an appropriate image. We must add a body to the soul of a doctrine, whenever we would make it palpable and enlivening. . . .

At the time when the words were uttered, there could not be a more melting address than, "If I, your Lord and Master, have washed your feet, ye also ought to wash one another's feet"; but when this touching sentiment is interpreted as a legal exaction, an argument for a Moravian or Romish ceremony, its poetic elegance is petrified into a prosaic blunder. There are moments in the stillness of our communion service, when we feel that our Lord is with us, when the bread and the wine so enliven our conceptions of his body and blood as, according to the law of vivid conception, to bring them into our ideal presence, and to make us *demand* the saying, as more pertinent and fit than any other, "This *is* my body, this *is* my blood." But no sooner are these phrases transmuted from hearty utterances into intellectual judgments than they merge their beautiful rhetoric into an absurd logic, and are at once repulsed by a sound mind into their pristine sphere. So there is a depth of significance which our superficial powers do not fathom, in the lamentation: "Behold! I was shapen in iniquity, and in sin did my mother conceive me." This will always remain the passage for the outflow of his grief, whose fountains of penitence are broken up. The channel is worn too deep into the affections to be easily changed. Let the schools reason about it just as, and as long as they please. Let them condemn it as indecorous, or false, or absurd, and the man who utters it as unreasonable, fanatical, bigoted. Let them challenge him for his meaning, and insist with the rigidness of the judge of Shylock that he weigh out the import of every word, every syllable, no more, no less: they do not move him one hair's breadth. He stands where he stood before, and where he will stand until disenthralled from the body. "My meaning," he says, "is exact enough for me, too exact for my repose of conscience; and I care just now for no proof clearer than this: 'Behold! I *was* shapen in iniquity, and in sin *did* my mother conceive me.' Here, on my heart the burden lies, and I *feel* that I am vile, a man of unclean lips, and dwell amid a people of unclean lips, and I went astray as soon as I was born, and am of a perverse, rebellious race, and there is a tide swelling within me and around me, and moving me on to actual transgression, and it is stayed by none of my unaided efforts, and all its billows roll over me, and I am so troubled that I cannot speak; and I am not content with merely saying that I am a transgressor; I long to heap infinite upon infinite, and crowd together all forms of self-reproach, for I am clad in sin as with a garment, I devour it as a sweet morsel, I breathe it, I live it, I *am* sin. My hands are stained with it, my feet are swift in it, all my bones are out of joint with it, my whole body is of tainted origin, and of death in its influence and end; and here is my definition and here is my proof, and, definition or no definition, proof or no proof, here I plant myself, and here I stay, for this is my feeling, and it comes up from the depths of an overflowing heart: '*Behold! I was shapen in iniquity, and in sin did my mother conceive me.*'" But when a theorist seizes at such living words as these, and puts them into his vice, and straightens or crooks them into the dogma, that man is blamable before he chooses to do wrong; deserving of punishment for the involuntary nature which he has never consented to gratify; really sinful before he actually sins, then the language of emotion, forced from its right place and treated as if it were a part of a nicely measured syllogism, hampers and confuses his reasonings, until it is given back to the use for which it was first intended, and from which it never ought to have been diverted. When men thus lose their sensitiveness to the discriminations between the style of judgment and that of feeling, and when they force the latter into the province of the former, they become prone to undervalue the conscience, and to be afraid of philosophy, and to shudder at the axioms of common sense, and to divorce faith from reason, to rely on *church government* rather than on fraternal discussion.

In conclusion allow me to observe that in some aspects our theme suggests a melancholy, in others a cheering train of thought. It grieves us by disclosing the ease with which we may slide into grave errors. Such errors have arisen from so simple a cause as that of confounding poetry with prose. Men whose reasoning instinct has absorbed their delicacy of taste have treated the language of a sensitive heart as if it were the guarded and wary style of the intellect. Intent on the sign more than on the thing signified, they have transubstantiated the living, spiritual truth into the very emblems which were designed to portray it. In the Bible there are pleasing hints of many things which were never designed to be doctrines, such as the literal and proper necessity of the will, passive and physical sin, baptismal regeneration, clerical absolution, the literal imputation of guilt to the innocent, transubstantiation, eternal genera-tion and procession. In that graceful volume, these metaphors bloom as the flowers of the field; *there* they toil not neither do they spin. But the schoolman has transplanted them to the rude exposure of logic; here they are frozen up, their fragrance is gone, their juices evaporated, and their withered leaves are preserved as specimens of that which in its rightful place surpassed the glory of the wisest sage. Or, if I may change the il-lustration, I would say that these ideas, as presented in the Bible, are like oriental kings and nobles, moving about in their free, flowing robes, but in many a scholastic system they are like the embalmed bodies of those ancient lords, their spirits fled, their eyes, which once had speculation in them, now lack lustre; they are dry bones, exceeding dry. . . .

From Edwards Amasa Park, "The Theology of the Intellect and That of the Feelings," *Bibliotheca Sacra* 7 (July 1850): 533–69.

Edwards Amasa Park

New England Theology (1852)

Charles Hodge was certain that Edwards Amasa Park had become an *in*consistent Calvinist and was using Jonathan Edwards's mantle to cover up his metamorphosis. In a lengthy series of articles published first in the *Princeton Review*, he attempted valiantly to prove this, severing Park from the vaunted source of his Edwardsean tradition and, more importantly to Hodge, from what he called the "great granitic formation" of orthodoxy.

Park retaliated with a historiographical coup, "New England Theology," a benchmark, fifty-page essay that offered the first-ever, comprehensive history of his tradition. He admitted that Edwards himself was not "a perfect exponent of what is now termed the Edwardean faith" and that the New England theologians "did not harmonize on every theme." But he insisted that the Edwardseans were faithful to Edwards's thought. "Idle, idle," he fumed, was Hodge's attempt to separate New England from the legacy of Edwards. The New England theologians not only stood in the line of Edwards but also developed Edwards's thought in "a system the *minutiae* of which" even "Calvin and Augustine would have . . . defended" had they "lived when the laws of interpretation and the philosophy of common sense had been as clear and prominent as they have been during and since the time of the Edwardses."

This essay did not put an end to New England's trouble with the Princetonians. Shortly after the Civil War, Hodge and Lyman Hotchkiss Atwater (a Taylorite turned Princetonian) debated George Park Fisher (a Yale professor and friend of Taylor) on the relationship between Edwards and the Edwardseans. Moreover, even in our day, Calvinists wrangle over the issues raised by Park's defense of New England—frequently in the manner of Hodge, Atwater, and Fisher. The weighty question of what it means to remain faithful to one's tradition will likely never go away. However, despite the amount of attention paid to these and related issues since the days of Park and Hodge, Park's "New England Theology" will ever stand as the *Urtext* for those assessing Edwards's role in New England's theological ancestry.

❦

In the preface to the first printed sermon ever preached in America is the following sentence: "So far as we can yet find, it [New England] is an island, and near about the quantity of England; being cut out from the main land in America, as England is from the main of Europe, by a great arm of the sea, which entereth in forty degrees, and runneth up north-west and by west, and goeth out either into the South Sea, or else into the Bay of Canada." This "great arm of the sea" means the Hudson river; the "South Sea" means the Pacific ocean, and the "Bay of Canada" means the river St. Lawrence. Now it were about as easy to learn the shape of New England from the preceding account as to learn the type of New England Theology from the statements which some of its recent opposers have deemed it wise to make.

We beg leave, therefore, first of all, to explain the term, New England Theology. It signifies the formal creed which a majority of the most eminent theologians in New England have explicitly or implicitly sanctioned, during and since the time of Edwards. It denotes the spirit and genius of the system openly avowed or logically involved, in their writings. It includes not the peculiarities in which Edwards differed, as he is known to have differed, from the larger part of his most eminent followers; nor the peculiarities in which any one of his followers differed, as some of them did, from the larger part of the others; but it comprehends the principles, with their logical sequences, which the greater number of our most celebrated divines have approved expressly or by implication. As German philosophy is not adopted by all Germans, and is adopted by some foreigners, so New England Theology is not embraced by all New Englanders, and is embraced by multitudes in other parts of the world. Its more prominent standards, however, are from these north-eastern States. It was first called New-light Divinity; then New Divinity; afterward, Edwardean; more recently, Hopkintonian or Hopkinsian. From the fact that Edwards, Hopkins, West, and Catlin resided in Berkshire County, it was once called Berkshire Divinity. When it was embraced by Andrew Fuller, Dr. Ryland, Robert Hall, Sutcliffe, Carey, Jay, and Erskine, it was called American Theology by the English, in order to discriminate it from the European systems. It has been denominated New England Theology by Americans, in order to distinguish it from the systems that have prevailed in other parts of the land. In 1756, two years before the death of Edwards, there were, according to Dr. Hopkins, not more than four or five clergymen who espoused this new theology. In 1773, according to Dr. Stiles, it was advocated by about forty-five ministers; and Dr. Hopkins says that, in 1796, it was favored by somewhat more than a hundred. Still, even while it was thus restricted in its influence, it was distinguished as a system peculiar to New England. In 1787, Dr. Stiles mentioned as among its champions the two Edwardses, Bellamy, Hopkins, Trumbull, Smalley, Judson, Spring, Robinson (father of Dr. Robinson of New York), Strong, Dwight, Emmons. In 1799, Hopkins appended the names of West, Levi, Hart, Backus, Presidents Balch and Fitch. We may now add such honored men as Dr. Catlin, President Appleton, Dr. Austin. Divines of this class were foremost in the Missionary enterprises of the day. They were conspicuous in the establishment of our oldest Theological Seminaries, as Andover and Bangor. They gave its form and pressure to our theological system. They were imperfect men. They did not harmonize on every theme, but a decided majority of them stood firm for the "three radical principles," that sin consists in choice, that our natural power equals, and that it also limits, our duty. Idle, idle is the late attempt to draw a line of demarcation between the elder Edwards, Bellamy, on the one side, and the younger Edwards, Emmons, West, on the other, with regard to these three principles. Hopkins was the beloved pupil of the first President Edwards, and through life was the most confidential of his friends; was with him in sickness and in health, in the house and on journeys, by day and often by night. He was also an adviser and more than a brother to Bellamy. He was the teacher and a spiritual father of the younger Edwards, West, Spring, and he was an intimate friend of Emmons. He serves, therefore, as a *commune vinculum* between the elder Edwards and Bellamy on the one hand, and the "choir leaders" of the "Exercise Scheme" on the other. But in more than two hundred of his free, private letters, and in all his published works, we have sought in vain for the slightest hint that, on these radical principles, there was even an approach to a disagreement between the two classes. He reached out his fraternal arms to Edwards and to Emmons, and gave them both his approval and his blessing in their maintenance of these three doctrines, and he often expressed as clearly as words can express, his hearty union with the forerunner and the follower. And all the theories which the original Edwardeans and the later Coryphaei of the Exercise Scheme were harmonious in espousing are parts of the New England system.

What worthy end, now, could our Reviewer aim to accomplish, by insinuating that we "regard the little coterie to which" we belong, "as all New England"? We belong to no party which has not been honored throughout the Christian world; but does our assailant dream that "*all* New England" must unite in the New England Theology? What! a single speculative creed for the Churchmen and Come-outers, the Presbyterians and the Quakers, the Baptists and the Swedenborgians, the Sublapsarians and the Supra-lapsarians, the Owenites and the Baxterians, the Burtonites and the Emmonites, of a community whose fathers were John Robinson and Roger Williams! We have never pretended that New England Theology is the dogmatic faith of every man, woman, and child, or of a majority of the laymen, or even clergymen, of these free States. It has, however, been the faith of certain elect minds, whom New England has loved and will ever love to venerate.

We now proceed to say, in the second place, that the Theology of New England is marked by certain new features. We have seen that for a hundred years it has been called "new"; it has been opposed as new, it has been admired as new. All its designations which we have just repeated show it to have been new. The younger Edwards wrote an essay on the "Improvements made in Theology by his father, President Edwards." We do not mean to say that the Edwardean school discovered principles which were never thought of before. They claim to have brought out into bold relief the obscurer faith of good men in all ages. They gave a new distinctness, a new prominence, to doctrines which had been more vaguely believed by the church. They produced new arguments for a faith which had been speculatively opposed by men who had practically sanctioned it. We say that Aristotle first discovered the syllogistic art, although Adam reasoned in syllogisms, whenever he reasoned at all. We say that Bacon first detected the law of induction, although Eve made obeisance to that law before she decided to eat the apple. We say that Longinus and Tully were among the first to find out the principles of rhetoric, and yet we are aware that all men, in all times, have known enough of those principles to comply with them in their speech. He is called a discoverer who makes that palpable which had been dim, and shows that to be reasonable which had formerly been held by an instinct.

We might illustrate these remarks by referring to several doctrines, but we will confine our illustration to the single truth, that an entirely depraved man has a natural power to do all which is required of him; a truth which has been so clearly unfolded by the New England divines, that it properly belongs to their distinctive system. All unsophisticated thinkers, we are aware, have poetically believed that a just God will not command men to do what they have no power to do; that he will not punish them with unending pain for doing as well as they can; that, in every case, physical ability is commensurate with obligation. In what sense, then, may so old a doctrine be called new? In this sense: the Edwardean school have made it more prominent and more effective than it has been made by some; have shown more fully than others have done its agreement with the truths of man's entire sinfulness and of God's decrees; have defended it against those metaphysical Calvinists who speculatively deny their own practical faith; have been the first to make obvious, prominent, and impressive the consistency of those two truths, which all good men have more or less secretly believed—that a sinner can perform what a reasonable law requires of him, and that he certainly will never do as well as he can, unless by a special interposition of Heaven. They deserve far more gratitude for their originality in developing these truths than Hume deserves for his originality in unfolding the laws of mental suggestion. . . .

. . . New England Theology is Calvinism in an improved form. It does not pretend to be a perfect system. Both Edwards and Hopkins reiterated the wish and hope that their successors would add to the improvements which the Genevan faith had already received. Neither does our system profess to be original in its cardinal truths. It has ever claimed that these great truths are the common faith of the church; that they are recognized in many evangelical creeds; that Calvinism contains the substance of New England Theology, not always well proportioned, not seldom intermingled with the remnants of an erring scholasticism, and sometimes enveloped in inconsistencies and expressed in a nervous style. "The voice is Jacob's voice, but the hands are the hands of Esau." The substance of our theology is Calvinistic; here it is old. Much of its self-consistency is Edwardean and Hopkinsian; here it is new. It is not mere Calvinism, but it is consistent Calvinism. Instead of pretending to be an entirely new revelation, it has always professed to be a revised and corrected edition of the Genevan creed. As such, it was extolled by its early friends, and ridiculed by its early foes. That Hopkins was far from having an ambition to shine as the originator of an altogether novel creed is apparent from the following modest words which he wrote in his eightieth year: "I believe that most of the doctrines, if not all, I have published, are to be found in the writings of former divines; viz., Calvin, Van Mastricht, Saurin, Boston, Manton, Goodwin, Owen, Bates, Baxter, Charnock, the Assembly of Divines at Westminster, Willard, Ridgley, Shepard, Hooker, etc. These, indeed, did not fully explain some of those doctrines which are asserted or implied in their writings; and many, if not most of them, are in some instances inconsistent with themselves, by advancing contrary doctrines." It was in reference to his labor in fitting together the heterogeneous parts of the Genevan creed that Emmons said, "I have spent half my life in making joints." Both he and Hopkins defended the substance of Calvinism earnestly and reverently; and the Genevan divine who now assails their memory must be ignorant of their controversial successes, or careless of that grace which is called "the memory of the heart." . . .

. . . New England divinity has been marked by strong, practical common sense. Its framers were remarkable men, invigorated by the scenes of an eventful era, and claiming our deference for their love of plain, wholesome truth. We might extol them as diligent readers. It is supposed that, on an average, Hopkins studied twelve hours a day, for more than half a century. He read in the original Latin the whole of Poole's five folios, nearly the whole of Calvin's nine folios, Turretin, Van Mastricht, and the standard treatises of English divines. For seventy years, Emmons remained like a fixture in his parsonage study, and like his brethren read "books which are books." Dr. West sat near his library so long that his feet wore away the wood-work in one part of his room, and left this enduring memorial of his sedentary habit. We care not, however, to extol our divines as readers. Many of them had been disciplined for practical life. The younger Edwards, who perused Van Mastricht seven times, was noted for his wisdom in his intercourse with men. It was a blessing not to be despised that some of our standard-bearers had been early trained to rural labors in a new country, and by this discipline they gained a healthy and practical judgment. Nearly all of them had been teachers of the common school, and Luther has well said that "no man is fit to be a theologian, who has not been a school-master." They were married men, and thus were saved from writing like the exsiccated monks of the Middle Ages. That melancholy phrase, "He hath no children," could not be applied to our divines, as to many who have speculated in favor of infant damnation. Our later theologians, as Dwight and Appleton, were adepts in the philosophy of Reid, Oswald, Campbell, Beattie, Stewart; and this has been termed *the philosophy of common sense.* The tendency of literature, during the last hundred years, has been to develop "the fundamental laws of human belief," and has aided our writers in shaping their faith according to those ethical axioms, which so many fathers in the church have undervalued. A modern reviewer has termed these axioms the germs of infidelity; but without them skepticism is our only refuge. There has never been a more independent class of thinkers than our Edwardean theologians. They lived under a free government in church and state. Nor council nor university could awe them down. Hence they did not copy after other men, so much as exercise, and thereby strengthen, their own judgment. They were peculiar, also, in being called to write a theology for the pulpit. In general, divines have written for the schools; but our fathers wrote for men, women, and children. The Germans have wondered that several of our theological systems are in the form of sermons. It is a practical form, and it was designed to exhibit a practical theology. We can say of it, as of few other systems, it is *fit* to be

261

preached. It has been accused of metaphysics, by men who distinguish between the sin belonging to us as natures, and the sin belonging to us inchoatively as bodies, and the sin belonging to us as persons. But the metaphysics of New England Theology is such as the yeomen of our fields drank down for the sincere milk of the word. It is the metaphysics of common sense. There are pious men, trained under other systems, who say in their creeds that let man do whatever he can possibly do, there is no atonement available for him, if he be of the non-elect. But when these pious men are preaching to the non-elect, they hide this notion, "like virtue." We can hardly repress a smile, when we hear good old Thomas Boston at one time exhort his impenitent hearers never to commit a sin, at another time assure them of their utter impotence to do anything which is not sin, and after all say to them, "Do what you *can*; and, it may be, while ye are doing what ye *can* for yourselves, God will do for you what ye *cannot*." It is because our theology has been practical in its aims that it has been, more than any other system, devoted to the ethical character of the acts preceding conversion, to the wisdom of demanding an immediate compliance with the law, and to the scientific refutation of all excuses for prolonged impenitence. Dr. Hopkins valued none of his speculations so highly as those in which he proved the duty of a sinner's instant surrender to God. . . .

. . . New England Theology is a comprehensive system of Biblical science. Hopkins says of President Edwards: "He studied the Bible more than all other books, and more than most other divines do." "He took his religious principles from the Bible, and not from any human system or body of divinity. Though his principles were Calvinistic, yet he called no man father. He thought and judged for himself, and was truly very much of an original." What had an Indian missionary, on the very bounds of civilized life, to fear from church authorities? The distance of our fathers from the old world made them cleave to the Word of God as their dearest standard. Who was ever more inwardly and thoroughly Protestant in his rule of faith than Samuel Hopkins? He expounded the entire Scriptures three several times to his congregation at Newport. Altogether too sternly would he have frowned upon the remark of Dr. Hodge: "If the point assailed can be shown to be a part of *the common faith of the church*, then we think the necessity for further debate is, in all ordinary cases, at an end." Altogether too severely would he have reprimanded the spirit of this remark, as leading its author into the unreasoning dogmatism of Rome. The more recent divines of New England have felt a similar preference for the Bible above creed. They have, accordingly, given such an impulse to Scriptural investigation as was previously unknown to the English world. . . .

The New England system is not only scriptural, but is scriptural *science*. Are its advocates condemned as too inquisitive? they *do* search for the truth; as too metaphysical? they do reason against a philosophy falsely so called; as too fond of novelties in speculation? they do love to "grow in knowledge"; as too ready to examine the foundations of their faith? they are not afraid of "open questions," nor of exposing their creed, in all its parts, to a rigid scrutiny. They know themselves to be imperfect. Free inquiry has made them humble; and can an arrogant temper, disdainful of all improvement be either the seed or the fruit of science? . . .

Because it is a science, it is comprehensive. A Unitarian opposer shrinks "with a feeling approaching horror," from the "stern and appalling theology" associated with the name of Hopkins. A Calvinistic opposer, as early as 1817, mourns over the Hopkinsian Seminary at Andover, because the doctrines taught there "do, in their nature and necessary consequences, lead to the Socinian ground." The vane of the Princeton Review points to Emmonism on one day as Pelagian, and on another day as ultra-Calvinistic. What is the source of these charges, that nullify each other? It is the comprehensiveness of the Edwardean scheme. This scheme unites a high, but not an ultra Calvinism, on the decrees and agency of God, with a philosophical, but not an Arminian theory, on the freedom and worth of the human soul. Its new element is seen in its harmonizing two great classes of truths; one relating to the untrammelled will of man, another relating to the supremacy of God. Because it has secured human liberty, it exalts the divine sovereignty; and its advocates have preached more than others on predestination, because they have prepared the way for it by showing that man's freedom has been predested. They have insisted on an eternally decreed liberty, and on a free submission to the eternal decrees. Their faith ascribes to man a noble structure of mind, and sinks him the lower for abusing it. In reprobating his wickedness, it exceeds all other systems; because it exceeds them all in unfolding the equity of the Sovereign against whom the subject, so richly endowed, has so needlessly rebelled. When its opposers think of its efforts to justify the ways of our Heavenly Father, they hastily accuse it of Arminianism; and when they turn their minds to its description of the Supreme, Universal Governor, they hastily accuse it of hyper-Calvinism. In these alternations between conflicting charges, they copy old replies to old theories, and misdirect them to a new doctrine. They overlook the element which Edwards disclosed to the church, the union between certainty and spontaneous choice. They forget the very genius of his system. This genius is to blend the loftiest truths concerning the Creator with the most equitable truths concerning the creature; to heighten our reverence for God, by disclosing his generosity to man, and to deepen our penitence for sin, by showing the ease with which it might have been avoided. A pious heart longs to glorify God; a sympathizing heart would arouse men to a free action; a comprehensive theology teaches in order to exhort freely, and exhorts freely in order to teach. . . .

From Edwards Amasa Park, "New England Theology," in *Bibliotheca Sacra* 9 (January 1852): 170–220.

PART 9

Things Sublime and Eternal

The New England Theology as Remembered by Harriet Beecher Stowe

Harriet Beecher Stowe (1811–96) is known for *Uncle Tom's Cabin* (1852), the best-selling novel of the entire nineteenth century. But she wrote historical novels that featured Edwardseans as well—clergy and laity—in scenes from daily life in old New England. Stowe was never completely happy with the New England Theology. She thought it exerted a crushing force on sensitive souls, especially those of females, and after her father died she joined the Episcopal Church. But as the daughter of Lyman Beecher (Nathaniel Taylor's closest friend), she came to know and even respect Edwardseanism in detail.

Stowe was born in Litchfield, Connecticut—a New Divinity stronghold—to Roxanna and the Rev. Lyman Beecher. Her father wished she had been a boy and trained her mind accordingly. Most of the men in her life were ministers—her father, seven brothers, and, eventually, her husband. Her mother died when she was five. She studied (and later taught as well) at her sister Catharine's school, the Hartford Female Seminary. Then in 1832, she moved with her family to Cincinnati, where her father became the president of Lane Theological Seminary. In 1836, she married a widower, Calvin Stowe, a Lane professor whom she met at a local literary club (the "Semi-Colons"). She gave birth to seven children (only three of whom survived her). In 1850, Calvin and Harriet moved their family to Brunswick, Maine, where Calvin accepted a teaching post at Bowdoin College. In 1853, they moved to Andover, Massachusetts. Calvin taught at Andover Seminary, and Harriet wrote books. Harriet's royalties enabled the family to build luxurious homes—first her dream home, Oakholm, and later another house in Hartford, as well as a winter home in rural Mandarin, Florida. Even after Calvin died (1886), Harriet kept these last two homes, dying in Hartford at the age of eighty-five.

The selections below are taken from Stowe's most beloved historical novels, *The Minister's Wooing* (1859) and *Oldtown Folks* (1869). Both of them fill out an understanding of the culture of the Edwardseans, as well as Stowe's apprehensions about its human casualties. Stowe knew from personal experience that, for better and for worse, New England demanded a lot of its Calvinists, rarely compensating them with emotional strokes or creature comforts. As she wrote in *The Minister's Wooing,* "It is impossible to write a story about New England life and manners for a thoughtless, shallow-minded person. If we represent things as they are, their intensity, their depth, their unworldly gravity and earnestness must inevitably repel lighter spirits, as the reverse pole of a magnet drives off sticks and straws."

This could be difficult for the "lighter spirits" living in New England. Indeed, it was difficult for Stowe and many others she knew well. But for those who thrived on the naked truth, on vital theological discourse, it could prove exhilarating. And to the extent that Stowe's novels are a reliable indicator, people like this were not uncommon in New England. Edwardsean sermons were "discussed by every farmer, in intervals of plough and hoe, by every woman and girl, at loom, spinning wheel, or wash-tub. New England was one vast sea, surging from depths to heights with thought and discussion on the most insoluble of mysteries. And it is to be added that no man or woman accepted any theory or speculation simply *as* theory or speculation; all was profoundly real and vital—a foundation on which actual life was based with intensest earnestness." No one surpasses Mrs. Stowe at making this real for the rest of us.

Harriet Beecher Stowe

THE MINISTER'S WOOING (1859)

The Minister's Wooing tells a fictional tale of the Rev. Samuel Hopkins and his parishioners in Newport at the end of the eighteenth century. A courageous opponent of slavery and an ardent disciple of Jonathan Edwards, Hopkins inspires the admiration of many members of his flock. But others view him as impractical, a threat to the social order in a seaport town whose commerce depends heavily on the traffic of the peculiar institution.

Hopkins boards with Mrs. Scudder, a prominent widow whose daughter Mary is the novel's central character. Mary respects Hopkins but falls in love with James Marvyn, a dashing but skeptical young man who seeks adventure on the high seas. Mary prays for James's soul, tries to secure his regeneration, and, when his ship is lost at sea, despairs of seeing him ever again. She consents to marry Hopkins, sure that her love for him will grow. But at the climax of the story, she and Hopkins exhibit the kind of truly disinterested benevolence that put the New Divinity on the map.

The selection below has little to do with the development of this plot. Rather, it testifies to the Spartan Calvinism of Dr. Hopkins, which could offer no assurance of James Marvyn's place in heaven to mourners doubtful of his soul's regeneration. In an excursus on the theological views of the New Divinity, Stowe unburdens her ambivalence toward clergymen like Hopkins, men of "unflinching consistency" unable to comfort weaker souls in time of need.

☙

Chapter XXIII: Views of Divine Government

We have said before, what we now repeat, that it is impossible to write a story of New England life and manners for superficial thought or shallow feeling. They who would fully understand the springs which moved the characters with whom we now associate must go down with us to the very depths.

Never was there a community where the roots of common life shot down so deeply, and were so intensely grappled around things sublime and eternal. The founders of it were a body of confessors and martyrs, who turned their backs on the whole glory of the visible, to found in the wilderness a republic of which the God of Heaven and Earth should be the sovereign power. For the first hundred years grew this community, shut out by a fathomless ocean from the existing world, and divided by an antagonism not less deep from all the reigning ideas of nominal Christendom.

In a community thus unworldly must have arisen a mode of thought, energetic, original, and sublime. The leaders of thought and feeling were the ministry, and we boldly assert that the spectacle of the early ministry of New England was one to which the world gives no parallel. Living an intense, earnest, practical life, mostly tilling the earth with their own hands, they yet carried on the most startling and original religious investigations with a simplicity that might have been deemed audacious, were it not so reverential. All old issues relating to government, religion, ritual, and forms of church organization having for them passed away, they went straight to the heart of things, and boldly confronted the problem of universal being. They had come out from the world as witnesses to the most solemn and sacred of human rights. They had accustomed themselves boldly to challenge and dispute all sham pretensions and idolatries of past ages—to question the right of kings in the State, and of prelates in the Church; and now they turned the same bold inquiries towards the Eternal Throne, and threw down their glove in the lists as authorized defenders of every mystery in the Eternal Government. The task they proposed to themselves was that of reconciling the most tremendous facts of sin and evil, present and eternal, with those conceptions of Infinite Power and Benevolence which their own strong and generous natures enabled them so vividly to realize. In the intervals of planting and harvesting, they were busy with the toils of adjusting the laws of a universe. Solemnly simple, they made long journeys in their old one-horse chaises, to settle with each other some nice point of celestial jurisprudence, and to compare their maps of the Infinite. Their letters to each other form a literature altogether unique. Hopkins sends to Edwards the younger his scheme of the universe, in which he starts with the proposition that God is infinitely above all obligations of any kind to his creatures. Edwards replies with the brusque comment—"This is wrong; God has no more right to injure a creature than a creature has to injure God"; and each probably about that time preached a sermon on his own views, which was discussed by every farmer, in intervals of plough and hoe, by every woman and girl, at loom, spinning-wheel, or wash-tub. New England was one vast sea, surging from depths to heights with thought and discussion on the most insoluble of mysteries. And it is to be added that no man or woman accepted any theory or speculation simply as theory or speculation; all was profoundly real and vital—a foundation on which actual life was based with intensest earnestness.

The views of human existence which resulted from this course of training were gloomy enough to oppress any heart which did not rise above them by triumphant faith or sink below them by brutish insensibility; for they included every moral problem of natural or revealed religion, divested of all those softening poetries and tender draperies which forms, ceremonies, and rituals had thrown around them in other parts and ages of Christendom. The human race, without exception, coming into existence "under God's wrath and curse," with a nature so fatally disordered, that, although perfect free agents, men were infallibly certain to do nothing to Divine acceptance until regenerated by the supernatural aid of God's Spirit—this aid being given only to a certain decreed number of the human race, the rest, with enough free agency to make them responsible, but without this indispensable assistance exposed to the malignant assaults of evil spirits versed in every art of temptation, were sure to fall hopelessly into perdition. The standard of what constituted a true regeneration, as presented in such treatises as Edwards on the Affections, and others of the times, made this change to be something so high, disinterested, and superhuman, so removed from all natural and common habits and feelings, that the most earnest and devoted, whose whole life had been a constant travail of endeavor, a tissue of almost unearthly disinterestedness, often lived and died with only a glimmering hope of its attainment.

According to any views then entertained of the evidences of a true regeneration, the number of the whole human race who could be supposed as yet to have received this grace was so small that, as to any numerical valuation, it must have been expressed as an infinitesimal. Dr. Hopkins in many places distinctly recognizes the fact that the greater part of the human race, up to his time, had been eternally lost—and boldly assumes the ground that this amount of sin and suffering, being the best and most necessary means of the greatest final amount of happiness, was not merely permitted, but distinctly chosen, decreed, and provided for, as essential in the schemes of Infinite Benevolence. He held that this decree not only *permitted* each individual act of sin, but also took measures to make it certain, though, by an exercise of infinite skill, it accomplished this result without violating human free agency.

The preaching of those times was animated by an unflinching consistency which never shrank from carrying an idea to its remotest logical verge. The sufferings of the lost were not kept from view, but proclaimed with a terrible power. Dr. Hopkins boldly asserts that "all the use which God will have for them is to suffer; this is all the end they can answer; therefore all their faculties, and their whole capacities, will be employed and used for this end. . . . The body can by omnipotence be made capable of suffering the greatest imaginable pain, without producing dissolution, or abating the least degree of life or sensibility. . . . One way in which God will show his power in punishing the wicked will be in strengthening and upholding their bodies and souls in torments which otherwise would be intolerable."

The sermons preached by President Edwards on this subject are so terrific in their refined poetry of torture that very few persons of quick sensibility could read them through without agony; and it is related that, when, in those calm and tender tones which never rose to passionate enunciation, he read these discourses, the house was often filled with shrieks and wailings, and that a brother minister once laid hold of his skirts, exclaiming, in an involuntary agony, "Oh! Mr. Edwards! Mr. Edwards! is God not a God of mercy?"

Not that these men were indifferent or insensible to the dread words they spoke; their whole lives and deportment bore thrilling witness to their sincerity. Edwards set apart special days of fasting, in view of the dreadful doom of the lost, in which he was wont to walk the floor, weeping and wringing his hands. Hopkins fasted every Saturday. David Brainerd gave up every refinement of civilized life to weep and pray at the feet of hardened savages, if by any means he might save *one*. All, by lives of eminent purity and earnestness, gave awful weight and sanction to their words.

If we add to this statement the fact that it was always proposed to every inquiring soul, as an evidence of regeneration, that it should truly and heartily accept all the ways of God thus declared right and lovely, and from the heart submit to Him as the only just and good, it will be seen what materials of tremendous internal conflict and agitation were all the while working in every bosom. Almost all the histories of religious experience of those times relate paroxysms of opposition to God and fierce rebellion, expressed in language which appalls the very soul—followed, at length, by mysterious elevations of faith and reactions of confiding love, the result of Divine interposition, which carried the soul far above the region of the intellect, into that of direct spiritual intuition.

President Edwards records that he was once in this state of enmity—
that the facts of the Divine administration seemed horrible to him—and
that this opposition was overcome by no course of reasoning, but by an
"inward and sweet sense," which came to him once when walking alone
in the fields, and, looking up into the blue sky, he saw the blending of the
Divine majesty with a calm, sweet, and almost infinite meekness.

The piety which grew up under such a system was, of necessity,
energetic—it was the uprousing of the whole energy of the human soul,
pierced and wrenched and probed from her lowest depths to her topmost
heights with every awful life-force possible to existence. He whose faith
in God came clear through these terrible tests would be sure never to
know greater ones. He might certainly challenge earth or heaven, things
present or things to come, to swerve him from this grand allegiance.

But it is to be conceded that these systems, so admirable in relation
to the energy, earnestness, and acuteness of their authors, when received
as absolute truth, and as a basis of actual life, had, on minds of a certain class, the effect of a slow poison, producing life-habits of morbid
action very different from any which ever followed the simple reading
of the Bible. They differ from the New Testament as the living embrace
of a friend does from his lifeless body, mapped out under the knife of
the anatomical demonstrator—every nerve and muscle is there, but to
a sensitive spirit there is the very chill of death in the analysis.

All systems that deal with the infinite are, besides, exposed to danger
from small, unsuspected admixtures of human error, which become
deadly when carried to such vast results. The smallest speck of earth's
dust, in the focus of an infinite lens, appears magnified among the heavenly orbs as a frightful monster.

Thus it happened that, while strong spirits walked, palm-crowned, with
victorious hymns, along these sublime paths, feebler and more sensitive
ones lay along the track, bleeding away in life-long despair. Fearful to
them were the shadows that lay over the cradle and the grave. The mother
clasped her babe to her bosom, and looked with shuddering to the awful
coming trial of free agency, with its terrible responsibilities and risks;
and, as she thought of the infinite chances against her beloved, almost
wished it might die in infancy. But when the stroke of death came, and
some young, thoughtless head was laid suddenly low, who can say what
silent anguish of loving hearts sounded the dread depths of eternity with
the awful question, *Where?*

In no other time or place of Christendom have so fearful issues been
presented to the mind. Some church interposed its protecting shield; the
Christian born and baptized child was supposed in some wise rescued
from the curse of the fall, and related to the great redemption—to be a
member of Christ's family, and, if ever so sinful, still infolded in some vague

sphere of hope and protection. Augustine solaced the dread anxieties of trembling love by prayers offered for the dead, in times when the Church above and on earth presented itself to the eye of the mourner as a great assembly with one accord lifting interceding hands for the parted soul.

But the clear logic and intense individualism of New England deepened the problems of the Augustinian faith, while they swept away all those softening provisions so earnestly clasped to the throbbing heart of that great poet of theology. No rite, no form, no paternal relation, no faith or prayer of church, earthly or heavenly, interposed the slightest shield between the trembling spirit and Eternal Justice. The individual entered eternity alone, as if he had no interceding relation in the universe.

This, then, was the awful dread which was constantly underlying life. This it was which caused the tolling bell in green hollows and lonely dells to be a sound which shook the soul and searched the heart with fearful questions. . . .

From Harriet Beecher Stowe, *The Minister's Wooing* (New York: Derby & Jackson, 1859), 332–50.

Harriet Beecher Stowe

OLDTOWN FOLKS (1869)

Oldtown Folks tracks the lives of two orphans, Harry and Tina, growing up in Massachusetts shortly after the Revolution. Much like she did in *The Minister's Wooing*, Harriet Beecher Stowe develops in this novel a series of portraits picturing everyday life in small-town New England before the Industrial Revolution changed its landscape and its culture. However, unlike *The Minister's Wooing, Oldtown Folks* features a cast of rather diverse Protestant pastors—from Oldtown's liberal Parson Lothrop to nearby Adams's Dr. Stern, a character based on Nathanael Emmons (one-time pastor to Catharine Beecher). As related by Horace Holyoke, the narrator of the story:

> Dr. Moses Stern's figure is well remembered by me as I saw it in my boy-hood. Everybody knew him, and when he appeared in the pulpit everybody trembled before him. He moved among men, but seemed not of men. An austere, inflexible, grand indifference to all things earthly seemed to give him the prestige and dignity of a supernatural being. His Calvinism was of so severe and ultra a type, and his statements were so little qualified either by pity of human infirmity, or fear of human censure, or desire of human approbation, that he reminded one of some ancient prophet, freighted with a mission of woe and wrath, which he must always speak, whether people would hear or whether they would forbear.

Two other ministers in the novel merit special attention here. The first is Joseph Bellamy, played in the novel by himself, though he appears not in person but through his book *True Religion*. Holyoke says of his grandmother, "who believed with heart and soul and life-blood everything that she believed at all,"

Her favorite books had different-colored covers, thriftily put on to preserve them from the wear of handling; and it was by these covers they were generally designated in the family. Hume's History of England was known as "the brown book"; Rollin's History was "the green book"; but there was one volume which she pondered oftener and with more intense earnestness than any other, which received the designation of "the blue book." This was a volume by the Rev. Dr. Bellamy of Connecticut, called "True Religion delineated, and distinguished from all Counterfeits." . . . It was written in a strong, nervous, condensed, popular style, such as is fallen into by a practical man speaking to a practical people, by a man thoroughly in earnest to men as deeply in earnest, and lastly, by a man who believed without the shadow of a doubt, and without even the comprehension of the possibility of a doubt.

Bellamy's "blue book," Stowe explains, was written originally for "a set of men and women brought up to *think*—to think not merely on agreeable subjects, but to wrestle and tug at the very severest problems."

The clerical star of *Oldtown Folks* is the redoubtable Mr. Avery, the preacher in Stowe's utopian mountain village of Cloudland. Sent there to study in the town's coeducational academy, the children find themselves in the midst of New Divinity territory, where they encounter a minister modeled after men like Stowe's father. Mr. Avery is depicted at length below.

☙

Chapter XXXIV: Our Minister in Cloudland

The picture of our life in Cloudland, and of the developing forces which were there brought to bear upon us, would be incomplete without the portrait of the minister.

Even during the course of my youth, the principles of democratic equality introduced and maintained in the American Revolution were greatly changing the social position and standing of the clergy. Ministers like Dr. Lothrop, noble men of the theocracy, men of the cocked hat, were beginning to pass away, or to appear among men only as venerable antiquities, and the present order of American citizen clergy was coming in.

Mr. Avery was a cheerful, busy, manly man, who posed himself among men as a companion and fellow-citizen, whose word on any subject was to go only so far as its own weight and momentum should carry it. . . .

Every person has a key-note to his mind which determines all its various harmonies. The key-note of Mr. Avery's was "the free agency of man." Free agency was with him the universal solvent, the philosopher's stone in theology; every line of his sermons said to every human being, "You are and you are able." And the great object was to intensify to its highest point, in every human being, the sense of individual personal responsibility.

Of course, as a Calvinist, he found food for abundant discourse in reconciling this absolute freedom of man with those declarations in the standards of the Church which assert the absolute government of God over all his creatures and all their actions. But the cheerfulness and vigor with which he drove and interpreted and hammered in the most contradictory statements, when they came in the way of his favorite ideas, was really quite inspiring.

During the year we had a whole course of systematic theology, beginning with the history of the introduction of moral evil, the fall of the angels, and the consequent fall of man and the work of redemption resulting therefrom. In the treatment of all these subjects, the theology and imagery of Milton figured so largely that one might receive the impression that Paradise Lost was part of the sacred canon.

Mr. Avery not only preached these things in the pulpit, but talked them out in his daily life. His system of theology was to him the vital breath of his being. His mind was always running upon it, and all nature was, in his sight, giving daily tributary illustrations to it. In his farming, gardening, hunting, or fishing, he was constantly finding new and graphic forms of presenting his favorite truths. The most abstract subject ceased to be abstract in his treatment of it, but became clothed upon with the homely, every-day similes of common life.

I have the image of the dear good man now, as I have seen him, seated on a hay-cart, mending a hoe-handle, and at the same moment vehemently explaining to an inquiring brother minister the exact way that Satan first came to fall, as illustrating how a perfectly holy mind can be tempted to sin. The familiarity that he showed with the celestial arcana—the zeal with which he vindicated his Maker—the perfect knowledge that he seemed to have of the strategic plans of the evil powers in the first great insurrection—are traits strongly impressed on my memory. They seemed as vivid and as much a matter of course to his mind as if he had read them out of a weekly newspaper. . . .

The Calvinism of Mr. Avery, though sharp and well defined, was not dull, as abstractions often are, nor gloomy and fateful like that of Dr. Stern. It was permeated through and through by cheerfulness and hope.

Mr. Avery was one of the kind of men who have a passion for saving souls. If there is such a thing as apostolic succession, this passion is what it ought to consist in. It is what ought to come with the laying on of hands, if the laying on of hands is what it is sometimes claimed to be.

275

Mr. Avery was a firm believer in hell, but he believed also that nobody need go there, and he was determined, so far as he was concerned, that nobody should go there if he could help it. Such a tragedy as the loss of any one soul in his parish he could not and would not contemplate for a moment; and he had such a firm belief in the truths he preached that he verily expected with them to save anybody that would listen to him.

Goethe says, "Blessed is the man who believes that he has an idea by which he may help his fellow-creatures." Mr. Avery was exactly that man. He had such faith in what preached he that he would have gone with it to Satan himself, could he have secured a dispassionate and unemployed hour, with a hope of bringing him round.

Generous and ardent in his social sympathies, Mr. Avery never could be brought to believe that any particular human being had finally perished. At every funeral he attended he contrived to see a ground for hope that the departed had found mercy. Even the slightest hints of repentance were magnified in his warm and hopeful mode of presentation. He has been known to suggest to a distracted mother, whose thoughtless boy had been suddenly killed by a fall from a horse, the possibilities of the merciful old couplet—

> "Between the saddle and the ground,
> Mercy was sought, and mercy found."

Like most of the New England ministers, Mr. Avery was a warm believer in the millennium. This millennium was the favorite recreation ground, solace, and pasture land, where the New England ministry fed their hopes and courage. Men of large hearts and warm benevolence, their theology would have filled them with gloom, were it not for this overplus of joy and peace to which human society on earth was in their view tending. Thousands of years, when the poor old earth should produce only a saintly race of perfected human beings, were to them some compensation for the darkness and losses of the great struggle.

Mr. Avery believed, not only that the millennium was coming, but that it was coming fast, and, in fact, was at the door. Every political and social change announced it. Our Revolution was a long step towards it, and the French Revolution, now in progress, was a part of that distress of nations which heralded it; and every month, when the Columbia Magazine brought in the news from Europe, Mr. Avery rushed over to Mr. Rossiter, and called him to come and hear how the thing was going. . . .

Calvinism is much berated in our days, but let us look at the political, social, and materialistic progress of countries, and ask if the world is yet far enough along to dispense with it altogether. Look at Spain at this hour, and look back at New England at the time of which I write—both having just finished a revolution, both feeling their way along the path of national independence—and compare the Spanish peasantry with the yeomen of New England, such as made up Mr. Avery's congregation—the one set made by reasoning, active-minded Calvinism, the other by pictures, statues, incense, architecture, and all the sentimental paraphernalia of ritualism.

If Spain had had not a single cathedral, if her Murillos had been all sunk in the sea, and if she had had, for a hundred years past, a set of schoolmasters and ministers working together as I have described Mr. Avery and Mr. Rossiter as working, would not Spain be infinitely better off for this life at least, whether there is any life to come or not? This is a point that I humbly present to the consideration of society. . . .

. . . Calvinistic doctrines, in their dry, abstract form, are, I confess, rather hard; but Calvinistic ministers, so far as I have ever had an opportunity to observe, are invariably a jolly set of fellows. In those early days the ministry had not yet felt the need of that generous decision which led them afterwards to forego all dangerous stimulants, as an example to their flock. A long green wooden case, full of tobacco-pipes and a quantity of papers of tobacco, used to be part of the hospitable stock prepared for the reception of the brethren. No less was there a quantity of spirituous liquor laid in. In those days its dispensation was regarded as one of the inevitable duties of hospitality. The New England ministry of this period were men full of interest. Each one was the intellectual centre of his own district, and supplied around him the stimulus which is now brought to bear through a thousand other sources. It was the minister who overlooked the school, who put parents upon the idea of giving their sons liberal educations. In poor districts the minister often practiced medicine, and drew wills and deeds, thus supplying the place of both lawyer and doctor. Apart from their doctrinal theology, which was a constant source of intellectual activity to them, their secluded life led them to many forms of literary labor.

As a specimen of these, it is recorded of the Rev. Mr. Taylor of Westfield that he took such delight in the writings of Origen that, being unable to purchase them, he copied them in four quarto volumes, that he might have them for his own study. These are still in the possession of his descendants. Other instances of literary perseverance and devotion, equally curious, might be cited.

The lives that these men led were simple and tranquil. Almost all of them were practical farmers, preserving about them the fresh sympathies and interests of the soil, and laboring enough with their hands to keep their muscles in good order, and prevent indigestion. Mingling very little with the world, each one a sort of autocrat in his way, in his own district, and with an idea of stability and perpetuity in his office, which, in these days, does not belong to the position of a minister anywhere, these men developed many originalities and peculiarities of character, to which the simple state of society then allowed full scope. They were humorists—like the mossy old apple-trees which each of them had in his orchard, bending this way and turning that, and throwing out their limbs with quaint twists and jerks, yet none the less acceptable, so long as the fruit they bore was sound and wholesome. . . .

From Harriet Beecher Stowe, *Oldtown Folks* (Boston: Fields, Osgood, 1869), 441–56.

Select Bibliography

This bibliography is not meant to be exhaustive. Rather, its purpose is to provide a reliable guide to the private papers, bibliographies, and major publications used to study the Edwardseans. After discussing the extant manuscripts of Jonathan Edwards and his followers and listing the key bibliographies for the study of their tradition, we orient readers to their best-known publications before concluding with a list of important secondary sources. (We have included only the writings of those featured in this anthology. Scores of other Edwardsean writers are not represented here, though a few of them authored works we count as secondary sources—using this category flexibly for the sake of comprehension—and have included here.)

Manuscripts

The vast majority of Jonathan Edwards's manuscripts is held in the Jonathan Edwards Collection of the Beinecke Rare Book and Manuscript Library, Yale University. (Many of the manuscripts in this collection are being reproduced on the website of the Jonathan Edwards Center; see below.) Most of the rest of Edwards's papers are held in the Jonathan Edwards Collection of the Franklin Trask Library, Andover-Newton Theological School.

The papers of the Edwardseans are scattered throughout the northeastern United States. Sizeable sets may be found at the Beinecke Rare Book and Manuscript Library, Yale University (which holds papers of Joseph Bellamy, Jonathan Edwards Jr., Sarah Osborn, John Smalley, and Edwards Amasa Park, among others); the Sterling Memorial Library, Yale University (Joseph Bellamy, Samuel Hopkins,

Asa Burton, Timothy Dwight, Nathaniel W. Taylor, Edwards Amasa Park, and others); the Yale Divinity School Library (Joseph Bellamy, Nathaniel W. Taylor, and others); the Franklin Trask Library, Andover-Newton Theological School (Samuel Hopkins, Jonathan Edwards Jr., Edwards Amasa Park, and others); the Case Memorial Library, Hartford Seminary (Joseph Bellamy, Samuel Hopkins, Jonathan Edwards Jr., the Tylerites, and others); the Historical Society of Pennsylvania, Philadelphia (Samuel Hopkins, Sarah Osborn, the Tylerites, and others); the Connecticut Historical Society, Hartford (Joseph Bellamy, Sarah Osborn, Nathaniel W. Taylor, and others); the Newport Historical Society (Samuel Hopkins, Sarah Osborn, and others); the Presbyterian Historical Society, Philadelphia (Joseph Bellamy, Nathaniel W. Taylor, and others); the Congregational Library, Boston (Samuel Hopkins, Nathanael Emmons, and others); the Boston Public Library (Samuel Hopkins and others); the Massachusetts Historical Society, Boston (Samuel Hopkins and others); the American Antiquarian Society, Worcester, Massachusetts (Joseph Bellamy, Sarah Osborn, and others); the Stowe-Day Foundation, Hartford (Harriet Beecher Stowe and others); the Oberlin College Archives (Charles G. Finney, James Harris Fairchild, and others); the Houghton Library, Harvard University (Joseph Bellamy and others); the Schlesinger Library, Radcliffe College, Harvard University (Harriet Beecher Stowe); and the Williams College Library (Samuel Hopkins).

Bibliographies

The Jonathan Edwards Center at Yale University sponsors a website containing multiple bibliographies on Edwards and his legacy (http://edwards.yale.edu). To access these aids, go to the center's home page and click on "Scholarly Resources."

Lesser, M. X. *Jonathan Edwards: An Annotated Bibliography, 1979–1993*. Bibliographies and Indexes in Religious Studies, no. 30. Westport, CT: Greenwood, 1994.

———. *Jonathan Edwards: A Reference Guide*. A Reference Guide to Literature. Boston: G. K. Hall, 1981.

———, ed. *The Printed Writings of Jonathan Edwards, 1703–1758: A Bibliography by Thomas H. Johnson*. Rev. ed. An Occasional Publication of Studies in Reformed Theology and History. Princeton: Princeton Theological Seminary, 2003.

Manspeaker, Nancy. *Jonathan Edwards: Bibliographical Synopses*. Studies in American Religion, vol. 3. Lewiston, NY: Edwin Mellen, 1981.

Works of the Major New England Theologians

General

In addition to the volumes listed below, there are several eighteenth- and nineteenth-century journals full of articles written by the Edwardseans. See especially the tables of contents of the *Massachusetts Missionary Magazine* (published primarily by the New Divinity ministers), the *Connecticut Evangelical Magazine* (New Divinity), the *Spirit of the Pilgrims* (Boston area evangelicals), the *Quarterly Christian Spectator* (New Haven theologians), the *Bibliotheca Sacra* (Andover theologians), the *Hopkinsian Magazine* (latter-day Hopkinsians), the *Evangelical Magazine* (the Tylerites), and the *Oberlin Evangelist* (Finney and company).

Beecher, Lyman. *The Autobiography of Lyman Beecher.* 2 vols. Edited by Barbara M. Cross. Cambridge: Harvard University Press, 1966.

Cooke, Parsons. *Recollections of Rev. E. D. Griffin; or, Incidents Illustrating His Character.* Boston: Sabbath School Society, 1855.

Kuklick, Bruce, ed. *American Religious Thought of the Eighteenth and Nineteenth Centuries.* New York: Garland Publishing, 1987.

Memoirs of American Missionaries, Formerly Connected with the Society of Inquiry Respecting Mission, in the Andover Theological Seminary. Boston: Peirce & Parker, 1833.

Park, Edwards A., ed. *The Atonement: Discourses and Treatises by Edwards, Smalley, Maxcy, Emmons, Griffin, Burge, and Weeks.* Boston: Congregational Board of Publication, 1859.

Spring, Gardiner. *Personal Reminiscences of the Life and Times of Gardiner Spring.* 2 vols. New York: Charles Scribner, 1866.

Jonathan Edwards

The definitive, critical edition of Jonathan Edwards's writings, both printed and manuscript, is *The Works of Jonathan Edwards* (New Haven: Yale University Press, 1957–). Nearly all of the Yale edition's projected twenty-seven volumes have been published. The entire set will soon be available on the website of the Jonathan Edwards Center at Yale University (see above).

Joseph Bellamy

A comprehensive bibliography of the writings of Joseph Bellamy is provided in Mark Valeri, *Law and Providence in Joseph Bellamy's New England: The Origins of the New Divinity in Revolutionary America,* Religion in America (New York: Oxford University Press, 1994), 180–82. What follows is a list of Bellamy's best-known publications.

A Blow at the Root of the Refined Antinomianism of the Present Age. Boston: S. Kneeland, 1763.

The Half-way Covenant: A Dialogue. New Haven: Thomas and Samuel Green, 1769.

A Letter to the Reverend Author of the Winter-Evening Conversation. Boston: S. Kneeland, 1758.

Sermons upon the Following Subjects, viz., the Divinity of Jesus Christ, the Millennium, the Wisdom of God in the Permission of Sin. Boston: Edes and Gill, and S. Kneeland, 1758.

That There Is but One Covenant, Whereof Baptism and the Lord's Supper Are Seals. New Haven: T. and S. Green, 1769.

Theron, Paulinas, and Aspasio, or Letters and Dialogues upon the Nature of Love to God, Faith in Christ, Assurance of Title to Eternal Life. Boston: S. Kneeland, 1759.

True Religion Delineated. Boston: S. Kneeland, 1750.

The Wisdom of God in the Permission of Sin, Vindicated. Boston: S. Kneeland, 1760.

The Works of Joseph Bellamy, D.D., First Pastor of the Church in Bethlem, Connecticut, with a Memoir of His Life and Character by Tryon Edwards. 2 vols. Boston: Doctrinal Tract and Book Society, 1850–53.

The Works of the Rev. Joseph Bellamy, D.D., Late of Bethlem, Connecticut. With "Funeral Sermon, with an Appendix" by Noah Benedict. 3 vols. New York: Stephen Dodge, 1811–12.

Samuel Hopkins

An Inquiry Concerning the Promises of the Gospel: Whether Any of Them Are Made to the Exercises and Doings of Persons in an Unregenerate State. Boston: W. M. Alpine and J. Flemming, 1765.

An Inquiry into the Nature of True Holiness. Newport: Solomon Southwick, 1773.

Sin, thro' Divine Interposition, an Advantage to the Universe. Boston: Daniel and John Kneeland, 1759.

Sketches of the Life of Samuel Hopkins. Edited by Stephen West. Hartford, CT: Hudson & Goodwin, 1805.

System of Doctrines Contained in Divine Revelation, Explained and Defended, Shewing Their Consistence and Connexion with Each Other, to Which Is Added, a Treatise on the Millennium. 2 vols. 2nd ed. 1793; repr., Boston: Lincoln & Edmands, 1811.

Twenty-One Sermons on a Variety of Interesting Subjects. Salem: Joshua Cushing, 1803.

Two Discourses: I. On the Necessity of the Knowledge of the Law of God, in Order to the Knowledge of Sin. II. A Particular and Critical Inquiry into the Cause, Nature, and Means of That Change in Which Men Are Born of God. Boston: n.p., 1768.
The Works of Samuel Hopkins, D.D. 3 vols. Edited by Edwards Amasa Park. Boston: Doctrinal Tract and Book Society, 1854.

Sarah Osborn

Memoirs of the Life of Mrs. Sarah Osborn Who Died at Newport, Rhode Island, on the Second Day of August, 1796. In the Eighty Third Year of Her Age. Edited by Samuel Hopkins. Worcester, MA: Leonard Worcester, 1799.
Nature, Certainty, and Evidence of True Christianity. Boston: S. Kneeland, 1755.
Osborn, Sarah, and Susanna Anthony. *Familiar Letters, Written by Mrs. Sarah Osborn, and Miss Susanna Anthony, Late of Newport, Rhode-Island.* Newport: Newport Mercury, 1807.

Nathan Strong

The Character of a Virtuous and Good Woman: A Discourse, Delivered by the Desire and in the Presence of the Female Beneficent Society, in Hartford, October 4, 1809. Hartford, CT: Hudson & Goodwin, 1809.
The Doctrine of Eternal Misery Reconcileable with the Infinite Benevolence of God. Hartford, CT: Hudson & Goodwin, 1796.
A Fast Sermon Delivered in the North Presbyterian Meeting House, in Hartford, July 23, 1812. Hartford, CT: Peter B. Gleason, 1812.
A Funeral Sermon: A Sermon Delivered at Hartford, January 6, 1807, at the Funeral of the Rev. James Cogswell, D.D., Late Pastor of the Church in Scotland, in the Town of Windham. Hartford, CT: Hudson & Goodwin, 1807.
The Mutability of Human Life: A Sermon Preached March 10, 1811. Hartford, CT: Hudson & Goodwin, 1811.
On the Universal Spread of the Gospel: A Sermon, Delivered January 4th, the First Sabbath in the Nineteenth Century of the Christian Era. Hartford, CT: Hudson & Goodwin, 1801.
Political Instruction from the Prophecies of God's Word: A Sermon Preached on the State Thanksgiving, Nov. 29, 1798. Hartford, CT: Hudson & Goodwin, 1798.
A Sermon at the Ordination of Thomas Robbins, at Norfolk, June 19, 1803, with Charge. Hartford, CT: Hudson & Goodwin, 1803.
A Sermon Delivered at the Consecration of the New Brick Church in Hartford, December 3, 1807. Hartford, CT: Hudson & Goodwin, 1808.
A Sermon Delivered in the North Presbyterian Church in Hartford, August 20th, at the Funeral of the Honorable Chauncey Goodrich, Lieutenant Governor of the State of Connecticut. Hartford, CT: Peter B. Gleason, 1815.
A Sermon on the Use of Time; Addressed to Men in the Several Ages of Life. Delivered at Hartford, January 10, 1813. Hartford, CT: Peter B. Gleason, 1813.

Sermons on Various Subjects, Doctrinal, Experimental, and Practical. 2 vols. Hartford, CT: Oliver D. and I. Cooke, 1798–1800.

Strong, Nathan, Abel Flint, and Joseph Steward, comps. *The Hartford Selection of Hymns. From the Most Approved Authors. To Which Are Added a Number Never before Published.* Hartford, CT: John Babcock, 1799.

A Thanksgiving Sermon, Delivered November 27th, 1800. Hartford, CT: Hudson & Goodwin, 1800.

Nathanael Emmons

The Works of Nathanael Emmons, D.D. Edited by Jacob Ide. 6 vols. Boston: Crocker & Brewster, 1842; seventh volume published, 1850.

The Works of Nathanael Emmons, D.D. Edited by Jacob Ide. 6 vols. Boston: Congregational Board of Publication, 1859–61.

Jonathan Edwards the Younger

A comprehensive bibliography of the writings of Jonathan Edwards the Younger, both published and unpublished, can be found in Robert L. Ferm, *Jonathan Edwards the Younger, 1745–1801, a Colonial Pastor* (Grand Rapids: Eerdmans, 1976), 184–94.

The Works of Jonathan Edwards, D.D., Late President of Union College. Edited by Tryon Edwards. 2 vols. Andover, MA: Allen, Morrill & Wardwell, 1842. Reprinted, Boston: Doctrinal Book and Tract Society, 1850.

Stephen West

An Essay on Moral Agency. Salem, MA: Thomas C. Cushing, 1794.

Evidence of the Divinity of the Lord Jesus Christ. Stockbridge, MA: R. H. Ashley, 1816.

The Scripture Doctrine of Atonement, Proposed to Careful Examination. New Haven: Meigs, Bowen & Dana, 1785.

A Sermon, Delivered on the Public Fast, April 9th, 1801. Stockbridge, MA: Heman Willard, 1801.

Sketches of the Life of the Late Rev. Samuel Hopkins, D.D. Hartford, CT: Hudson & Goodwin, 1805.

John Smalley

The Consistency of the Sinner's Inability to Comply with the Gospel; with His Inexcusable Guilt in Not Complying with It, Illustrated and Confirmed. Hartford, CT: Green & Watson, 1769.

The Law in All Respects Satisfied by Our Saviour, in Regard to Those Only Who Belong to Him; or, None but Believers Saved, through the All-Sufficient Satisfaction of Christ. A Second Sermon, Preached at Wallingford, with a View to the Universalists. Hartford, CT: Hudson & Goodwin, 1786.

On the Evils of a Weak Government: A Sermon Preached on the General Election at Hartford, in Connecticut, May 8, 1800. Hartford, CT: Hudson & Goodwin, 1800.

Sermons on a Number of Connected Subjects. 1784; repr., Hartford, CT: Oliver D. Cooke, 1803.

Sermons on Various Subjects, Doctrinal and Practical. Middletown, CT: Hart & Lincoln, 1814.

Asa Burton

Essays on Some of the First Principles of Metaphysicks, Ethicks, and Theology. Portland, ME: A. Shirley, 1824.

The Life of Asa Burton, Written by Himself. Edited by Charles Latham Jr. Thetford, VT: First Congregational Church, 1973.

Theological Tracts. 3 vols. Edited by John Brown. London: A. Fullerton, 1853.

Timothy Dwight

A comprehensive bibliography of the writings of Timothy Dwight can be found in John R. Fitzmier, *New England's Moral Legislator: Timothy Dwight, 1752–1817* (Bloomington: Indiana University Press, 1998), 241–45. What follows is a list of Dwight's best-known publications.

America: Or a Poem on the Settlement of the British Colonies; Addressed to the Friends of Freedom and Their Country. New Haven: Thomas and Samuel Green, 1780.

The Conquest of Canaan: A Poem in Eleven Books. Hartford, CT: Elisha Babcock, 1785.

The Duty of Americans at the Present Crisis, Illustrated in a Discourse, Preached on the Fourth of July, 1798, at the Request of the Citizens of New-Haven. New Haven: Thomas and Samuel Green, 1798.

Greenfield Hill: A Poem in Seven Parts. New York: Child & Swaine, 1794.

The Nature and Danger of Infidel Philosophy, Exhibited in Two Discourses Addressed to the Candidates for the Baccalaureate, in Yale College, September 9, 1797. New Haven: George Bunce, 1798.

Remarks on the Review of Inchiquin's Letters, Published in the Quarterly Review, Addressed to the Right Honourable George Canning, Esq., by an Inhabitant of New-England. 1815; repr., New York: Garrett Press, 1970.

Sermons by Timothy Dwight, D.D., LL.D., Late President of Yale College. 2 vols. New Haven: Hezekiah Howe, and Durrie & Peck, 1828.

Theology, Explained and Defended, in a Series of Sermons. 5 vols. Middletown, CT: Charles Lyman, 1818–19.

Travels in New England and New York. 4 vols. Edited by Barbara Miller Solomon, with the assistance of Patricia M. King. 1821–22; repr., Cambridge, MA: Belknap Press of Harvard University Press, 1969.

The Triumph of Infidelity: A Poem. N.p.: "Printed in the World," 1788.

The True Means of Establishing Public Happiness: A Sermon Delivered on the 7th of July, before the Connecticut Society of Cincinnati, and Published at Their Request. New Haven: T. & S. Green, 1795.

Virtuous Rulers a National Blessing: A Sermon Preached at the General Election, May 12, 1791. Hartford, CT: Hudson & Goodwin, 1791.

Nathaniel W. Taylor

Most of Nathaniel W. Taylor's writings were published in theological quarterlies, most significantly Yale's *Quarterly Christian Spectator.* For information on these, consult Douglas A. Sweeney, *Nathaniel Taylor, New Haven Theology and the Legacy of Jonathan Edwards* (New York: Oxford University Press, 2003). What follows is a list of Taylor's essential publications, some of which appeared in the quarterlies but all of which were also published separately.

Concio ad Clerum: A Sermon Delivered in the Chapel of Yale College, September 10, 1828. New Haven: Hezekiah Howe, 1828.

Essays, Lectures, Etc., upon Select Topics in Revealed Theology. New York: Clark, Austin & Smith, 1859.

Essays on the Means of Regeneration. New Haven: Baldwin & Teadway, 1829.

An Inquiry into the Nature of Sin, as Exhibited in Dr. Dwight's Theology. A Letter to a Friend, by Clericus. New Haven: Hezekiah Howe, 1829.

Introduction to *Yahveh Christ, or, the Memorial Name,* by Alexander MacWhorter. Boston: Gould & Lincoln, 1857.

Lectures on the Moral Government of God. 2 vols. New York: Clark, Austin & Smith, 1859.

Man, a Free Agent without the Aid of Divine Grace. Tracts Designed to Illustrate and Enforce the Most Important Doctrines of the Gospel, no. 2. New Haven, 1818.

Practical Sermons. New York: Clark, Austin & Smith, 1858.

Regeneration the Beginning of Holiness in the Human Heart: A Sermon. New Haven: Nathan Whiting, 1816.

A Sermon, Addressed to the Legislature of the State of Connecticut, at the Annual Election in Hartford, May 7, 1823. Hartford, CT: Charles Babcock, 1823.

James Harris Fairchild

James Harris Fairchild published extensively in ecclesiastical quarterlies such as the *Oberlin Quarterly Review* and the *Congregational Quarterly*. What follows is a list of other, separately published writings.

Educational Arrangements and College Life at Oberlin: Inaugural Address of President J. H. Fairchild, Delivered at the Commencement of Oberlin College. New York: E. D. Jenkins, 1866.

Elements of Theology, Natural and Revealed. Oberlin, OH: Edward J. Goodrich, 1892.

Moral Philosophy; or, the Science of Obligation. New York: Sheldon & Co., 1869.

Oberlin: Its Origin, Progress, and Results. Oberlin, OH: Butler, 1871.

Oberlin: The Colony and the College, 1833–83. Oberlin, OH: Goodrich, 1883.

Present Demand of the Missionary Work: A Sermon Preached at the Sixty-Eighth Annual Meeting of the American Board of Commissioners for Foreign Missions, Providence, Oct. 2, 1877. Boston: Beacon, 1877.

Underground Railroad . . . An Address Delivered for the Society in Association Hall, Cleveland, January 24, 1895. N.p., 1895.

Charles G. Finney

Extensive bibliographies of the writings of Charles G. Finney can be found in Garth M. Rosell and Richard A. G. Dupuis, eds., *The Memoirs of Charles G. Finney: The Complete Restored Text* (Grand Rapids: Zondervan, 1989), 671–701; and Keith J. Hardman, *Charles Grandison Finney, 1792–1875: Revivalist and Reformer* (Syracuse: Syracuse University Press, 1987), 502–3. What follows is a list of Finney's best-known publications.

Guide to the Savior, or Conditions of Attaining to and Abiding in Entire Holiness of Heart and Life. Oberlin, OH: James M. Fitch, 1848.

Lectures on Revivals of Religion. Edited by William G. McLoughlin. 1835; repr., Cambridge: Harvard University Press, 1960.

Lectures on Systematic Theology. 2 vols. Oberlin, OH: James M. Fitch, 1846–47.

Lectures to Professing Christians. New York: John S. Taylor, 1837.

The Prevailing Prayer Meeting. London: Ward, 1859.

Sermons on Gospel Themes. Oberlin, OH: Goodrich, 1876.

Sermons on Important Subjects. New York: John S. Taylor, 1836.

Sermons on Various Subjects. New York: Taylor, 1834.

Views of Sanctification. Oberlin, OH: James Steele, 1840.

Edwards Amasa Park

In addition to the volumes listed below, Edwards Amasa Park published dozens of articles in the *Bibliotheca Sacra,* a journal he edited for over forty years. Both of the entries by Park in this volume, in fact, were published first in the pages of that journal.

The Associate Creed of Andover Theological Seminary. Boston: Franklin Press, 1883.

The Atonement: Discourse and Treatises by Edwards, Smalley, Maxcy, Emmons, Griffin, Burge, and Weeks, with an Introductory Essay. Boston: Congregational Board of Publication, 1859.

A Discourse Delivered at the Funeral of Professor Moses Stuart. Boston: Tappan & Whittemore, 1852.

Essay on the Imprecatory Psalms Viewed in the Light of the Southern Rebellion. Andover, MA: Draper, 1862.

Memoir of Nathanael Emmons, with Sketches of His Friends and Pupils. Boston: Congregational Board of Publication, 1861.

Memoir of the Life and Character of Samuel Hopkins, D.D. In *The Works of Samuel Hopkins, D.D.* 3 vols. Edited by Edwards Amasa Park. Boston: Doctrinal Tract and Book Society, 1852.

Memorial Collection of Sermons. Compiled by Agnes Park. Boston: Pilgrim, 1902.

New England Theology: With Comments on a Third Article in the Princeton Review, Relating to a Convention Sermon. Andover, MA: W. F. Draper, 1852.

The Theology of the Intellect and That of the Feelings: A Discourse Delivered before the Convention of the Congregational Ministers of Massachusetts . . . May 30, 1850. Boston: Perkins & Whipple, 1850.

Harriet Beecher Stowe (and the Edwardsean Tradition)

The Minister's Wooing. New York: Derby & Jackson, 1859.

"New England Ministers." *Atlantic Monthly* 1 (February 1858): 487.

Oldtown Folks. Boston: Fields, Osgood, 1869.

Poganuc People. New York: Fords, Howard & Hulbert, 1878.

Secondary Sources

General

Abzug, Robert H. *Passionate Liberator: Theodore Dwight Weld and the Dilemma of Reform.* New York: Oxford University Press, 1980.

Ahlstrom, Sydney E. "Theology in America: A Historical Survey." In *The Shaping of American Religion,* edited by James Ward Smith and A. Leland Jamison. Princeton: Princeton University Press, 1961.

———, ed. *Theology in America: The Major Protestant Voices from Puritanism to Neo-Orthodoxy.* Indianapolis: Bobbs-Merrill, 1967.

"The Alleged Collapse of New England Theology." *Bibliotheca Sacra* 65 (October 1908): 601–10.

Allen, Alexander V. G. "The Transition in New England Theology." *Atlantic Monthly* 68 (December 1891): 767–80.

Allmendinger, David F. "Mount Holyoke Students Encounter the Need for Life Planning, 1837–1850." *History of Education Quarterly* 19 (1979): 27–43.

———. *Paupers and Scholars: The Transformation of Student Life in Nineteenth-Century New England.* New York: St. Martin's, 1975.

Andrew, John A., III. *From Revivals to Removal: Jeremiah Evarts, the Cherokee Nation, and the Search for the Soul of America.* Athens: University of Georgia Press, 1991.

———. *Rebuilding the Christian Commonwealth: New England Congregationalists and Foreign Missions, 1800–1830.* Lexington: University Press of Kentucky, 1976.

Atkins, Gaius Glenn. "New England Theology." In *An Encyclopedia of Religion,* edited by Vergilius Ferm. New York: Philosophical Library, 1945.

———, and Frederick L. Fagley. *History of American Congregationalism.* Boston: Pilgrim, 1942.

Atwater, Lyman Hotchkiss. "Jonathan Edwards and the Successive Forms of New Divinity." *Princeton Review* 30 (October 1858): 585–620.

———. "Old Orthodoxy, New Divinity, and Unitarianism." *Biblical Repertory and Princeton Review* 29 (October 1857): 561–98.

Bacon, Leonard. *A Commemorative Discourse, on the Completion of Fifty Years from the Founding of the Theological Seminary at Andover.* Andover, MA: W. F. Draper, 1858.

———. *The Story of the Churches: The Congregationalists.* New York: Baker & Taylor, 1904.

Bailey, Sarah Loring. *Historical Sketches of Andover.* Boston: Houghton, 1880.

Bainton, Roland H. *Yale and the Ministry: A History of Education for Christian Ministry at Yale from the Founding in 1701.* New York: Harper & Brothers, 1957.

Baird, Samuel J. "Edwards and the Theology of New England." *Southern Presbyterian Review* 10 (January 1858): 574–92.

———. *A History of the New School, and of Questions Involved in the Disruption of the Presbyterian Church in 1838.* Philadelphia: Claxton, Remsen & Haffelfinger, 1868.

Baldwin, Ebenezer. *The History of Yale College, from Its Foundation, A.D. 1700, to the Year 1838.* New Haven: Benjamin and William Noyes, 1841.

289

Birdsall, Richard D. *Berkshire County: A Cultural History.* New Haven: Yale University Press, 1959.

———. "Ezra Stiles versus the New Divinity Men." *American Quarterly* 17 (Summer 1965): 248–58.

———. "The Second Great Awakening and the New England Social Order." *Church History* 39 (September 1970): 345–64.

Birney, George Hugh, Jr. "The Life and Letters of Asahel Nettleton, 1783–1844." Ph.D. diss., Hartford Theological Seminary, 1943.

Bloch, Ruth H. *Visionary Republic: Millennial Themes in American Thought, 1756–1800.* Cambridge: Cambridge University Press, 1985.

Boardman, George Nye. *A History of New England Theology.* New York: A. D. F. Randolph, 1899.

Bogin, Ruth. "'Liberty Further Extended': A 1776 Antislavery Manuscript by Lemuel Haynes." *William and Mary Quarterly* 40 (January 1983): 85–105.

Breitenbach, William. "The Consistent Calvinism of the New Divinity Movement." *William and Mary Quarterly* 41 (April 1984): 241–64.

———. "New Divinity Theology and the Idea of Moral Accountability." Ph.D. diss., Yale University, 1978.

———. "Unregenerate Doings: Selflessness and Selfishness in New Divinity Theology." *American Quarterly* 34 (Winter 1982): 479–502.

Brown, Jerry Wayne. *The Rise of Biblical Criticism in America, 1800–1870.* Middletown, CT: Wesleyan University Press, 1969.

Bryant, M. Darrol. "From Edwards to Hopkins: A Millennialist Critique of Political Culture." In *The Coming Kingdom: Essays in American Millennialism and Eschatology,* edited by M. Darrol Bryant and Donald W. Dayton. Barrytown, NY: New Era Books, 1983.

Buckham, John Wright. "The New England Theologians." *American Journal of Theology* 24 (January 1920): 19–29.

Chaney, Charles L. "God's Glorious Work: The Theological Foundations of the Early Missionary Societies in America, 1787–1817." Ph.D. diss., University of Chicago, 1973.

Channing, William Henry. "Edwards and the Revivalists." *Christian Examiner* 43 (November 1847): 374–94.

Cherry, Conrad. *Nature and Religious Imagination from Edwards to Bushnell.* Philadelphia: Fortress, 1980.

Clark, Joseph S. *A Historical Sketch of the Congregational Churches in Massachusetts from 1620 to 1858.* Boston: Congregational Board of Publication, 1858.

Clark, Sereno D. *The New England Ministry Sixty Years Ago: The Memoir of John Woodbridge, D.D.* Boston: Lee & Shepard, 1877.

Clebsch, William A. *American Religious Thought: A History.* Chicago: University of Chicago Press, 1973.

Cole, Arthur C. *A Hundred Years of Mount Holyoke College: The Evolution of an Educational Ideal.* New Haven: Yale University Press, 1940.

Committee of the Synod of New York and New Jersey. *A History of the Division of the Presbyterian Church in the United States of America.* New York: Dodd, 1852.

Conforti, Joseph. "Edwardsians, Unitarians, and the Memory of the Great Awakening, 1800–1840." In *American Unitarianism: 1805–1865,* edited by Conrad Edick Wright. Boston: Northeastern University Press, 1989.

———. "Jonathan Edwards and American Studies." *American Quarterly* 41 (March 1989): 165–71.

———. *Jonathan Edwards, Religious Tradition, and American Culture.* Chapel Hill: University of North Carolina Press, 1995.

———. "The Rise of the New Divinity in Western New England, 1740–1800." *Historical Journal of Western Massachusetts* 8 (January 1980): 37–47.

Conkin, Paul K. *The Uneasy Center: Reformed Christianity in Antebellum America.* Chapel Hill: University of North Carolina Press, 1995.

Constantin, Charles Joseph, Jr. "The New Divinity Men." Ph.D. diss., University of California at Berkeley, 1972.

Contributions to the Ecclesiastical History of Connecticut. New Haven: William L. Kingsley, 1861.

Cooke, Parson. *Views in New England Theology No. I: The New England Theology Contrasted with the New Arminianism.* Boston: Crocker & Brewster, 1859.

———. *Views in New England Theology No. II: The New Apostasy, or a Word to the Laodiceans.* Boston: Crocker & Brewster, 1860.

Cott, Nancy F. "Young Women in the Second Great Awakening in New England." *Feminist Studies* 3 (Fall 1975): 15–29.

Crocker, Zebulon. *The Catastrophe of the Presbyterian Church, in 1837, Including a Full View of the Recent Theological Controversies in New England.* New Haven: B. and W. Noyes, 1838.

Davidson, James West. *The Logic of Millennial Thought: Eighteenth-Century New England.* New Haven: Yale University Press, 1977.

Davis, Hugh. *Leonard Bacon: New England Reformer and Antislavery Moderate.* Baton Rouge: Louisiana State University Press, 1998.

———. "Leonard Bacon, the Congregational Church, and Slavery, 1845–1861." In *Religion and the Antebellum Debate over Slavery,* edited by John R. McKivigan. Athens: University of Georgia Press, 1998.

de Jong, J. A. *As the Waters Cover the Sea: Millennial Expectations in the Rise of Anglo-American Missions.* Kampen, Neth.: J. H. Kok, 1970.

DeJong, Peter Y. *The Covenant Idea in New England Theology, 1620–1847.* Grand Rapids: Eerdmans, 1945.

Dexter, Franklin B. *Biographical Sketches of the Graduates of Yale College, with Annals of the College History.* 6 vols. New York: H. Holt, 1885–1912.

Dexter, Henry Martyn. *The Congregationalism of the Last Three Hundred Years as Seen in Its Literature.* New York: Harper, 1880.

Douglas, Ann. *The Feminization of American Culture.* New York: Knopf, 1977.

Dugdale, Antony, J. J. Fueser, and J. Celso de Castro Alves. *Yale, Slavery, and Abolition.* New Haven: Amistad Committee, 2001.

Dunning, Albert E. *Congregationalists in America: A Popular History of Their Origins, Belief, Polity, Growth, and Work.* Boston: Pilgrim, 1894.

Durfee, Calvin. *A History of Williams College.* Boston: A. Williams, 1860.

Dwight, William Theodore. *Characteristics of New England Theology: A Discourse, Delivered at the First Public Anniversary of the Congregational Board of Publication, at the Tremont Temple, Boston.* Boston: Congregational Board of Publication, 1855.

Education for Christian Service, by Members of the Faculty of the Divinity School of Yale University: A Volume in Commemoration of Its One Hundredth Anniversary. New Haven: Yale University Press, 1922.

Elsbree, Oliver W. *The Rise of the Missionary Spirit in America, 1790–1815.* Williamsport, PA: Williamsport Printing, 1928.

Ely, Ezra Stiles. *A Contrast between Calvinism and Hopkinsianism.* New York: S. Whiting, 1811.

Essig, James D. *The Bonds of Wickedness: American Evangelicals against Slavery, 1770–1808.* Philadelphia: Temple University Press, 1982.

Exercises Commemorating the Two-Hundredth Anniversary of the Birth of Jonathan Edwards, Held at Andover Theological Seminary, October 4 and 5, 1903. Andover, MA: Andover Press, 1904.

Fisher, George Park. "The Augustinian and the Federal Theologies of Original Sin Compared." *New Englander* 27 (June 1868): 468–516.

———. *A Discourse, Commemorative of the History of the Church of Christ in Yale College.* New Haven: Thomas H. Pease, 1858.

———. *Discussions in History and Theology.* New York: Charles Scribner's Sons, 1880.

Fisk, Fidelia. *Recollections of Mary Lyon, with Selections from Her Instruction to the Pupils in Mt. Holyoke Female Seminary.* Boston: American Tract Society, 1866.

Fisk, Wilbur. *Calvinistic Controversy.* New York: T. Mason and G. Lane, 1837.

Fiske, Daniel T. *The Creed of Andover Theological Seminary.* Boston: Cupples, Upham, 1887.

———. "New England Theology." *Bibliotheca Sacra* 22 (July 1865): 467–512; (October 1865): 568–88.

Foster, Frank Hugh. "The Eschatology of the New England Divines." *Bibliotheca Sacra* 43 (1886): 1–32.

———. *A Genetic History of the New England Theology.* Chicago: University of Chicago Press, 1907.

———. "New England Theology." In *The New Schaff-Herzog Encyclopedia of Religious Knowledge,* edited by Samuel McCauley Jackson. 12 vols. New York: Funk & Wagnalls, 1910.

Fraser, James W. *Pedagogue for God's Kingdom: Lyman Beecher and the Second Great Awakening.* Lanham, MD: University Press of America, 1985.

Fuess, Claude Moore. *Andover: Symbol of New England.* Andover, MA: Andover Historical Society, 1959.

Gabriel, Ralph Henry. *Religion and Learning at Yale: The Church of Christ in the College and University, 1757–1957.* New Haven: Yale University Press, 1958.

Gale, Nahum. *Memoir of Bennet Tyler.* Boston: J. E. Tilton, 1859.

Gambrell, Mary Latimer. *Ministerial Training in Eighteenth-Century New England.* New York: Columbia University Press, 1937.

Geer, Curtis Manning. *The Hartford Theological Seminary, 1834–1934.* Hartford, CT: Case, Lockwood & Brainard, 1934.

Geissler, Suzanne. *Jonathan Edwards to Aaron Burr, Jr.: From the Great Awakening to Democratic Politics.* New York: Edwin Mellen, 1981.

General Catalogue of the Theological Seminary, Andover, Massachusetts, 1808–1908. Boston: T. Todd, 1909.

German, James. "The Social Utility of Wicked Self-Love: Calvinism, Capitalism, and Public Policy in Revolutionary New England." *Journal of American History* 82 (December 1995): 965–98.

Gerstner, John H. "American Calvinism until the Twentieth Century Especially in New England." In *American Calvinism: A Survey,* edited by Jacob T. Hoogstra. Grand Rapids: Baker, 1957.

Gilchrist, Beth Bradford. *The Life of Mary Lyon.* Boston: Houghton Mifflin, 1910.

Giltner, John H. "The Fragmentation of New England Congregationalism and the Founding of Andover Seminary." *Journal of Religious Thought* 20 (1963–64): 27–42.

———. *Moses Stuart: The Father of Biblical Science in America.* Atlanta: Scholars Press, 1988.

Ginzberg, Lori D. "Women in an Evangelical Community: Oberlin 1835–1850." *Ohio History* 89 (Winter 1980): 78–88.

Goodenough, Arthur. *The Clergy of Litchfield County.* Litchfield, CT: N.p., 1909.

Gordon, George A. "The Collapse of the New England Theology." *Harvard Theological Review* 1 (April 1908): 127–68.

———. "The Contrast and Agreement between the New Orthodoxy and the Old." *Andover Review* 19 (January 1893): 1–18.

———. *Humanism in New England Theology.* Boston: Houghton Mifflin, 1920.

———. "The Significance of Edwards Today." *Congregationalist* 85 (June 28, 1900): 944–46.

Granquist, Mark. "The Role of 'Common Sense' in the Hermeneutics of Moses Stuart." *Harvard Theological Review* 83 (1990): 305–19.

Grasso, Christopher. *A Speaking Aristocracy: Transforming Public Discourse in Eighteenth-Century Connecticut.* Chapel Hill: University of North Carolina Press, 1999.

Green, Elizabeth Alden. *Mary Lyon and Mount Holyoke: Opening the Gates.* Hanover, NH: University Press of New England, 1979.

Grossbart, Stephen R. "Seeking the Divine Favor: Conversion and Admission in Eastern Connecticut, 1711–1832." *William and Mary Quarterly* 46 (October 1989): 696–740.

Guelzo, Allen C. *Edwards on the Will: A Century of American Theological Debate.* Middletown, CT: Wesleyan University Press, 1989.

———. "From Calvinist Metaphysics to Republican Theory: Jonathan Edwards and James Dana on the Freedom of the Will." *Journal of the History of Ideas* 56 (July 1995): 413–18.

———. "Jonathan Edwards and the New Divinity: Change and Continuity in New England Calvinism, 1758–1858." In *Pressing Toward the Mark: Essays Commemorating Fifty Years of the Orthodox Presbyterian Church,* edited by Charles G. Dennison and Richard C. Gamble. Philadelphia: Committee for the History of the Orthodox Presbyterian Church, 1986.

Hannah, John D. "The Doctrine of Original Sin in Postrevolutionary America." *Bibliotheca Sacra* 134 (July–September 1977): 238–56.

Harding, Vincent. "Lyman Beecher and the Transformation of American Protestantism." Ph.D. diss., University of Chicago, 1965.

Haroutunian, Joseph. *Piety versus Moralism: The Passing of the New England Theology.* New York: Henry Holt, 1932.

Harpole, Ralph Orin. "The Development of the Doctrine of Atonement in American Thought from Jonathan Edwards to Horace Bushnell." Ph.D. diss., Yale University, 1924.

Hart, D. G., Sean Michael Lucas, and Stephen J. Nichols, eds. *The Legacy of Jonathan Edwards: American Religion and the Evangelical Tradition.* Grand Rapids: Baker, 2003.

Hatch, Nathan O., and Harry S. Stout, eds. *Jonathan Edwards and the American Experience.* New York: Oxford University Press, 1988.

Heimert, Alan. *Religion and the American Mind: From the Great Awakening to the Revolution.* Cambridge: Harvard University Press, 1966.

Henry, Stuart C. *Unvanquished Puritan: A Portrait of Lyman Beecher.* Grand Rapids: Eerdmans, 1973.

Hirrel, Leo P. *Children of Wrath: New School Calvinism and Antebellum Reform.* Lexington: University Press of Kentucky, 1998.

Hitchcock, Edward. *The Power of Christian Benevolence, Illustrated in the Life and Labors of Mary Lyon.* Northampton, MA: Hopkins, Bridgman, 1851.

Hodge, Charles. "Clap's Defence of the Doctrines of the New England Churches." *Biblical Repertory and Princeton Review* 11 (July 1839): 369–404.

Hodges, Alpheus C. "Yale Graduates in Western Massachusetts." *Papers of the New Haven Colony Historical Society* 4 (1888): 253–98.

Holifield, E. Brooks. *Theology in America: Christian Thought from the Age of the Puritans to the Civil War.* New Haven: Yale University Press, 2003.

Holland, David F. "Anne Hutchinson to Horace Bushnell: A New Take on the New England Sequence." *New England Quarterly* 78 (June 2005): 163–201.

Hoopes, James. *Consciousness in New England: From Puritanism and Ideas to Psychoanalysis and Semiotics.* Baltimore: Johns Hopkins University Press, 1989.

Howard, Victor B. *Conscience and Slavery: The Evangelistic Calvinist Domestic Missions, 1837–1861.* Kent, OH: Kent State University Press, 1990.

Howe, Daniel Walker. "The Decline of Calvinism: An Approach to Its Study." *Comparative Studies in Society and History* 14 (1972): 306–27.

———. *Making the American Self: Jonathan Edwards to Abraham Lincoln.* Cambridge: Harvard University Press, 1997.

Humphrey, Heman. *Revival Sketches and Manual.* New York: American Tract Society, 1859.

Hutchinson, George P. *The Problem of Original Sin in American Presbyterian Theology.* Nutley, NJ: Presbyterian & Reformed, 1972.

Keller, Charles Roy. *The Second Great Awakening in Connecticut.* New Haven: Yale University Press, 1942.

Kelley, Brooks Mather. *Yale: A History.* New Haven: Yale University Press, 1974.

Kennedy, William S. *The Plan of Union.* Hudson, OH: Pentagon Steam Press, 1856.

Kling, David W. *A Field of Divine Wonders: The New Divinity and Village Revivals in Northwestern Connecticut, 1792–1822.* University Park: Pennsylvania State University Press, 1993.

———. "The New Divinity and Schools of the Prophets, 1750–1825." In *Theological Education in the Evangelical Tradition,* edited by R. Albert Mohler and D. G. Hart. Grand Rapids: Baker, 1996.

———. "The New Divinity and the Origins of the American Board of Commissioners for Foreign Missions." *Church History* 72 (December 2003): 791–819. Reprinted in Wilbert R. Shenk, ed. *North American Foreign Missions, 1810–1914: Theology, Theory, and Policy.* Studies in the History of Christian Missions. Grand Rapids: Eerdmans, 2004.

———. "The New Divinity and Williams College, 1793–1836." *Religion and American Culture* 6 (Summer 1996): 195–223.

———. "New Divinity Schools of the Prophets, 1750–1825: A Case Study in Ministerial Education." *History of Education Quarterly* 37 (Summer 1997): 185–206.

———, and Douglas A. Sweeney, eds. *Jonathan Edwards at Home and Abroad: Historical Memories, Cultural Movements, Global Horizons.* Columbia, SC: University of South Carolina Press, 2003.

Kuehne, Dale S. *Massachusetts Congregationalist Political Thought, 1760–1790: The Design of Heaven.* Columbia, MO: University of Missouri Press, 1996.

Kuklick, Bruce. *Churchmen and Philosophers: From Jonathan Edwards to John Dewey.* New Haven: Yale University Press, 1985.

Lawrence, Edward Alexander. "New England Theology Historically Considered." *American Theological Review* 2 (May 1860): 209–32.

———. "New England Theology: The Edwardean Period." *American Theological Review* 3 (January 1861): 36–69.

———. "The Old School in New England Theology." *Bibliotheca Sacra* 20 (April 1863): 311–48.

Lesick, Lawrence Thomas. *The Lane Rebels: Evangelicalism and Antislavery in Antebellum America.* Studies in Evangelicalism, no. 2. Metuchen, NJ: Scarecrow, 1980.

Lewis, Donald M., ed. *The Blackwell Dictionary of Evangelical Biography, 1730–1860.* 2 vols. Oxford: Blackwell, 1995.

Linden, Marshall. "In and beyond Joseph Bellamy's Shadow: A Life of Azel Backus (1765–1816)." *Bulletin of the Congregational Library* 42 (Winter 1991): 4–17.

Long, Gary Dale. "The Doctrine of Original Sin in New England Theology from Jonathan Edwards to Edwards Amasa Park." Th.D. diss., Dallas Theological Seminary, 1972.

Lowe, Wolfgang E. "The First American Foreign Missionaries: The Students, 1810–1829: An Inquiry into Their Theological Motives." Ph.D. diss., Brown University, 1962.

Marsden, George M. *The Evangelical Mind and the New School Presbyterian Experience: A Case Study of Thought and Theology in Nineteenth-Century America.* New Haven: Yale University Press, 1970.

———. "The New School Heritage and Presbyterian Fundamentalism." *Westminster Theological Journal* 33 (1970): 129–47.

Matthews, Lyman. *Memoir of the Life and Character of Ebenezer Porter, D.D., Late President of the Theological Seminary, Andover.* Boston: Perkins & Marvin, 1837.

May, Sherry Pierpont. "Asahel Nettleton: Nineteenth-Century American Revivalist." Ph.D. diss., Drew University, 1969.

McCoy, Genevieve. "The Women of the ABCFM Oregon Mission and the Conflicted Language of Calvinism." *Church History* 64 (March 1995): 62–82.

McKivigan, John R. *The War against Proslavery Religion: Abolitionism and the Northern Churches, 1830–1865.* Ithaca: Cornell University Press, 1984.

Memorial: Twenty-Fifth Anniversary of the Mount Holyoke Female Seminary. Springfield, MA: S. Bowles, 1862.

Meyer, Donald. "The Dissolution of Calvinism." In *Paths of American Thought,* edited by Arthur M. Schlesinger Jr. and Morton White. Boston: Houghton Mifflin, 1963.

Miller, Perry. *Errand into the Wilderness.* Cambridge: Belknap Press of Harvard University Press, 1956.

———. *The Life of the Mind in America: From the Revolution to the Civil War.* New York: Harcourt, Brace & World, 1965.

Minkema, Kenneth P., and Harry S. Stout. "The Edwardsean Tradition and the Antislavery Debate, 1740–1865." *Journal of American History* 92 (June 2005): 47–74.

Mitchell, Mary Hewitt. *The Great Awakening and Other Revivals in the Religious Life of Connecticut.* New Haven: Yale University Press, 1934.

Morris, Edward D. *The Presbyterian Church New School, 1837–1869: An Historical Review.* Columbus: Chaplin Press, 1905.

Morse, James King. *Jedidiah Morse: A Champion of New England Orthodoxy.* New York: Columbia University Press, 1939.

Murray, Iain H. *Revival and Revivalism: The Making and Marring of American Evangelicalism, 1750–1858.* Carlisle, PA: Banner of Truth Trust, 1994.

Nash, Ansel. "Memoir of Edward Dorr Griffin." *American Quarterly Register* 13 (May 1841): 365–85.

"New and Old Calvinism." *Methodist Review* 13 (April 1831): 222–27.

"New England Theology." *Church Review* 5 (October 1852): 349–60.

Niebuhr, H. Richard. *The Kingdom of God in America.* New York: Harper & Brothers, 1937.

Noll, Mark A. *America's God, from Jonathan Edwards to Abraham Lincoln.* New York: Oxford University Press, 2002.

———. "The Contested Legacy of Jonathan Edwards in Antebellum Calvinism: Theological Conflict and the Evolution of Thought in America." *Canadian Review of American Studies* 19 (Summer 1988): 149–64.

———. "Moses Mather (Old Calvinist) and the Evolution of Edwardseanism." *Church History* 49 (September 1980): 273–85.

———. "Revival, Enlightenment, Civic Humanism, and the Development of Dogma: Scotland and America, 1735–1843." *Tyndale Bulletin* 40 (1989): 49–76.

Noricks, Ronald Harold. "'To Turn Them from Darkness': The Missionary Society of Connecticut on the Early Frontier." Ph.D. diss., University of California, Riverside, 1975.

"Old Orthodoxy, New Divinity, and Unitarianism." *Biblical Repertory and Princeton Review* 29 (October 1857): 561–98.

Opie, John, Jr. "Conversion and Revivalism: An Internal History from Jonathan Edwards through Charles Grandison Finney." Ph.D. diss., University of Chicago, 1964.

Osgood, Samuel. "Jonathan Edwards and the New Calvinism." In *Studies in Christian Biography: or, Hours with Theologians and Reformers.* New York: C. S. Francis, 1850.

Peabody, Andrew P. "Hopkinsianism." *Proceedings of the American Antiquarian Society* 5 (1898): 437–61.

Phillips, Joseph W. *Jedidiah Morse and New England Congregationalism*. New Brunswick: Rutgers University Press, 1983.

Piper, John, and Justin Taylor, eds. *A God-Entranced Vision of All Things: The Legacy of Jonathan Edwards*. Wheaton: Crossway, 2003.

Pond, Enoch. *The Autobiography of the Rev. Enoch Pond*. Edited by Enoch Pond Parker. Boston: Congregational Sunday School and Publishing Society, 1883.

———. *Sketches of the Theological History of New England*. Boston: Congregational Publishing Society, 1880.

Pope, Earl. *New England Calvinism and the Disruption of the Presbyterian Church*. 1962; repr., New York: Garland, 1987.

Porter, Ebenezer. *Letters on the Religious Revivals Which Prevailed about the Beginning of the Present Century*. Boston: Congregational Board of Publication, 1858.

Porterfield, Amanda. *Feminine Spirituality in America: From Sarah Edwards to Martha Graham*. Philadelphia: Temple University Press, 1980.

———. *Mary Lyon and the Mount Holyoke Missionaries*. New York: Oxford University Press, 1997.

Post, Stephen G. *Christian Love and Self-Denial: An Historical and Normative Study of Jonathan Edwards, Samuel Hopkins, and American Theological Ethics*. Lanham, MD: University Press of America, 1987.

———. "Disinterested Benevolence: An American Debate over the Nature of Christian Love." *Journal of Religious Ethics* 14 (Fall 1986): 356–68.

———. *A Theory of Agape: On the Meaning of Christian Love*. Lewisburg, PA: Bucknell University Press, 1990.

"The Power of Contrary Choice." *Princeton Review* 12 (October 1840): 532–49.

Purcell, Richard. *Connecticut in Transition: 1755–1818*. 1918; repr., Middletown, CT: Wesleyan University Press, 1963.

Rabinowitz, Richard. *The Spiritual Self in Everyday Life: The Transformation of Personal Religious Experience in Nineteenth-Century New England*. Boston: Northeastern University Press, 1989.

Robbins, Sarah Stuart. *Old Andover Days: Memories of a Puritan Childhood*. Boston: Pilgrim, 1908.

Rohrer, James R. *Keepers of the Covenant: Frontier Missions and the Decline of Congregationalism, 1774–1818*. Religion in America Series. New York: Oxford University Press, 1995.

Rowe, Henry K. *History of Andover Theological Seminary*. Newton, MA: Thomas Todd, 1933.

Rudisill, Dorus Paul. *The Doctrine of the Atonement in Jonathan Edwards and His Successors*. New York: Poseidon Books, 1971.

Rudolph, Frederick. *Mark Hopkins and the Log: Williams College, 1836–1872*. New Haven: Yale University Press, 1956.

Saillant, John. *Black Puritan, Black Republican: The Life and Thought of Lemuel Haynes, 1753–1833*. Religion in America Series. New York: Oxford University Press, 2003.

———. *Black, White, and "The Charitable Blessed": Race and Philanthropy in the American Early Republic*. Bloomington: Indiana University Center on Philanthropy, 1993.

———. "A Doctrinal Controversy between the Hopkintonian (Lemuel Haynes) and the Universalist (Hosea Ballou)." *Vermont Historical Review* 61 (Fall 1993): 177–216.

———. "Lemuel Haynes and the Revolutionary Origins of Black Theology, 1776–1801." *Religion and American Culture* 2 (Winter 1992): 79–102.

———. "Slavery and Divine Providence in New England Congregationalism: The New Divinity and a Black Protest, 1775–1805." *New England Quarterly* 68 (December 1995): 584–608.

———. "'Wipe Away All Tears from Their Eyes': John Marrant's Theology in the Black Atlantic, 1785–1808." *Journal of Millennial Studies* 1 (Winter 1999), http://www.mille.org/journal.html (accessed January 26, 2006).

Sargent, Mark L. "The New Divinity in the Old Colony: Chandler Robbins and the Legend of the Pilgrims." In *Puritanism in America: The Seventeenth through the Nineteenth Centuries*. Studies in Puritan American Spirituality, vol. 4. Lewiston, NY: Edwin Mellen, 1994.

Sassi, Jonathan D. *A Republic of Righteousness: The Public Christianity of the Post-Revolutionary New England Clergy*. Religion in America Series. New York: Oxford University Press, 2001.

Schafer, Thomas A. "The Role of Jonathan Edwards in American Religious History." *Encounter* 30 (Summer 1969): 212–23.

Schmotter, James W. "Ministerial Careers in Eighteenth-Century New England." *Journal of Social History* 9 (Winter 1975): 249–67.

Scott, Donald M. *From Office to Profession: The New England Ministry, 1750–1850*. Philadelphia: University of Pennsylvania Press, 1978.

Scott, Lee Osborne. "The Concept of Love as Universal Disinterested Benevolence in the Early Edwardseans." Ph.D. diss., Yale University, 1952.

The Semi-Centennial Anniversary of the Divinity School of Yale College, May 15th and 16th, 1872. New Haven: Tuttle, Morehouse & Taylor, 1872.

Senior, Robert C. "New England Congregationalists and the Anti-Slavery Movement." Ph.D. diss., Yale University, 1954.

Shea, Daniel B. "Jonathan Edwards: The First Two Hundred Years." *Journal of American Studies* 14 (August 1980): 181–97.

Sherman, David. *Sketches of New England Divines*. New York: Carlton & Porter, 1860.

Shewmaker, William Orpheus. "The Training of the Protestant Ministry in the United States of America, before the Establishment of Theological Seminaries." *Papers of the American Society of Church History* 6 (1921): 71–202.

Shiels, Richard Douglas. "The Connecticut Clergy in the Second Great Awakening." Ph.D. diss., Boston University, 1976.

———. "The Feminization of American Congregationalism, 1730–1835." *American Quarterly* 33 (Spring 1981): 46–62.

———. "The Scope of the Second Great Awakening: Andover, Massachusetts, as a Case Study." *Journal of the Early Republic* 5 (Summer 1985): 223–46.

———. "The Second Great Awakening in Connecticut: Critique of the Traditional Interpretation." *Church History* 49 (December 1980): 401–15.

Sklar, Kathryn Kish. "The Founding of Mount Holyoke College." In *Women of America: A History,* edited by Carol Ruth Berkin and Mary Beth Norton. Boston: Houghton Mifflin, 1979.

Slater, Peter Gregg. *Children in the New England Mind—In Death and in Life.* Hamden, CT: Archon Books, 1977.

Smith, H. Shelton. *Changing Conceptions of Original Sin: A Study in American Theology since 1750.* New York: Charles Scribner's Sons, 1955.

Smith, Henry Boynton. *Faith and Philosophy: Discourses and Essays.* Edited by George L. Prentiss. New York: Scribner, Armstrong, 1877.

Sprague, William B. *Annals of the American Pulpit; or Commemorative Notices of Distinguished American Clergymen of Various Denominations.* 9 vols. New York: R. Carter and Brothers, 1857–69.

———. *Lectures on Revivals of Religion.* Albany: J. P. Haven and J. Leavitt, 1832.

———. *The Life of Jedidiah Morse.* New York: Anson D. F. Randolph, 1874.

———. *Memoir of the Rev. Edward D. Griffin, D.D.* New York: Taylor & Dodd, 1839.

Spring, Gardiner. *Memoir of Samuel John Mills.* 2nd ed. New York: Saxton & Miles, 1842.

Squires, William Harder, ed. *The Edwardean: A Quarterly Devoted to the History of Thought in America.* 1903–4; repr., Lewiston, NY: Edwin Mellen, 1991.

R. P. Stebbins. "The Andover and Princeton Theologies." *Christian Examiner and Religious Miscellany* 52 (May 1852): 309–35.

Stephens, Bruce M. "An Appeal to the Universe: The Doctrine of the Atonement in American Protestant Thought from Jonathan Edwards to Edwards Amasa Park." *Encounter* 60 (Winter 1999): 55–72.

———. "Changing Conceptions of the Holy Spirit in American Protestant Theology from Jonathan Edwards to Charles G. Finney." *Saint Luke's Journal of Theology* 33 (June 1990): 209–23.

———. *God's Last Metaphor: The Doctrine of the Trinity in New England Theology.* Chico, CA: Scholars Press, 1981.

———. "Horace Bushnell and New England Theology." *Dialog* 14 (Fall 1975): 268–73.

———. *The Prism of Time and Eternity: Images of Christ in American Protestant Thought, from Jonathan Edwards to Horace Bushnell.* Metuchen, NJ: Scarecrow, 1996.

———. "A Theological Patois: The Eternal Sonship of Christ in New England Theology." In *American Religion: 1974 Proceedings,* compiled by Edwin S. Gaustad. Missoula, MT: Scholars Press, 1974.

Stevenson, Louise L. "Between the Old Time College and the Modern University: Noah Porter and the New Haven Scholars." *History of Higher Education Annual* 3 (1983): 39–55.

———. *Scholarly Means to Evangelical Ends: The New Haven Scholars and the Transformation of Higher Learning in America, 1830–1890.* Baltimore: Johns Hopkins University Press, 1986.

Stewart, George C., Jr. *A History of Religious Education in Connecticut to the Middle of the Nineteenth Century.* New Haven: Yale University Press, 1924.

Stokes, Anson Phelps. *Memorials of Eminent Yale Men: A Biographical Study of Student Life and University Influences during the Eighteenth and Nineteenth Centuries.* New Haven: Yale University Press, 1914.

Stout, Harry S. *The New England Soul: Preaching and Religious Culture in Colonial New England.* New York: Oxford University Press, 1986.

———. "Rhetoric and Reality in the Early Republic: The Case of the Federalist Clergy." In *Religion and American Politics: From the Colonial Period to the 1980s,* edited by Mark A. Noll. New York: Oxford University Press, 1990.

Stow, Sarah D. Locke. *History of Mount Holyoke Seminary, South Hadley, Mass., during the First Half Century, 1837–1887.* South Hadley, MA: Mount Holyoke Female Seminary, 1887.

Stowe, C. E. "Sketches and Recollections of Dr. Lyman Beecher." *Congregational Quarterly* 6 (July 1864): 221–35.

Strong, Douglas M. *Perfectionist Politics: Abolitionism and the Religious Tensions of American Democracy.* Religion and Politics. Syracuse: Syracuse University Press, 1999.

Strong, William E. *The Story of the American Board: An Account of the First Hundred Years of the American Board of Commissioners for Foreign Missions.* Boston: Pilgrim, 1910.

Sweeney, Douglas A. "Edwards and His Mantle: The Historiography of the New England Theology." *New England Quarterly* 71 (1998): 97–110.

Taylor, J. L., ed. *A Memorial of the Semi-Centennial Celebration of the Founding of the Theological Seminary at Andover.* Andover, MA: W. F. Draper, 1859.

Taylor, Oliver A. "Sketches, Statistics, Etc., of the Theological Seminary of Andover." *American Quarterly Register* 11 (1839): 63–81.

Thayer, Eli. *The New England Emigrant Aid Company and Its Influence, through the Kansas Contest, upon National History.* Worcester, MA: Franklin P. Rice, 1887.

Thayer, William. *Poor Girl and True Woman: Or, Elements of Woman's Success Drawn from the Life of Mary Lyon and Others.* Boston: Gould, Lincoln, 1859.

Thomas, C. Richards. *Samuel J. Mills: Missionary Pathfinder, Pioneer, and Promoter.* Boston: Pilgrim, 1906.

Thomas, Louise P. *Seminary Militant: An Account of the Missionary Movement at Mount Holyoke Seminary and College.* South Hadley, MA: Department of English, Mount Holyoke College, 1937.

Thompson, J. Earl, Jr. "Abolitionism and Theological Education at Andover." *New England Quarterly* 47 (June 1974): 238–61.

———. "Lyman Beecher's Long Road to Conservative Abolitionism." *Church History* 42 (March 1973): 89–109.

Thompson, Joseph P. "Jonathan Edwards, His Character, Teaching, and Influence." *Bibliotheca Sacra* 18 (October 1861): 809–39.

Thornbury, John F. *God Sent Revival: The Story of Asahel Nettleton and the Second Great Awakening.* Grand Rapids: Evangelical Press, 1977.

Tracy, Frederick P. "Historical View of the Calvinistic Theology of New England." *Methodist Review* 18 (October 1836): 408–23.

Trumbull, Benjamin. *A Complete History of Connecticut, Civil and Ecclesiastical.* 2 vols. New Haven: Maltby, Goldsmith, 1818.

Tyler, Bennet. *An Address to the Alumni of the Theological Institute of Connecticut, Delivered July 15, 1857, on the Occasion of the Author's Resigning His Office of President and Professor of Christian Theology.* Hartford, CT: Case, Lockwood, 1857.

———. *Memoir of the Life and Character of Rev. Asahel Nettleton, D.D.* 2nd ed. Hartford, CT: Robins & Smith, 1845.

———. *New England Revivals, as They Existed at the Close of the Eighteenth, and the Beginning of the Nineteenth Centuries. Compiled Principally from Narratives First Published in the Connecticut Evangelical Magazine.* Boston: Massachusetts Sabbath School Society, 1846.

Vaill, Joseph. "Theological Education in Connecticut Seventy Years Ago; as Connected with Charles Backus's Divinity School." *Congregational Quarterly* 6 (April 1864): 137–42.

Valeri, Mark. "The New Divinity and the American Revolution." *William and Mary Quarterly* 46 (October 1989): 741–69.

Vanderpool, Harold Young. "The Andover Conservatives: Apologetics, Biblical Criticism, and Theological Change at the Andover Theological Seminary, 1808–1880." Ph.D. diss., Harvard University, 1971.

Walker, George Leon. *Some Aspects of the Religious Life of New England with Special Reference to the Congregationalists.* New York: Silver, Burdett, 1897.

Walker, Williston. "Changes in Theology among American Congregationalists." *American Journal of Theology* 10 (April 1906): 204–18.

———. *The Creeds and Platforms of Congregationalism.* 1893; repr., New York: Pilgrim, 1991.

———. *A History of the Congregational Churches in the United States.* American Church History Series. Vol. 3. New York: Christian Literature Company, 1894.

———. *Ten New England Leaders.* New York: Silver, Burdett, 1901.

Wallace, David A. *The Theology of New England.* Boston: Crocker & Brewster, 1856.

Walsh, James. "The Pure Church in Eighteenth-Century Connecticut." Ph.D. diss., Columbia University, 1967.

Warch, Richard. *School of the Prophets: Yale College, 1701–1740.* New Haven: Yale University Press, 1973.

Warfield, Benjamin Breckinridge. "Edwards and the New England Theology." In *Encyclopedia of Religion and Ethics,* vol. 5, edited by James Hastings. New York: Charles Scribner's Sons, 1912.

Warren, Austin. *The New England Conscience.* Ann Arbor: University of Michigan Press, 1966.

Washburn, Owen Redington. *John Calvin in New England, 1620–1947.* North Montpelier, VT: Driftwood Press, 1948.

Wayland, John T. *The Theological Department in Yale College, 1822–58.* 1933; repr., New York: Garland, 1987.

Weber, Donald. "The Figure of Jonathan Edwards." *American Quarterly* 35 (Winter 1983): 556–64.

———. "The Image of Jonathan Edwards in American Culture." Ph.D. diss., Columbia University, 1978.

———. *Rhetoric and History in Revolutionary New England.* New York: Oxford University Press, 1988.

Weddle, David L. "The Law and the Revival: A 'New Divinity' for the Settlements." *Church History* 47 (June 1978): 196–214.

Wells, David F. "The Debate over the Atonement in Nineteenth-Century America." *Bibliotheca Sacra* 144 (April–June 1987): 123–43; (July–September 1987): 243–53; (October–December 1987): 363–76.

———. *Reformed Theology in America: A History of Its Modern Development.* Grand Rapids: Eerdmans, 1985.

Whittemore, Robert C. *The Transformation of the New England Theology.* New York: Peter Lang, 1987.

Widenhouse, Ernest Cornelius. "The Doctrine of the Atonement in the New England Theology from Jonathan Edwards to Horace Bushnell." Th.D. diss., Hartford Seminary, 1931.

Winship, Albert E. *Jukes-Edwards: A Study in Education and Heredity.* Harrisburg, PA: R. L. Myers, 1900.

Wood, James. *The Doctrinal Differences Which Have Agitated and Divided the Presbyterian Church, or, Old and New Theology.* Philadelphia: Presbyterian Board of Publication, 1853.

Woods, Leonard. *History of the Andover Theological Seminary.* Boston: James R. Osgood, 1885.

———. *Memoirs of the American Missionaries Formerly Connected with the Society of Inquiry Respecting Missions in the Andover Theological Seminary.* Boston: Peirce & Parker, 1833.

Wyatt-Brown, Bertram. *Lewis Tappan and the Evangelical War against Slavery.* Cleveland: Press of Case Western Reserve University, 1969.

Youngs, J. William T., Jr. *The Congregationalists.* New York: Greenwood, 1990.

Jonathan Edwards

There are thousands of publications on Jonathan Edwards's life, times, and thought. M. X. Lesser's bibliographies are the best guides to these scholarly works (see above). What follows is a list of the most important books on Edwards published since 1993, the last year covered by Lesser.

Brown, Robert E. *Jonathan Edwards and the Bible.* Bloomington: Indiana University Press, 2002.

Caldwell, Robert W. *Communion in the Spirit.* Carlisle, UK: Paternoster, 2006.

Chai, Leon. *Jonathan Edwards and the Limits of Enlightenment Philosophy.* New York: Oxford University Press, 1998.

Crisp, Oliver D. *Jonathan Edwards and the Metaphysics of Sin.* Aldershot, UK: Ashgate, 2005.

Danaher, William J. *The Trinitarian Ethics of Jonathan Edwards.* Louisville: Westminster John Knox, 2004.

Daniel, Stephen H. *The Philosophy of Jonathan Edwards*: *A Study of Divine Semiotics.* Bloomington: Indiana University Press, 1994.

Davies, Ronald E. *Jonathan Edwards and His Influence on the Development of the Missionary Movement from Britain.* Cambridge: Currents in World Christianity Project, 1996.

Gura, Philip F. *Jonathan Edwards: America's Evangelical.* An American Portrait. New York: Hill & Wang, 2005.

Helm, Paul, and Oliver D. Crisp, eds. *Jonathan Edwards: Philosophical Theologian.* Aldershot, U.K.: Ashgate, 2003.

Holmes, Stephen R. *God of Grace and God of Glory: An Account of the Theology of Jonathan Edwards.* Grand Rapids: Eerdmans, 2000.

Kreider, Glenn R. *Jonathan Edwards's Interpretation of Revelation 4:1–8:1.* Lanham, MD: University Press of America, 2004.

Lee, Sang Hyun, ed. *The Princeton Companion to Jonathan Edwards.* Princeton: Princeton University Press, 2005.

———, and Allen C. Guelzo, eds. *Edwards in Our Time: Jonathan Edwards and the Shaping of American Religion.* Grand Rapids: Eerdmans, 1999.

Marsden, George. *Jonathan Edwards: A Life*. New Haven: Yale University Press, 2003.

McClymond, Michael J. *Encounters with God: An Approach to the Theology of Jonathan Edwards*. New York: Oxford University Press, 1998.

McDermott, Gerald R. *Jonathan Edwards Confronts the Gods: Christian Theology, Enlightenment Religion, and Non-Christian Faith*. New York: Oxford University Press, 2000.

Mitchell, Louis J. *Jonathan Edwards on the Experience of Beauty*. Studies in Reformed Theology and History. Princeton: Princeton Theological Seminary, 2003.

Moody, Josh. *Jonathan Edwards and the Enlightenment: Knowing the Presence of God*. Lanham, MD: University Press of America, 2005.

Morimoto, Anri. *Jonathan Edwards and the Catholic Vision of Salvation*. University Park: Pennsylvania State University Press, 1995.

Nichols, Stephen A. *An Absolute Sort of Certainty: The Holy Spirit and the Apologetics of Jonathan Edwards*. Phillipsburg, NJ: Presbyterian & Reformed, 2003.

Pauw, Amy Plantinga. *The Supreme Harmony of All: The Trinitarian Theology of Jonathan Edwards*. Grand Rapids: Eerdmans, 2003.

Stein, Stephen J., ed. *The Cambridge Companion to Jonathan Edwards*. Cambridge: Cambridge University Press, forthcoming.

———, ed. *Jonathan Edwards' Writings: Text, Context, Interpretation*. Bloomington: Indiana University Press, 1996.

Stout, Harry S., Kenneth P. Minkema, and Caleb J. D. Maskell, eds. *Jonathan Edwards at 300: Essays on the Tercentenary of His Birth*. Lanham, MD: University Press of America, 2005.

Wilson, Stephen A. *Virtue Reformed: Rereading Jonathan Edwards's Ethics*. Brill's Studies in Intellectual History. Leiden: Brill, 2005.

Zakai, Avihu. *Jonathan Edwards' Philosophy of History: The Re-enchantment of the World in the Age of Enlightenment*. Princeton: Princeton University Press, 2003.

Joseph Bellamy

Anderson, Glenn Paul. "Joseph Bellamy (1719–1790): The Man and His Work." Ph.D. diss., Boston University, 1971.

Anderson, Michael P. "The Pope of Lichfield County: An Intellectual Biography of Joseph Bellamy, 1719–1790." Ph.D. diss., Claremont Graduate School, 1980.

Battles, Ford Lewis. "Bellamy Papers." *Hartford Quarterly* 8 (1967): 64–91.

Conforti, Joseph A. "Joseph Bellamy and the New Divinity Movement." *New England Historical and Genealogical Register* 137 (1983): 126–38.

Eggleston, Percy Coe. *A Man of Bethlehem, Joseph Bellamy, D.D., and His Divinity School*. New London, CT: Printed for the Bethlehem, Connecticut, Tercentenary, 1908.

Valeri, Mark. *Law and Providence in Joseph Bellamy's New England: The Origins of the New Divinity in Revolutionary America.* Religion in America Series. New York: Oxford University Press, 1994.

Williams, Stanley T. "Six Letters of Jonathan Edwards to Joseph Bellamy." *New England Quarterly* 1 (1928): 226–42.

Samuel Hopkins

Beecher, Edward. "The Works of Samuel Hopkins." *Bibliotheca Sacra* 10 (January 1853): 63–82.

Conforti, Joseph Anthony. *Samuel Hopkins and the New Divinity Movement: Calvinism, the Congregational Ministry, and Reform in New England between the Great Awakenings.* Grand Rapids: Christian University Press, 1981.

———. "Samuel Hopkins and the New Divinity: Theology, Ethics, and Social Reform in Eighteenth-Century New England." *William and Mary Quarterly* 34 (October 1977): 572–89.

Elsbree, Oliver Wendell. "Samuel Hopkins and His Doctrine of Benevolence." *New England Quarterly* 8 (December 1935): 534–50.

Ferguson, John. *Memoir of the Life and Character of the Rev. Samuel Hopkins, D.D.* Boston: Leonard W. Kimball, 1830.

Gillett, E. H. "Hopkinsianism before Hopkins." *American Presbyterian Review* 2 (October 1870): 680–99.

Jauhiainen, Peter Dan. "An Enlightenment Calvinist: Samuel Hopkins and the Pursuit of Benevolence." Ph.D. diss., University of Iowa, 1997.

Knapp, Hugh Heath. "The Early Career of Samuel Hopkins and the End of the Awakening Style." *Bulletin of the Connecticut Historical Society* 39 (1974): 54–64.

———. "Samuel Hopkins and the New Divinity." Ph.D. diss., University of Wisconsin, 1971.

Lovejoy, David S. "Samuel Hopkins: Religion, Slavery, and the Revolution." *New England Quarterly* 40 (June 1967): 227–43.

Park, Edwards Amasa. *Memoir of the Life and Character of Samuel Hopkins, D.D.* Vol. 1 of *The Works of Samuel Hopkins, D.D.* Boston: Doctrinal Tract Society, 1852.

Patten, William. *Reminiscences of the Late Rev. Samuel Hopkins, D.D.* Boston: Crocker & Brewster, 1843.

Pond, Enoch. "Hopkinsianism." *Bibliotheca Sacra* 19 (July 1862): 633–70.

Sassi, Jonathan D. "'This Whole Country Have Their Hands Full of Blood This Day': Transcription and Introduction of an Antislavery Sermon Manuscript Attributed to the Reverend Samuel Hopkins." *Proceedings of the American Antiquarian Society* 112 (2004): 24–92.

Swift, David E. "Samuel Hopkins: Calvinist Social Concern in Eighteenth-Century New England." *Journal of Presbyterian History* 47 (March 1969): 31–54.

Van Halsema, Dick L. "Samuel Hopkins, 1721–1803: New England Calvinist." Th.D. diss., Union Theological Seminary, 1956.

West, Stephen, ed. *Sketches of the Life of the Late Rev. Samuel Hopkins, D.D.* Hartford, CT: Hudson & Goodwin, 1805.

Sarah Osborn

Brekus, Catherine. *Sarah Osborn's World: Popular Christianity in Early America.* New York: Knopf, forthcoming.

Hambrick-Stowe, Charles E. "The Spiritual Pilgrimage of Sarah Osborn (1714–1796)." *Church History* 61 (December 1992): 408–21.

Hopkins, Samuel, ed. *Memoirs of the Life of Mrs. Sarah Osborn.* Worcester, MA: Leonard Worcester, 1799.

Kujawa, Sheryl Anne. "'A Precious Season at the Throne of Grace': Sarah Haggar Wheaten Osborne, 1714–1796." Ph.D. diss., Boston College, 1993.

Norton, Mary Beth, ed. "'My Resting Reaping Times': Sarah Osborne's Defense of Her 'Unfeminine' Activities, 1767." *Signs: Journal of Women in Culture and Society* 2 (Winter 1976): 515–29.

Nathan Strong

Riddel, Samuel H. "Memoir of the Rev. Nathan Strong, D.D." *American Quarterly Register* 13 (November 1840): 129–43.

Nathanael Emmons

Baker, Abijah R. *Memoir of Rev. Nathanael Emmons, D.D., Pastor of the Church in Franklin, Massachusetts.* Boston: T. R. Marvin, 1842.

Blake, Mortimer. *A History of the Town of Franklin, Massachusetts.* Franklin, MA: Committee of the Town, 1879.

Dahlquist, John Terrence. "Nathanael Emmons: His Life and Work." Ph.D. diss., Boston University, 1963.

Ellis, George E. "Memoir of Nathanael Emmons." *Christian Examiner and Religious Miscellany* 71 (September 1861): 287–91.

Fisher, George Park. "Professor Park's Memoir of Dr. Emmons." *New Englander* 19 (July 1861): 709–31.

Ide, Jacob. "Memoir." In *The Works of Nathaniel Emmons*, vol. 1, edited by Jacob Ide, ix–xxxvii. Boston: Crocker & Brewster, 1842.

Niles, Nathaniel. *A Letter to a Friend, Who Received His Theological Education under the Instruction of Dr. Emmons, Concerning the Doctrine Which Teaches That Impenitent Sinners Have Natural Power to Make Themselves New Hearts.* Windsor, VT: Alden Spooner, 1809.

Park, Edwards Amasa. *Memoir of Nathanael Emmons; with Sketches of His Friends and Pupils.* Boston: Congregational Board of Publication, 1861.

Pond, Enoch. "The Life and Character of Emmons." *American Theological Review* 3 (October 1861): 632–69.

Smalley, E. "The Theology of Emmons." *Bibliotheca Sacra* 7 (April 1850): 253–80; (July 1850): 479–501.

Smith, Henry Boynton. "The Theological System of Emmons." In *Faith and Philosophy: Discourses and Essays*, edited by George L. Prentiss. New York: Scribner, Armstrong, 1877.

Williams, Thomas. *The Official Character of Rev. Nathanael Emmons, D.D.: Taught and Shown in a Sermon on His Life and Death*. Boston: Ferdinand Andrews, 1840.

Jonathan Edwards the Younger

Birney, George Hugh, Jr. "The Edwards Papers in the Case Memorial Library." S.T.M. thesis, Hartford Theological Seminary, 1942.

Edwards, Tryon, ed. *The Works of Jonathan Edwards, D.D., Late President of Union College*. 2 vols. Andover, MA: Allen, Morrill & Wardwell, 1842.

Ewert, Wesley C. "Jonathan Edwards the Younger: A Biographical Essay." Th.D. diss., Hartford Theological Seminary, 1953.

Ferm, Robert L. *Jonathan Edwards the Younger, 1745–1801: A Colonial Pastor*. Grand Rapids: Eerdmans, 1976.

Minkema, Kenneth Pieter. "The Edwardses: A Ministerial Family in Eighteenth-Century New England." Ph.D. diss., University of Connecticut, 1988.

Stephen West

Egleston, Nathaniel Hillyer. *In Memoriam: A Discourse Preached November 1st, 1868, on the Occasion of the Erection of Tablets in the Old Church at Stockbridge, Mass., in Memory of Its Former Pastors: John Sergeant, Jonathan Edwards, Stephen West, and David D. Field*. New York: Baker & Godwin, 1869.

Hyde, Alvan. *Sketches of the Life, Ministry, and Writings of the Rev. Stephen West, D.D.: Late Pastor of the Church in Stockbridge, Massachusetts*. Stockbridge: Charles Webster, 1819.

John Smalley

Garver, Daniel C. "John Smalley (1734–1820)." In *American Writers before 1800*, edited by James Levernier and Douglas R. Wilmes. Westport, CT: Greenwood, 1983.

Goodell, C. L. "John Smalley." *Congregational Quarterly* 15 (July 1873): 351–64.

Asa Burton

Latham, Charles, Jr., ed. *The Life of Asa Burton, Written by Himself.* Thetford, VT: First Congregational Church, 1973.

Pond, Enoch. "Dr. Burton on Metaphysics." *Bibliotheca Sacra* 32 (October 1875): 773–82.

Timothy Dwight

Addison, Daniel Dulany. "Timothy Dwight." In *The Clergy in American Life and Letters.* New York: Macmillan, 1900.

Anonymous. "Biographical Memoir of the Rev. Timothy Dwight, S.T.D., LL.D." *Port Folio* 4 (1817): 355–69.

———. "Biographical Notice of the Rev. Timothy Dwight, S.T.D., LL.D., Late President and Professor of Divinity of Yale College." *Analectic Magazine* 9 (1817): 265–81.

———. "Timothy Dwight and the Greenfield Academy." *American Historical Record* 2 (1873): 385–87.

Berk, Stephen E. *Calvinism vs. Democracy: Timothy Dwight and the Origins of American Evangelical Orthodoxy.* Hamden, CT: Archon Books, 1974.

Briggs, Peter. "Timothy Dwight 'Composes' a Landscape for New England." *American Quarterly* 40 (1988): 359–77.

Buchanan, Lewis. "The Ethical Ideas of Timothy Dwight." *Research Studies, State College of Washington* 13 (1945): 185–99.

Buss, Dietrich. "The Millennial Vision of Motive for Religious Benevolence and Reform: Timothy Dwight and the New England Evangelicals Reconsidered." *Fides et Historia* 16 (1983): 18–34.

Chapin, Calvin. *A Sermon Delivered 14th January, 1817, at the Funeral of the Rev. Timothy Dwight, D.D., LL.D., President of Yale College, in New Haven, and Professor of Divinity in the Institution, Who Died January 11th, 1817, in the Sixty-Fifth Year of His Age and Twenty-Second of His Presidency.* New Haven: Maltby & Goldsmith, 1817.

Clark, Gregory. "Timothy Dwight's Moral Rhetoric at Yale College, 1795–1817." *Rhetorica* 5 (1987): 149–61.

Cuningham, Charles. *Timothy Dwight, 1752–1817: A Biography.* New York: Macmillan, 1942.

Fain, William M. "A Study of the Preaching of Timothy Dwight." Th.D. diss., New Orleans Baptist Theological Seminary, 1970.

Fitzmier, John R. *New England's Moral Legislator: Timothy Dwight, 1752–1817.* Bloomington: Indiana University Press, 1998.

Freimarck, Vincent. "Timothy Dwight's Dissertation on the Bible." *American Literature* 26 (1952): 73–77.

Good, L. Douglas. "The Christian Nation in the Mind of Timothy Dwight." *Fides et Historia* 7 (1974): 1–18.

Gribbin, William. "The Legacy of Timothy Dwight: A Reappraisal." *Connecticut Historical Society Bulletin* 37 (1972): 33–41.

Griffith, John. *"The Columbiad* and *Greenfield Hill*: History, Poetry, and Ideology in the Late Eighteenth Century." *Early American Literature* 10 (1975–76): 235–50.

Harding, Walter. "Timothy Dwight and Thoreau." *Boston Public Library Quarterly* 10 (1958): 109–15.

Harris, Marc L. "Revelation and the American Republic: Timothy Dwight's Civic Participation." *Journal of the History of Ideas* 54 (1993): 449–68.

Hoffelt, R. David. "Pragmatics of Persuasion and Disciplines of Piety: The Influence of Timothy Dwight in American Preaching." Ph.D. diss., Princeton Theological Seminary, 1983.

Howard, Leon. *The Connecticut Wits*. Chicago: University of Chicago Press, 1943.

Imholt, Robert J. "Timothy Dwight, Federalist Pope of Connecticut." *New England Quarterly* 73 (September 2000): 386–411.

Kafer, Peter K. "The Making of Timothy Dwight: A Connecticut Morality Tale." *William and Mary Quarterly* 47 (1990): 189–209.

Kamensky, Jane. "'In These Contrasted Climes, How Chang'd the Scene': Progress, Declension, and Balance in the Landscapes of Timothy Dwight." *New England Quarterly* 63 (1990): 80–108.

Leary, Lewis. "The Author of the Triumph of Infidelity." *New England Quarterly* 20 (1947): 377–85.

Lee, Robert Edson. "Timothy Dwight and the Boston Palladium." *New England Quarterly* 35 (1962): 229–38.

Morgan, Edmund S. "Ezra Stiles and Timothy Dwight." *Proceedings of the Massachusetts Historical Society* 72 (1963): 101–17.

Olmstead, Denison. "Timothy Dwight as a Teacher." *Journal of American Education* 6 (1858): 567–85.

Ravitz, Abe C. "Timothy Dwight: Professor of Rhetoric." *New England Quarterly* 39 (1956): 63–72.

———. "Timothy Dwight's Decisions." *New England Quarterly* 31 (1958): 514–19.

Sears, John F. "Timothy Dwight and the American Landscape: The Composing Eye in Dwight's *Travels in New England and New York.*" *Early American Literature* 11 (1976–77): 311–21.

Shiber, Paul T. "The Conquest of Canaan as a Youthful Expression of Timothy Dwight's New Divinity and Political Thought." Ph.D. diss., University of Miami, 1972.

Silliman, Benjamin. *A Sketch of the Life and Character of President Dwight, Delivered as a Eulogium, in New Haven, February 12, 1817, before the Academic Body of Yale College, Composed of the Senatus Academic, Faculty, and Students.* New Haven: Maltby & Goldsmith, 1817.

Silverman, Kenneth. *Timothy Dwight*. New York: Twayne Publishers, 1969.

Snyder, K. Alan. "Foundations of Liberty: The Christian Republicanism of Timothy Dwight and Jedidiah Morse." *New England Quarterly* 56 (1983): 382–97.

Spears, Timothy B. "Common Observations: Timothy Dwight's *Travels in New England and New York*." *American Studies* 30 (1989): 35–52.

Spring, Gardiner. *An Oration on the Evening of the Fifth of February, before the Alumni of Yale College, Resident in the City of New York, in Commemoration of Their Late President, Timothy Dwight, D.D., LL.D.* New York: Dodge & Sayre, 1817.

Stillinger, Jack. "Dwight's *Triumph of Infidelity*: Text and Interpretation." *Studies in Bibliography: Papers of the Bibliography Society of the University of Virginia* 15 (1962): 259–66.

Tyner, Wayne Conrad. "The Theology of Timothy Dwight in Historical Perspective." Ph.D. diss., University of North Carolina at Chapel Hill, 1971.

Volkomer, Walter E. "Timothy Dwight and New England Federalism." *Connecticut Review* 3 (1970): 72–82.

Wells, Colin. *The Devil and Doctor Dwight: Satire and Theology in the Early American Republic*. Chapel Hill: University of North Carolina Press, 2002.

Wenzke, Anabelle S. *Timothy Dwight (1752–1817)*. Lewiston, NY: Edwin Mellen, 1989.

Whitford, Kathryn. "Excursions in Romanticism: Timothy Dwight's Travels." *Papers on Language and Literature* 2 (1966): 225–33.

———, and Philip Whitford. "Timothy Dwight's Place in Eighteenth-Century American Science." *Proceedings of the American Philosophical Association* 114 (1970): 60–71.

Nathaniel W. Taylor

Anonymous. *An Address, to the Congregational Churches in Connecticut, on the Present State of Their Religious Concerns*. Hartford, CT: Peter B. Gleason, 1833.

———. "Dr. Taylor's Lectures on the Moral Government of God." *Biblical Repertory and Princeton Review* 31 (July 1859): 489–538.

———. "Memorial of Nathaniel Taylor." *Biblical Repertory* 30 (July 1858): 573–76.

Atwater, Lyman Hotchiss. "Professor Fisher on the Princeton Review and Dr. Taylor's Theology." *Princeton Review* 40 (July 1868): 368–98.

Bacon, Leonard, Samuel W. S. Dutton, and George P. Fisher. *Memorial of Nathaniel W. Taylor, D.D., Three Sermons*. New Haven: Thomas H. Pease, 1858.

Cherry, Conrad. "Nature and the Republic: The New Haven Theology." *New England Quarterly* 51 (1978): 509–26.

DeLashmutt, Michael W. "Nathaniel William Taylor and Thomas Reid: Scottish Common-sense Philosophy's Impact upon the Formation of New Haven

Theology in Antebellum America." *Scottish Journal of Theology* 58 (February 2005): 59–82.

Dow, Daniel. *New Haven Theology, Alias Taylorism, Alias Neology; In Its Own Language.* Thompson, CT: George Roberts, 1834.

Dutton, Samuel W. S. "A Sketch of the Life and Character of Rev. Nathaniel W. Taylor, D.D." *Congregational Quarterly* 2 (July 1860): 245–66.

Fisher, George Park. "Dr. N. W. Taylor's Theology: A Rejoinder to the 'Princeton Review.'" *New Englander* 27 (October 1868): 740–63.

———. "Historical Address." In *The Semi-Centennial Anniversary of the Divinity School of Yale College, May 15th and 16th, 1872.* New Haven: Tuttle, Morehouse & Taylor, 1872.

———. "The 'Princeton Review' on the Theology of Dr. N. W. Taylor." *New Englander* 27 (April 1868): 284–348.

Fowler, William Chauncey. "The Appointment of Nathaniel William Taylor to the Chair of the Dwight Professorship of Didactic Theology in Yale College." In *Essays: Historical, Literary, Educational.* Hartford, CT: Case, Lockwood & Brainard, 1876.

Griffin, Edward D. *The Doctrine of Divine Efficiency, Defended against Certain Modern Speculations.* New York: J. Leavitt, 1833.

Hansen, Wayne S. "Nathaniel William Taylor's Use of Scripture in Theology." Ph.D. diss., Drew University, 1995.

Harvey, Joseph. *An Examination of a Review of Dr. Taylor's Sermon on Human Depravity, and Mr. Harvey's Strictures on That Sermon.* Hartford, CT: Goodwin, 1829.

———. *Letters on the Present State and Probable Results of Theological Speculations in Connecticut.* N.p., 1832.

———. *A Review of a Sermon Delivered in the Chapel of Yale College, September 10, 1828, by Nathaniel W. Taylor.* Hartford, CT: Goodwin, 1829.

Hatch, Rebecca Taylor. *Personal Reminiscences and Memorials.* New York: Gilliss Press, 1905.

Martin, B. N. "Dr. Taylor on Moral Government." *New Englander* 17 (November 1859): 903–67.

Mead, Sidney. *Nathaniel William Taylor, 1786–1858: A Connecticut Liberal.* Chicago: University of Chicago Press, 1942.

Munger, Theodore T. "Dr. Nathaniel W. Taylor—Master Theologian." *Yale Divinity Quarterly* 5 (February 1909): 233–40.

Nicholls, Jason A. "'Certainty' with 'Power to the Contrary': Nathaniel William Taylor (1786–1858) on the Will." Ph.D. diss., Marquette University, 2002.

Pope, Earl A. "The Rise of the New Haven Theology." *Journal of Presbyterian History* 44 (March 1966): 24–44; (June 1966): 106–21.

Porter, Noah. "The Princeton Review on Dr. Taylor and the Edwardean Theology." *New Englander* 18 (August 1860): 726–73.

Rayner, Menzies. *Review of the Rev. Mr. Taylor's Sermon on Regeneration, Preached and Published at New Haven, 1816.* New Haven: Steele & Gray, 1817.

Stephens, Bruce M. "Nathaniel W. Taylor (1786–1858): On Speaking of the Trinity." *Princeton Seminary Bulletin* 66 (1973): 113–19.

Sutton, William R. "Benevolent Calvinism and the Moral Government of God: The Influence of Nathaniel W. Taylor on Revivalism in the Second Great Awakening." *Religion and American Culture* 2 (Winter 1992): 23–47.

Sweeney, Douglas A. *Nathaniel Taylor, New Haven Theology, and the Legacy of Jonathan Edwards.* New York: Oxford University Press, 2003.

Thacher, Tyler. *Taylorism Examined: Or a Review of the New Haven Theology.* North Wrentham, MA: Telegraph Press, 1834.

Tyler, Bennet. "Dr. Tyler's Examination of Dr. Taylor's Theological Views." *Spirit of the Pilgrims* 5 (June 1832): 325–36.

———. "Dr. Tyler's Letter to the Editor of the Spirit of the Pilgrims." *Spirit of the Pilgrims* 6 (May 1833): 284–306.

———. "Dr. Tyler's Reply to Dr. Taylor." *Spirit of the Pilgrims* 5 (September 1832): 508–23; (October 1832): 545–63.

———. *Letters on the Origin and Progress of the New Haven Theology.* New York: Robert Carter and Ezra Collier, 1837.

———. *Strictures on the Review of Dr. Spring's Dissertation on the Means of Regeneration, in the Christian Spectator for 1829.* Portland, ME: Shirley & Hyde, 1829.

———. *A Vindication of the Strictures on the Review of Dr. Spring's Dissertation on the Means of Regeneration, in the Christian Spectator for 1829, in Reply to the Reviewer and Evangelus Pacificus.* Portland, ME: Shirley & Hyde, 1830.

Whedon, Daniel Denison. "Wesleyanism and Taylorism—Reply to the New Englander." *Methodist Review* 42 (October 1860): 656–69.

———. "Wesleyanism and Taylorism—Second Reply to the New Englander." *Methodist Review* 44 (January 1862): 129–51.

Winslow, Hubbard. *An Evangelical View of the Nature and Means of Regeneration; Comprising a Review of "Dr. Tyler's Strictures."* Boston: Perkins & Marvin, 1830.

Woods, Leonard. *Letters to Rev. Nathaniel Taylor.* Andover, MA: Mark Newman, 1830.

James Harris Fairchild

Swing, Albert Temple. *James Harris Fairchild, or, Sixty-Eight Years with a Christian College.* New York: Revell, 1907.

Charles G. Finney

Charles G. Finney has attracted a great deal of scholarly attention since his death in 1875. What follows is a select list of essential secondary sources.

"Are There Two Roads to Holiness? Charles G. Finney and the Reinterpretation of Wesleyan/Holiness Origins: A Conversation between Allen Guelzo and Douglas A. Sweeney." *Wesleyan/Holiness Studies Center Bulletin* 6 (Spring 1998): 1–3.

Barnard, John. *From Evangelicalism to Progressivism at Oberlin College, 1866–1917.* Columbus: Ohio State University Press, 1969.

Beecher, Lyman, and Asahel Nettleton. *Letters of the Rev. Dr. Beecher and Rev. Mr. Nettleton, on the "New Measures" in Conducting Revivals of Religion, with a Review of a Sermon by Novanglus.* New York: G. and C. Carvill, 1828.

Brand, James, and John M. Ellis. *Memorial Addresses on the Occasion of the One Hundredth Anniversary of the Birth of President Charles G. Finney.* Oberlin, OH: E. J. Goodrich, 1893.

Cox, Helen Finney. "Charles Finney." In *Lives of the Leaders of Our Church Universal,* edited by Ferdinand Piper. Philadelphia: Presbyterian Board of Publication, 1879.

Cross, Whitney R. *The Burned-Over District: The Social and Intellectual History of Enthusiastic Religion in Western New York, 1800–1850.* 1950; repr., New York: Harper & Row, 1965.

Essig, James D. "The Lord's Free Man: Charles G. Finney and His Abolitionism." In *Abolition and American Religion,* edited by John R. McKivigan. New York: Garland, 1999.

Fletcher, Robert Samuel. *A History of Oberlin College: From Its Foundation through the Civil War.* 2 vols. Oberlin, OH: Oberlin College, 1943.

Griffin, Edward D. *A Letter to a Friend on the Connexion between the New Doctrines and the New Measures.* Albany: Hosford & Wait, 1833.

Guelzo, Allen C. "An Heir or a Rebel? Charles Grandison Finney and the New England Theology." *Journal of the Early Republic* 17 (Spring 1997): 61–94.

———. "Oberlin Perfectionism and Its Edwardsian Origins, 1835–1870." In *Jonathan Edwards's Writings: Text, Context, Interpretation,* edited by Stephen J. Stein. Bloomington: Indiana University Press, 1996.

Hambrick-Stowe, Charles. *Charles G. Finney and the Spirit of American Evangelicalism.* Library of Religious Biography. Grand Rapids: Eerdmans, 1996.

Hamilton, James, and Edward H. Madden. "Edwards, Finney, and Mahan on the Derivation of Duty." *Journal of the History of Philosophy* 13 (July 1975): 347–60.

Hardesty, Nancy A. *Your Daughters Shall Prophesy: Revivalism and Feminism in the Age of Finney.* Chicago Studies in the History of American Religion. Brooklyn, NY: Carlson, 1991.

Hardman, Keith J. *Charles Grandison Finney 1792–1875: Revivalist and Reformer.* Syracuse: Syracuse University Press, 1987.

Hewitt, Glenn A. *Regeneration and Morality: A Study of Charles Finney, Charles Hodge, John W. Nevin, and Horace Bushnell.* Brooklyn, NY: Carlson, 1991.

Hodge, Charles. "Review of 'The New Divinity Tried'; or, an Examination of the Rev. Mr. Rand's Strictures on a Sermon Delivered by the Rev. C. Finney, on Making a New Heart." *Biblical Repertory and Theological Review* 4 (April 1832): 278–304.

Johnson, James E. "Charles G. Finney and a Theology of Revivalism." *Church History* 38 (September 1969): 1–21.

———. "Charles G. Finney and Oberlin Perfectionism." *Journal of Presbyterian History* 46 (March–June 1968): 42–57.

———. "Charles G. Finney and the Great 'Western' Revivals." *Fides et Historia* 6 (Spring 1974): 13–30.

Johnson, Paul. *A Shopkeeper's Millennium: Society and Revivals in Rochester, New York, 1815–1837.* New York: Hill & Wang, 1978.

Leonard, Delavan L. *Story of Oberlin: The Institution, the Community, the Idea, the Movement.* Boston: Pilgrim, 1898.

Mattson, John Stanley. "Charles Grandison Finney and the Emerging Tradition of 'New Measures' Revivalism." Ph.D. diss., University of North Carolina at Chapel Hill, 1970.

Mead, Hiram. "Charles Grandison Finney." *Congregational Quarterly* 19 (January 1877): 1–28.

Morrison, Howard Alexander. "The Finney Takeover of the Second Great Awakening during the Oneida Revivals of 1825–1827." *New York History* 59 (January 1978): 27–53.

Opie, John. "Finney's Failure of Nerve: The Untimely Demise of Evangelical Theology." *Journal of Presbyterian History* 51 (Summer 1973): 155–73.

Perciaccante, Marianne. *Calling Down Fire: Charles Grandison Finney and Revivalism in Jefferson County, New York, 1800–1840.* Albany: State University of New York Press, 2003.

Rand, Asa. *The New Divinity Tried, Being an Examination of a Sermon Delivered by the Rev. C. G. Finney, on Making a New Heart.* Boston: Lyceum, 1832.

———. *A Vindication of "The New Divinity Tried," in Reply to a "Review" of the Same.* Boston: Peirce & Parker, 1832.

Reminiscences of Rev. Charles G. Finney. Speeches and Sketches at the Gathering of His Friends and Pupils, in Oberlin, July 28th, 1876, Together with President Fairchild's Memorial Sermon, Delivered before the Graduating Class, July 30, 1876. Oberlin, OH: E. J. Goodrich, 1876.

Rosell, Garth M. "Charles G. Finney: His Place in the Stream." In *The Evangelical Tradition in America,* edited by Leonard I. Sweet. Macon, GA: Mercer University Press, 1984.

Smith, Timothy L. "The Doctrine of the Sanctifying Spirit: Charles G. Finney's Synthesis of Wesleyan and Covenant Theology." *Wesleyan Theological Journal* 13 (Spring 1978): 92–113.

Sweet, Leonard I. "The View of Man Inherent in New Measures Revivalism." *Church History* 45 (June 1976): 206–21.

Weddle, David L. *Law as Gospel: Revival and Reform in the Theology of Charles G. Finney.* Metuchen, NJ: Scarecrow, 1985.

Wilkinson, William Cleaver. "Charles G. Finney as a Preacher." *Independent* (New York), September 9, 1875, 1–2.

———. "Charles Grandison Finney." In *Modern Masters of Pulpit Discourse,* edited by William C. Wilkinson. New York: Funk & Wagnalls, 1905.

Wright, George Frederick. *Charles Grandison Finney.* American Religious Leaders. Boston: Houghton Mifflin, 1891.

Edwards Amasa Park

Allen, George. *The Andover Fuss, or, Dr. Woods versus Dr. Dana on the Imputation of Heresy against Professor Park Respecting the Doctrine of Original Sin.* Boston: Tappan & Whittemore, 1853.

Catalogue of the Theological Library of the Late Professor Edwards A. Park of Andover, Massachusetts. Boston: C. F. Libbie, 1903.

Cecil, Anthony C., Jr. *The Theological Development of Edwards Amasa Park: Last of the "Consistent Calvinists."* Missoula, MT: Scholars Press, 1974.

Conforti, Joseph. "Edwards A. Park and the Creation of the New England Theology, 1840–1870." In *Jonathan Edwards's Writings: Text, Context, Interpretation,* edited by Stephen J. Stein. Bloomington: Indiana University Press, 1996.

Fisher, George P. "Professor Park as a Theologian." *Congregationalist* 85 (June 14, 1900): 871–72.

Foster, Frank Hugh. *The Life of Edwards Amasa Park, Abbot Professor, Andover Theological Seminary.* New York: Revell, 1936.

———. "Professor Park's Theological System." *Bibliotheca Sacra* 61 (January 1904): 55–79.

Furber, D. L., et al., eds. *Professor Park and His Pupils.* Boston: Samuel Usher, 1899.

Gordon, George A. "The Achilles in Our Camp: An Acute and Inspiring Characterization of the Late Dr. Edwards A. Park." *Congregationalist* 88 (June 13, 1903): 840.

Hodge, Charles. "Professor Park and the Princeton Review." *Princeton Review* 23 (October 1851): 674–95.

———. "Professor Park's Sermon." *Biblical Repertory and Princeton Review* 22 (October 1850): 642–74.

———. "Prof. Park's Remarks on the Princeton Review." *Biblical Repertory and Princeton Review* 23 (April 1851): 306–47.

Lord, Nathan. *A Letter to the Rev. Daniel Dana, D.D., on Professor Park's Theology of New England.* Boston: Crocker & Brewster, 1852.

McKenzie, Alexander. *Memoir of Professor Edwards Amasa Park.* Cambridge, MA: John Wilson & Son, 1901.

Rowe, Kenneth E. "Nestor of Orthodoxy New England Style: A Study in the Theology of Edwards Amasa Park, 1808–1900." Ph.D. diss., Drew University, 1969.

Storrs, Richard Salter. *Edwards Amasa Park: Memorial Address.* Boston: S. Usher, 1900.

———. *Professor Park and His Pupils.* Boston: S. Usher, 1899.

Harriet Beecher Stowe (and the Edwardsean Tradition)

Buell, Lawrence E. "Calvinism Romanticized: Harriet Beecher Stowe, Samuel Hopkins, and *The Minister's Wooing.*" *Emerson Society Quarterly* 24 (1978): 119–32.

———. *New England Literary Culture: From Revolution through Renaissance.* Cambridge: Cambridge University Press, 1986.

Caskey, Marie. *Chariot of Fire: Religion and the Beecher Family.* New Haven: Yale University Press, 1978.

Foster, Charles H. "The Genesis of Harriet Beecher Stowe's *The Minister's Wooing.*" *New England Quarterly* 21 (December 1948): 493–517.

———. *The Rungless Ladder: Harriet Beecher Stowe and New England Puritanism.* Durham, NC: Duke University Press, 1954.

Goldman, Maureen. "American Women and the Puritan Heritage: Anne Hutchinson to Harriet Beecher Stowe." Ph.D. diss., Boston University, 1975.

Hedrick, Joan D. *Harriet Beecher Stowe: A Life.* New York: Oxford University Press, 1994.

Kimball, Gayle. "Harriet Beecher Stowe's Revision of New England Theology." *Journal of Presbyterian History* 58 (Spring 1980): 64–81.

———. *The Religious Ideas of Harriet Beecher Stowe: Her Gospel of Womanhood.* Lewiston, NY: Edwin Mellen, 1982.

Rourke, Constance Mayfield. *Trumpets of Jubilee: Henry Ward Beecher, Harriet Beecher Stowe, Lyman Beecher, Horace Greeley, P. T. Barnum.* New York: Harcourt, Brace, 1927.

Rugoff, Milton. *The Beechers: An American Family in the Nineteenth Century.* New York: Harper & Row, 1981.

Index

ability, natural. *See* agency, moral; inability, Edwardsean; will, freedom of
absolutism, ethical. *See* benevolence, disinterested; ethics, Edwardsean
accountability, moral. *See* agency, moral
activity, moral, 173–78. *See also* agency, moral; will, freedom of
affection, natural, 30
affections, religious. *See* conversion
agency, moral
    free will and, 63–68, 173–78, 222
    motivation and, 183–86
    natural ability and, 118–22, 241–42
    regeneration and, 130–31
    See also will, freedom of
anxious seat, 235–36
atheism, 190–93
atonement, 128, 133–48. *See also* government, God's; justification
authority, moral, 217–18. *See also* government, God's

backsliding, 230
baptism, 79–85
Bellamy, Joseph, 15–16, 69–71, 73–74
benevolence, disinterested
    free will and, 223–25
    motivation and, 182
    piety and, 76–77, 91–97, 127–28
    selfishness and, 114, 131
    See also ethics, Edwardsean
birth, new. *See* conversion
blameworthiness. *See* agency, moral
born again. *See* conversion
Brainerd, David, 47–56
Burton, Asa, 179–80

Calvinism, consistent. *See* New Divinity
choice, freedom of. *See* will, freedom of
church and state, 16–17
communion, holy, 79–85
complacence, 92

conscience, 223–24
contingency, 64, 124. *See also* necessity, Edwardsean; will, freedom of
conversion
    natural ability and, 70–71, 118–22
    piety and, 38–46, 73–78
    regeneration and, 87–90, 238–41
    revelation and, 37
    revival and, 25–26, 230–31
    sanctification and, 225–26
    See also regeneration, spiritual; revivalism; sanctification
conviction, natural, 29–30, 89, 113–17
covenant, half-way, 79–85
creation, the, 124–25

delight, spiritual, 77–78
denominations, New Divinity and, 21–24
dependence, moral, 173–78. *See also* agency, moral; will, freedom of
depravity. *See* sin
disinterest. *See* benevolence, disinterested
disposition, moral. *See* habituality, moral
divine efficiency scheme, 240
divine moral suasion, 240–41
Dwight, Timothy, 187, 189–90

Edwards, Jonathan, 14–15, 21–24, 25–26, 69, 124–32
Edwards, Jonathan, the Younger, 123–24, 157
Edwardseanism. *See* New Divinity
efficiency, divine, 240
elect, the, 133–34
Emmons, Nathanael, 113–14, 118–19, 173–74, 179
empathy, natural. *See* affection, natural
Enlightenment, the, 16
enthusiasm, religious, 51–54. *See also* revivalism
esteem, 75–76, 92
ethics, Edwardsean
    justification and, 109–12

moral agency and, 70, 222–26
piety and, 73–78
slavery and, 21, 149–70
See also benevolence, disinterested
evil. *See* sin
example, Christian, 47–56
exercise, moral, 172–78, 240–41. *See also* inability, Edwardsean; piety
exhortation, lay, 234
experience, Christian, 41–43, 131
experiment, religious. *See* experience, Christian

Fairchild, James Harris, 221
feeling, theology of, 247–55
female religious societies, 98–101, 234
Finney, Charles Grandison, 18, 219–20, 227–28, 237
forgiveness. *See* justification
freedom, human. *See* liberty, human; will, freedom of
Freedom of the Will (Edwards), 15–16

generality, moral. *See* habituality, moral
government, God's, 133–48, 190–93, 214–18, 222–23, 231. *See also* justification
grace, common. *See* conviction, natural
grace, God's, 43–46, 89–90, 145–48, 242
gratitude, love of, 92, 95
guilt, natural. *See* conviction, natural

habituality, moral
free will and, 61–62, 64–68
government of, 216–17
motivation and, 77–78
original sin and, 129–30, 194–204
piety and, 109–12
regeneration and, 209–12, 240
slavery and, 161
truth and, 190–92
See also necessity, Edwardsean
happiness, 127, 180–83, 209–11
heart. *See* conversion; feeling, theology of; substance, spiritual
holiness, lived. *See* piety
Hopkins, Samuel, 15–16, 69–71, 86–87, 98, 151–52

imagination, natural, 30
imputation, doctrine of, 109–10, 128–30. *See also* government, God's; justification
inability, Edwardsean
habituation and, 60–63

moral agency and, 16, 70–71, 118–22, 125–27
motivation and, 184–86
refutation of, 237, 241–42
revival and, 229
See also agency, moral; necessity, Edwardsean; will, freedom of
indifference, freedom and, 64, 65. *See also* will, freedom of
inspiration, 30
intellect. *See* reason
interest, selfish. *See* selfishness

judicial justification, 133–34. *See also* justification
justice. *See* benevolence, disinterested
justification, 43–46, 109–12, 128–30, 133–48

knowledge, spiritual, 74–75. *See also* revelation

law, God's, 74–78, 133–43, 215–18
lay participation, 233–34
legalism. *See* works, Christian
liberty, human, 63–64, 65, 125–27, 241–42. *See also* will, freedom of
light, spiritual. *See* revelation
limited atonement, 133–34, 140–41, 145. *See also* atonement
love. *See* benevolence, disinterested

means, use of, 86, 92, 205–13, 229, 231–36. *See also* covenant, half-way
measures, revivalist, 233–36. *See also* means, use of
membership, church, 79–85
missions, ethics and, 149–50, 165–70
moral inability, 60–63. *See also* inability, Edwardsean
moral necessity, 15–16, 58–60, 64–68, 126
motivation, moral, 78, 171–86, 192. *See also* habituality, moral

natural inability, 60. *See also* inability, Edwardsean
natural necessity, 15, 58–60, 67–68, 126. *See also* habituality, moral; necessity, Edwardsean
nature, human. *See* habituality, moral; inability, Edwardsean; substance, spiritual
necessity, Edwardsean, 15–16, 58–60, 64–68, 125–27, 176–77. *See also* habituality, moral
new birth. *See* conversion

New Divinity, 15–24, 69–71, 256–64
New England Theology. *See* New Divinity
new measures, revivalist, 233–36. *See also* means, use of

Oberlin Theology, 221–26
occasionality, moral, 61–62
Osborn, Sarah, 98–108

Park, Edwards Amasa, 245–46, 256–57
particularity, moral. *See* occasionality, moral
perfectionism, moral. *See* ethics, Edwardsean
piety
  benevolence as, 127–28
  conversion and, 38–46
  justification and, 109–12
  motivation and, 172–78
  revelation and, 37
  truth and, 190–92
pleasure. *See* happiness
power, efficient. *See* inability, Edwardsean
practice, Christian, 39–46, 109–12. *See also* piety
praiseworthiness. *See* agency, moral
prayer, lay, 233–34
preaching, lay, 234
predestination, 15–16. *See also* agency, moral; will, freedom of
propensities, sinful. *See* habituality, moral

rationality. *See* reason
reason, 32–33, 34–36, 247–55
Reformed theology, 21–24
regeneration, spiritual, 88–90, 118–22, 131–32, 205–13, 238–41. *See also* conversion; revelation
religion, experimental. *See* experience, Christian
repentance, 222. *See also* conversion; regeneration, spiritual
responsibility, moral. *See* agency, moral
revelation, 27–37
revivalism, 13–18, 69–70, 227–36. *See also* conversion
righteousness, imputation of, 109–10, 128–30. *See also* government, God's; justification

sacraments, the, 79–85
sanctification, 225–26, 242–43. *See also* conversion; regeneration, spiritual
Scripture, 33–34
seat, anxious, 235–36

self-determination, 64, 125–27. *See also* will, freedom of
selfishness, 93–97, 114–17, 182, 197–99, 209–12. *See also* sin
self-love, 93–97, 209–11
separatism, religious, 17, 70
sin
  atonement and, 133–39, 145–48
  benevolence and, 224–25
  human nature and, 129–30, 194–204
  moral agency and, 128, 173–78, 184–86
  regeneration and, 87–90
  truth and, 190–92
  See also selfishness
sincerity, Christian, 109–12
situationality, moral. *See* occasionality, moral
slavery, ethics and, 150–64
Smalley, John, 144–45
societies, female religious, 98–101, 234
sovereignty. *See* government, God's
spontaneity, volitional, 125–27
state, church and, 16–17
Stowe, Harriet Beecher, 265–66
Strong, Nathan, 109–10
suasion, divine moral, 240–41
substance, spiritual, 171–72, 179–86, 238–39
susceptibility scheme, 240
sympathy, natural. *See* affection, natural

taste, moral, 172, 179–86, 190–92, 240. *See also* habituality, moral
Taylor, Nathaniel, 187–88, 194–95, 205–6
temptation, 196

utility, ethical, 183

views, philosophical, 191–92
virtue. *See* piety
volition. *See* will, freedom of

West, Stephen, 135–36
will, freedom of
  ethics and, 223–26
  moral agency and, 15–16, 57–68, 118–22, 125–27
  motivation and, 171–86
  natural ability and, 241–43
  original sin and, 194–204
  regeneration and, 239
women, New Divinity and, 98–101, 234
works, Christian, 43–46, 109–12